MAGILL'S
SURVEY
OF
WORLD
LITERATURE

MAGILL'S SURVEY OF WORLD LITERATURE

Volume 4

Kundera–Osborne

Edited by
FRANK N. MAGILL

Marshall Cavendish Corporation
New York • London • Toronto • Sydney • Singapore

Published By
Marshall Cavendish Corporation
2415 Jerusalem Avenue
P.O. Box 587
North Bellmore, New York 11710
United States of America

∞ The paper used in these volumes conforms to the American National Standard for Permanence of Paper for Printed Library Materials, Z39.48-1984.

Library of Congress Cataloging-in-Publication Data
Magill's survey of world literature. Edited by Frank N. Magill.
    p. cm.
Includes bibliographical references and index.
    1. Literature—History and criticism. 2. Literature—Stories, plots, etc. 3. Literature—Bio-bibliography. 4. Authors—Biography—Dictionaries. I. Magill, Frank Northen, 1907-
PN523.M29 1992
809—dc20
ISBN 1-85435-482-5 (set)   92-11198
ISBN 1-85435-486-8 (volume 4)   CIP

Second Printing

PRINTED IN THE UNITED STATES OF AMERICA

CONTENTS

MAGILL'S SURVEY OF WORLD LITERATURE

MILAN KUNDERA

Born: Brno, Czechoslovakia
April 1, 1929

Principal Literary Achievement

Kundera is an internationally acclaimed Czech émigré writer whose novels have used experiments in form to examine fundamental existential questions through explorations of the role of sex and politics in the lives of his characters.

Biography

Milan Kundera was born on April 1, 1929, in Brno, Czechoslovakia, to Ludvík and Milada Janosikova Kundera. He grew up in the provincial capital of Brno and then went to Prague to attend Charles University and the Film Faculty of the Prague Academy of Music and Dramatic Arts. In 1947, he joined the Communist Party. Like the majority of his compatriots, he initially celebrated the Communists' rise to power after the war as a victory of the future over the past. Like the majority of his compatriots, he soon regretted this decision and found himself at odds with the party. In 1950, he was expelled for "ideological differences" and left Prague to work as a laborer and jazz pianist in the provinces. In 1956, he was reinstated in the party, and two years later he became an assistant professor at the Institute for Advanced Cinematographic Studies of the Academy of Music and Dramatic Arts.

In 1963, he became a member of the Central Committee of the Czechoslovak Writers Union. Between 1963 and 1968, Kundera emerged as one of the most important literary figures in Prague. His three collections of short stories, entitled *Směšne lásky* (1969; partial translation as *Laughable Loves*, 1974), were immensely popular and were awarded the Czechoslovak Writers' Publishing House Prize. His first novel *Žert* (1967; *The Joke*, 1969, revised, 1982) which was finally published, unchanged, after a two-year battle with the censors, quickly went through three editions and received the Union of Czechoslovak Writers' Prize. With other prominent writers such as Ludvik Vaculik and Ivan Klima, Kundera used his stature in the Writers' Union to press for "socialism with a human face" and thereby helped to usher in the Prague Spring.

When the Soviet tanks rolled into Czechoslovakia and crushed this reform movement, Kundera and these other writers were immediately classified as enemies of the state. His books were removed from libraries and bookstores, his plays were banned, he was fired from his teaching position and denied the right to publish in his own country. (Although he continued to write in Czech, beginning in 1970 the first edi-

tions of his books were all foreign translations.) Between 1970 and 1975, he was both forbidden to work in Czechoslovakia and prevented from traveling abroad. To support himself at one point, he wrote several thousand horoscopes for Prague clients and published a monthly astrology column under a pseudonym.

At the same moment that Kundera was denied publication in his own country, an international readership began to discover him. *The Joke* was quickly translated into a dozen languages. His second novel, *La Vie est ailleurs* (1973; *Life Is Elsewhere*, 1974; in Czech as *Život de jinde*, 1979), was awarded the French Prix Médicis; his third, *La Valse aux adieux* (1976; *The Farewell Party*, 1976; in Czech as *Valcik no rozloučenou*, 1979), received the Italian Premio Mondello. Philip Roth enthusiastically introduced his works to American readers by publishing both *Laughable Loves* and *The Farewell Party* in his Writers from the Other Europe series.

In 1975, the Czech authorities finally permitted Kundera and his wife to leave the country so that he could accept a visiting professorship in comparative literature at the University of Rennes. He arrived in France, at age forty-five, with two suitcases, a few books, and some records. *Le Livre du rire et de l'oubli* (1979; *The Book of Laughter and Forgetting*, 1980; in Czech as *Kniha smíchu a zapomnění*, 1981) both established Kundera's place in contemporary world literature and led to the revocation of his Czech citizenship. In 1980, he moved to Paris to become a professor at the École des Hautes Études en Sciences Sociales, and in 1981 President François Mitterrand made him a French citizen. Two novels, *L'Insoutenable Légèreté de l'être* (1984; *The Unbearable Lightness of Being*, 1984; in Czech as *Nesnesitelná lehkost bytí*, 1985) and *Nesmertelnost* (1990; *Immortality*, 1991), the play *Jacques et son maître: Hommage à Denis Diderot* (1970), a series of widely read and frequently quoted essays on the history and fate of central Europe, and a collection of essays and interviews entitled *L'Art du roman* (1986; *The Art of the Novel*, 1988) followed—along with the Commonwealth Award (1981), the Prix Europa (1982), and the Jerusalem Prize for Literature on the Freedom of Man in Society (1985).

Analysis

"I tried a lot of things" before turning to fiction, Kundera has said. "[c]inema, painting, music, poetry, criticism, theory, aesthetics. But none of it was serious; I think of all that now as a kind of prehistory." Intellectually and artistically, he has repeatedly emphasized, "I am attached to nothing apart from the European novel, that unrecognized inheritance that comes to us from Cervantes." As Kundera sees it, that inheritance is a record of both an extraordinary sequence of discoveries and a series of roads not taken. With English novelist Samuel Richardson, he argues, the novel discovered psychological realism, and, ever since, most novels have followed the nearly inviolable standards of that tradition. In the second half of the twentieth century, Kundera notes, it has often been argued that the novel is dead. He disagrees, insisting instead that, since Richardson, the novel has ignored many of its possibilities. One of the most important of those unexplored possibilities, he argues, is the one suggested by Laurence Sterne's *The Life and Opinions of Tristram Shandy, Gent.*

(1759-1767) and Denis Diderot's *Jacques le fataliste et son maître* (1796; *Jacques the Fatalist and His Master*, 1797): the idea of the novel as a game rather than a representation of reality.

After Sterne and Diderot, Kundera owes his aesthetic of the novel to the examples of central European novelists and artists of the past century—especially to Hermann Broch and to the Czech composer Leoš Janáček. He shares Broch's view that every serious novel must discover something that the novel—and no other form—can discover. He has also experimented with several of the formal ideas contained in his favorite Broch novel, *Die Schlafwandler* (1931-1932; *The Sleepwalkers* 1932): The novel's traditional unity of action can be replaced by a unity of theme; the musical technique known as polyphony—the simultaneous presentation of two or more voices or melodic lines that are both bound together and independent—can be adapted to enrich the form of the novel; such novelistic polyphony can allow the author to combine radically different nonnovelistic genres within the text. From Janáček, his favorite composer, Kundera learned to upset technical conventions through ellipsis: to replace traditional transitions with harsh, abrupt juxtapositions, to replace repetition with variations, to eliminate the superfluous.

For Kundera, then, "a novel is a long piece of synthetic prose based on play with invented characters. These are the only limits." By "synthetic," he told Philip Roth, he means

> the novelist's desire to grasp his subject from all sides and in the fullest possible completeness. Ironic essay, novelistic narrative, autobiographical fragment, historic fact, flight of fantasy: The synthetic power of the novel is capable of combining everything into a unified whole like the voices of polyphonic music. The unity of the book need not stem from the plot, but can be provided by the theme.

A novel, he believes, should search and pose questions. The questions that his own works pose are existential: Who am I? What is a self? To what extent do I define my self, and to what extent is it defined by others? Do my choices define me, or does chance? What does life, living, being a human being, really mean? The fact that Kundera can explore such weighty questions in novels that are also witty and entertaining is an essential aspect of his art and his appeal.

In each of his novels, from *The Joke* to *Immortality*, his exploration of these existential questions is structured around a series of key words (or themes) that appear and reappear from book to book. *Immortality*, he says of that novel, would have been called *The Unbearable Lightness of Being* if he had not already used the title. All of his novels, he told an interviewer, might have been called *The Joke* or *Laughable Loves*. Moreover, each is a book of laughter and forgetting.

THE BOOK OF LAUGHTER AND FORGETTING

First published: *Le Livre du rire et de l'oubli*, 1979 (English translation, 1980)

Type of work: Novel

A novel in the form of variations on the themes of laughter and forgetting, this work examines both the lives of a series of characters in Prague and Paris and the implications of history and memory for individuals and nations.

The Book of Laughter and Forgetting, which was finally published in Czech as *Kniha smíchu a zapomnění* (1981), like all of Kundera's novels except *The Farewell Party*, is divided into seven parts. Several of the parts have the same titles—two are entitled "Lost Letters," two are entitled "Angels"—to underline the idea that the novel is a series of variations on a set of themes. Two parts focus on a young woman named Tamina, but each of the other five focuses on unrelated characters who appear only in that part. Each of the seven parts combines several genres, such as traditional novelistic narrative, autobiography, philosophical essay, dream, political commentary, linguistic analysis, realistic description, and fantasy. The parts are not linked by a single plot, but by their direct or indirect relationship to Kundera's exploration of the meanings that he attaches to words such as "laughter," "forgetting," "angels," the "circle," "litost," and "border"; by his reflections on Czech history; by his voice and presence as the authorial "I."

They are also connected—to one another, and to all of Kundera's other fiction—by their exploration of the interrelationship of public and private life. In Kundera's work, the threat that the border between public and private life will disappear—the fear that it already has—is the nightmare that lies behind all the verbal and sexual high jinks. Most often, this threat is expressed as an invasion of private life by public life, seen as a distortion of the sexual by the political. In Kundera, sexual relations are an arena where the politically powerless exercise power, where the oppressed oppress, where public tragedy begets private comedy. Yet they are also the sphere where character reveals itself most fully. One of the paradoxes at the heart of his novels is that, in their most intimate moments, his characters are both most themselves and most the product of the external forces acting upon them.

The first part of *The Book of Laughter and Forgetting* perfectly demonstrates Kundera's novelistic method. Each of its sections presents private and public variations on the theme of forgetting. The love story of Mirek and Zdena is intimately connected to both their individual political histories and the history of their country. Mirek's desire to forget his former love, Zdena, to "airbrush" her out of the picture of his past and his life, is a private reflection of the public effort of the Czech people to erase the past deed that *they* would like to forget—their support of the communists in 1947-1948. The party is also engaged in an effort to forget when it seeks to eliminate its own past mistakes by airbrushing Clementis from the photograph described on the novel's first page. The bare space on the wall where Clementis once stood in the photograph is tied to the bare space in his history where Mirek's memories of Zdena should be. Zdena's passionate love of Mirek is presented as both a product of, and the impulse behind, the passionate singlemindedness that also made her a loyal party member; Mirek's decision to become a political dissident is connected to his desire to forget the embarrassment of his youthful relationship with Zdena. The hat on Gottwald's head is an emblem of all the personal and public pasts that cannot be erased.

Similar variations on the theme of forgetting continue throughout the novel, joined by new themes that are introduced with their own variations in each of the succeeding parts. The novel, Kundera writes, is "about Tamina. . . . She is its main character and main audience, and all the other stories are variations on her story and come together in her life as in a mirror." In other words, the parts devoted to Tamina—the fourth and sixth parts, which are the parts that repeat the titles of the earlier parts "Lost Letters" and "Angels"—are the heart of *The Book of Laughter and Forgetting*. There, the novel's themes echo and reverberate in a story that combines sex, love, exile, memory, forgetting, laughter, the circle, angels, politics, and borders in both startling and extremely subtle ways. There, they come together in a story that also introduces the thematic notes upon which Kundera's next novel would be composed. To Tamina, the unbearable lightness of being represented by the island of memoryless children is the ultimate nightmare: a world in which meaning disappears and nothing matters. Like Tereza (even their names echo each other), Tamina clings to meaning, to memory, to mortality—and to the existential burden of spiritual heaviness that comes with them—because, for her, that is what it means to be human. The alternative, Kundera seems to suggest in the novel's final section and coda, is a freedom without meaning and a life without purpose.

THE UNBEARABLE LIGHTNESS OF BEING

First published: *L'Insoutenable Légèreté de l'être*, 1984 (English translation, 1984)

Type of work: Novel

This novel explores the nature of responsibility and identity through the story of two romantic triangles set before, during, and after the Russian invasion of Czechoslovakia in 1968.

In many ways, *The Unbearable Lightness of Being*, published in Czech as *Nesnesitelná lehkost bytí* (1985), is a more traditional novel than *The Book of Laughter and Forgetting*. It, too, mixes genres and is tied together by variations on a series of themes: lightness and heaviness, body and soul, vertigo and eternal return, the Grand March. It also tells several clearly related stories about four fully developed characters: the waitress/photographer Tereza, the doctor Tomas, the painter Sabina, and the professor Franz. This novel does not follow the conventions of the realistic novel: The fact of the main characters' deaths is revealed long before it occurs, thereby undermining the plot's suspense, a major character is introduced toward the end of the novel and then disappears, and a section is told from the point of view of Tereza and Tomas' dog. It does, however, create and resolve a central conflict among these characters, and it does occur within a recognizable social and historical context.

The main characters are carefully paired, both romantically and thematically. Tereza and Tomas, Tomas and Sabina, and Sabina and Franz are each involved in love affairs. Tereza and Franz are both associated with the theme of weight and heaviness; Tomas and Sabina, with the theme of lightness. Weight and heaviness are associated with the soul, commitment, seriousness, responsibility; lightness, with the body, betrayal, infidelity, and selfishness. Through Tereza's influence, in the course of the novel Tomas makes the moral journey from lightness to heaviness. Sabina and Franz remain largely unchanged.

Tereza first comes to Prague from the country because of her love for Tomas, a man whose personal life is dominated by his numerous sexual conquests. When they and Sabina join the flood of émigrés after the Russian invasion and arrive in Switzerland, Sabina finds Tereza's counterpart in Franz. When Tereza feels adrift in Zurich and returns to Czechoslovakia, Tomas follows her, although he has lost his position at the hospital and is forced to become a window washer. Although his commitment to her is real, he continues to spend every free moment in dalliances with other women until his love for Tereza finally leads him to agree to leave the city and its temptations for a collective farm. There, they eventually die together in a truck accident. Sabina rejects Franz's desire for commitment and becomes a fashionable artist who travels throughout Europe and America. Franz joins a group of European leftists who travel to Cambodia, drawn by the idea of the Grand March of international revolution, which he sees as somehow related to his love for Sabina; there, he is fatally injured.

As Kundera tells the story, the personal and sexual lives of these four characters are intimately bound up with the social and political realities of Czechoslovakia before and after the Russian invasion. He presents vivid glimpses of the Prague Spring, of the Russian invasion, of post-1968 life in Prague, of the emigration of Czechs to the West, and of Western political attitudes toward émigrés and toward the idea of revolutionary change. Moreover, in spite of his many comments about the unreality of fictional characters, in *The Unbearable Lightness of Being* he creates four believable and interesting characters whose fates matter to the reader. As a consequence, perhaps, this work has been the most widely read and highly praised of his novels.

Summary

Milan Kundera has often objected to political readings of his fiction, emphasizing that his novels are about the existential dilemmas of his characters and complaining that Western readers are drawn to the work of writers from "the other Europe" for the wrong reasons. He has also spoken often of his ideas about the novel, the fate of central Europe, and the role of Central Europe in the culture of the West. His interviews, essays, and comments are required reading for anyone who is interested in any of these matters. Finally, however, Kundera will be remembered for the power and accomplishment of his novels themselves. Together with those of his contemporaries from Eastern, Central, and Western Europe and North, Central, and South America, his works amply demonstrate that the contemporary novel is anything but exhausted or dead.

Bibliography

Atlas, James. "The Wounded Exile." *Vanity Fair* 3 (January, 1985): 53-55.

Baranczak, Stanislaw. "Life Is Elsewhere." *New Republic* 205 (July 29, 1991): 36-39.

Boyers, Robert. *Atrocity and Amnesia: The Political Novel Since 1945.* New York: Oxford University Press, 1985.

Carlisle, Olga. "A Talk with Milan Kundera." *The New York Times Magazine* 134 (May 19, 1985): 2-76.

Webb, Igor. "Milan Kundera and the Limits of Skepticism." *Massachusetts Review* 31 (Autumn, 1990): 357-368.

Bernard F. Rodgers, Jr.

PHILIP LARKIN

Born: Coventry, Warwickshire, England
August 9, 1922
Died: Hull, England
December 2, 1985

Principal Literary Achievement

A major English poet of the post-World War II era, Larkin is admired for crafted, readable poems that speak honestly, with sad wit and irony, of the modern isolated life.

Biography

Philip Arthur Larkin was born in Coventry, England, on August 9, 1922, the son of Sydney and Eva Emily (Day) Larkin. His bookish father was city treasurer. Larkin tended to dismiss his Coventry childhood as uneventful but recalled that during the 1930's he "wrote ceaselessly," both prose and verse, while attending King Henry VIII School. As a youth, he kept booklets of his writings—a practice he followed throughout his life, later using typescripts—and published poems in his school magazine, *The Coventrian*. At St. John's College, Oxford, he earned the B.A. with distinction in English literature (1943) and then the M.A. (1947). He failed his physical for military service in World War II. Close friends at Oxford encouraged his literary efforts, and in his mid-twenties he published the novels *Jill* (1946, 1964) and *A Girl in Winter* (1947). Though Larkin at first wanted to be a novelist and much later said he found novels "richer, broader, deeper, more enjoyable than poems," poetry proved to be his real vocation. Influenced by W. H. Auden and, after 1943, by the Irish poet William Butler Yeats, Larkin published verses at Oxford and brought out *The North Ship* (1945, 1966), poems that revealed a solitary persona and gained little notice. Larkin later "disowned" the book but allowed its reissue.

Larkin's poems from the late 1940's were the first in his new, representative voice—"less poetic," he said, and "freer of the late Mr. W. B. Yeats also." From 1949 onward, his notebook texts show careful, laborious revision, sometimes extending over months or years. Alternating scarce and fruitful periods were the norm throughout the poet's life.

In 1951, Larkin, by then a gainfully employed librarian, had one hundred copies of a volume titled *XX Poems* printed in Belfast and circulated privately, with little effect. Pressed in 1943 by the Ministry of Labour to find employment, Larkin had found

his first job at the public library in Wellington, Shropshire, where, in his reading of the English poet and novelist Thomas Hardy, he found ironic and sober views compatible with his own. Larkin worked at academic libraries in Leicester and Belfast before taking over in 1955 as librarian at the University of Hull, England, a growing institution that thereafter demanded much of his professional energy. Larkin's reclusive and unassuming life-style earned for him the epithet the "Hermit of Hull." As his fame grew, he consistently shunned the limelight by giving few readings, interviews, and lectures.

In Larkin's *The Less Deceived* (1955), his now-familiar poetic personality emerged. Thrusting Larkin into prominence among critics and a growing readership, the book brought numerous formal recognitions—the Queen's Gold Medal (1965), other awards, and offers of honorary degrees and fellowships. Behind Larkin's apparently sudden emergence in his thirties as a major poet lay more than a decade of serious effort. *The Whitsun Weddings* (1964) confirmed and broadened his reputation. The title poem, begun in May, 1957, like others in the book combines social observation with a strong personal voice. (The poet's reading of this widely acclaimed poem on radio in 1973 was a "first and last" concession to public demand that his voice emerge from the closet.)

From his youth onward, Larkin was a jazz buff. Features he wrote for the London *Daily Telegraph* were collected as *All What Jazz: A Record Diary 1961-68* (1970).

As editor of *The Oxford Book of Twentieth-Century English Verse* (1973), Larkin took on a large, prestigious task that had been Yeats's task before him. The results led some to charge that Larkin had inordinately favored traditional forms and minor poets. "At any rate," he said, "I made a readable book. I made twentieth-century poetry sound nice."

In the year that Larkin moved from his "high windows" flat to another residence in Hull that was to be his last, his final volume, *High Windows* (1974), appeared. Photos from mid-life onward show Larkin bald, with heavy dark-rimmed glasses, inscrutable and impish. He traveled little and never married. After 1974, he made only eight poems public, including slight occasional pieces. An interview in *The Paris Review* appeared in 1982. *Required Writing: Miscellaneous Pieces, 1955-1982* (1983) assembled prose pieces that add to an understanding of his career.

The year before his death, Larkin refused the offer of the laureateship, Britain's highest honor for poets, reportedly on the grounds that he found his previous decade too unproductive of poetry to make him worthy. Larkin, a smoker, died in Hull, England, on December 2, 1985, after surgery for throat cancer. His *Collected Poems* (1988) has been a surprise best-seller in England.

Analysis

The list of contemporary literary luminaries responding in the media to Larkin's *Collected Poems* helps suggest the stature as a modern English poet that Larkin achieved during his lifetime. Seamus Heaney, Stephen Spender, Howard Nemerov, Ian Hamilton, and Derek Walcott figure among Larkin's many admiring reviewers.

Some discussion focuses on whether the canon of Larkin's poems should exceed what the poet himself chose to include in the four slim volumes he published—the 115 poems collectively constituting *The North Ship, The Less Deceived, The Whitsun Weddings*, and *High Windows*. Even the 30 poems of his first volume are marginal, since Larkin allowed that book's reprinting in 1966 "with considerable hesitation"; Larkin's characteristic style and voice, the collective features that give him his uniqueness, appear definitively in the last three volumes. Still, editor Anthony Thwaite salvages 242 poems that Larkin wrote, mostly between 1946 and his death, with a few · from 1938 through 1945. "Aubade," written in November, 1977, and published on December 23 in *The Times Literary Supplement*, is an important, previously uncollected poem from Larkin's late period, during which his nonproductivity led him to think himself unworthy of the proffered laureateship and to reject it. The "morning song" of an aging insomniac who wakes before "all the uncaring/ Intricate rented world begins to rouse," "Aubade" is vintage Larkin: "I work all day, and get half-drunk at night," he starts. "Being brave/ Lets no one off the grave," he concludes.

In variants of just such an authoritative yet self-demeaning voice, Larkin speaks to his readers, sharing calmly depressing, undogmatic glimpses of postimperial (and especially working-class) Britain. In what poet/biographer Alan Brownjohn calls a "vigorous colloquial mode"—language both ordinary and formal, serious and witty, figurative and literal—the Hermit of Hull himself seems to come through, at once thoughtful, intimate, wry, sad, and playful. Poems in Larkin's voice accumulate the collective features of the Larkin persona, a detached and bemused, sometimes misogynistic bachelor. Modestly ranging themes include choice and its fated limits, work, aging, the elusiveness of personal happiness, marriage and singleness, and, in general, the ordinary experiences of unpretentious people, lucidly and often tenderly rendered.

The notable regularity with which Larkin's small volumes appeared—exactly one a decade—says much about his craftsmanship. External evidence of painstaking revision supports the feel that his best poems have of having ripened thoughtfully. ("The Whitsun Weddings," for example, was begun in May, 1957, resumed in 1958, reworked through twenty-three pages, and finished later that year.) Though "quietly English," Larkin's poems after 1960 often show diction—and graphic concerns with sex and bodies—sure to make shy readers redden. Still, a gentleman's formality always remains. Irregularized meter, stanza, and rhyme undergird even the most random-sounding of Larkin's verses.

The paradox of colloquial formality, of course, is not unique to Larkin and in fact has a long history in English poetry. Larkin's underpinning of talk with the organizational structures of traditional verse thus creates frequent random echoes of John Donne and the other Metaphysical poets, of Robert Browning's artfully "natural" monologues, of T. S. Eliot (the Prufrock persona is never far out of hearing distance), of Lord Byron (especially in the witty rhymes), or of Alexander Pope (with his parallels and wordplay). As to the poet's worldview, the sardonic pessimism of Thomas Hardy is the important influence that Larkin has acknowledged.

Since Larkin invented no geninely new formal mode for writing poems, the impulse to link him not only with earlier poets but also with contemporaries is strong. An association between Larkin and "The Movement" in English letters began soon after the appearance of *The Less Deceived*. The collective tendencies of this loose "school" include a rejection of both Romanticism and the extreme principles of modernist experimentalism. Movement writers think that common sense, honesty, clarity, realism, and empiricism should govern art. Robert Conquest's anthology *New Lines* (1956) epitomized features of The Movement.

The Larkin persona, of foreground interest in most poems, is also often an unenthusiastic witness to life. Thus Larkin is both social critic and realist. His ordinary people marry and start their lives ("The Whitsun Weddings"), go to weekend fairs ("Show Saturday"), play cards, visit bars, get sick ("Ambulances"), and die ("The Explosion"). Meanwhile, the Empire's soldiers come "home/ For lack of money" ("Homage to a Government"), and England's omnipresent churches stand as taunting residues of a dying religion ("Church Going"). Larkin's social concerns appear as early as the novel *Jill*, a bellwether among postwar British novels for its working-class hero; his poems persist in showing something of the novelist's sense of place and situation. One risks equating poet with persona to say that Larkin's foiled plan to become a novelist seems but one more ironic instance of his "falling short."

Larkin's poems of wistful isolation show sadness and failure and treat the mundane and mediocre; however, they also imply persistent communal values. In "Show Saturday," for example, a weekend fair reveals "something [people] share/ That breaks ancestrally each year into/ Regenerate union. Let it always be there." Young lovers in "High Windows" or "The Whitsun Weddings" find at least brief pleasure in each other, even as the speaker is excluded. Indeed, there is everywhere in Larkin's poems the sense of a "perfect happiness/ I can't confront" ("Mother, Summer, I").

A Larkin dichotomy that reminds posterity of his successes, not his failures, sounds in a later poem that begins "The daily things we do/ for money or for fun/ Can disappear like dew/ Or harden and live on."

TOADS

First published: 1955
Type of work: Poem

The speaker, after berating himself for letting "the toad *work*" spoil his life, decides that he is fated for an unromantic existence.

Memorable among the poems in *The Less Deceived* (1955) that brought Larkin his first fame, "Toads" is a comically exaggerated, self-directed harangue whose speaker seems easily identifiable with the Hermit of Hull. The poem's work-driven man trades six days of his week for economic security, meanwhile giving up "The fame and the girl and the money" that "windfall" types might get with their "wits" or "blarney." The strong sensory impact of the opening rhetorical question makes the poem hard to forget: "Why should I let the toad *work*/ Squat on my life?" In nine quatrains of rough dactyls, the persona goes on to reach a partial, chilling answer: "something sufficiently toad-like/ Squats in me, too;/ Its hunkers are heavy as hard luck,/ And cold as snow."

The poem's main image provides an "objective correlative"—to use the term suggested by the Anglo-American poet/critic T. S. Eliot—for oppressive daily work that suppresses the life of which the individual dreams. (A pun in "toady" as "fawning underling" urks under the conceit.) The other life that the speaker decides is not for him, the unrealized romantic alternative to a workaday world, gives the poem its main contrast. The word "Toads" rules the poem as image, witty symbol, personification (or animation), metaphor, and analogy; but the text engages many other "poetic" devices. A second rhetorical question, echoing the first, heightens its animated little comic drama with simile: "Can't I use my wit as a pitchfork/ And drive the brute off?" ("Wit" is echoed later as "wits" and finally identified with "blarney." Since the poet as crafty talker is at work in the poem, the foils of librarian and happy-go-lucky poet may be partly what the speaker imagines.) The phrases "skinny as whippets," "Toad-like," and "heavy as hard luck,/ . . . cold as snow" show other similes that sharpen the imagery. Further details sketch manly risk-takers living "up lanes/ With fires in a bucket," eating "windfalls and tinned sardines." The Popean wit of this last image (technically called zeugma) derives from Larkin's pairing of things intangible and sensibly concrete, both objects of the verb "Eat." Hyperalliteration in the third stanza, especially, reinforces the poem's comic tone, even as the catalog "Lecturers, lispers,/ Losels, loblolly-men, louts" is congruent with the mock-epic, one remote model for the poem.

The speaker's mention of the inaccessible "stuff/ That dreams are made on," echoing William Shakespeare's *The Tempest* (1611) helps set up the poem's romantic foil. In this detail, the text is reminiscent of Eliot's "The Love Song of J. Alfred Prufrock," where Prufrock thinks of the inimitable actions of Hamlet as the obverse of his own. Ultimately, in fact, it is hard not to compare Larkin's resigned persona with Prufrock, for both are timid men whose "love songs" go unsung. Like Eliot and others, Larkin shows skill at using startling conceits to make the "stuff" of his poem memorable. While Prufrock's mind drifts toward the genteel (and Eliot's toward free verse), Larkin's speaker stanzaically envisions a downscale society where something chancier would replace propriety.

Formally, the quatrains of "Toads" exemplify rowdy versions of the four-line "common meter" stanza, long serviceable in English verse. The dactylic meter is an "oomp-pah-pah" that blusters on. Half-rhymes typify the *abab* scheme: In fact, no exact rhymes occur. Such pairings as "poison/ proportion" and "bucket/ like it" are clever in the manner of Lord Byron. Larkin's conversational "blarney" also employs colloquial diction, disruptive dashes, exclamations, italicized phrases, and contractions. The phrase "All at one sitting" is a pun full of irony, given both the toad's "squatting" stance and the nonsedentary life needed for one to get fame, love, or wealth. Dialectal words help individualize Larkin's speaker, who speaks of "losels" (worthless persons), "loblolly-men" (louts), "nippers" (children), and "hunkers" (haunches), and who says, "*Stuff your pension!*"

Unlike the rest, the poem's last stanza is obscure; the pronouns are ambiguous, the antecedents remote. The verb "bodies" seems vaguely transitive. Probably "one" and "the other" (and "either" and "both") refer to the "two toads" previously mentioned—one squatting "on my life," the other squatting "in me, too." The plural title seems to be a main clue that helps identify these two referents. Thus "one bodies the other/ One's spiritual truth" means that the outward tendency to be a workaholic, symbolized by the outward "toad," is an emblem of one's inner reality. If the first "one" is the squatting toad and the second "One" the man on whom it sits, the idea may be that work gives an individual his or her "spiritual truth." The fact that the speaker rejects the affirmation he asserts makes his last pontification doubly gnomic. Here the pedantic librarian's voice supplants the breezier blarney that dominates the poem—though wit is a common denominator in both modes. However one reads its end, the poem's serious theme is that a fatal temperamental workaholism, while paying the bills and securing the pension, fails to bring such footloose fulfillment as one can fancy.

CHURCH GOING

First published: 1955
Type of work: Poem

An English cyclist's weekday visit to an empty church provokes his serious, skeptical reverie on the appeal, and future, of Christianity.

Written the same summer as "Toads," "Church Going" also first appeared in Larkin's remarkable little book *The Less Deceived*. Each of the two much-admired poems illustrates the book's emphatic focus on relative disillusionment. The punning title "Church Going" is typically Larkinesque, implying both "attending church" and "the vanishing church." A further irony is that Larkin's "church goer" is a sole drop-in to whom the empty edifice is alien and puzzling, not supportive or enlightening.

As sobriety varies from playfulness, the persona of "Church Going" varies from that of "Toads." Yet the loneliness and dissociation from human company that one perceives in the speaker and the recognition that he contemplates an important modern dilemma tie him to the "toad-dominated" worker. One added strength of "Church Going" is its firm grounding in a concrete setting and situation, allowing Larkin's skeptical preachment about the irrelevance of the church to occur without much offense, from the ironic opening phrase onward: "I am sure there's nothing going on/ . . .

inside." Eventually the speaker wonders "who/ Will be the last, the very last, to seek/ This place for what it was." Imagery of a church in ruins dominates the poem at its climax: "Grass, weedy pavement, brambles, buttress, sky." (Conjured images of Tintern Abbey, or other stereotypically English ruins, here summarize the coming fate of churches in England that the speaker sees.) The balanced melancholy of the poem finds the church, though a "place . . . not worth stopping for," to be nonetheless "A serious house on serious earth" that pulls people toward it, a place "proper to grow wise in,/ If only that so many dead lie round." The imaginative range of the poem, moving as it does from the concrete to the abstract and universal, from "disbelief" to a future time when even that may be a forgotten human stage, gives it distinction and significance.

Formally "Church Going" is like an ode, a stanzaic lyric poem that develops and explores a serious topic at some length. Each of its seven stanzas comprises nine iambic pentameter lines—the numerology seeming, like religion itself, to tap into the prerational. A complex stanzaic rhyme scheme, *ababcadcd*, employs full and approximate (half or slant) rhymes freely. Skill with subtle metrical variations— trochaic substitutions, caesuras, enjambments, feminine endings—keeps the lines flowing like talk, much in the manner to which readers of Robert Browning's monologues, or of Larkin's lyrics, are accustomed. As usual Larkin's speaker is syntactic, at once colloquial and formal in his assertions. His sharp imagery draws the church interior in the first two stanzas: "sprawlings of flowers, cut/ For Sunday, brownish now; some brass and stuff/ Up at the holy end; the small neat organ." The "musty, unignorable silence" has "Brewed God knows how long." When the man reads "Here endeth" to an empty sanctuary, "The echoes snigger briefly."

As in "Toads"—and following the lead of his disavowed mentor Yeats—Larkin has his speaker engage in questions, a useful device for exploring alternatives: "Shall we avoid [churches] as unlucky places?" "And what remains when disbelief has gone?" and "I wonder who/ Will be the last . . . to seek/ This place for what it was?" "Some ruin-bibber, randy for antique,/ Or Christmas-addict?" In such an inquisitive context, the speaker's varied assertions hold their ground: "Power of some sort or other will go on," "It pleases me to stand in silence here," or "someone will forever be surprising/ A hunger in himself to be more serious,/ And gravitating with it to this ground."

In this serious meditation on the post-Christian age, Larkin's witty glints lighten the tone. As the persona, for example, wonders if in future eras "we shall keep/ A few cathedrals chronically on show" and "let the rest rent-free to rain and sheep," his word "chronically" plays on "perpetually" while suggesting something like a lingering illness, and "let" as "lease" introduces a playful figurative situation, with sheep as renters. The "crew" of cathedral-hounds who "tap and jot and know what rood-lofts were" are mildly satirized as the eventual last "church goers," just as the phrases "this accoutred frowsty barn" (where "frowsty" means unkempt and musty), "randy for antique," and "Christmas-addict" all trigger weak smiles. The mild self-denigration that occurs in various details, hinting that the biker is a bit of a perplexed bumblehead, likewise entertains.

The speaker's "serious" view is clearly that the church is irrelevant and "obsolete," appeals to superstition, plays a riddling power game, and is destined to fade into vague memory, even as so many church structures in England already have. Nonetheless, nostalgia for inaccessible certainties remains. In that tangential respect, the speakers in "Church Going" and "Toads" are alike: Each looks wistfully at a pattern of living that he seems constitutionally unsuited to embracing and suffers an emotional isolation that seems to be his fate. As in Hardy's poems and novels, there is no possibility that by strength of will the persona can remake himself into something he is not. The final lines hint bleakly that one "grows wise" only in the company of the dead.

THE WHITSUN WEDDINGS

First published: 1964
Type of work: Poem

Taking the train down to London on a Maytime Saturday, a man observes newlyweds boarding at successive stations and contemplates the convergent pattern.

Written in October, 1958, and published as the title poem in Larkin's 1964 volume, the ode-like poem "The Whitsun Weddings" bears formal and thematic resemblances to "Church Going" but shifts its focus away from the Larkin speaker and toward the collective social event that he witnesses, voyeuristically, while making "A slow and stopping curve southwards" from Hull to London. The poem is thus only partly "about" the speaker, whose presumed bachelorhood serves as foil for the "dozen" wedded couples who, at stop after stop, board the train to journey with him toward their separate and communal destinies. The details of the poem that focus on the speaker seem little more than a cumulative medium for framing what he sees: "I was late getting away;" "At first, I didn't notice what a noise/ The weddings made/ Each station that we stopped at;" and, near the end, "I thought of London spread out in the sun,/ Its postal districts packed like squares of wheat." Through much of the poem the speaker says "we," including others on the train with himself and—incrementally—all the couples who join their microcosmic ride.

The poem seems provocative and mildly fatalistic in its conclusions about what the observed phenomena mean. The ironic sense that the couples are wrapped in their own excitement so as to be unaware of participating in any larger pattern governs the poet's conclusion, where "none/ Thought of the others they would never meet/ Or how their lives would all contain this hour." Several details in the poem underscore how destiny operates in ways no person among the passengers can understand: "There [at London] we were aimed," "it was nearly done, this frail/ Travelling coincidence," and finally, "there swelled/ A sense of falling, like an arrow-shower/

Sent out of sight, somewhere becoming rain." In the moment lives a sense of "all the power/ That being changed can give." The train ride becomes finally a metaphor for life as it moves onward, propelled by a common stream of marriages. Mutability, the inevitable pattern of change that governs life while remaining so unsusceptible to understanding or governance, is one large theme here.

Much of the poem's appeal lies in its snapshot social realism. In minutely observed if mildly satiric detail, Larkin's observer represents the working-class wedding parties: men "grinning and pomaded, girls/ In parodies of fashion, heels and veils," "mothers loud and fat;/ An uncle shouting smut," young girls who "stared/ At a religious wounding," imagining some bride's impending surrender. The note that "each face seemed to define/ Just what it saw departing" is precise in its relativism. Images of "short-shadowed cattle" and "the reek of buttoned carriage-cloth" vivify the witnessed drama. Meanwhile, unobtrusive figures enrich the poem's texture: "tall heat that slept," a typical personification, and the similes of the last two stanzas are examples.

Formally "The Whitsun Weddings" is much like "Church Going." Its eight stanzas are each ten lines long, all lines but the second (which is two-stressed) showing the elegantly "natural" iambic pentameter that Larkin managed with such skill. The *ababcdecde* rhyme scheme suggests that the poet conceived of his stanza as quatrain-plus-sestet, the latter in the manner of Italian sonnets; enjambment, however, usually blurs the division, and run-ons in syntax between stanzas occur often.

HIGH WINDOWS

First published: 1974
Type of work: Poem

Eying a young couple lasciviously, an aging man thinks of his youth before imagining blank "high windows."

"High Windows," finished in 1967 and included as the title poem in Larkin's last volume, shows modest departures in method and new symbolic indirections. Though the windows are no doubt symbols, literally they are sashes set high in a wall (perhaps in a tall building) so that one looking out "the sun-comprehending glass" from inside sees only "the deep blue air, that shows/ Nothing, and is nowhere, and is endless." These apertures onto heaven, but not into eternity, are clouded over with a Larkinesque nihilism, an agnostic's philosophical nothingness. The image of the windows occurs to the speaker "Rather than words," suggesting the skeptic's truth that what lies beyond cannot be stated. Thus the poem's epiphany, its moment of revelation, reveals "Nothing"; the parallelism with *"No God any more,"* occurring earlier, heightens the figurative message. The hint in "high windows" of cathedral panes doubles the irony.

This poem seems a aging man's piece but also surely reflects something of the youth-led and freedom-intent 1960's—with "Bonds and gestures pushed to one side"— in its relatively licentious language and loosened style. Like "Church Going," the poem is a reverie on the absence of viable religion, but the method of exploration here is associative, not quietly rational and syntactic: Seeing the young couple and imagining their sex life makes the speaker think about his lost youth and how he might have appeared then. In turn, that thought triggers the image of the windows. (The cinematic technique of the skyward fadeout may lie in the background of the poem's closing effect.) The poem's unbalanced three-part structure highlights its "middle" section with italicized type.

Formally, the poem is stanzaic but not metrical. Like "Toads," it intentionally abuses "common meter," settling into an *abab* rhyme scheme. A notable, witty irony is that "kids" and "diaphragm" are early nonrhymes.

Reading the poem with established notions about the "Larkin persona" overlaid on it, one thinks inevitably of the librarian of Hull in his university-owned "high windowed" apartment, aging and unmarried. Thus irony dominates—whoever imagined the young Larkin among the youthful "lot" that would eventually "*all go down the long slide/ Like free bloody birds*" surely misread things. Typically for Larkin, a set of foils operates: While the speaker can now imagine the young couple in "Paradise" and can think of "everyone young going down the long slide/ To happiness," that destiny seems to have escaped him personally; even his early freedom from a fearful faith has not left him romantically happy or sensually fulfilled. The poem's image of "an outdated combine harvester" that has "reaped" little is a quiet, innuendo-filled analogue for the poem's persona.

Summary

Though an Oxford graduate and university librarian, Philip Larkin is not "academic." Acclaimed by scholars and general readers alike, Larkin is a principal English poet of the post-World War II era. Formally conservative, his poems nonetheless adapt colloquial talk and explore contemporary life. His persona's voice is sad, ironic, balanced, wise, witty, stoic, and capable of surprise. Missing access to the fulfillments of love or faith that others may have, the poet/voyeur looks out wistfully onto the world—but not far into the heavens. Critical discussion of Larkin after 1955 as a part of The Movement in English literature acknowledges his pragmatic rejection of the excesses of both Romanticism and modern experimentation.

Bibliography

Brownjohn, Alan. *Philip Larkin*. Harlow, Essex: Longman Group, 1975.

Hoffpauir, Richard. *English Poetry from Hardy to Larkin*. London: Associated University Presses, 1991.

Martin, Bruce K. *Philip Larkin*. Boston: Twayne, 1978.

Petch, Simon. *The Art of Philip Larkin*. Sydney: Sydney University Press, 1981.

Rossen, Janice. *Philip Larkin: His Life's Work*. Iowa City: University of Iowa Press, 1989.

Salwak, Dale, ed. *Philip Larkin: The Man and His Work*. Basingstoke, England: Macmillan, 1988.

Thwaite, Anthony. Introduction to *Philip Larkin: Collected Poems*. London: Marvell Press, 1988.

Whalen, Terry. *Philip Larkin and English Poetry*. Vancouver: University of British Columbia Press, 1986.

Roy Neil Graves

MARGARET LAURENCE

Born: Neepawa, Manitoba, Canada
July 18, 1926
Died: Lakefield, Ontario, Canada
January 5, 1987

Principal Literary Achievement

Laurence contributed to the development of Canadian fiction, and particularly to themes relating to women's experiences, through her creation of the Manawaka Cycle, five novels based on a fictional Canadian town.

Biography

Margaret Laurence was born Jean Margaret Wemyss on July 18, 1926, in Neepawa, Manitoba. Her ancestry was a mixture of Scottish and Irish-Canadian. She was an inveterate reader as a child and began to write stories in her childhood. She wrote stories for the school magazine; by the age of thirteen she had imagined a fictional town of Manawaka, clearly based on Neepawa. Later she would portray that town of Manawaka as the context for her heroines' varied experiences.

Laurence's father, Robert Wemyss, was a lawyer, and her mother, Verna Simpson, was a musician. Her maternal grandfather was a cabinetmaker and became the town undertaker. Laurence's youth was marked with tragic losses and remarkable adaptations on the part of her family. When Laurence was four, her mother died suddenly, and her aunt came to live with her father and her. This aunt, Margaret Simpson, married Laurence's father a year later, and the couple had one child, Robert. Laurence and her stepmother developed a close relationship that persisted throughout Laurence's formative years. Tragedy struck again four years later when Laurence's father died. Laurence's stepmother faced an uncertain future since she was a woman rearing two children alone. Help arrived in the person of Laurence's maternal grandfather, eighty-two years old and also recently widowed, who came to live with them. The grandfather was in good health and became a strong influence in Laurence's life. Although her stepmother often became engaged in bitter conflicts with her stubborn grandfather, the two provided a stable environment for Laurence and her brother.

Laurence went to college in Winnipeg and continued to write. In 1947, she was graduated and became a reporter. That same year she married an engineer, Jack Laurence, and the two moved to England in 1949. The next year the Laurences moved to Somaliland, West Africa, where Jack built dams to retain rainwater for villagers. Two

1111

years later the Laurences moved to the British Colony that became Ghana. The Laurence's two children, Jocelyn and David, were born there. Her first book, *A Tree for Poverty: Somali Poetry and Prose* (1954), was a translation of Somali literature.

In 1957, the Laurences moved to Vancouver, British Columbia, where Laurence began to write about her African experiences from a fictional perspective. The outcome was *This Side Jordan* (1960), a novel that reflected the turbulent era of emerging independence of the Ghanaian people. She also wrote about her African experience in stories she had published in Canadian magazines from 1954 to 1962. The resulting collection, *The Tomorrow-Tamer*, was published in 1963, a year after Laurence separated from her husband and moved with her children to Buckinghamshire, England. She lived in England for twelve years.

During that period she composed the primary body of works that secured her reputation as one of Canada's foremost novelists. The year 1963 also saw the appearance of *The Prophet's Camel Bell* (published in the United States as *New Wind in a Dry Land*, 1964), based upon her experience a decade earlier in Somaliland. In 1968, *Long Drums and Cannons: Nigerian Dramatists and Novelists, 1952-1966* appeared. In 1969 she divorced Jack Laurence.

Five works published between 1964 and 1974 are the basis of her fame. These five novels, called the Manawaka Cycle, begin with *The Stone Angel* (1964) and *A Jest of God* (1966). Both novels introduce heroines who live in Manawaka, a small prairie town in Canada, and who struggle to gain insights into their families and their identities. In 1969, Laurence completed *The Fire-Dwellers*, which draws upon autobiographical elements and treats the experiences of a sister of the main character in *A Jest of God*. The fourth novel in the cycle, *A Bird in the House* (1970), is largely autobiographical and focuses on Laurence's childhood. Her body of work was acknowledged in 1971, when she received the honor of Companion, Order of Canada. In 1974, Laurence returned to Canada to live in Ontario. In that year *The Diviners*, the last novel in the Manawaka Cycle, appeared. A year later, Laurence was honored again with the Molson Award.

The five Manawaka novels were the climax of her writing career. She wrote four children's books from 1970 through 1981; *Heart of a Stranger*, a book of travel writings based on her African experiences, appeared in 1976. After the *The Diviners*, she published no more fiction for adults. She became chancellor of Trent University in Ontario in 1981; she died in 1987 in Ontario, Canada.

Analysis

In an autobiographical essay, "Books That Mattered to Me" (1981), Laurence recalled that in college she discovered Canadian writers who were striving to understand what it meant to be Canadian. From her exposure to these writers, Laurence learned that as a writer she would have to "write out of my own place, my own time, my own people." This declaration serves as a good starting point for understanding Laurence's strengths as a Canadian author. She is first and foremost Canadian in her identity and in her values. Readers of her books will gain insights into the ways in which the vast Canadian landscape affects the choices and struggles faced by individuals and by families. When Laurence discovered her roots, she also discovered her strengths. In doing so, she set the foundation for her finest writing.

The importance of that sense of "place" and its relationship to a character's identity and values is best reflected in her creation of a specific fictional town she called Manawaka, based to a great extent on her hometown of Neepawa, Manitoba, Canada. Her creation of Manawaka reflects also the primacy of the autobiographical elements of Laurence's fiction. All the heroines in the five Manawaka novels can trace their backgrounds or roots in some way to the fictional Manawaka. Often Laurence used specific settings, such as the town cemetery, her grandfather's funeral parlor, the dance hall, or the junkyard, as symbolic settings in which her characters could interact. Just as William Faulkner did in his creation of Yoknapatawpha County (the county seat of Jefferson is based in part on Oxford, Mississippi), Laurence transformed the townspeople and the literal settings to serve the purposes of her art. It is impossible to separate the meanings of Laurence's characterizations, conflicts, and themes from the sense of place that is generated by her blending of autobiography and fiction.

Her experiences in Somaliland and Ghana in the 1950's certainly were formative ones in her career as a writer. The works based on her African experiences reflect the struggles of individuals from diverse cultures trying to communicate with one another and accommodate one another's needs. Similarly, these works concern the problems faced by a country preparing itself for independence. Many of her stories emphasize the outsider's point of view, perhaps reflecting her own status as a Westerner living in an alien culture.

Laurence was acutely aware of the theme of the insider/outsider. She was able to empathize with the plight of people who lived under the domination of colonial powers and thus were, in many respects, outsiders in their own lands because they were subject to oppression. As a Canadian author, she understood that feeling of being outside the main political and economic power base in the Western Hemisphere. As a woman, she was aware of the struggle of women to free themselves from the domination of men. In her creation of the town of Manawaka, she was identifying with the conflicts that arise between the narrow-minded citizens of a small town and the outsiders who dared to challenge the security of the status quo. Laurence gave voice in her characters to a diverse set of ideas that challenged old assumptions.

Whereas men were the dominant characters in her African stories, women are the dominant characters in her Canadian fiction. Each of the five Manawaka novels features the experiences of a separate heroine. Four of the women are from Manawaka; the fifth, Morag Gunn, is an outsider who seeks to escape from the town after she has become part of its fabric. Morag is also a novelist and thus perhaps most closely represents the viewpoint of someone who, like Laurence, had to stand on the outside in order to portray objectively the experiences of Manawaka natives. In many respects Laurence is a feminist author. Her women are engaged in a process of reflection and self-discovery. They resist the domination of men and seek insights into their own strengths (and even failings) of character.

Many of her novels and stories portray problems of communication between individuals. Laurence suggests that although people seek closeness and understanding in relationships, they often undermine successful relationships because of deep-seated personal conflicts that remain hidden from them. In Laurence's fictional world relationships are fragile, sometimes fleeting, but always complicated. Characters necessarily have difficulty relating to others when they do not know themselves fully.

THE STONE ANGEL

First published: 1964
Type of work: Novel

An old woman's struggle with cancer stimulates her to reevaluate her life.

Hagar Shipley, ninety years old, dominates the action in *The Stone Angel*, the first of Laurence's five novels that treat the experiences of women whose lives intersect with the fictional town of Manawaka, Manitoba. Hagar tells her story in the first person, and a review of her past life is woven into the narrative. Hagar was born in Manawaka; her mother died giving birth to her. Hagar has never accepted this loss. She associates any weakness on the part of others as symbolic of the weakness of her mother, who was not able to survive childbirth. To compensate, Hagar has always been a stern, unremitting judge of others. She has lost touch with the sensitive side of herself.

Laurence provides a compelling symbol of Hagar early in the novel. The town cemetery is dominated by the statue of a stone angel placed there in her mother's honor. In an ironic twist of fate, the carver did not add the eyes of the angel, and the author suggests that this symbolic "blindness" is reflected in Hagar's view of herself, her relationships with her father and her brothers, her marriage to Bram Shipley, and her attitudes toward her two sons, Marvin and John. Hagar has never seen herself for who she truly is. Reared by a maiden aunt, Hagar was dominated by her father, who had a narrow conception of how a young woman should act and what role she should fulfill. Hagar tries to escape her father's domination by marrying Shipley, an uncouth farmer who shows little promise for managing his property. Before long, Hagar and Bram argue constantly; soon they live separate lives even though they live together. Eventually, they decide to separate when Hagar leaves with their younger son, John.

Hagar invests all of her emotional energy in her son John. She rears him alone and becomes blind to his character as it develops in a direction similar to that of Bram. John becomes all that Hagar desires that he not become. He defies her just as she defied her father and just as Bram defied her. John even falls in love with a woman whom his mother considers beneath him. Unfortunately, Hagar cannot see and accept the deep affection the two feel toward each other. John and his lover die a tragic death, the result of another defiant act on John's part. Hagar never forgives herself for driving him away and, in her mind, indirectly causing his death. The day she sees her dead son in the hospital is the day her grieving heart turns to stone.

The image of stone is an important part of the symbolic meaning of the stone angel. If stone is a common symbol of the heart numbed forever by grief, stone also represents what is cold, hard, and unforgiving in the human heart. Hagar's judgments throughout the novel are unrelenting and enduring. She refuses to change her mind once she has made a decision, and this behavior leaves her isolated from the warmth of human contact.

Hagar lives with her son Marvin and his wife Doris. These caregivers are in their sixties and finding it increasingly difficult to live in harmony with a quarrelsome old woman. Laurence ably treats the theme of adult caregivers facing the limitations of old age while trying to provide adequate care for an older parent. Added to these concerns is Marvin's long-standing unresolved relationship with his mother. John was always her favorite son. Although Marvin has cared for Hagar for more than twenty years, she has never recognized him for being a good son. Near the end of the novel, when Hagar enters the hospital to receive treatment for the symptoms of advanced cancer, she does acknowledge Marvin's devotion to her. Laurence treats their interaction ironically, however, for when Hagar releases Marvin from his burden, she does so as an act of kindness toward him, not because she believes what she tells him. In fact, she calls her recognition of Marvin's efforts a "lie"; but then reconsiders by saying that it was "not a lie, for it was spoken at least and at last with what may perhaps be a kind of love."

Although Hagar's interaction with Marvin reflects ambivalent feelings on her part, it reflects one of the few times in the novel that she seizes an opportunity to communicate honestly and openly with another person. An important theme in the novel is that of missed opportunities for communication. When Hagar's brother dies, she misses the chance to share her feelings with her other brother; she never tells her father what her needs are; she never tells her husband how much she loves him; she never acknowledges Marvin's appeals for affection when he is a boy; she never tells her son John that it would be all right to see his girlfriend in the house whenever he wants to see her.

Laurence suggests that lost opportunities for communication are related to excessive pride and a fear of dependency or loss of control. In old age, Hagar begins to realize what she has lost; before she dies, she realizes that what she has always wanted was to experience joy and fullness of life. Yet her need for privacy, her rigid exclusion of contrary points of view, and her pride held her back.

Hagar is an enigma to the end. The epigram for the novel is an excerpt from Dylan Thomas' famous poem, "Do Not Go Gentle into That Good Night." Hagar lives out the imperative that the narrator makes to his father in that poem. Hagar "rages" from the beginning to the end of this novel. She rages against the loss of control she feels as the object of caregiving; she rages against her aging body and the cancer that afflicts her; she rages against the lack of communication between the generations; she rages at the failed choices she has made throughout her life; and she rages against

God for not making the terms of communication between people more accessible and easy to follow.

THE FIRE-DWELLERS

First published: 1969
Type of work: Novel

A woman overcomes feelings of self-doubt, struggles to resolve ongoing conflicts with her husband, and discovers untapped sources of strength in her character.

The Fire-Dwellers is the third in the series of Laurence's five Manawaka novels. Its heroine, Stacey MacAindra, is the sister of Rachel Cameron, the heroine in the second novel in the series, *A Jest of God* (1966). Whereas Rachel seemed doomed to spend her life in the narrow confines of the small town of Manawaka, her sister Stacey escaped the town and moved to Vancouver, British Columbia, at the age of nineteen. At the age of twenty-three she married Cliff MacAindra, a salesman. Now thirty-nine, Stacey is not happy with her life. She feels unattractive, trapped by the pressures of motherhood, confused by her husband's lack of communication with her, and frustrated with her husband's decision to begin a new job working for a man who appears to be a manipulative and overbearing charlatan.

Laurence tells the story through Stacey's eyes, using the form of interior monologue as the character reacts to events in the present and reflects upon events in the past. Stacey's world is dominated by her responsibilities as a mother of four children, each of whom is an individual with unique needs. At first Stacey feels she has reached an impasse as a caregiver. The burden of responding to the children's diverse requests seems too much to bear. Stacey retreats into a private world. At one point she laments that she is neither a good mother nor a good wife.

In time, Stacey's experiences contradict this declaration. She survives several crises facing her children. At the end of the novel she feels her strength of will renewed. Finally, she declares, "I used to think there would be a blinding flash of light someday, and then I would be wise and calm and would know how to cope with everything and my kids would rise up and call me blessed. Now I see that whatever I'm like, I'm pretty well stuck with it for life." She realizes that she is a good mother and possesses an internal reservoir of strength and determination.

The strains in the relationship between Stacey and her husband reflect Laurence's interest in the theme of the fragile nature of human communication. Stacey complains that Mac will not share his thoughts or fears with her. Initially, she concludes that his lack of disclosure reveals his lack of caring; eventually, she understands that his reticence masks his fears that he will not be able to take care of the family's financial needs and that he is inadequate at his job. As soon as Stacey grasps the true state of her husband's crisis, she is empowered to act on his behalf against all odds. By the end of the novel, she demonstrates skills for reconciliation, adaptation, and a willingness to take on new challenges on behalf of her family.

Stacey's personal struggle to regain a sense of her own identity reflects Laurence's abiding concern with the process of reflection and self-discovery in women's lives. Stacey constantly seeks answers as to who she is, what her purpose in life should be, and what suitable roles she can fulfill. In despair at her inability to communicate with her husband, Stacey meets a young man by chance and begins a love affair with him. Although Stacey gains a sense of fulfillment from this affair, she does not know how to resolve her relationships at this point.

Eventually, several crises occur that propel her toward a resolution of all relationships. Stacey decides to stay with Mac after he begins to share some of his fears; she does not return to her lover; and she decides to take care of Mac's father after the old man has a bad fall. Mac escapes his intimidating boss when the latter is promoted to a position in Montreal. Stacey cannot help but marvel at the workings of fate and human will. At the end of the novel, Laurence emphasizes a newfound harmony in their relationship after both survive respective periods of self-imposed isolation and introspection. Now the two have each other, not as each would like the other to be but as each accepts the other despite imperfections and limitations of character or will.

In a sense, Stacey has always wanted her husband to speak to her in her language—articulate, expressive, sharing openly, willing to disclose any and all feelings. Yet he cannot speak this way. After one of many family emergencies is overcome late in the novel, Stacey recognizes that Mac and her oldest son speak the same language, a language in many respects foreign to her own. Finally, she comes to accept this difference in how communication works within this family. To Stacey, the world will always be a dangerous place. Everyone is a "fire-dweller"—Stacey's experiences in the novel reflect innumerable close calls and crises. Yet Stacey finally learns to accept the uncertainties and risks associated with the future.

Summary

Margaret Laurence was always faithful to her Canadian roots as a writer. Her depiction of life on the harsh prairie landscape, particularly her creation of the fictional town of Manawaka, which functions as the setting for five of her novels, is an integral part of the sense of place in her works. Her creation of strong women characters and her treatment of themes relevant to women's experiences, place her in the forefront of feminist writing. Laurence portrays women who overcome problems of identity, limited roles, the complexities of motherhood, and the perils of marriage relationships. Laurence probes the nuances of communication in human relationships and exposes the difficulties faced by individuals who seek to uncover secrets about their pasts and about themselves.

Bibliography

Gunnars, Kristjana, ed. *Crossing the River: Essays in Honour of Margaret Laurence.* Winnipeg, Canada: Turnstone Press, 1988.

Nicholson, Colin. *Critical Approaches to the Fiction of Margaret Laurence.* Vancouver, Canada: University of British Columbia Press, 1990.

Thomas, Clara. *The Manawaka World of Margaret Laurence.* Toronto, Canada: McClelland and Stewart, 1976.

Verduyn, Christl, ed. *Margaret Laurence: An Appreciation.* Peterborough, Canada: Broadview Press, 1988.

Woodcock, George. *Introducing Margaret Laurence's "The Stone Angel": A Reader's Guide.* Toronto, Canada: ECW Press, 1989.

_____. *The World of Canadian Writing: Critiques and Recollections.* Vancouver, Canada: Douglas & McIntyre, 1980.

Robert E. Yahnke

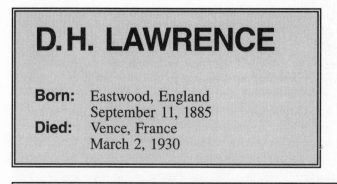

D. H. LAWRENCE

Born: Eastwood, England
September 11, 1885
Died: Vence, France
March 2, 1930

Principal Literary Achievement

A major British author of the twentieth century, Lawrence probed with great intensity and occasional audacity themes of human sexual psychology and questions of moral behavior.

Biography

David Herbert Lawrence was born in Eastwood, a coal mining town in Nottingham, England, on September 11, 1885. His father, Arthur John Lawrence, was a gregarious, hard-drinking collier whose marriage to Lydia Beardsall, formerly a schoolteacher of genteel refinements, was a continuous struggle for mastery. D. H. Lawrence was the third son born into this household, along with two sisters. A gentle, studious, sissified boy, Lawrence was sometimes scorned by the more robust colliers' sons of the town; shunning their athletic games, he enjoyed instead the company of his sisters or of their young female friends, whom he charmed with his skill at charades and games of mimicry. Above all, he enjoyed excursions in the Derbyshire countryside not far from the grimy mines, near the lush Sherwood Forest area surrounding Eastwood, a retreat that Lawrence once called "the country of my heart."

Although he did not enter school until he was seven, when he was enrolled in the Beauvale Board School, he made rapid progress there, and at the age of twelve he was awarded a North County Council scholarship to Nottingham High School, eight miles from his town. After he left high school in 1901, he was briefly employed in Nottingham at the office of a surgical supply factory. At sixteen, he suffered from a severe bout with pneumonia and required a long time to recuperate. Earlier in 1901, his older brother, Ernest, had died of respiratory illness; frantic, his mother began to focus all of her attention on her convalescent son. So intense was the affectionate relationship between mother and son that Lawrence later came to believe that it had diverted his sexual development from a more normal path.

Some time before his illness, during the summer of 1901, Lawrence had met Jessie Chambers, then fourteen, who was living at the Haggs' farm, three miles from Eastwood. In the convivial household of the Chambers family, so different from his own,

1120

Lawrence enjoyed a friendship, especially with the brothers, that was relaxed and spontaneous; with Jessie he enjoyed a deeper, more intimate relationship, although his mother disapproved of the girl.

In 1902, Lawrence was a pupil-teacher at the Eastwood British School, where he taught both in Eastwood and at Ilkeston, Derbyshire, until September, 1906, when he entered Nottingham University. Having placed in the First Division of the First Class on the National King's Scholarship Examination, he was admitted to a two-year academic program leading to an arts degree. Qualified as a teacher in 1908, he became a junior assistant-master at the Davidson Road School in Croydon, a suburb of London. He worked there until November, 1911, when a second severe attack of pneumonia forced him to take a leave of absence.

Yet as early as 1905 Lawrence had begun writing, and with Jessie Chambers as his sounding board, he experimented in fiction and poetry. When his mother died in January, 1911, he suffered a terrible emotional blow, yet in that year he published his first novel, *The White Peacock*. Reviewed favorably by most critics—one compared Lawrence as a regionalist to Thomas Hardy—the novel established a thematic pattern that would become fairly typical for the author. Narrated by a Lawrence-like character, the book treats the mating choice of a young woman for one of two suitors, one overcerebral and overcivilized, the other an earthy, vital man. The novel also urges the need for honesty, for naturalness in the relationships between men and men, as well as between men and women.

Lawrence's second novel, *The Trespasser* (1912), based upon the experiences of his friend Helen Corke, was less successful. Yet with the publication of *Sons and Lovers* in 1913, his reputation began to grow. Along with the publication of his first book of poetry in the same year, the novel marked a major advance in his professional career. A year earlier, in April, 1912, Lawrence's personal life had also changed dramatically. After a month's courtship, he had eloped with Frieda von Richthofen Weekley, mother of three small children and wife of a professor of French at Nottingham University.

With Frieda by his side (the couple was not to marry until 1914, when her divorce became final), Lawrence traveled the world extensively—usually in self-imposed exile from England. In the midst of packing and unpacking, seeking warm places more favorable to his tuberculosis, he continued to write major fiction, such as *The Rainbow* (1915), *Women in Love* (1920)—generally regarded as his masterpiece—and *Lady Chatterley's Lover* (1928). Lawrence also published other novels, including *The Lost Girl* (1920), *Aaron's Rod* (1922), *Kangaroo* (1923), *The Boy in the Bush* (1924), and *The Plumed Serpent* (1926). Lawrence also published collections of novellas; nearly a dozen volumes of poetry, eight volumes of short stories, four volumes of travel sketches, and other collections of essays and plays. By 1928, following the publication of *Lady Chatterley's Lover*, Lawrence's health began to fail. After staying a month at a sanatorium, he insisted upon being moved to a villa at Vence, near Cannes (France). There on March 2, 1930, with Frieda at his side, he died. After burial, his body was later reinterred at Taos, New Mexico.

Analysis

In an essay entitled "The State of Funk," Lawrence discusses his moral vision as an artist:

> My field is to know the feelings inside a man, and to make new feelings conscious. What really torments civilised people is that they are full of feelings they know nothing about; they can't realise them, they can't fulfil them, they can't live them. And so they are tortured. It is like having energy you can't use—it destroys you. And feelings are a form of vital energy.

In Lawrence's worldview, people either possess or lack vital energy—that is to say, *anima*, or spirit. Those whose vital spark fires into passionate energy are truly alive; the rest—those whose natural feelings are dulled by the mechanical routine of "civilization," so that their responses are cerebral, not instinctive—might as well be dead, no matter how successful they may appear to be, no matter how attractive or wealthy or powerful they may seem.

Lawrence's novels, short stories, poems, and miscellaneous writings advance the same moral vision: that men and women (indeed, whole cultures) must discover their true selves, a quality epitomized in *Studies in Classic American Literature* (1923) as the "*IT.*" The IT, or essential self, was once, among primitive cultures, celebrated as a life-force of vital energy. When Lawrence visited sites of Etruscan culture, in *Etruscan Places* (1932), he half described, half invented an archaic world during a period when its people took passionate pride in the human body, when they exulted the sacredness of the whole living universe. According to Lawrence, Etruscans and other old civilizations regarded the universe as an organism, a living whole, to which all living things, and even seemingly inanimate things, belong. Now, Lawrence believes, human beings have lost sight of their interconnectedness with the organic universe; they have lost their connection with *anima*, the vital spirit. Through constant mechanical repetition, their feelings, even their sexual feelings, have grown dull, repetitious, lacking spontaneity or natural warmth.

Rejecting the scientific positivism dominant in twentieth century philosophy, Lawrence urges instead a "religion of the blood," a primitivistic belief in the power of instinct rather than mind. For him, the "dark gods" of the blood, of the subconscious intuitive self, not the light of cerebral rationality, must rule human conduct.

Yet how can modern men and women, forced to work in a mechanized, technologically complex world, tap their deepest feelings? For Lawrence, reared in a mining town that symbolized for him the mechanical horrors of a rigid, artificial, inhuman universe, the answer was both simple and complicated. On a simple level, they must learn to reeducate their native instincts, almost stultified by the repetitions of work, almost blighted by meaningless social intercourse.

To renew these instincts, Lawrence as an artist would educate the sensibility of people, so that they might confront their secret hearts. Typically, his stories concern confrontations or encounters in which characters discover their true sensual identity and either achieve fulfillment or fail. Because the sexual urge, in Lawrence's view, is the last powerful human feeling that resists the mechanization of intellect, he usually shows how characters can reeducate their passionate selves in order to become authentic human beings. Thus, sex—usually identified in the public mind as the writer's central theme—is actually the means, not the end, of vital education. Lawrence once complained bitterly about the vulgar image of him as a "lurid" propagandist for sexuality. His theme, indeed, is not sex, but love. In a sense, Lawrence is the most "romantic" of major twentieth century writers, for he believes not only in the redemptive powers of love but also that human beings have a narrow choice: They will either love or die—they will either become part of the vital flow of energy, or they will dry up, shrink in heart, and become one of the living dead.

If Lawrence's moral vision is simple (or, to his detractors, simplistic), his purposes as an artist are often complicated. Although his plots are generally direct enough—he brings two or three major characters into direct confrontation—the means by which characters confront one another are calculated to expose their intrinsic psychological urges. Commonly, Lawrence will structure a plot around the conflict of three persons in a triangle confrontation. In this pattern, a woman has a choice between two suitors. One is inhibited, "civilized," meticulous to a fault, often limited by a weak or ambiguous sexual drive; the other is virile, healthy, unaffected, but often coarse in manner. Stories such as "The Old Adam" and "A Modern Lover" are typical. Sometimes the pattern is varied, with a fastidious male character forced to choose between a prim, gentle, sexually undemanding (or unresponsive) potential mate and a more earthy, vital, but sexually assertive female, as in "The Witch a la Mode" and *Sons and Lovers*.

A second common pattern of Lawrence's plots is that involving the mating of two couples, one seemingly more compatible or "lucky" in its robust sexuality, the other experiencing a serious, early complication in its romance. In this pattern, Lawrence usually shows how the members of the "lucky" couple actually are ill-suited to each other, whereas the problematic couple resolves its difficulties to achieve a measure of happiness as in *Love Among the Haystacks* (1930) and *Women in Love*.

Forced to confront their authentic natures, Lawrence's characters either come to terms with their "blood," their subconscious psychological urges, or fail—usually because they attempt to dominate their lover. For Lawrence, love's psychology is inextricably connected with the psychology of mastery, the urge to control another person. When the impulse toward dominance is stronger than that toward eros, as in "The Prussian Officer," the character will fail to achieve vital fulfillment. When one character succeeds in achieving ruthless domination over the other in spite of the partner's resistance, the result is also tragic, as in *The Fox* (1922). Only when Lawrence's love-partners acquiesce to a passionate relationship that is both sexual (phallic) and tender, is the pattern perfected in mutual love, as in *Lady Chatterley's Lover*.

As for characters who fail to achieve any vital connection with another human being, they are either humiliated, as Bertie Reid is in "The Blind Man," or, like expiring vampires, decompose, as Pauline Attenborough does in "The Lovely Lady." For Lawrence, the human vampires, those who feed off the vital energy of others to maintain a semblance, but not the reality, of life, are among the living dead. Lawrence's characters are not so much good or evil as they are alive or dead, either life enlarging or life limiting, either those who worship the dark gods or those who worship the gods of machinery and of money.

SONS AND LOVERS

First published: 1913
Type of work: Novel

In this famous psychological novel, a sensitive Midlands youth cannot reciprocate the love of women of his class because of his Oedipal attraction to his mother.

Sons and Lovers, Lawrence's third book, is an apprenticeship novel that, in many respects, defies the conventions of its genre. Among early twentieth century English apprenticeship novels that preceded Lawrence's work, the main character usually undergoes an "education" or "apprenticeship" toward a meaningful life experience. As part of his (or, rarely, her) apprenticeship, the protagonist begins with innocent, often mistaken notions about the nature of reality; only after some painful experiences does he grow to mastery in the game of life. Specifically, he learns valuable lessons about himself, especially his limitations and illusions, but by the completion of his youth he often can answer three questions: What is the nature of love? What vocation is appropriate for me? and What is the meaning of life?

In contrast with the main characters in earlier apprenticeship novels or in subsequent ones, Paul Morel, Lawrence's protagonist, fails to find answers to any of these questions. By the end of his life apprenticeship, he has learned only that he is incapable of intense sexual feelings to sustain a relationship with a young woman, that he lacks a true vocation for his considerable talents, and that he cannot fathom the "meaning of life," exept narrowly in terms of his own sensibility.

Grappling with a modern version of the classic Oedipal problem, Paul loathes his father, the hard-drinking but convivial miner, Walter, and he attaches himself emotionally to his mother, Gertrude. As a result of this psychological conditioning, in Freudian theory, Paul has been crippled emotionally. Following his mother's death from cancer, Paul is a "derelict," isolated from all meaningful emotional contact with women. His proposal of marriage to Miriam Leivers, whom he had earlier seduced, is merely formalistic, and she rejects him. He turns back Clara Dawes, his paramour, to her husband, Baxter, for he knows that he cannot give her the fullness of love that she deserves.

Yet the clinical phrase "Oedipal complex" does not quite get to the heart of Paul's dilemma. As Lawrence understands his protagonist, Paul has indeed been crippled in his vitality through his mother's excessive love for him, for her identification of soul with his soul. In Lawrence's variation on the Freudian paradigm, Paul has invested his vital force, his *anima*, so deeply into identification with his mother that they are truly one. He has no more vital energy to surrender to any other woman. Gentle, passive Miriam threatens him because, in his imagination, she wishes to absorb his soul, to destroy what is left of his independence. Although he loves her on a spiritual level, he subconsciously fears her physical sexual presence. His "test" on her sexuality has really been a test of his own capacity to feel erotic emotion through her stimulus—and he fails. His love affair with Clara, sexual enough to satisfy him physically, lacks a dimension of the spirit. In either case, he shrinks from being absorbed—from losing his independence through love with either a passive or an assertive woman.

Even as he fails in his quest for love, Paul also fails to discover a life's vocation. Although he has dabbled in painting, has worked as a spiral clerk at a surgical supply factory, and has taught school briefly, he concludes his youth without ever selecting a foundation for his future labors. His vocation, by the end of the novel, is not to work at all, at least not to work at mechanical, dehumanizing tasks. In a sense, his work at Jordan's—which symbolically manufactures artificial limbs and prostheses—prepares him for the larger world beyond Nottingham. He learns that every person is crippled to some degree, some obviously, like the hunchback, Fanny, others emotionally, like Paul.

Finally, he fails to solve the great mystery of the meaning of life. By the end of the novel, he has made only one crucial decision: to go on living. He has decided not to follow his mother in death, presumably by his own suicide. Yet this decision, considering the great emotional stress that Paul has endured, is no small victory of the spirit. The lights of the town that urge him onward are symbols of his renewed spark of vital force. By moving toward these lights "quickly," he shows the reader that he accepts the challenge eagerly.

WOMEN IN LOVE

First published: 1920
Type of work: Novel

In this novel treating the mating of two sisters with their lovers, one couple is relatively successful, while the other concludes its relationship in tragedy.

Women in Love, begun as early as 1913, was tentatively entitled "The Sisters," then later "The Wedding Ring." As the sprawling manuscript began to take shape over the next two years, Lawrence published the first part as *The Rainbow* (1915). With considerable revisions and a complete rethinking of the material, he published a second Brangwen novel in 1920. In its final form, *Women in Love* is less a continuation of *The Rainbow* than an altogether different novel. To be sure, Ursula and Gudrun

Brangwen persist in their quest for happiness. Yet the Gudrun of *The Rainbow* was a minor figure; in *Women in Love*, she is a major protagonist, with a fully developed psychology. Ursula's change is even more dramatic. In the earlier novel, she was a woman of passionate independence, whereas in *Women in Love* she is subdued—less impulsive, less heroic, more nearly domesticated.

Their lovers, Gerald Crich and Rupert Birkin, complement the sisters' essential temperaments. Like the fiery, strong-willed Gudrun, Gerald is a controlling, domineering sensualist—one as habituated to subduing horses to his iron command as to overworking his laborers in the coal mines. In contrast, Rupert (a Lawrence-like personality) is sensitive, introspective, emotionally fragile in spite of his intellectual vitality and his charm.

Unless one reads Lawrence's canceled prologue to *Women in Love*, a chapter that can be examined in the author's posthumous volume *Phoenix II: Uncollected, Unpublished and Other Prose Works* (1968), one cannot fully understand the reason for Rupert's timorousness as a lover. Yet this prologue is an essential key to perceiving what follows in the novel. Even as Rupert was pursuing with dutiful but passionless zeal his affair with Hermione Roddice, he was attempting to put behind him a far more satisfactory emotional friendship with Gerald. Whether the men's earlier relationship had become one of physical homosexuality is not entirely clear (although Lawrence seems to exclude the physical element). Nevertheless, Rupert is erotically stimulated more by men than by women and certainly not by Hermione, in spite of his frantic lovemaking or his earnest wishes to love her with tenderness:

> He wanted all the time to love women. He wanted all the while to feel this kindled, loving attraction toward a beautiful woman, that he would often feel towards a handsome man. But he could not. Whenever it was a case of a woman, there entered in too much spiritual, sisterly love; or else, in reaction, there was only a brutal, callous sort of lust.

As the novel itself begins, a reader ignorant of this complication in Rupert's psychosexual orientation may not fully understand why the character experiences so much trouble in his relationship with Ursula. The couple, after all, seems to be well suited culturally, intellectually, even emotionally. The two share a similar background in education and social class, are both intelligent, sensitive, tolerant, and certainly "love" each other. Yet their love must be tested and refined. Many readers will wonder at the lengthy disputations between Ursula and Rupert—the continuing, often circular debates over the meaning of love, the subtle defining of roles that each partner must adopt to make the relationship work. Precisely this test is the core of Ursula and Rupert's mating, for it results in compromises that make it possible for the couple to marry.

Ursula wisely and lovingly diminishes Rupert's secret fear that women will dominate him sexually. He is actually more comfortable with the embraces of a man. In the chapter "Gladiatorial," Rupert and Gerald release their tensions (and sublimate their repressed eroticism) by wrestling; more than that, for Rupert the touching is a sign of hope for "blood-brotherhood," a deep friendship and binding between the males. When Gerald dies, Rupert is a broken man. Although he has mated successfully with Ursula and loves her as deeply as ever he can a woman, he regrets the loss of another form of fulfillment: bonding for life with a male friend.

If Ursula's vacillating relationship with Rupert ends at last with bittersweet success, Gudrun's passionate affair with Gerald concludes in tragic failure. Yet their love had seemed at first to be grounded firmly on their similar temperaments. Both are controlling, emotionally vehement, erotically charged persons. Yet their seeming "luck" in discovering passion so easily is, in fact, a cause for failure in love. Even as Gerald exerts despotic and capricious force to control his miners, so he tries to subdue the strong-willed Gudrun. Yet she is as defiant, independent, and proud a person as he: She battles him sexually for dominance, so that their lovemaking assumes the qualities of a battle, without tenderness or consideration for the other partner. Less cruel than Gerald, she is nevertheless as perverse in diminishing his self-confidence. Near the conclusion of the novel, his suicide seems inevitable.

Yet how can one explain Gudrun's infatuation with Loerke, a physically unattractive homosexual? Why should this sexually vital woman follow after a man who seems to contrast with Gerald's powerful, athletic virility? The answer is that Loerke is also, like Gerald, a willful, controlling, arrogant brute. He attracts Gudrun through both his magnetism and his dedication to art; in his drawings and sculpture, he achieves works that are mechanical, starkly industrial, rather than human. Through her servant-to-master role with Loerke, Gudrun will complete her destruction (in Lawrence's image, her reduction), eventually to become as mechanical as Loerke.

For Lawrence, Gerald's tragic fate is caused partly by Gudrun's reductive energy, which corrodes his vital spirit, and partly by his own self-destructive egoism. In contrast, Ursula and Rupert are "lucky" in love because they nurture, rather than diminish, the vital energy of their partner. Artists such as Loerke—clever, manipulative, independent—may survive with their ego intact; but unless their lives, as well as their art, are established on human principles, they too fail to reach fulfillment.

THE HORSE DEALER'S DAUGHTER

First published: 1922
Type of work: Short story

In this modern psychological fairy tale of rebirth, a desperate woman and her rescuer are redeemed by love.

"The Horse Dealer's Daughter," resembling such fairy or folktales of transformation as "Cinderella" or variations on themes of "The Ugly Duckling," treats a sullen country girl whose condition is wonderfully altered from humble (or ugly) to attractive and marriageable. Mabel Pervin's transformation also resembles that of tales concerning Princess Aurora or of Snow White, in which a maiden and her world are cast under a spell (or curse), only to revive, along with the revival of life everywhere, upon the magic of a lover's kiss. As a psychological tale, Lawrence's story also resembles coming-of-age rituals, in which the protagonist moves from sexual latency to mature fulfillment, from sterility to fecundity, from passivity to vitality.

At twenty-seven, with a fixed expression on her face described as "bull-dog," Mabel first appears to be an unattractive spinster; worse, she suffers from a depression that brings her to the verge of suicide. Her mother dead, her father and her brothers indifferent to her, she is the drudge of an otherwise all-male household. The men enjoy a vital, jovial connection through their drinking and hearty companionship. Yet Mabel, symbolized by the draught horses tied head to tail, is as captive as a brute animal, in spite of her slumbering, subdued animal strength. Like the horses, she seems to be asleep—helpless to demonstrate her vitality.

When Dr. Jack Ferguson, a friend of the Pervins, especially of Mabel's boisterous brothers, views her wading into the water moments before she submerges into the turgid, "dead" pond, he perceives at once that she wishes to end her life. He rescues her not simply as a physician but also as a concerned human being. In sinking beneath the cold water, he nearly drowns. In a sense, he has saved two persons, Mabel and himself. Yet the immersion, resembling baptism, is a renewal of life—from near death to rebirth—so that both persons are symbolically "reborn."

Mabel's confused words, when she discovers that Ferguson has removed her muddy clothing, challenge him: "Who undressed me?" Certainly it was the doctor, who had in mind only the welfare of his patient. Her next challenge, striking to the heart of her deepest yearning, arouses in him a response that is equally authentic: "Do you love me, then?" For many readers, this challenge appears to be illogical, even absurd. Before the incident, Ferguson had never indicated to her any feeling of love. Yet his response is affirmative. He is compelled to love her, not because of any particular quality in the girl, but because of his need to love. In a sense, his existence has been heretofore as devoid of vital force as hers. He, too, had been dying to his passional self, although he had not been aware of this reduction. In a leap of intuition, he "connects" with Mabel's elliptical meaning. If he does not love her, she might as well be dead. Without intellectual reflection, he knows instantly, subconsciously, that his case is the same.

Ferguson's insistence that the woman marry him at once, the next day if possible, is appropriate to his heart's deepest needs, even as it is to Mabel's. She fears only that his intense, fierce desire will overwhelm her. When she speaks of her "horrible" qualities, she is only human. To Lawrence, all people fear that they are "horrible" despite their exterior attractiveness or charm; only the power of love redeems them from their fears of incapacity. In this most explicitly romantic of Lawrence's stories, his theme must be understood directly, without reading into it any sense of implied irony or satire: Lawrence truly means that Mabel and Jack must either love or die. Awakened into life by the enchantment of flowing vitality, these lovers, like those of fairy-tale romance, successfully complete their ritual of rebirth and are saved.

SNAKE

First published: 1921
Type of work: Poem

From his encounter with a snake, the narrator confronts on a symbolic level his attitudes toward sex.

"Snake" can be understood on two levels, as narrative and as symbol. On the simpler level, a Lawrence-like speaker encounters a snake at "his" water trough. Rapt by nearly hypnotic fascination, he allows the snake to drink, without taking action. Soliloquizing like Hamlet, the speaker wonders whether he is a coward not to kill the snake, because in Sicily the gold snakes are venomous. The snake continues to drink until, satisfied, it climbs the broken bank of the wall face, puts its head into "that dreadful hole," and withdraws "going into blackness." At this point, the speaker throws a log at the water trough yet fails to hit the snake. Immediately, he regrets his "pettiness" and wishes that the snake would come back, for it seemed to be like a king. The speaker has missed his chance with "one of the lords of life."

On the narrative level, the poem is perplexing because a reader cannot fathom why the speaker expresses his internal debate with such vehemence over the question of killing the snake. One is not necessarily a "coward" in avoiding a poisonous snake, nor is one "perverse" in longing to talk to one. What "voices" of his education demand that he kill the snake? Are they the voices of Judaic-Christian tradition concerning the serpent in the Garden of Eden? Are they the voices of scientific rationalism that define a venomous snake as dangerous? Moreover, why should the speaker feel such regret at the act of throwing a log at the snake? After all, the snake had escaped the blow. Why should the snake seem to the speaker to be "like a king in exile, uncrowned in the underworld"? To be sure, in non-Western cultures the snake (or, in ancient Egypt, the crocodile) is often worshiped as a divine symbol of fertility. In India and in Mexico among the ancient Aztecs, the snake has been revered as a god of sexuality and life. Yet why should a twentieth century European speaker suppose that the snake is "due to be crowned again" as a lord of life?

Answers to these questions can best be determined by analyzing the symbolic structure of the poem. The snake is clearly a phallic image—at least to the speaker. When the snake first emerges, reaching down from "a fissure in the earth-wall," the speaker perceives, on a subconscious level, the male organ emerging from the female. Lawrence uses the vulva image of "fissure" or "earth-lipped fissure" deliberately. When the speaker, almost trancelike, stares at the snake "withdrawing into that horrid black hole," he imagines on a symbolic level the act of sexual intercourse. As a result of his "education," he has repressed his sexuality; his fears of the woman are expressed by the word "horrid." By throwing a phallic-shaped log at the disappearing snake, he has suddenly snapped the tension. Now he regrets the voices of his "accursed human education." Even as the Ancient Mariner in Samuel Taylor Coleridge's poem suffered guilt after slaying the albatross, so the speaker feels guilt at his "mean" act. For the snake, in Lawrence's symbolism, is indeed a lord of life. Like Pluto, who in Greek mythology ruled the underworld, the sexual force (phallus) rules the subconscious and is "due to be crowned again," this time as king of the dark gods of the blood—of vitality. Because the snake inhabits two worlds—that of light and of darkness, of the consciousness and of the subconsciousness—it represents to Lawrence (as do "Bavarian Gentians") a union or wedding of the opposing elements of the universe into a single symbol of the life force.

Summary

In "The Rocking-Horse Winner," D. H. Lawrence makes clear his belief that the only "luck" that a person ever achieves in life is the good fortune—or capability—to love. Yet not all forms of love are life enhancing. As a moralist, Lawrence urges his readers to discriminate between incomplete, self-involved, or perverse love and love represented by phallic tenderness. In *Lady Chatterley's Lover*, particularly, he shows how good sex (which is natural, spontaneous, springing from tender feelings toward one's partner) renews life, whereas bad sex (which is cerebral, mechanical, springing from self-involvement and the urge to dominate another human being) results in emotional sterility.

In his essay "Why the Novel Matters," Lawrence wrote that "the novel is the book of life." By that he did not mean simply that the novel provides a reader with vicarious experiences that resemble life. Instead, he meant that the novel actually gives the reader life, because the novelist transmits part of his life force to the reader. As a novelist and as a writer of different genres, Lawrence is generous in providing not only the simulation of life, but also life itself.

Bibliography

Delaney, Paul. *D. H. Lawrence's Nightmare: The Writer and His Circle in the Years of the Great War*. New York: Basic Books, 1978.

Freeman, Mary. *D. H. Lawrence: A Basic Study of His Ideas*. Gainesville: University of Florida Press, 1955.

Garnett, David. *Great Friends: Portraits of Seventeen Writers*. New York: Atheneum, 1980.

Gregory, Horace. *D. H. Lawrence: Pilgrim of the Apocalypse*. New York: Grove Press, 1957.

Hough, Graham. *The Dark Sun: A Study of D. H. Lawrence*. New York: Macmillan, 1957.

Leavis, F. R. *D. H. Lawrence: Novelist*. London: Chatto & Windus, 1955.

Moore, Harry T. *The Intelligent Heart: The Story of D. H. Lawrence*. New York: Farrar, Straus, and Young, 1954.

Spilka, Mark. *The Love Ethic of D. H. Lawrence.* Bloomington: Indiana University Press, 1955.
Tindall, William York. *D. H. Lawrence and Susan His Cow.* New York: Columbia University Press, 1939.

Leslie B. Mittleman

STEPHEN LEACOCK

Born: Swanmoor, Hampshire, England
December 30, 1869
Died: Toronto, Canada
March 28, 1944

Principal Literary Achievement

Although Leacock wrote authoritatively on political economics, the profession for which he was trained, he became Canada's finest writer of parody and burlesque.

Biography

Stephen Butler Leacock was born at Swanmoor, Hampshire, England (in the Isle of Wight), on December 30, 1869, the son of W. P. Leacock and Agnes Butler Leacock. He was taken in 1876 to live on a farm near Lake Simcoe in Ontario, Canada. Stephen Leacock was educated at Upper Canada College in Toronto, where he was head boy in 1887. He was graduated from the University of Toronto in 1891 and earned a Ph.D. in economics from the University of Chicago in 1903. He then began a distinguished academic career that was to last until he was past sixty-five years of age. From 1891 to 1899, he taught at his old preparatory school and found the job of schoolmaster deeply depressing. He joined the faculty at McGill University in Montreal as a temporary lecturer, however, and eventually became professor of political economy. He was named head of the department of economics and political science in 1908 and taught at the university until 1936.

He was widely known for his professional writings, publishing many learned studies in economics. *Elements of Political Science* (1906) was an early academic work, and *Economic Prosperity in the British Empire* (1930) was a major late work. Their author whimsically observed that he hoped that no one would ever have to read them. Certainly, the larger reading audience knew him as the author of humorous essays and burlesques. In fact, so enormously successful were his books of humor and his lectures that, in time, his scholarly writings may have been unjustly neglected.

Leacock made his appearance as a humorist in *Literary Lapses* (1910). This well-received collection was followed in rapid succession by *Nonsense Novels* (1911), *Sunshine Sketches of a Little Town* (1912), and *Arcadian Adventures with the Idle Rich* (1914). Volumes with similarly playful and alliterative titles are *Moonbeams from the Larger Lunacy* (1915) and *Frenzied Fiction* (1918).

Works from the latter half of Leacock's career are *Laugh with Leacock* (1930), *Afternoons in Utopia* (1932), *Mark Twain* (1932), *Charles Dickens: His Life and Work* (1933), *Humor: Its Theory and Technique* (1935), and *Funny Pieces: A Book of Random Sketches* (1936). His books on Twain and Dickens are studies of other writers who made liberal use of humor in their work. In *Humor: Its Theory and Technique*, the college professor brings his analytic powers to the study of comic writing. Books from the prolific writer's last decade are *Laugh Parade* (1940), *Our British Empire: Its Structure, Its History, Its Strength* (1940), *My Remarkable Uncle, and Other Sketches* (1942), *How to Write* (1943), *Last Leaves* (1945), and *The Boy I Left Behind Me* (1946).

The sketches in *Literary Lapses* were actually written between 1891 and 1899, Leacock's period as an unhappy schoolmaster, and had appeared in various periodicals. When he offered them to the publishers of his *Elements of Political Science*, they did not take the proposal seriously. He then printed the sketches at his own expense and, using a news company as distributor, sold three thousand copies in two months. Soon thereafter, the book was published in more conventional form, and Leacock's career as a popular writer was launched.

In August, 1900, Leacock married Beatrix Hamilton of Toronto at the Little Church Around the Corner in New York City. He joined the University Club and, as he became more prosperous, established a summer home in Orillia, Ontario, Canada. Leacock's humor is gently teasing (as opposed to the blistering satire of Twain, to whom he is often compared), but the residents of Orillia were deeply offended by *Sunshine Sketches of a Little Town*. In August, 1915, his only son, Stephen Lushington Leacock, was born. Mrs. Leacock died in 1925. Gradually, Leacock accumulated a host of honorary degrees: Litt.D., LL.D., and D.C.L.

Leacock's comments on himself are usually so playful and self-mocking as to warn the reader against taking them at face value. For example, in the preface to *Sunshine Sketches of a Little Town*, he offers his membership in the Political Science Association of America, the Royal Colonial Institute, and the Church of England as a proof of his respectability. He goes on to say that he is a member of the Canadian Conservative Party but has failed utterly at politics, since he has never been awarded a contract to build a bridge or anything else.

Following a throat operation, Leacock died in the General Hospital at Toronto, Canada, on March 28, 1944. He was seventy-four years of age and left behind four chapters of his autobiography.

Analysis

Leacock has often been compared to Twain. Perhaps it is inevitable that any North American humorist who has won a wide reading audience and whose work is not largely urban and ethnic in nature will be compared to Twain. Moreover, it is true that superficial similarities between the two writers do exist. Both are at their best in the sketch or self-contained episode, and their books, even Twain's novels, are usually collections of short pieces. Both gave humorous lectures that showed them to be skilled performers, as well as writers. Both use a prose that depends little upon quaint-ness or wordplay. The style of each is simple and straightforward, allowing the com-edy to flow from the closely observed absurdities of daily life rather than from verbal pyrotechnics. Finally, of course, Leacock expressed his fascination with Twain by becoming his biographer.

The differences between the two writers, however, are as marked as the similar-ities. Twain's satire, from his first book onward, is often characterized by antipathy and disgust for his subjects. Leacock's dominant mood, on the other hand, is one of amused tolerance. Twain is more truly a writer of fiction. Leacock's pieces are not usually short stories in the sense in which that term is traditionally applied. They are fictional to be sure, in that the reader has no illusions that those anecdotes featuring Leacock himself as protagonist recount actual occurrences. The author-narrator usu-ally represents himself as a naïve bumbler, a persona belied by the skill of his story-telling. Apart from such anecdotes, the bulk of Leacock's humor is parody. He wrote many hilarious spoofs of the romantic novels, detective stories, and theatrical melo-dramas of his day.

It could be argued that all humor is aggressive, that every joke is on someone. Humor is the result of someone's embarrassment, discomposure, loss of status or control, however slight. The ways in which Twain and Leacock express this aggres-sion mark the major difference between them. Leacock writes often about Prohibi-tion in the United States, an undertaking by which he was both amused and bemused. Had Twain lived to see the enactment of the Eighteenth Amendment, the reader can easily imagine the virulence with which he would have assaulted the fools, scoun-drels, and hypocrites who would abridge the freedom of others through such a high-handed measure. Leacock, however, greeted the noble experiment of the Americans (and similar laws enacted in some Canadian provinces) with a feigned amazement and a gentle skepticism.

Leacock alludes obliquely to the professional stresses created by his books of hu-mor. To his professional colleagues, he was first and foremost a political economist. To those most closely associated with him, he was the department head—the man who determined teaching assignments, who recommended raises in pay and promo-tions in rank. In the previously mentioned preface to *Sunshine Sketches of a Little Town*, Leacock complains that many of his friends believe that he writes humorous trifles only in those hours during which he is too weary to perform his true work. He protests that the truth is the exact opposite of this notion, that his academic writing is easy, while his imaginative work is arduous and succeeds only upon occasion. He concludes that he would rather have written *Alice's Adventures in Wonderland* (1865) than the entire *Encyclopædia Britannica* (1768-1771). There, Leacock compares him-self, by implication, not to Mark Twain but to Lewis Carroll, another gentle humorist and university professor. Leacock attests to the seriousness with which he approached the writing of humor in *Humor: Its Theory and Technique* and *How to Write*.

In typically self-deprecating fashion, Leacock writes that, immediately after he had lectured extensively on Imperial organization throughout the British Empire, the

Union of South Africa came into being, and riots and wars threatened the empire elsewhere. These events, he says with mock seriousness, will give the reader some idea of the importance of his addresses. The admirer of Leacock's comic writings, however, should not make the same error in reverse that the author attributes to his academic colleagues. Leacok's serious works are not insignificant.

In 1930, while putting together a collection of Leacock's best comic pieces up to that time, the humorist's editor writes that he polled more than a dozen of the wittiest minds of the day regarding what the selections should be. The single most requested piece was not humorous at all. It was a discussion of present-day education under the title, "Oxford as I See It." Even though the volume is to be called *Laugh with Leacock*, the editor says that he is obliged to include this shrewd analysis in the collection. The presence of "Oxford as I See it," surrounded by parodies, burlesques, and pieces of inspired nonsense, suggests a nice metaphor for Leacock's work—the gift of wisdom and common sense found within the extravagantly wrapped package.

LITERARY LAPSES

First published: 1910
Type of work: Short stories

This little book is a mixture of fanciful short stories, literary parodies, and mock-serious essays by an eccentric persona.

Literary Lapses is Leacock's first book of humor. It is not an easy volume to classify. Russel Nye calls it a collection of esssays, but only a handful of the sketches are truly essays. It is composed of twenty-six short pieces, ranging from short stories to burlesques of severely condensed romantic novels to essays that solemnly develop mad premises. Leacock's typical narrator is established in the very first sketch, "My Financial Career." After several ludicrous missteps, he succeeds in opening his first bank account; then, because of the bank's intimidating ambiance, he inadvertently draws a check for the total amount of his deposit. Thereafter, he keeps his savings in a sock.

The literary parodies, although comprising only a fraction of the text, appear to give the volume its title. "Lord Oxhead's Secret" is subtitled "A Romance in One Chapter." The peer's daughter, Gwendoline, is a beautiful "girl" of thirty-three who is being courted by the dashing Edwin Einstein of Oshkosh, Wisconsin. At the climactic moment, as the father and the unsuitable suitor come face to face, Lord Oxhead falls dead, taking his secret with him to the grave. It is too complicated to be of interest anyway, concludes the narrator. In "Getting the Thread of It," the narrator's friend Sinclair attempts, by fits and starts, to familiarize him with the plot of the historical novel that Sinclair is reading. It is set in Italy in the time of Pius the something and features such characters as Carlo Carlotti the Condottiere and the Dog of

Venice. "A Lesson in Fiction" is a sort of quiz on the modern melodramatic novel. The reader is asked to predict the behavior of the hero, Gaspard de Vaux, boy lieutenant, and is able to do so at every juncture of the plot. The critic in "Saloonio: A Study of Shakespearean Criticism" is Colonel Hogshead who, after amassing a fortune from cattle trading in Wyoming, has turned to the study of Shakespeare. Unshakably fixed in his head is the idea that a character named Saloonio is central to the action of *The Merchant of Venice* (c. 1596-1597). This notion meets such spirited resistance from the narrator and others that Colonel Hogshead is actually driven to reading the play. The fact that no Saloonio appears in the text, the Colonel finds unpersuasive—the book in hand, he insists, is unlike those that he consulted in Wyoming.

The short stories often have absurdly tragic endings. In "The New Food," Professor Plumb of the University of Chicago has invented a highly concentrated form of food. A happy family is gathered around the small pill that represents their 350-pound Christmas dinner, when baby Gustavus Adolphus snatches the pill and swallows it. The distracted mother gives him water, a fatal error. After the explosion, only the smiling lips of a child who has had thirteen Christmas dinners remain. In "Borrowing a Match," the passerby of whom the narrator asks this favor eventually throws away all of his possessions and rips his clothing to shreds in search of the requested item. He finally extracts from the lining of his coat—a toothpick. The narrator pushes him under the wheels of a trolley car and runs. In "An Experiment with Policeman Hogan," as the officer walks his beat in front of the *Daily Eclipse* at two o'clock in the morning, journalist Scalper is at work in the office above. Scalper writes a column in which he delineates the character of readers by examining their handwriting. As he moves from one sample of handwriting to the next, he drinks from a dark bottle, which he shares with Policeman Hogan by periodically lowering it to the street on the end of a string. Scalper's analysis of each sample coincides suspiciously with the degree of his progressive inebriation, so that by five o'clock in the morning he is telling Emily, a timid maiden in her teens, that she is on the verge of delirium tremens and that her liquor habit is so advanced as to preclude all hope.

A few of these pieces are dated, but it is a testimony to Leacock's understanding of human nature and to the subtlety of his style that the public found sketches written twenty years earlier still fresh and amusing. Indeed, a century after their composition, most are still fresh and amusing.

SUNSHINE SKETCHES OF A LITTLE TOWN

First published: 1912
Type of work: Novel

A deadpan narrator amusingly describes the character types and the folkways of a fictional Canadian town.

The episodic plot of *Sunshine Sketches of a Little Town* is developed through a conversation between Leacock's chatty narrator and another resident, or former resident, of Mariposa. The reader takes the part of the former resident, whose responses are minimal and are recorded only occasionally as the narrator repeats them. Mariposa is a sunlit town of five thousand, according to the Canadian census, or ten thousand, according to the natives, lying along a hillside next to little Lake Wissanotti. The narrator is extremely proud of the progressive nature of Mariposa, the showplace of Missinaba County. He purports to take every occurrence at face value, never challenging the way that the characters represent their actions or their motives. The discrepancy between the interpretations of the narrator and those of the reader account for much of the book's humor.

Leacock presents a fine gallery of small town characters. Josh Smith is a hotel keeper who possesses an imposing size and manner, as well as a shadowy past. Some of his business practices are sharp almost to the point of criminality. He is also the *deus ex machina* of the novel. When, during the Knights of Pythias' Excursion Day on Lake Wissanotti, the *Mariposa Belle* sinks (in six feet of water), it is Mr. Smith who raises her. When the heavily mortgaged (and insured) sanctuary of the Church of England burns to the ground, it is Mr. Smith who saves the rest of Mariposa. Evidence that Mr. Smith was seen earlier carrying a can of kerosene through the streets is quite sensibly dismissed by Judge Pepperleigh, who immediately finds for the Church of England and against the insurance company. In the novel's penultimate chapter, Mr. Smith stands as the Conservative candidate from Missinaba County. He finds his inability to read and write no true impediment and, by means of his usual skillful maneuvering, defeats the long-entrenched Liberal member, John Henry Bagshaw.

Other residents of Mariposa are Jefferson Thorpe, barber and speculator in mining stocks; Golgotha Gingham, undertaker and longtime Liberal, who announces on the day of Mr. Smith's election that he supported Bagshaw only with the deepest misgivings; Peter Pupkin, heroic junior bank teller who, along with Gillis, the caretaker, foils a robbery of the Exchange Bank at three o'clock one morning—both men fire at the intruder, and Pupkin is slightly wounded when the robber fires back (although, strangely, only two shots are heard by witnesses); and Myra Thorpe and Zena Pepperleigh, beauties who quicken the pulses of young Mariposan males. One of the most appealing characters is the elderly Dean Drone. The dean's poor head for arithmetic has sunk his church deep into debt. He insists that the fault lies with the mathematical professor at the Anglican college who, fifty-two years earlier, stopped the lesson right at the point where the book discussed logarithms.

The final chapter in the book is an equal mixture of humor and nostalgia. The reader has become a rich businessman in the city. At the Mausoleum Club, he nods and dreams of returning to the little sunlit town of his birth. Yet, of course, he never has—and he never will.

Summary

Stephen Leacock published almost a book for each year between the appearance of his first collection of humor, *Literary Lapses*, and the posthumous *The Boy I Left Behind Me*. He wrote in a number of genres: scholarly studies in his academic specialty, humor, literary biography, literary theory, and autobiography. At the time of his death in 1944, he was regarded as one of the finest writers in Canada and the foremost humorist of North America.

His fame has diminished with the passage of time, and newer Mark Twains have been put forward by the critics. Still, the droll persona of his narrator, the tolerance and generosity of spirit that soften his satire, and the simplicity and clarity of his style have not lost their appeal.

Bibliography

Adcock, Arthur St. John. "Stephen Leacock." In *The Glory That Was Grub Street: Impressions of Contemporary Authors*. 1928. Reprint. Freeport, N.Y.: Books for Libraries Press, 1969.

Beharriell, S. Ross. "Writers of Fiction, 1880-1920." In *Literary History of Canada: Canadian Literature in English*. Edited by Carl F. Klinck. Toronto: University of Toronto Press, 1966.

Davies, Robertson. "Stephen Leacock." In *Our Living Tradition: Seven Canadians*. Edited by Claude T. Bissell. Toronto: University of Toronto Press, 1957.

Legate, David. *Stephen Leacock*. Garden City, N.Y.: Doubleday, 1971.

McArthur, Peter. *Stephen Leacock*. Toronto: Ryerson, 1923.

Nye, Russel, ed. *Modern Essays*. Chicago: Scott, Foresman, 1957.

Sedgewick, G. G. "Stephen Leacock as Man of Letters." *University of Toronto Quarterly*, October, 1945, 17-26.

Patrick Adcock

JOHN LE CARRÉ

Born: Poole, Dorsetshire, England
October 19, 1931

Principal Literary Achievement

Le Carré created spy novels that were more realistic and intelligent than those that previously typified the genre, thereby demonstrating that they could be serious literature.

Biography

John le Carré is the pseudonym of David Moore Cornwell, who was born in the town of Poole in Dorsetshire, England, on October 19, 1931, the son of Ronald Thomas Archibald Cornwell and the former Olive Glassy. His mother deserted the family when John was a little boy; his father had innumerable mistresses who created emotional confusion in the boy's life by serving as unreliable transient mothers. It is probably because of the early loss of his mother that the major theme of all le Carré's fiction has to do with betrayal. Le Carré's semiautobiographical novel *A Perfect Spy* (1986) paints a picture of a lonely, hypersensitive boy whose father was a philanderer, a heavy drinker, and a flamboyant con artist who once served a term in prison for fraud. Le Carré was sent to prestigious English boarding schools but felt out of place because he did not belong to the same social class as the majority of the students. His father caused him humiliation by paying the tuition with bad checks. His precarious situation left him with ambivalent feelings toward the upper class; he was taught to share their values but did not identify with them. These feelings are evident in many of his novels, but particularly in *A Perfect Spy*.

Le Carré attended Berne University in Switzerland for a year, where he perfected his knowledge of German. He has stated that "the strongest literary influence was all that German literature that I devoured either compulsorily or voluntarily." Because he was fluent in German, he spent his obligatory period of military service as an intelligence officer in occupied Austria in the aftermath of World War II. Le Carré became a retiring and secretive man, reticent about his activities as an intelligence officer; many broad hints of his former life are given in *A Perfect Spy*, which is the most comprehensive source of information about his real life. After his period of national service, Le Carré attended the University of Oxford, where he specialized in modern languages. Upon graduation, he obtained a position as a German instructor at Eton. He was not happy there. He never really liked the English upper class and

made his feelings apparent in many of his novels.

After quitting his post at Eton, le Carré engaged in somewhat ambiguous pursuits. Many people have claimed that he was working for a branch of the British Secret Intelligence Service. He himself says, "I have always tried to deny it and keep away from the subject, and I intend to go on doing so." On the strength of his knowledge of European languages, le Carré joined the British Foreign Service in 1960, and it is widely believed that he continued to work as a spy, using his diplomatic cover to recruit agents in foreign countries.

Le Carré was still employed by the Foreign Office when he wrote his first three novels. He was required by department rules to use a pseudonym, and he chose the name John le Carré. His first two novels, *Call for the Dead* (1961) and *A Murder of Quality* (1962), feature a protagonist named George Smiley, who acts more as a private detective than as a secret intelligence officer. Both books were well reviewed but had only modest sales. It was not until le Carré published *The Spy Who Came in from the Cold* in 1963 that he became famous in both Great Britain and the United States and began to earn enough money to devote full time to writing.

Since 1964, he has become one of the world's most successful writers. Many of his novels have been made into motion pictures. The most elaborate productions were film adaptations of *The Little Drummer Girl* (1983), starring Diane Keaton, and *The Russia House* (1989), starring Sean Connery; but the most faithful and the most aesthetically satisfying adaptations were the British productions of *Tinker, Tailor, Soldier, Spy* (1974) and *Smiley's People* (1980), both starring the great English actor Sir Alec Guinness as George Smiley.

John le Carré, a tall, distinguished-looking man, became an accomplished raconteur and mimic. His two marriages produced four sons. He procured a secluded home in Cornwall, England, and settled there with his second wife.

Analysis

John le Carré does for the spy novel what Raymond Chandler did for the detective novel in works such as *The Big Sleep* (1939) and *Farewell, My Lovely* (1940). Le Carré demonstrates how a popular genre can be used to explore serious issues in a realistic manner. Le Carré's first two novels, though they are impeccably written, are rather inhibited and conventional detective-type novels. It was with the publication of his third novel, *The Spy Who Came in from the Cold*, that he found himself as a writer.

Before le Carré's time, most spy thrillers featured impossibly patriotic, courageous heroes who were always getting involved in violent action. The hero's country was always right and the other side always wrong. The hero used ethical methods and acted in self-defense while the villains could be counted upon to use murder and fiendish physical and psychological torture. One of the rare exceptions was W. Somerset Maugham's intellectual spy-hero who appeared in a series of short stories collected under the title *Ashenden: Or, The British Agent* (1928). These realistic stories attempted to show spies and counterspies as real human beings. Other exceptions to the stereotypical romantic spy-thriller, and another major influence on le Carré, were the thrillers or "entertainments" of Graham Greene. Greene's brooding, paranoic *Stamboul Train: An Entertainment* (1932; published in the United States as *Orient Express: An Entertainment*, 1933), *A Gun for Sale: An Entertainment* (1936; published in the United States as *This Gun for Hire: An Entertainment*), and *The Confidential Agent* (1939) still make excellent reading after more than half a century. A third important influence on le Carré was Joseph Conrad, who was known primarily as an author of sea stories but turned out one memorable spy story in his novel *The Secret Agent* (1907).

The best representative of the romantic spy-heroes before le Carré's time is the famous James Bond. While the Bond stories such as *From Russia, with Love* (1957) and *Dr. No* (1958) have given readers and moviegoers many hours of escapist entertainment, even their own author Ian Fleming never took them seriously. Le Carré had plenty of exposure to the unpleasant realities of espionage in his years of government service. Just as Raymond Chandler wanted to show how real cops and real crooks talked and acted, le Carré wants to show how real spying is conducted and what sort of people are involved. In *The Spy Who Came in from the Cold*, le Carré reveals to the reading public what Phillip Knightley has called "the sordid world of espionage with its easily bought loyalties, loose morals, mind-boggling complexities, and, if it were not for its murderous consequences, comic inanity."

That novel is impressive in its characterization and apparent authenticity; however, it still has unmistakable traces of the old-style spy-thriller with its action-oriented hero taking on the whole communist world single-handedly and throwing his life away in a final romantic gesture. *The Spy Who Came in from the Cold* was only le Carré's third novel. He had started writing fairly late in life; he was still struggling to find the right creative groove. It is obvious from his writings that le Carré's own personality is more cerebral than athletic and that his experience as a secret agent must have involved more organizational work than derring-do. He finally found the right formula for his spy-fiction by focusing on the character of George Smiley and giving Smiley a formidable counterpart on the other side of the Iron Curtain.

Smiley is the least heroic hero ever featured in genre fiction. The character he most closely resembles is the sedentary, hyper-intellectual Sherlock Holmes. While James Bond was appropriately portrayed on the screen by the handsome, dynamic Sean Connery, George Smiley was portrayed equally appropriately by the pudgy, soft-spoken Sir Alec Guinness. While James Bond is a man of action, Smiley is definitely an intellectual. Bond is an extrovert and Smiley is an introvert. Bond likes high-powered cars and exotic weapons; Smiley does not like to drive at all and never carries a gun. Bond is famous for his affairs with beautiful women, while Smiley is extremely shy with both men and women and is married to a woman who is outrageously unfaithful. Bond represents the kind of man the average male reader would like to be, while Smiley represents the kind of man the average armchair-spy suspects himself to be.

The Quest for Karla represents the high point in le Carré's career. Besides George Smiley, the three novels in this trilogy contain other memorable characters. The Leninlike Karla becomes one of fiction's great characters even though he remains offstage until the last chapter of the last book. The rivalry between these two strong-willed, brilliant antagonists resembles nothing in literature so much as the classic rivalry between Sherlock Holmes and Professor James Moriarty ("The Final Problem," in *The Memoirs of Sherlock Holmes*, 1894). It took an author with le Carré's intelligence, creativity, and insider knowledge to capture in fictional form the essence of the worldwide ideological, propagandistic, diplomatic, economic, technological, and military struggle called the Cold War. With the spy-heroes of Conrad, Maugham, Greene, and Fleming, the reader is confined to the agent level of espionage; with le Carré, the reader is admitted to the highest levels of spying and diplomacy.

A Perfect Spy reads like an addendum to *The Quest for Karla*, dealing with a minor theater of the Cold War but focusing with revealing autobiographical detail on the personality of a British spy turned traitor. The hero, Magnus Pym, resembles George Smiley in being a man who relies on his brain and his powers of persuasion rather than on brawn and athletic ability. *A Perfect Spy* reveals the psychological stress experienced by the British, as well as the Europeans in general, and even members of the Third World, as they were crushed between the enormous economic, military, and ideological pressure being exerted by the United States and the Soviet Union, with the threat of nuclear annihilation facing humankind for more than forty years.

THE SPY WHO CAME IN FROM THE COLD

First published: 1963
Type of work: Novel

A British spy deliberately disgraces himself in order to get recruited as a double agent by the East Germans in a story of multiple betrayals.

The Spy Who Came in from the Cold begins with a dramatic nighttime scene in which a British spy is shot down while trying to escape from East Germany. Alec Leamas, a British agent, harbors hatred toward Hans-Dieter Mundt, second in command of the Abteilung (East German Intelligence Service), who is responsible for the extermination of Leamas' entire spy network. Back in England, Leamas is recruited for a sting operation against Mundt. Leamas is dismissed from the "Circus" (a special department of the British Intelligence Service) and pretends to go through a period of moral disintegration in order to make himself seem like a good candidate for recruitment as a double agent. During this period he meets Liz Gold, a shy, lonely librarian, who falls in love with him. She happens to be a member of the British Communist Party but is more interested in personal relationships than in causes.

Leamas is approached and agrees to betray his service for a price. He is taken into

East Germany, where he meets Jens Fiedler, a brilliant Jewish intellectual deeply committed to Marxist-Leninist ideology. Fiedler is Mundt's chief rival in the Abteilung. Leamas disingenuously feeds Fiedler rehearsed information intended to make it appear that Mundt has been working for the British. The zealous and ambitious Fiedler accuses Mundt of treason and a trial is staged with Leamas as the star witness. Leamas, however, learns that George Smiley and his associates at the Circus have been clumsily covering up his tracks in England. For example, it is brought out by Mundt's defense that Leamas had "friends" who paid his overdue rent and other bills.

Then Liz Gold is called as a surprise witness. She has been lured to East Germany on a bogus tour for members of the British Communist Party. She reveals that men calling themselves friends of Leamas came to her apartment and gave her money. One had identified himself as George Smiley, well known to the Abteilung as a highly placed member of the British Secret Intelligence Service. Leamas cannot understand how Smiley could have been so clumsy but begins to realize that the whole scheme was concocted to make it appear that Fiedler has been involved with the Circus in a conspiracy to destroy Mundt. That is exactly what the court decides is the truth. Fiedler is arrested and is certain to be executed as an *agent provocateur*. Mundt, a neo-Nazi and longtime British mole, is totally exonerated and obviously destined to become the most important figure in the Abteilung.

Leamas will probably be executed. Liz is heartbroken: She feels responsible for betraying her lover. The disgusted Leamas tells Liz: "What do you think spies are: priests, saints and martyrs? They're a squalid procession of vain fools, traitors too, yes; pansies, sadists and drunkards, people who play cowboys and Indians to brighten their rotten lives." Here le Carré is spelling out the theme that would serve to structure all of his future spy novels. In the Cold War, both sides are equally despicable. Human values are being outraged by the ideological clash of communism and capitalism.

Mundt proves the correctness of these conclusions by releasing Leamas and Liz and providing transportation to the Berlin Wall. Here is an echo of traditional spy novels featuring daring escapes from enemy territory under a hail of bullets. Le Carré, however, deliberately violates the conventions of the genre by allowing hero and heroine to be caught in spotlights while trying to scale the infamous Berlin Wall and dying within sight of freedom.

TINKER, TAILOR, SOLDIER, SPY

First published: 1974
Type of work: Novel

George Smiley is brought out of forced retirement in a desperate attempt to uncover a traitor in the British secret service.

Tinker, Tailor, Soldier, Spy is the first novel in a trilogy that came to be called *The Quest for Karla*. The novels are set in different parts of the world but have in common the British protagonist George Smiley and the Soviet antagonist known only as Karla. Oddly enough, Karla actually apears only at the very end of the last novel; yet his powerful personality, his unbending will, and his fanatical disregard for human feelings are felt throughout the approximately one thousand pages that make up these three wonderful books. The novels were inspired by the most famous case of treason in British history. Kim Philby, an upper-class, Oxford-educated intellectual who rose to the top echelon in the British Secret Intelligence Service, defected to Russia and was discovered to have been a mole—a double agent who had been revealing ultra-sensitive information to Moscow Centre for decades. What made Philby's treachery even more devastating was that he had been in close contact with the American Central Intelligence Agency (CIA) and the Federal Bureau of Investigation (FBI) in Washington, D.C., and was in a position to betray vital American secrets as well. This treachery poisoned relations between the secret services of the two allies. The British and Americans were unable to have confidence in their informants or operatives anywhere in the world.

In *Tinker, Tailor, Soldier, Spy*, George Smiley is brought back out of semiretirement on a mission of the utmost urgency and confidentiality. It has been learned through a Soviet defector that Moscow Centre has a high placed mole in the Circus who has been taking orders directly from Karla for years and has been systematically sabotaging the Circus. The mole has caused loyal employees to be fired and probably has been responsible for hiring agents who are working for Moscow Centre. Since Smiley has no way of knowing whom he can trust, he has to act as a counterspy against his own organization. *Tinker, Tailor, Soldier, Spy* contains little overt action. Smiley spends most of his days and nights examining musty files, trying to trace people's movements and link them with significant events. He is greatly aided by one of le Carré's most interesting characters, Connie Sachs, an arthritic, asthmatic old lesbian with a brilliant mind and a photographic memory.

The shy, self-effacing Smiley discreetly interviews various individuals and eventually finds a pattern of activities that enables him to identify the mole. He sets up an elaborate trap to lure the traitor to a safe house for a supposedly secret meeting with a Soviet agent. When the highly regarded Bill Haydon appears, he is caught red-handed and confesses that he has been the Soviet mole since his undergraduate days at Oxford. It is common knowledge within the Circus that Bill Haydon had an affair with Smiley's aristocratic wife, Ann. Smiley is horrified and outraged by the realization that Haydon initiated the affair on Karla's orders, because Karla considered Smiley his most dangerous opponent and wanted Haydon to obtain confidential information through the unsuspecting Ann Smiley. George Smiley is reinstated and becomes acting head of the Circus with the awesome responsibility of repairing all the damage that has been done throughout the years.

Jim Prideaux, one of the men whom Haydon betrayed, murders this former friend and superior while Haydon is being held in custody. As a character, Prideaux exists in order to provide some physical action in this otherwise highly intellectual plot; however, his role is tangential to the story and mostly covered in flashbacks. On the other hand, in the sequel, *The Honourable Schoolboy* (1977), le Carré attempts to create a role for a vigorous, sexually active young hero while retaining the sedentary Smiley in the vital role of master planner.

THE HONOURABLE SCHOOLBOY

First published: 1977
Type of work: Novel

George Smiley, now head of the Circus, sends an agent to the war-torn Orient to capture a Soviet mole in the Red Chinese government.

In *The Honourable Schoolboy*, le Carré moves to a different theater of the Cold War, the Far East. Smiley learns that Karla has a mole in Communist China supplying him with information. Capturing this mole would help revive morale within the Circus and also help repair its relationship with its counterparts in the United States. It would also damage relations between Red China and the Soviet Union and secure badly needed information about what is going on inside mainland China.

Smiley sends a young agent named Jerry Westerby to Hong Kong to obtain information about a secret bank account into which Karla has been funneling American dollars for years. Westerby, posing as a journalist, spends much of his time drinking and womanizing. His investigations take him to various theaters of one of the bloodiest wars in history. Guerrilla armies in Thailand, Cambodia, and Vietnam, aided and abetted by the Red Chinese, are trying to topple the established governments, which are being held together only by massive military and economic support from the United States. The descriptions of military action, streams of fleeing civilians, the total demoralization of the population, and the collapse of the Western presence on the Asian mainland represent some of the best writing le Carré has ever done.

In this novel, le Carré makes his anti-American sentiments more obvious than in any of his other works. He deplores the way in which the Americans are obliterating

ancient cultures with napalm and other explosives dropped indiscriminately on innocent civilians. Le Carré is popular with American readers in spite of the fact that he
has never treated American characters kindly and has never been successful in portraying them.

Westerby discovers that the mole inside Communist China is Nelson Ko, brother
of a powerful Hong Kong businessman named Drake Ko. On Smiley's orders, Westerby begins leaking such sensitive information that Drake realizes he must get his
brother out of mainland China before he is exposed. Unfortunately, Westerby falls in
love with Drake Ko's English mistress Elizabeth Worthington and nearly foils the
entire Anglo-American plot by trying to make a private deal with Drake to exchange
Nelson for Elizabeth. Westerby is killed by the Americans. Nelson is captured and
taken to the United States for interrogation. Smiley's operation is successful, but he
has been double-crossed by his own associates in the Circus who have colluded with
their American counterparts to force Smiley out and replace him with Saul Enderby,
a stupid aristocrat who toadies to the CIA.

While the plot abundantly illustrates le Carré's favorite themes of betrayal and
dehumanization, *The Honourable Schoolboy* is weakened by being broken into two
widely separated points of view: that of Westerby in the Orient and that of Smiley in
England. When Smiley comes to Hong Kong in the final chapters to participate in
the capture of Nelson Ko, this is an awkward attempt to tie the two separate plot
lines together for artistic neatness. In *Smiley's People*, however, le Carré finally writes
the perfect spy novel by making George Smiley both the thinker and the doer, the
intellectual and the man of action all in one central hero.

SMILEY'S PEOPLE

First published: 1980
Type of work: Novel

George Smiley organizes a complex multinational espionage operation to force
his archenemy Karla to defect from the Soviet Union.

Smiley's People brings to a satisfying conclusion the battle of wits that has been
going on between Smiley and Karla for many years. Smiley is called out of retirement to help the Circus investigate the recent murder of a former Red Army general
living in exile in London. The general had been in contact with a Russian woman
living in Paris who had recently been approached by Soviet agents with an offer to
allow her daughter to leave Russia and move to France. Smiley deduces that the general was assassinated because the old man suspected that Karla was only using the
woman's daughter to create a false identity for some young woman he wanted to
send to France. Smiley goes to the European continent to investigate. He appears as a
major or minor character in many of le Carré's earlier novels, but *Smiley's People* is

the first book in which the reader is able to develop a full appreciation of Smiley's talents as a secret agent. He is in grave danger, because Karla can have people murdered by agents in any country of the world and would certainly eliminate Smiley if he suspected that the British secret service agent was trying to unravel his secret.

Karla had an illegitimate daughter named Tatiana who is now in her early twenties. Tatiana is a schizophrenic, and Karla has had her secretly moved from Russia to a sanatorium in Switzerland where she can receive better treatment. The nuns who operate the sanatorium know virtually nothing about her. Karla sends money to pay for her treatment via a minor official named Grigoriev. Karla must keep this a dark secret because his enemies in the Kremlin could destroy him if they could show he was using the Soviet diplomatic and espionage apparatus to further his purely personal interests. Smiley gets damaging information about Grigoriev's adulterous affairs and forces him to become a double agent, promising him safe asylum in Australia. Through the terrified Russian diplomat, Smiley sends a confidential letter to Karla, offering him a carrot-and-stick proposition: If Karla will defect to the British, he will receive asylum and Tatiana will continue to receive high-quality psychiatric care; otherwise, Smiley will expose him. Karla will be executed, and his daughter will become a charity case without money, friends, or even an identity.

At the appointed deadline, Smiley and his assistants wait in the fog. If Karla crosses the bridge into West Berlin, it will be the greatest triumph in the history of the Circus. They will be able to learn everything about Soviet internal and external affairs. Suspense mounts as minutes tick by. Finally Karla, disguised as a working man, crosses the bridge, hesitates, and then delivers himself into British hands.

Characteristically, Smiley is not exultant. He feels ashamed for using Karla's genuine paternal love to destroy his archenemy. One of le Carré's major concerns in all of his novels has been the destruction of human values by the clash of godless ideologies. Smiley realizes that he has not really defeated Karla because he has not proved that Western values are superior to those of Communism. Furthermore, Smiley cannot help but reflect that Karla destroyed his relationship with Ann, condemning him to a life of loneliness, and that in a sense Karla destroyed Smiley as a human being long before Smiley was able to do the same thing to Karla.

A PERFECT SPY

First published: 1986
Type of work: Novel

A high-ranking member of the British diplomatic corps reveals in a lengthy confession that he has been a double agent for many years.

A Perfect Spy is the most autobiographical of all le Carré's novels. Since many of the facts about his life are obscure, it is difficult to determine exactly how much of the novel is factual and how much has been fabricated for dramatic effect. The central theme probably comes close to the truth about the author himself: His father was the most important influence in his life. Rick Pym, the father of the hero Magnus Pym, closely corresponds to what is known about le Carré's own father. It was through Rick that Magnus learned how easy it is to deceive people if it is done with charm and on a lavish scale. Both the fictional and the real father expected the most of their sons but set for them bad moral examples.

In the novel, Magnus Pym is a high-ranking diplomat who secretly manages espionage operations in foreign countries. He creates great alarm in government circles by disappearing without informing his wife about where he is going. The suspicion is that he has defected to the Soviet Union, in which case all the undercover agents behind the Iron Curtain who were known to him would be in immediate danger.

Pym is actually living in a private home on the Devon coast with an old woman who has no knowledge of his true identity. Miss Dubbers mothers him, and he treats her with kindness and generosity, revealing that he is a good man who had been led astray by circumstances beyond his control. His relationship with his landlady is central to the story. Like le Carré himself, Pym lost his mother at an early age and, because of his loveless childhood, was never able to relate to people in a normal manner.

Pym is writing an elaborate confession and suicide note in the form of a letter to his own son. This letter makes up much of the novel. He reveals how he began to take delight in secretly betraying people even as a boy in boarding school. His whole life has been a pattern of winning people's confidence, learning their secrets, and then betraying them. His only real friendship appears to have been with the brilliant Axel Hampel, whom he met while attending a university in Switzerland. Their relationship comes suspiciously close to being overtly homosexual, the type of thing at which le Carré often hints in his works but that he never explores in detail.

Eventually Axel becomes a spy for the Eastern Bloc, operating out of Czechoslovakia. He and Pym hit upon the scheme of exchanging secret information to advance their careers, and both are spectacularly successful for years. Then their superiors on both sides begin to deduce the truth. With the British secret service closing in on his pathetic foster home, Pym puts a pistol to his head and pulls the trigger.

The convoluted story leaps backward and forward in time and shifts to several different viewpoints, most notably that of Jack Brotherhood, Pym's older, father-figure friend who is trying to track Pym down. In addition to being made up of many lengthy flashbacks, the story leaps about geographically, with scenes taking place in England, Germany, Czechoslovakia, Switzerland, and the United States. It is le Carré's most autobiographical, complex, experimental, and ambitious novel. It is only partially successful because it departs from the conventions of the espionage genre to some degree but does not do so completely; it is neither mainstream nor genre fiction.

Summary

John le Carré's early experiences fitted him for a career as a spy novelist. He had the creative genius to see that the spy, living from day to day in paranoid terror, was the ideal symbol of the alienated modern individual living in the shadow of nuclear annihilation. Le Carré elevates the spy-thriller to the level of enduring literature. His best novels will outlive many more pretentious contemporary works and will probably tell future readers more about the psychological and moral issues of the Cold War than any number of scholarly history books.

Bibliography

Barley, Tony. *Taking Sides: The Fiction of John le Carré.* Milton Keynes, England: Open University Press, 1986.

Bold, Alan, ed. *The Quest for le Carré.* London: Vision Press, 1988.

Homberger, Eric. *John le Carré.* London: Methuen, 1986.

Knightley, Phillip. *The Second Oldest Profession: Spies and Spying in the Twentieth Century.* New York: W. W. Norton, 1986.

Lewis, Peter. *John le Carré.* New York: Frederick Ungar, 1985.

Monaghan, David. *The Novels of John le Carré.* Oxford, England: Basil Blackwell, 1985.

_____. *Smiley's Circus: A Guide to the Secret World of John le Carré.* London: Orbis Book Publishing, 1986.

Wolfe, Peter. *Corridors of Deceit: The World of John le Carré.* Bowling Green, Ohio: Bowling Green State University Popular Press, 1987.

Bill Delaney

DORIS LESSING

Born: Kermanshah, Persia
October 22, 1919

Principal Literary Achievement

A major post-World War II novelist, Lessing uses her craft to explore the educative value of human experience and to examine the effects of institutions, or collectives, on the human psyche.

Biography

Doris May Tayler Lessing was born in Kermanshah, Persia (later Iran), on October 22, 1919, the daughter of Alfred Cook Tayler and Emily Maude McVeagh. As a soldier during World War I, Alfred Tayler sustained a serious injury that left him an amputee. While convalescing, he fell in love with his nurse, Emily McVeagh, and married her. After the war ended, they moved to Persia, where Alfred began working in a bank. Soon after the young couple were settled in Persia, financial incentives enticed them to try their luck in Rhodesia, South Africa, a recently established British colony. They made plans to relocate; by the time that Alfred and Emily were ready to move into their Rhodesian farmhouse, a daughter, Doris May Tayler, had been born. Once engaged in farming, Alfred and Emily Tayler found that the dream that they had pursued did not bring the promise of riches envisioned earlier. For one reason or another, their expectations for amassing wealth were never realized, and they were forced to accommodate themselves to a life that was disappointingly modest by local white standards.

Doris, as a young girl growing up in frontier country, however, did not feel the disappointment of her parents. The veld, bordering their farm, held for her an array of attractions. As an adolescent, she would take long solitary walks across the unspoiled countryside, often carrying a rifle to shoot small game. Given unlimited opportunity to observe nature on the vast canvas of the veld and given countless occasions to pit her cunning and skill against the survival instincts of prey, she became unusually independent and introspective, traits that influenced greatly the paths that she chose to explore as a writer.

Tayler began her schooling in Salisbury, about one hundred miles from her home. She enrolled first in a Roman Catholic convent school and later attended Girls' High School. Although a lover of books, she increasingly grew to despise the regimentation of school life. At age fourteen, she dispensed with formal education and went to

work as an au pair girl in Salisbury.

Two years later, Tayler returned to the family farm and began to write. Books by such nineteenth century realists as Fyodor Dostoevski, Honoré de Balzac, Stendhal, Anton Chekhov, Ivan Turgenev, and Leo Tolstoy helped her shape her ideas and learn the elements of good writing. She was also influenced philosophically by her reading of political and social tracts, which included Adolf Hitler's *Mein Kampf* (1925-1927; English translation, 1933) and the sexual studies of Henry Havelock Ellis.

In 1938, Tayler yet again declared her independence and went to work as a telephone operator in Salisbury. The following year, she married a civil servant named Frank Wisdom. During their four-year marriage, two children were born. Finding the life-style of a suburban housewife constricting, Doris joined a Marxist group in 1942. Political and domestic conflicts probably contributed to the dissolution of her marriage and familial responsibilities in 1943. After resuming a single life-style, later that same year, she published her first pieces of short fiction and poems in local journals. In 1945, she married a German refugee and fellow Marxist by the name of Gottfried Anton Lessing. This marriage produced a son, Peter. When it ended in divorce in 1949, Doris Lessing (retaining her married name) decided to take her son and move to London, England.

Analysis

The years spanning Lessing's adolescence and her young adulthood provide seed plots for her five related novels, the Children of Violence series, which were written over a twenty-year span. The first novel in the series, *Martha Quest*, was published in 1952. It was followed by *A Proper Marriage* in 1954, *A Ripple from the Storm* in 1958, *Landlocked* in 1965, and *The Four-Gated City* in 1969. Between the appearance of these serial books, Lessing wrote two other novels, as well as a considerable number of plays and short stories. Her most significant work, written during an interval between the Children of Violence novels, is *The Golden Notebook* (1962), which first brought her world acclaim. More than any other work, *The Golden Notebook*, still considered her masterpiece, affirmed her reputation as a major talent. The five books in the Children of Violence series and the single most definitive of Lessing's novels, *The Golden Notebook*, are representative of the author's prolific body of fiction, in that they contain all the themes and dominant imagery appearing throughout her work. Her reworking of basic material reveals the variety of her narrative techniques, that is, her ability to rework ideas through different story lines with novel and engaging effects.

Lessing's fascination with opposition may be traced to her early experiences on the veld, where she was first impressed with the majesty and wonder of nature, deriving her first inkling of the human capacity for reaching a state of harmony with the universe. The integrity of the veld presented a sharp contrast to the divisions that she observed in her colonial community. Living in a divided society stratified by race and class caused her to develop an understanding of the opposition between the privileged and the oppressed. The cruelty of the collective that claimed her as one of its own not only sharpened her sense of morality but also sparked her intellect and instilled in her the drive to examine the system and its larger ramifications. Lessing, therefore, deliberately embarked upon a long process of self-education. At different times in her life, she became involved in most of the significant political and intellectual movements of her day: Jungian and Freudian psychology, Sufi mysticism, existentialism, sociobiology, futuristic scientific theories, Communism, and Marxism. Her narratives reflect the influence of all of these movements. In her stories, she uses insight gained from these various theories of the world to define and explore other oppositions such as the gap between the public self and the private self, and the gap between the visionary and the pragmatic.

The reality of the ethical conflict that often exists between collectives and the commitment that one must make to his or her inner being is at the heart of Lessing's fiction. On at least one occasion, she expressed surprise when critics, in their reviews of the first two books of the Children of Violence series, missed the point that she had written the series as a study of the relationship between individual conscience in opposition to the demands of the collective (*A Small Personal Voice*, 1974).

Lessing weaves her plots around a core of imagery that recurs in a number of key scenes throughout the novels. Visions of the veld, houses, and cities materialize at critical moments to represent conditions related to either the individual or the collective in different situations. The prevailing image of the veld comes straight from Lessing's childhood experiences—the veld being the enduring reality that can be equated to unity and wholeness. The symbolic meaning of the veld as representative of the cosmic whole is contrasted with the compartmentalizations people make in their civilizing activities of building houses and cities.

Houses as images can represent one's inner world or the socially constructed outer world at various times. For example, when Martha, the protagonist of the series, envisions herself in *Landlocked* as a house with many rooms but without a center to hold the compartments together, she perceives the condition of her inner being and concludes that the space will have to be filled by some outside unifying agent, a man. When the image of the house appears in *The Four-Gated City*, however, Martha is herself the free agent wandering inside the divided, uncentered structure that represents the various duties imposed by collectives that she had neglected. At this point, Martha places herself inside the empty space to begin the healing process for her life. Also, in this final book, houses are used to represent the public world. The four houses that Martha enters during the course of the novel become, as Frederick Karl points out, a "microcosm" of British society, fragmented and out of harmony with nature.

The image of the city can also have both public and private applications depending on the situation in which the image appears. When the vision first comes to Martha Quest on the veld, it is not the *city*, but rather the *City*—a noble construction with "flower bordered terraces" and "splashing fountains." It is a man-made place but still in harmony with nature. It is a place on the veld where all groups "smile with pleasure at the sight of children" and all races of children "walk hand in hand"

(*Martha Quest*). Yet the city that Martha Quest encounters in England in *The Four-Gated City* and in *The Golden Notebook* is in opposition to nature. It represents nature compartmentalized by the collective mind.

Through her writings, Lessing expresses faith in the ability of humankind to transform both the individual and the world despite the proclivity of the collective mind to pervert nature and cause individuals to act often against their own best interests. Indeed, the abiding message of the author's narrative, as she states in *A Small Personal Voice*, is: "though we may not be able to prevent evil, we are capable of reinforcing a vision of good and using it to defeat evil." At the end of *The Four-Gated City*, Lessing's optimism for humanity is summarized in her vision of evolution. She conceives of the future as belonging to a new kind of evolving individual—one who will transcend history and ultimately will be assessed by his or her ability to endure suffering and grow as a result of it.

MARTHA QUEST

First published: 1952
Type of work: Novel

In a complex, racially stratified society caught between two world wars, a confused young girl renounces the conventional prejudices of her elders and seeks fulfillment through a man.

Martha Quest, the first book in the Children of Violence series, covers the years 1934 to 1938. The central character of the novel, Martha Quest, experiences an adolescence of disquiet, troubled by the turbulence of a world recently rocked by one world war and fast approaching a second. She is an intelligent observer of a world that seems to have gone awry. She feels at odds both with the awesome history of human beings acting in large collectives and with the reality of their petty pursuits in smaller social arenas.

From the time that Martha Quest notices discrepancies between the words people speak and their behaviors, she begins to feel displaced and unhappy. To allay despair, Martha turns to literature for ideas and spiritual support, usually borrowing books from two young Jewish intellects living in town. As she uses great books to structure her theory of the world, she is compelled to face the grim realities of her own life:

> She was adolescent, and therefore bound to be unhappy; British and therefore uneasy and defensive; in the fourth decade of the twentieth century, and therefore inescapably beset with problems of race and class; female, and obliged to repudiate the shackled women of the past.

Hoping to escape her current misery and dismal prospect for her future, fifteen-year-old Martha decides to leave her provincial rural community and live in the nearby fictional city, Zambesia, South Africa.

Although Martha is learning to fear biological and historical entrapment, she ironically decides that her salvation has to include sexual relations with a man. Martha's
search for self-expression and fulfillment through a romantic liaison leads her to make
several unfortunate choices. Finally, she allows a Jewish musician, Adolph (Dolly, for
short), to enter her life and become her first sexual experience. Martha chooses to
have relations with Dolly, not because she feels real passion for him, but because the
anti-Semitism directed toward him makes him seem more worthy than he actually is.

During the first two years of Martha's independent life, she becomes a regular with
a loosely knit gang of irresponsible white semiadults from a variety of national backgrounds. Her time is divided between work and sundowner parties at local restau-
rants.

As the winds of World War II gather, Martha enters into a relationship with Douglas, a civil servant who is several years her senior. War fever causes a wave of marriages and pregnancies among Martha's contemporaries, and nineteen-year-old Martha is influenced by the tide, as well. She, like her friends, is carried along in a rush
to the altar. Despite the fact that she does not love Douglas, Martha decides to legiti-
mize her relationship; they marry. Martha is puzzled by her madness:

> It was as if half a dozen entirely different people inhabited her body, and they violently
> disliked each other, bound together by only one thing, a strong pulse of longing; anony-
> mous, impersonal, formless, like water."

The novel ends with Martha trying to persuade herself that what she feels overall
for Douglas could pass for love, not merely sexual desire. Yet a nagging, unvoiced
conviction makes her understand that this marriage will not last.

A PROPER MARRIAGE

First published: 1954
Type of work: novel

   Biology and history are portrayed as determining factors for the limitations
that women face in life.

A Proper Marriage covers the years 1939 to 1941 in Martha Quest's life. After
leaving home and symbolically taking her life into her own hands, Martha is confused by the events that have placed her in a situation that is no more free than the
one that she left. Lessing's ironic view of the gap between one's personal desires and
the compelling power of collectives is brilliantly focused through the protagonist's
inexplicable acts of self-sabotage.

The first few weeks of Martha's marriage to Douglas Knowell are marked by strange
physical sensations, the early signs of pregancy. When Martha recognizes the symp-

toms, she realizes that she must have been pregnant before her wedding. Immediately, she feels trapped. Feeling that her choices thus far have eliminated her options, however, she decides to suppress her repulsion toward pregnancy and to surrender to her maternal instincts. While concentrating on her pregnancy, she is uneasily aware that she is reenacting a basic process in evolution. Additionally, she fears more than ever that her future will become a replication of her mother's life. Although Martha recognizes the awful possibility, she still lets the fog of happiness envelop her as long as she can envision the eventual pleasure of regaining her own body.

Meanwhile, Martha is influenced by the patriotic hoopla surrounding the advent of World War II, and she enrolls in Sister Doll's Red Cross course. One day after starting classes, Martha suddenly realizes that all her recent actions have been drawing her closer to the repetitive circle of history. She now sees herself in her mother's position during World War I, when Mrs. Quest and her female contemporaries assisted in the campaign and lost their lovers to the machines of war. It now seems possible to Martha that Douglas could become her war sacrifice, and that she might carry his memory as her mother's generation of women was carrying its memories.

To be near Martha during her pregnancy, Mr. and Mrs. Quest move to the city. Initially, Martha reacts negatively to their relocation. In her mind, their separation from the veld signifies severance of her childhood roots. Martha becomes reconciled to the change, however, after she impulsively joins another pregnant friend in a ritual-like mud bath on an open field one rainy night, symbolically merging herself and her unborn baby with the wholeness of the veld. Soon after this reconnecting event, Martha's daughter, Caroline Knowell, is born.

Meanwhile, Douglas becomes a soldier and leaves Martha alone for nearly a year. Upon his return, he and Martha resume conjugal relations, but Martha becomes fearful of another pregnancy. She is further harassed by Mrs. Quest, who tells her that she looks pregnant and criticizes her for allowing her servants too many privileges. While Martha silently rejects her mother, she gains sudden insight. She sees Mrs. Quest as a woman so disappointed in her own life that she needs to live vicariously through her daughter. Martha reasons that, in the light of Mrs. Quest's experiences, her behavior is "natural . . . even harmless and pathetic." Making a cognitive leap, she sees what may lie in store for her. She realizes that, if she continues to act against her own desires, by age fifty she could be like Mrs. Quest: "narrow, conventional, intolerant, insensitive."

Once Martha discovers that she is not again pregnant, she hastens to end her marriage. As the marriage dissolves messily, Martha finds direction for her life in the Communist Party. Communism seems to offer both the bases for the eradication of the family and an end to Martha's fear of repetition. Ironically, as Martha seizes Communism as a means of liberation, she once again uses a man to lead the way. By the end of the novel, Martha is romantically entangled with William, a comrade in Communism and a member of the British Royal Air Force.

A RIPPLE FROM THE STORM

First published: 1958
Type of work: novel

> After expending incredible amounts of energy working for the local Communist Party, Martha Quest is overtaken by a strange illness; after recovery, she sinks further into depression.

A Ripple from the Storm covers the years 1941 to 1943. The portrayal of Martha Quest's emotional, personal life and her tenuous relationship to the mainstream society of white South Africa continues in this novel. Her deep involvement in the secret world of Communism adds further complications to her life.

Following the example of her friend Jasmine, Martha—recently divorced and alienated from her mother and daughter—becomes the ideal hard-working Communist. Believing that Russia has created the framework for an ideal society, Martha glorifies the country at every opportunity. Her worship of Russia, however, is assailed when Solly Cohen, Martha's childhood friend, informs her that Stalin is responsible for executing Red Army officers. Although she does not at first accept this information, subsequent corruption from within her local party forces her to see that comrades do not have an automatic claim to virtue.

As Martha continues to present herself as a willing tool for the good of the Communist Party, she reaches a point of physical breakdown and has to take extended bed rest. During her illness, she is nursed by Anton Hesse, leader of the local Communist group. As Anton guards Martha's well-being, her former lover, William, fades into the background. Martha allows Anton to take over her mind and body. Her lack of spunk also allows her to accept passively Mrs. Quest's accusation that she has abandoned Caroline, her daughter.

Despite the fact that she does not love Anton and realizes that they are sexually incompatible, Martha moves in with Anton after she recovers. Later, she marries him to save him from an internment camp. For a period of time, she allows herself to think that they can live together harmoniously because she truly respects Anton's mind and his position in the local party. Soon after the marriage, however, Martha sees that Anton wants to live with a "real" wife, not a fellow communist; she grows to despise him. Still, she stays in the marriage so that Anton can remain in the country.

When the Communist group dissolves, mainly because of Anton's overbearing manner and snobbery, Martha is overwhelmed by feelings of futility. Nevertheless, she believes that the end results were inevitable. At this point in her life, she loses her faith in Communism and despairs of ever finding her true self: "I am not a person at all, I'm nothing yet—perhaps I never will be." Her journey toward self-identification seems to have ended in a blind alley.

LANDLOCKED

First published: 1965
Type of work: Novel

Suffering from a sense of self-division, Martha Quest seeks to unify her fragmented character by finding the right man and, in the process, learns something about the nature of self-destruction.

Landlocked covers the years 1944 to 1949 in Martha Quest's life. In an irrational world of organizational corruptions and personal frustrations, Martha Quest enters a love affair and finds a temporary solace. Paradoxically, this relationship becomes both a balm for her troubled soul and the most profound emotional experience of her entire life. The visionary heights that Martha achieves through her sexual expression with her new lover reflect Lessing's view that, from the release of intense feeling and passion, one can achieve a sense of connection and balance in the universe.

At the outset, Martha is offered a promotion at her law firm. Instead of being happy for the opportunity, she refuses the offer, believing further commitment to a collective that she does not esteem will only detract from her search for self. After refusing the job, she dreams that she is a "large house . . . with half a dozen different rooms in it," but that in the center the house is empty, ready to be filled. She accepts the dream as an "image of her position" and reasons that a man is needed to fill her inner space.

Martha's choice becomes Thomas Stern, a Polish Jew who escaped from Poland but discovered later that the Nazis murdered all members of the family that he left behind. Thomas' passionate outrage toward Nazis stirs Martha and alerts her to his potential for filling her empty center with emotions that could ignite her true self. Although Martha is still married to Anton Hesse, she has no reservations about becoming Thomas' lover because the marriage is an acknowledged sham by both herself and Anton. She responds to Thomas in a way that she can compare only to pregnancy. With Thomas, her body becomes "a newly discovered country with laws of its own."

Yet Thomas is a tormented man, having the "eye of an insane artist." The lack of continuity in his life because of his loss of generations to the Holocaust, proves too much for him to bear. Feelings of alienation lead him to "the long process of breaking down." As Martha watches Thomas slip into madness, her imagination expands, and she starts to comprehend the incipient darkness that she knows will soon take him away.

By the end of *Landlocked*, Martha has ended her "in name only" marriage; she has abandoned her revolutionary dream; she is now suspicious that, in leaving Caroline, her daughter, she has not released her from being victimized by history; finally, she has lost the love of her life to a bizarre illness, which he has recorded in a final rambling manuscript. With these disappointments from the outside world heavy on her mind, Martha makes the decision to look inward and develop her inner self.

THE FOUR-GATED CITY

First published: 1969
Type of work: novel

In continuing her self-development, Martha Quest works through the roles that she had shunned in the past, traveling a road to spiritual growth that takes her to the edge of madness and then to self-integration.

The Four-Gated City covers the years 1950 through 1997, focusing centrally on Martha Quest's middle-age years. The novel derives its title from the Book of Revelation, but the title refers specifically to four types of houses that represent for Lessing the man-made world. Martha's passing between the houses connects the gates of the houses in postwar London, which she depicts as violent and corrupt. It is little wonder that perfect sanity seems like insanity in such a world. The question of mental balance in an imbalanced world is one that Lessing undertakes in this novel.

Since Martha has severed all ties with the collectives that once had placed restrictions on her life, she now relinquishes her public self, Matty, and asserts her inner character, Martha. Soon after her arrival in London, she finds sexual communion with a man named Jack. During a critical sexual experience with him, she has a vision in which she sees the golden age of her youth on the veld and a picture of herself as a middle-aged woman living in a house filled with sad-faced children.

When financial necessity presses Martha to find a job, she accepts a position as secretary to an aristocratic English novelist, Mark Coldridge. Her duties expand as Mark's eccentric family life becomes more complicated. Soon, Martha is running the entire household, which consists of Mark's insane wife, Lynda, Mark's troubled, orphaned nephew, Paul, and Mark's own star-crossed son, Francis. Martha functions as a surrogate wife to Mark and as a surrogate mother for the two boys. When Mark's nieces, Gwen and Jill, enter the picture, Martha also extends herself to them.

In a central scene in the book, Martha walks through the Coldridge house announcing dinner and daydreams that the house has no center. While suspended in this surrealistic state, she loses part of her memory and then realizes that, like the house, she does not have a center; there is nothing to hold the pieces of her life together. This experience is followed by news that Mrs. Quest is coming to London to see her. The impending visit causes Martha to panic and sends her back to the psychiatrist, who tells her that she has to work through her troubled bond with her mother.

In preparation for Mrs. Quest's visit, Martha places herself mentally at the center of the Coldridge house. She becomes so attuned to members of the household that she can overhear what they are thinking. When Martha shares this information with Lynda, she learns that Lynda has the same sensitivity and that it was this ability that first caused society to label her insane. Martha wishes to learn more about Lynda's insanity, which she now believes was induced by collectives in society. Through starvation and wakefulness, she descends with Lynda into the dark world of sound and begins to understand different psychic levels where people like Lynda can be trapped. Martha learns how to move through this frightening psychic world, developing resources that allow her to eradicate her guilty feelings about her mother.

At the end of the book, about the year 1965, Martha has put her life into focus, and she has reached a stage of self-integration. The futuristic appendix to the book takes the reader up to the year 1997 and charts events leading to some kind of nuclear holocaust. Survivors of the catastrophe are stranded in remote places, and the future of the world now seems to belong to the Third World.

THE GOLDEN NOTEBOOK

First published: 1962
Type of work: Novel

A fragmented woman writer, seeking to avoid chaos, writes about different pieces of her life in four notebooks; during a breakdown, imagined reels of her experiences merge to make a coherent movie, and she is healed.

The Golden Notebook encompasses the years 1950 through 1957. It is divided into five sections called Free Women 1-5. The first four sections contain a part of the main story (the conventional novel) and excerpts from four differently colored notebooks. The fourth section of the novel also contains the golden notebook. The last section is a straightforward ending to the main story, which presents an integrated character who no longer needs to compartmentalize experiences. When the story begins, the central character, Anna Wulf, has already published a single successful book, "Frontiers of War," set in central Africa, detailing "colour-bar hatreds and cruelties." This 1951 novel was so successful that Anna has been able to live off the royalties from it for the next six years while she suffers from writer's block.

The main story line evolves around two women, Anna and Molly, who seem to be extensions of each other politically and responsively. Their common enemy is Molly's ex-husband, Richard, a rich business executive who seems a perfect specimen of the British capitalist society. Richard continues to be very intrusive in Molly's life because they share a son, Tommy. Consequently, Richard assumes a relationship with Anna that is much like his relationship with Molly. Even Richard's second wife, Marion, becomes a part of the circle, vacillating, in an inebriated state, between Molly and Anna, trying to unburden herself of hurt feelings stemming from her bad marriage.

Once Tommy reaches the age when he should decide upon a career, he is torn between the idealistic world of his mother and Anna and the capitalistic world of tycoons. The "paralysis of the will" that Tommy suffers reaches its highest point when Tommy goes to Anna to have her confirm for him that her life-style, which seems to him morally superior, is truly viable. After reading Anna's notebooks, Tommy understands the chaos awaiting a person who tries to operate outside collectives; yet he cannot formulate the proper balance necessary for advancement. In a fit of depression, Tommy shoots himself in the head. Against the odds, he survives, though he is left totally blind. Ironically, he eventually leads the life of a successful businessman and joins forces with Marion, who leaves Richard to be with him.

At the end of *The Golden Notebook*, Molly decides to remarry, and Anna sees the end of yet another affair. Nevertheless, Anna has gained a better understanding of herself as a result of working through dark areas of her personality with a sexual partner who was in crisis himself during their relationship. He, too, is able to heal his life.

A brief description of the contents of each of the notebooks follows.

In the black notebook, Anna gives the African background for her novel "Frontiers of War." Although the first entry in this notebook is 1952, entries flash back to 1944. The story is a study of the cruelty of the colonial mind as seen through the eyes of the young idealist, Anna.

The red notebook is the contemporary notebook in which Anna records everyday events. It contains her present politics and gives an account of her disillusionment with the Communist Party. In it are a number of parodies of dedicated communists and newspaper clippings of such horrors as the testing of the hydrogen bomb, the bombing of Quemoy and Matsu, and the execution of the Rosenbergs in the United States.

The yellow notebook is a novel-within-the-novel. It contains Anna's fictional, unpublished second novel, called "The Shadow of the Third." The characters and actions in it are direct doubles for the main story.

The blue notebook is used by Anna as a diary. It contains commentary on her affiliation with the British Communist Party; details of the most intense love affair of her life, a five-year period when she truly loved a man named Michael; reports on her lengthy psychoanalysis with Mrs. Marks, whose therapy helps lead Anna into an emotional transformation when Anna has an affair with Saul Green, the man with whom she descends into chaos and learns how to self-unite.

The *Golden Notebook* symbolizes Anna's ultimate recognition that experience is fluid and connected. It is the notebook that both she and Saul Green want to use. They both contribute to it, and, through it, they give each other new beginnings.

Summary

Although Doris Lessing is a writer of a great narrative range, the themes that run throughout her work have been constant. Her concentration on such important extraliterary themes as colonialism, racial inequities, male-female relations, nuclear war possibilities, and the continuing evolution of humankind reveals her commitment to the betterment of humanity and underscores her belief in the serious role of the artist in society.

In reading a Doris Lessing book, one soon realizes that the undertaking is essentially expansive, for the writer's intent is not only to engage the reader's imagination through a literary experience but also to enlarge the reader's concept of what it means to live in harmony with oneself, with the world, and with the universe.

Bibliography

Draine, Betsy. *Substance Under Pressure: Artistic Coherence and Evolving Forms in the Novels of Doris Lessing.* Madison: University of Wisconsin Press, 1983.

Karl, Frederick. "The Four-Gaited Beast of the Apocalypse: Doris Lessing's *The Four-Gated City.*" In *Old Lines, New Forces: Essays on the Contemporary British Novel.* Edited by Robert K. Morris. Rutherford, N.J.: Fairleigh Dickinson University Press, 1976.

Pickering, Jean. *Understanding Doris Lessing.* Columbia: University of South Carolina Press, 1990.

Rubenstein, Roberta. *The Novelistic Vision of Doris Lessing: Breaking the Forms of Consciousness.* Urbana: University of Illinois Press, 1979.

Schlueter, Paul, ed. *A Small Personal Voice: Essays, Reviews, Interviews.* New York: Alfred A. Knopf, 1974.

Sarah Smith Ducksworth

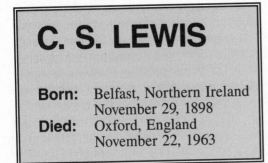

C. S. LEWIS

Born: Belfast, Northern Ireland
November 29, 1898
Died: Oxford, England
November 22, 1963

Principal Literary Achievement
An important scholar of English medieval and Renaissance literature, Lewis is best known as a novelist and religious apologist.

Biography

C. S. Lewis was born in Belfast, Northern Ireland, on November 29, 1898, the younger son of Albert and Flora Hamilton Lewis. His pleasant childhood with his brother Warren ended at age ten when his mother died. Already Lewis had begun to compose stories of imaginary worlds, featuring talking animals. After their mother's death, both boys were sent to English boarding schools, a separation that permanently estranged Lewis emotionally from his father. The next six years were the worst of his life, as Lewis makes clear in *Surprised by Joy: The Shape of My Early Life* (1955). Finally, in 1914, Albert sent him to a tutor, W. T. Kirkpatrick, who had instructed Albert himself, to prepare for college. Kirkpatrick strengthened Lewis' atheism and his skills in language and debate.

In 1916, Lewis won a scholarship to University College, Oxford; he failed the university entrance examination, however, because of weakness in mathematics. He was permitted to attend in 1917 so that he could join the army through enlistment in the University Officers' Training Corps. He left for France in November, 1917, was wounded in April, 1918, and returned to England.

While he convalesced, Lewis maintained a friendship with the mother of an Oxford companion, Paddy Moore. Both had promised to care for the other's family should his friend be killed, and Moore's death led Lewis to fulfill his promise. He supported Mrs. Moore and her daughter Maureen until Maureen reached adulthood; Mrs. Moore lived in his home until her death in 1951. Lewis' relationship with Mrs. Moore is unclear; he may have found a mother figure in her that replaced the loss of his own mother. She was not apparently sympathetic either to his academic work or to his later conversion to Christianity. During his convalescence, *Spirits in Bondage* (1919), a book of poems, was published.

Lewis returned to Oxford in 1919, graduating in 1922 with a B.A. while earning

highest honors in classics and philosophy. Unable to find work, he continued his studies in English literature, completing the standard two-year program in less than a year with highest honors. A temporary teaching position led in 1925 to a post as tutor in English at Magdalen College, which he held until his election to Cambridge in 1954. His position involved weekly meetings with students to discuss readings and essays, and college-wide lectures. In 1926, his poem *Dymer* was published. His friends in these years included fellow scholars such as J. R. R. Tolkien, who shared his love of Norse literature.

In 1929, Lewis' father died in Ireland. After selling the family home, the brothers purchased property in Headington, a suburb of Oxford, and moved there with Mrs. Moore and her daughter. Although they had never been close, his father's death struck Lewis very deeply. Over a number of months, Lewis was led to reflect on religious issues, and his friends Tolkien, Owen Barfield, and Hugo Dyson all discussed Christianity with him. His atheism, representing fifteen years of his life, he abandoned by 1929. He described himself only as a theist, however, believing in a God, until in 1931 he became a convert to Christianity. Central to his conversion, as he wrote in *Surprised by Joy*, was his pursuit of "Joy," a longing for something wonderful that this world cannot supply. He illustrated this quest in his allegorical narrative *The Pilgrim's Regress* (1933; revised, 1943).

His scholarly reputation was made with *The Allegory of Love* (1936), although he was professionally active throughout his career. Other scholarly publications included *A Preface to "Paradise Lost"* (1942). Nineteen years of study resulted in *English Literature in the Sixteenth Century, Excluding Drama* (1954), a volume in the Oxford History of English Literature series.

He found support from a group of colleagues, known as "The Inklings," who met twice a week to discuss works in progress. Tolkien's *The Hobbit* (1937) was first read in this context. The group also heard Lewis' first theological essay, *The Problem of Pain* (1940), the science-fiction trilogy, *The Screwtape Letters* (1942), and *The Great Divorce* (1945).

The Screwtape Letters established his popular audience. Originally serialized weekly in the newspaper *The Guardian*, when the letters were published together Lewis had a best-seller. Subsequent speaking engagements produced the famous wartime radio addresses collected as *Mere Christianity* (1952). Later, his lectures linked teaching with values in *The Abolition of Man* (1943). From 1947 to 1960, he wrote three more works on Christian doctrine. In the same period, his children's books, *The Chronicles of Narnia* (1950-1956), appeared.

Lewis' life changed dramatically in the mid-1950's. Professionally, his election in 1954 as professor of medieval and Renaissance literature at Cambridge permitted him freedom to lecture on topics of his choosing. Personally, it meant marriage. In the early 1950's, he had met Helen Joy Davidman, the wife of William Gresham. The Gresham marriage was failing, and after her divorce, she and her sons moved from the United States to Oxford in 1955. Their friendship influenced his most mature novel, *Till We Have Faces: A Myth Retold* (1956). In 1956, they were married in a civil ceremony, in part to secure British citizenship for Joy and for her sons. Joy was shortly afterward diagnosed with bone cancer, and in March of 1957, while Joy was hospitalized, they were formally married by an Anglican priest. Her almost miraculous recovery permitted them a honeymoon, and the next two years were the happiest of Lewis' life. Her cancer returned, however, and she died in July, 1960. Lewis recorded his loss in *A Grief Observed* (1961).

In his last years, he published little original material beyond *An Experiment in Criticism* (1961). He remained active at Cambridge until, in 1963, in failing health, he resigned his position. He died at his home in Oxford on November 22, 1963.

Analysis

As a literary scholar, as well as a creative writer, Lewis was sensitive to issues of technique, style, and purpose in writing. In his essays, he suggested some of his preferences about literature generally. Published after completing all of his "science-fiction" novels but before he had begun the Narnia stories, his essay "On Stories," in *Essays Presented to Charles Williams* (1947), illuminates some of these concerns. He distinguishes between exciting, suspenseful plots and the "whole world" of a novel. He rejects an adventure novel such as Alexandre Dumas' *Les Trois Mousquetaires* (1844; *The Three Musketeers*, 1846).

> The total lack of atmosphere repels me. There is no country in the book—save as a storehouse of inns and ambushes. There is no weather. When they cross to London there is no feeling that London differs from Paris. There is not a moment's rest from the "adventures": one's nose is kept ruthlessly to the grindstone.

Lewis' critics occasionally fault his fiction for its conventional plot structure, similarity of characterization, and occasionally unnatural dialogue. In "On Stories," however, he argues that to be preoccupied with character or plot is to miss an even more compelling element of the story. Plot, he suggests, is "a net" to "catch something else," a sense of perceiving another world. Against Dumas, he cites David Lindsay's science-fiction novel *A Voyage to Arcturus* (1920), where "physical dangers . . . count for nothing":

> He is the first writer to discover what "other planets" are really good for in fiction. No merely physical strangeness or merely spatial distance will realize that idea of otherness which is what we are always trying to grasp in a story about voyaging through space. . . . To construct plausible and moving "other worlds" you must draw on the only real "other world" we know, that of the spirit.

Lewis sees stories, then, as opportunities to portray spiritual journeys, to discover "otherness." All of his novels are conventional "quest" stories, involving tasks to be fulfilled and knowledge to be gained. In his first two science-fiction novels, the character Ransom is taken off the Earth, undergoes psychological, physical, and spiritual trials, and returns with knowledge and faith that yield him a new perspective on his society. Common to these stories and to his children's novels is the education of the spiritual innocent. Variety in his plots lies chiefly in the types of obstacles that confront characters and the means to overcome them. Often, a trial turns out to be quite different from its initial appearance, so that the protagonist's intellect, as well as courage, is tested.

In the process, characters must often learn to see the world around them in radically new ways. The earliest example of this is Ransom, in *Out of the Silent Planet* (1938), who is unable at first to perceive the giant shapes around him on Mars as mountains, since they seem unnaturally tall because of that planet's lighter gravity. "Reperceptions" can be physical or moral, as when Jane Studdock, in *That Hideous Strength: A Modern Fairy Tale for Grownups* (1945), discovers the existence of a moral hierarchy in which she is called upon to subordinate herself to God and to her husband. Similarly, her husband Mark sees his callous treatment of Jane and his selfishness as a moral and spiritual failure.

Occasionally, the novels appear static as characters are caught up in moral and religious argument, as in *Perelandra* (1943) and *The Silver Chair* (1953). In both novels, characters must defend the intellectual integrity of their beliefs. While Lewis was a well-known debater, and the scenes illustrate his concern for an intellectually informed faith, they are rare in his fiction. Instead, where Lewis places his energy, in creating the "atmosphere," the "weather" of another world, he is extremely successful. In creating Malacandra, Perelandra, or Narnia, he invests sensory details with a suggestion of the symbolic and the mythic. Narnia varies little from England in its plants and animals, yet contains centaurs, dryads, and talking beasts. Its charm lies in part in its distance from mechanized England, so that time slows down and moments may be savored. Lewis' only novel written about contemporary England, *That Hideous Strength*, points up the contrast: Only in Bragdon Wood, where the magician Merlin is buried, and at St. Anne's, where Ransom is, are there moments of stillness and joy.

Lewis has been accused by some of writing allegory, particularly in the Narnia stories, in which Aslan the lion, creator of Narnia, appears to take on the qualities of Christ. He responded to the charge by describing the genesis of the stories in scenes recalled from dreams, and commenting that the central figure, Aslan, suddenly intruded into *The Lion, the Witch, and the Wardrobe* (1950), the first story, unbidden. A distinction that Lewis made in *Perelandra* seems appropriate, that between myth, truth, and fact. In the sacraments, particularly in Holy Communion, participants eat bread and drink wine or grape juice, in *fact*; yet they participate in and reenact a *mythic* celebration, in which a man who said he was God offered himself for all humanity. Lewis' fiction, then, has sometimes been described as "sacramental," in this sense; it is not allegory, which Lewis did use in *The Pilgrim's Regress*. Allegory implies a simple retelling of a story with different names—England becomes Puritania, the Church becomes Mother Kirk. Instead, characters in his fiction are called to act as Christ might have acted, or to act on His behalf, in their separate stories. This is as true of the human "patient" to be tempted in *The Screwtape Letters* as it is of the Pevensie children in Narnia.

THE SPACE TRILOGY

First published: *Out of the Silent Planet*, 1938; *Perelandra*, 1943; *That Hideous Strength*, 1945
Type of work: Novels

Contemporary Englishmen discover that they are participants in a battle against spiritual powers seeking to enslave humanity.

Lewis' science-fiction trilogy is sometimes called the Ransom Trilogy, after the central figure of *Out of the Silent Planet* and *Perelandra*. Elwin Ransom, a middle-aged linguistics professor at the University of Cambridge, grows in the course of the novels from a lonely independence to find relationships with others, maturing into a leader against hostile nonhuman forces. Lewis transforms a conventional science-fiction pattern by making his villains demonic powers and his protagonists Christians literally on the side of the angels. While science fiction has frequently dealt with issues of religion, Lewis lays aside the typical dualistic "good against evil" plot for an explicitly Christian worldview. All three of the novels attempt to make believable the presence of a spiritual reality transcending the everyday life.

Out of the Silent Planet opens as Ransom, on a walking tour of England, falls in with two acquaintances, one an old friend from his prep school. His friend Devine and the scientist Weston kidnap Ransom, carrying him to Mars, or Malacandra, in Weston's spaceship. Late in the voyage, Ransom learns that the others were commanded to bring another human back as the condition of their return. When they land, Ransom escapes. The novel is so far entirely conventional: mad scientist, greedy assistant, innocent victim, threatening aliens.

Here, however, Lewis diverges from convention. Ransom finds Mars inhabited by three species of rational beings, all friendly. More, he finds present a fourth species, the eldila, something on the order of angels. After Ransom learns the Martian language, he is reunited with Weston and Devine, who have killed a Martian. Judged by the ruling eldil, the Oyarsa, all three are exiled to Earth. Ransom learns from the Oyarsa that Earth is the "Silent Planet" because of the rebellion of its Oyarsa millennia ago. It becomes clear to Ransom, already a Christian, that the biblical story of the Incarnation of God in Christ is historically true, one incident in a war that has left Earth isolated and dominated by evil powers.

Two elements of the story are particularly significant: first, the minimal place of "science" in the action, and second, the "reperceptions" that Ransom experiences. The "good society" of the Martians is almost Rousseauvian in its rejection of technology, and the one species with which Ransom spends much time is a tribe of hunters and farmers. Ransom must repeatedly adjust his perception of the landscape, his understanding of culture, and his sense of what it is to be "human." He discovers a new sense of his own place and that of humanity in a universe of many intelligent species, and a new humility, in that humankind is the sole species in need of redemption.

In *Perelandra*, Ransom is summoned to Venus to defend its inhabitants from an unknown threat. He discovers that only two "humans" have been created, the Adam and Eve of their race. Like Adam and Eve, they have a single commandment given them, which they must obey to show their love for God. Weston's sudden arrival in a new spaceship makes clear the nature of the threat. Proclaiming himself the servant of the demonic Oyarsa of Earth, Weston begins a campaign of temptation against the unfallen Eve, the Queen.

Lewis' study of John Milton's *Paradise Lost* (1671) lies behind many of the novel's scenes; the temptation, for example, recapitulates Milton, not the Bible. Like Milton, Lewis faced the problem of portraying "goodness," unfallenness, in the Queen. The difficulty of successful characterization is enormous: She is simultaneously innocent, gracious, wise, and naked. At the same time, Lewis must portray the decaying personality of Weston as suggesting the sterility and misery of the Satanic.

Ransom matures in this novel, and at its climax he must physically battle Weston, in a scene recalling *Beowulf* (c. sixth century) or Homer's *Odyssey* (c. 800 B.C.). Before he can bring himself to kill Weston, however, his understanding of Christianity itself must change. Previously, his faith has been intellectual and passive; he discovers that as a Christian warrior he stands, for the moment, in the place of Christ defending innocence.

In treating the temptation that the Queen endures, for the first time Lewis focuses on the necessity of intellectual maturity in Christians. The twisted arguments Weston develops, suggesting the abuse and perversion of language itself, Lewis had foreshadowed in a comic scene in *Out of the Silent Planet*. In *Perelandra* and in *That Hideous Strength*, the intellectual theme of armament against evil is much more prominent.

That Hideous Strength, the only story set in modern England, Lewis subtitled *A Modern Fairy Tale for Grownups*. He seems not to suggest the simplicity of the traditional tale, but its associations with magic intruding into everyday life. That is precisely what happens. The story is not from Ransom's perspective, but from that of an ordinary English university community. The protagonists, Jane and Mark Studdock, are a modern, well-educated postwar newlywed couple; Mark teaches sociology at Bracton College, and Jane is working on a degree in literature.

Both long for professional success and personal recognition. Neither realizes the selfishness these goals represent or what means they must use to achieve them. Mark, greedy for peer approval and power, joins a scientific and industrial combine, the National Institute for Co-ordinated Experiments (NICE). Behind the NICE, however, is a demonic conspiracy to conquer England. Jane's latent psychic powers make her a desirable pawn to NICE, as well, and she eventually flees to sanctuary in Ransom's household.

In the previous novels, Lewis' criticism of modern life had been a minor element. Here, he sharpened his critique of Western culture, particularly its materialism and skepticism. Jane and Mark, in their self-enclosed worlds, are forced to reckon with a spiritual reality and authority their culture has denied. What eventually saves them is a core of genuine love for one another, which leads them to repentance. Many in the novel, however, never rise above a self-consuming self-love.

THE SCREWTAPE LETTERS

First published: 1942
Type of work: Novel

In a series of letters, a senior tempter advises a junior devil how to succeed with a patient.

The Screwtape Letters made Lewis' popular reputation. An epistolary novel from a senior tempter, Screwtape, the letters advise his junior colleague and nephew, Wormwood. The narrative traces Wormwood's attempts to enslave the soul of a "patient," a human on Earth, so that he may end in Hell at his death. Over the course of thirty-one letters, set in contemporary England during the Blitzkrieg, Screwtape reviews strategies based on exploitations of human nature.

Lewis' purpose is frankly didactic, although his use of Screwtape as a narrator means that readers must often "invert" the truths he reveals. In the process, Lewis' satire ranges over much of modern life, for Screwtape is ironically aware of human failings invisible to humans. Yet Screwtape himself is satirized, too; at moments, he appears confused, contradicting himself, admitting truths about God that he later denies. Lewis succeeds in creating both a character and an atmosphere: Hell is the mindset in which selfishness becomes self-absorption.

Early in the novel, the patient experiences a religious conversion, permitting Screwtape to discuss how the Christian life may itself be perverted. This development becomes the major interest of the work, for the Church is the real enemy of the demonic. As Screwtape provides advice, Lewis is able to portray the Christian faith in opposition to those facets of modern life that are diabolical.

Over the course of the novel, Screwtape encourages Wormwood to promote four illusions held by moderns. The first is that total freedom and independence lie in casting off inhibitions and that God is somehow opposed to this. By contrast, Screwtape casually notes that God intends that humans grow to maturity and intellectual and emotional independence. God intends that they be free from whatever might enslave them, including themselves, and thus offers them the power of self-transcendence through the Church. He lures them toward his freedom with joy and love, and to that end provides both in human life as shadows of what awaits those who love Him.

A second illusion lies in modern beliefs about the Christian church. Screwtape reveals that the Church is, first of all, mostly invisible, for it includes all of its members in time and eternity. The Church opposes modern culture in its emphasis on interdependence, while industrial life emphasizes competition. Screwtape notes that interdependent life in community can be maintained only by love, while selfishness motivates competition. Since Christianity demands love and condemns selfishness, competitive attitudes are a direct threat to it. Further, the Church offers access to permanence and security, while modern culture perceives these as stodginess.

A third illusion is that emotions, rather than the intellect, are trustworthy. Lewis implicity stresses repeatedly the role of reason in everyday life, especially for the Christian. Screwtape cautions Wormwood to confuse, rather than argue with, his patient, and especially to employ jargon or emotion-laden terms to motivate him.

Finally, Screwtape gives the lie to the belief that personal faith has no social implications. He urges Wormwood repeatedly to separate his patient's convictions, especially his religious faith, from outward conduct and habits. Because most men and women lack consistent intellectual and moral beliefs, they remain inactive when called to moral choice. To Lewis, a mature Christian life is one in which the central attitudes and beliefs work their way into every moment. Screwtape reviews a catalog of occasions to separate conduct from belief, including relationships within the family, moments under stress, attitudes toward Christians of differing faith, and relationships with non-Christian companions.

THE CHRONICLES OF NARNIA

First published: *The Lion, the Witch, and the Wardrobe*, 1950; *Prince Caspian*, 1951; *The Voyage of the Dawn Treader*, 1952; *The Silver Chair*, 1953; *The Horse and His Boy*, 1954; *The Magician's Nephew*, 1955; *The Last Battle*, 1956.

Type of work: Novels

Into the parallel world of Narnia come a series of English children who meet the lion Aslan, confront evil, and grow to maturity.

The Chronicles of Narnia traces the experience of a number of modern children in their encounter with a "medieval" world. Lewis apparently envisioned key scenes in the story when he was in his adolescence but may have had no thought of developing a series of stories until he was well into them. Into the stories flow memories of the works of authors such as Kenneth Grahame, E. Nesbit, and George MacDonald. Each story portrays the growing maturity of the children who find their way into Narnia, and the plots are, in that respect, very similar. Each child must confront wickedness, spiritual evil localized in some individual, and overcome it. Perhaps more significant than the plot, Lewis creates settings that are richly described, in which magic is possible and everyday actions may have deeply symbolic value. If any of his fiction succeeds in creating that longing for "Joy" that he experienced in his own life, the Narnia stories do.

The Lion, the Witch, and the Wardrobe introduces the Pevensie children, Peter, Susan, Edmund, and Lucy, who discover Narnia, where the White Witch has brought a hundred-year winter without Christmas. Although the children enter Narnia apparently by accident, they are expected, and welcomed. Humans are meant to rule in Narnia, despite the fact that its chief inhabitants are talking beasts and creatures such as centaurs, satyrs, nymphs, and dryads. When the children learn that a prophecy of their arrival means that humans may help to free Narnia, three enlist to fight the White Witch. Yet she has already enchanted Edmund into betraying them.

Christian truth is never far under the surface of Narnia, though children who read the stories may not notice it. Each story demonstrates the necessity of relying on Aslan, the lion who is a thinly veiled image of Christ. His entrance into *The Lion, the Witch, and the Wardrobe* transforms it from fairy tale to spiritual romance. Edmund is saved when Aslan offers himself to the White Witch to die as a substitution, and Lewis thus makes understandable to children the Incarnation and Crucifixion of Christ. One of the novel's most effective scenes is Aslan's return to life the next morning. With his power, the children swiftly defeat the witch's army of monsters, and spring is renewed.

Prince Caspian returns the Pevensies to a Narnia again enslaved. This time the materialistic humans, the Telmarines, are at fault. Fearful of the talking animals and other intelligent Narnian creatures, they first drove them out to the forest, then in later years denied their existence. The Telmarine Caspian's battle on behalf of "Old Narnia" fails until he depends on Aslan, and the Pevensie children similarly must listen to Aslan and trust him before they can be effective. A comic element of the story is the failure of adults to recognize the moral authority of children when directed by Aslan.

The Voyage of the Dawn Treader brings together Caspian, Lucy, and Edmund. They return to Narnia, this time with their cousin Eustace Scrubb, an insufferably modern child. Caspian has resolved to find seven missing noblemen who sailed east from Narnia. At first glance, the story might simply be an adventure like any other children's novel. Again, however, Lewis develops lessons of religious truth through the children's adventures. The journey results in a literal transformation of Eustace, who must be freed from a physical enchantment and, simultaneously, from the enchantment of modern skepticism.

The Silver Chair returns Eustace to Narnia, with a schoolmate, Jill Pole. They arrive in Aslan's country, escaping the persecution of schoolchildren at their "modern" school, and are dispatched to rescue Caspian's grown son, Rilian, kidnapped by a witch. The children and a companion eventually defeat her enchantment in what is explicitly a test of faith, of faithfully remembering Aslan's directions. At the novel's conclusion, Lewis includes the comic scene of Jill, Eustace, and Caspian, still in armor, terrifying the bullies who had persecuted Jill.

The Horse and His Boy is an episode from the rule of the Pevensie children during the time of the first novel. The story line reminds one of intrigue and mistaken-identity novels, or even of William Shakespeare's *The Comedy of Errors* (c. 1592-

1594), and is the slightest of the stories in symbolic depth. Shasta, a young boy, though the son of the King of Archenland, near Narnia, had been kidnapped as an infant. Later, he escapes to Narnia with a Calormene girl, Aravis, and two Narnian talking horses. In the process they foil a planned Calormene attack on Narnia. Aslan appears to guide Shasta and disciplines Aravis, whose selfishness has resulted in suffering for others.

In the last two books of the series, Lewis completes the story of Narnia by narrating its creation and its final destruction. *The Magician's Nephew* describes how Digory and his friend Polly discover Narnia and inadvertently bring evil into it. Lewis' picture of the creation as spoken and sung by the power of Aslan's voice is a remarkable evocation of the biblical story in *Genesis*. The story accounts for several mysteries in the series, not the least of which is the source of evil in an unfallen world.

The Last Battle is Narnia's version of the Book of Revelation. Narnia is overthrown, the servants of evil triumph, and Eustace and Jill and the Narnian defenders are flung into a stable to die. What they find inside, however, is another Narnia, one so intensely real that the world outside the door seems a shadow. This is Heaven, and Aslan welcomes them and the Pevensies to their real home. When Aslan judges and unmakes the world, they see him retain in the new Narnia all the good things in the old. It is clear that Lewis focuses in this last novel on consolation, both for the fears children have about death and for their anxiety at the scriptural theme of the end of the world. Yet, as in *That Hideous Strength*, Lewis attacks the unbelief, decadence, and corruption of modern life, which make inevitable the final battle. Further, he shows the self-destructive nature of evil, for the triumph of evil is the occasion for Aslan to end Narnia itself.

Summary

C. S. Lewis' fantasies center on the discovery of the reality of the supernatural. In an age when the "theology" of most fantasies is confused or dualistic, he employs the tools of fiction to awaken audiences to Christianity. One may fairly argue that Lewis never varies his essential plot, the story of individuals whose moral choices move them either toward themselves or toward God. He might have responded that all stories can, finally, be reduced to this. His real strength lies in the creation of fantasy worlds that are "desirable," in which audiences can sense the otherness that leads to a new perception of human life.

Bibliography

Carpenter, Humphrey. *The Inklings: C. S. Lewis, J. R. R. Tolkien, Charles Williams, and Their Friends.* London: Allen & Unwin, 1979.

Glover, Donald E. *C. S. Lewis: The Art of Enchantment.* Athens: Ohio University Press, 1981.

Green, Roger L., and Walter Hooper. *C. S. Lewis: A Biography.* New York: Harcourt Brace Jovanovich, 1974.

Howard, Thomas. *The Achievement of C. S. Lewis: A Reading of His Fiction.* Wheaton, Ill.: Harold Shaw, 1980.

Meilaender, Gilbert. *The Taste for the Other: The Social and Ethical Thought of C. S. Lewis.* Grand Rapids, Mich.: Wm. B. Eerdmans, 1978.

Schakel, Peter J., ed. *The Longing for a Form: Essays on the Fiction of C. S. Lewis.* Kent, Ohio: Kent State University Press, 1977.

——————. *Reason and Imagination in C. S. Lewis.* Grand Rapids, Mich.: Wm. B. Eerdmans, 1984.

Willis, John R. *Pleasures Forevermore: The Theology of C. S. Lewis.* Chicago: Loyola University Press, 1983.

Richard J. Sherry

WYNDHAM LEWIS

Born: Amherst, Nova Scotia, Canada
November 18, 1882
Died: London, England
March 7, 1957

Principal Literary Achievement
Lewis applied principles of the graphic arts to writing, promoted vorticism, and produced more than forty volumes, including novels, short stories, essays, poetry, autobiography, and criticism.

Biography
A beginning like Percy Wyndham Lewis' could hardly yield a conventional adult. Lewis first saw the light of day aboard the family yacht anchored off Amherst, Nova Scotia, Canada, on November 18, 1882, when his British mother, Anne Prickett Lewis, gave birth to him. Although his father, Charles Lewis, was an American who had attended West Point, been an army officer, and fought in the Civil War, the infant was officially a Canadian citizen, bearing for life the citizenship of neither parent.

When Percy Lewis was six, the family, which had lived in coastal Maine and on the Chesapeake Bay, resettled in England. The Lewis marriage was teetering and before long ended. Anne's finances were limited although Charles had sufficient means to live the life of a gentleman, having no pressing need to work. Young Percy, as he was then called, lived with his mother in genteel poverty.

The lad, nevertheless, was able to enter the Rugby School in 1897, supported in part by his father. Percy proved a disappointing scholar who ranked last in his class. At Rugby, however, he acquired the bearing and accent of a proper British gentleman; he was also encouraged in his art work, probably because art was the only pursuit for which he showed both an enthusiasm and an aptitude.

Lewis' mother encouraged the boy's painting. She used some of her meager resources every summer to take Percy abroad for as long as she could afford to stay. He was regularly exposed to the art works of the Louvre and the museums at Luxembourg. It was natural that when Lewis finished Rugby, he would seek instruction in the one thing at which he was good. He entered London's Slade School of Art in 1898 and remained there for three years, receiving a scholarship to help finance his final year of study.

Slade was not the sort of school to push its students in daring artistic directions.

Its teaching was traditional and conventional. Still, Lewis benefited greatly both from the regularity that the school's routine imposed and from the basic instruction that taught him something about form, graphic representation, and art forms that were practiced in other parts of the world. He also began associating with artists who were alive with ideas, among them Augustus John and William Rothstein, with whom he remained friends for the rest of his life.

Upon leaving Slade, Lewis traveled abroad extensively, financed by an allowance that his father settled upon him. He traveled to the Continent, haunting museums and formally studying painting in Paris, Madrid, Haarlem, and Munich, imbibing the best of the artistic techniques that these disparate cultures had to offer. During the seven years that he spent abroad, Lewis spent most of his time in Paris.

Although Lewis' stay in Paris occurred more than a decade before the literary excitement of the "lost generation" infected the city, the Paris of Lewis' day bristled with ideas and was a magnet to many literary figures. Lewis' first novel, *Tarr* (1918), is based upon his life in Paris and on the artists and writers whom he knew there. During this period, Lewis strove to shake the conventionality of being the British gentleman that Rugby had sought to make him and became something of an *enfant terrible*, doing everything he could to be outrageous in an effort to attract attention and publicity.

When he returned to England in 1909, Lewis turned to his mother for support, although he was beginning to attract art commissions and was regarded as an important emerging painter. He was working on *Tarr* at this time and also tried unsuccessfully to market a trashy novel that he had written to make some quick money. It was during this period that Lewis began friendships and long associations with Ezra Pound, Rebecca West, William Butler Yeats, and Ford Maddox Ford. Lewis' first published story, "The Pole," appeared in Ford's *English Review*.

Lewis associated regularly with people trying experimental literary and artistic forms, including T. S. Eliot. Pound had moved a step beyond Imagism to vorticism, an art that emphasized detachment and geometric form. Before long, Lewis was viewed as the organizing force of the vorticists. In June, 1914, Lewis published the first issue of *Blast*, a journal devoted to cubism, futurism, Imagism, and other forms of modern art. Although this journal survived for just two issues, it marked a significant direction in painting and literature.

As World War I raged, Lewis volunteered for military service early in 1916. After training as a gunner and bombardier, he was commissioned in 1917 and sent to France, at the time that the serial publication of *Tarr* began in *The Egoist*. Avoiding combat, he survived the war and by 1919 was back in London, where he published *The Caliph's Design* (1919), a call for an ideal in architecture.

For the next six years, Lewis remained semiretired, painting, reading, writing criticism. With the publication of *The Art of Being Ruled* (1926), he entered a highly productive period of writing. His political conservatism was now pronounced, and several of his books of the early 1930's diminished his reputation.

Lewis' *The Apes of God* (1930) satirized savagely the Sitwells and the Bloomsbury

Group, causing much of London's genteel literary community to eschew its author. To make matters worse, Lewis published *Hitler* (1931) the following year, casting his lot with the national socialism that the Nazis were spreading in Germany. His *Men Without Art* (1934) attacked Ernest Hemingway and D. H. Lawrence mercilessly, further alienating Lewis from segments of the literary community.

When World War II erupted, Lewis was lecturing in Canada. He and his wife remained in North America throughout the war, eking out an uncertain living on Lewis' lecture fees and painting commissions. At war's end, the Lewises were literally on the first passenger ship to leave Canada for England. Lewis' vision was failing; by 1953, he was totally blind. He continued, however, to write, producing eight books between 1948 and his death in London on March 7, 1957.

Analysis

Lewis was not good at school things and turned in a weak performance as a student at Rugby. It is interesting, therefore, to realize how, by cultivating the one field in which he had both an interest and an aptitude, he opened other opportunities for himself. Essentially, it is through his work as an artist that he developed his interest in literature and established himself as a productive writer and critic. That his writing often makes its impact through visual means suggests that it is the artist's keen eye and sensitivity to form that shaped it.

The intellectual ferment that Lewis experienced as an art student in Paris became a part of his life in London after he returned there in 1909. Meeting Pound was crucial in Lewis' life, because Pound was at that time emerging from his Imagist period, in which he sought to write precise, spare, visual poetry aimed at projecting single, vivid images and was moving toward vorticism, a literary and artistic movement closely connected to Imagism. Lewis, attracted to this new movement, became its reigning guru.

The overt art of the vorticist is a geometrical art of surfaces. It was this element of vorticism that affected Lewis' writing. He wrote of surfaces, not of substrata. He is not the penetrating psychological writer that Henry James was, because it would have been philosophically abhorrent to Lewis to write that way. In *Men Without Art*, he calls James a creator of "great disembodied romances," something he himself never could or would be.

Lewis spent his first thirty years trying to find himself. Just as he was finding his niche, World War I intervened. The society that he had created for himself was disrupted by the war. *Blast*, his greatest literary triumph to that point, was discontinued in 1915. Within the year, Lewis was in military service, although much of his service was as a member of the Canadian War Artists rather than as a combatant. He was involved in only one combat, the battle of Passchendaele; within a short time, he was reassigned to London to do two large war paintings. His war experience, however, left him bitter. He believed that it had robbed him of productive time.

Philosophically, Lewis had already revealed some of his feelings about Friedrich Wilhelm Nietzsche in *Tarr*, where the notion that artists must dominate women is a central theme. His association with Pound, Yeats, and Eliot confirmed his own elitist views and encouraged his political conservatism. Just as Pound became a voice for the Fascists in Italy, Lewis sided with Adolf Hitler's Nazi Party that was beginning to take hold in Germany in the late 1920's.

Although Lewis repudiated his earlier, pro-Nazi stand in two long essays, *The Hitler Cult* (1939) and *The Jews, Are They Human?* (1939), his image as a Fascist sympathizer was difficult to dispel. The same currents that underlay his pro-Nazi sympathies were reflected in much of his superbly written literary criticism, which, despite its excellence of style, was based upon such wrongheaded prejudices that it created a breach between him and some of the most notable intellectuals of his day.

Lewis' attack in *The Apes of God* on the Sitwells and the Bloomsbury Group was in a sense an outgrowth of the vorticism that he had earlier tried to promote. Satire is always cutting, but Lewis' satire has an acerbic quality beyond all expectation. This quality emerges again in *Men Without Art*, in which Lewis' attack upon Ernest Hemingway so infuriated the renowned novelist that he eventually retaliated by presenting a scathing portrait of Lewis in *A Moveable Feast* (1964).

Lewis' earliest writing was characterized by vigor, by strong visual imagery, and by striking use of stream-of-consciousness. All of these characteristics became hallmarks of his style as his writing progressed. He was a writer well in control of language and all of its effects. His juxtaposition of characters creates the dramatic tensions that make his books bristle with excitement. The cutting satiric edge that discomfited some readers of Lewis' books is clearly evident in *The Art of Being Ruled* and *The Apes of God*, both of which are polemical. *The Lion and the Fox: The Role of the Hero in Shakespeare's Plays* (1927), *Time and Western Man* (1927), *The Childermass* (1928), and *Paleface: The Philosophy of the Melting Pot* (1929) are all products of the same approach to society, each of them addressing the ills of the world in heterodox ways.

Lewis' emphasis is usually on the place of artists in modern society. He examined the artists of his day—Ezra Pound, James Joyce, Virginia Woolf, Henry James, and others—and found them sometimes superficial and derivative, practitioners of style at the expense of ideas. He had unqualified kind words for few writers of his own period.

Along with his bitterness about the war, Lewis later cultivated a bitterness at not having received the recognition that he felt was his due. He turned against democracy, adapting an attitude quite like that of the American journalist and writer H. L. Mencken, whose term "boobocracy" coincided well with Lewis' view of government by the people. In Lewis' eyes, fascism offered artists greater hope than a government that had no elite class. He considered Hitler a man of peace and downplayed his anti-Semitism. The publication of his ill-conceived and badly researched *Hitler* in 1931 drew harsh condemnation and resulted in Lewis' losing a number of painting commissions.

Lewis' writing of the 1930's did not sell well. Additionally, Lewis suffered from continuing bouts of ill health, some of it related to venereal diseases contracted almost two decades earlier. He lived a financially precarious existence, which caused his bitterness to accelerate. The six-year exile in North America that World War II imposed upon him did little to assuage his feeling of alienation and neglect. When they returned to England, the Lewises found a nation in disarray. They endured food shortages and other inconveniences, but perhaps Lewis felt more at home in England now than ever before. His *Rotting Hill* (1951) is a collection of stories that depicts postwar Britain, and it has less invective than Lewis' earlier work. He entered into a period of intense productivity that continued until his death.

TARR

First published: 1918
Type of work: Novel

Lewis focuses on a group of artists in Paris before World War I, using the protagonist, Tarr, to espouse his own aesthetic and moral philosophy.

Although *Tarr* is concerned largely with two artists, one English and one German, involved with the same woman, Lewis is concerned more broadly with reaching generalizations about the English and German temperaments and about the perceptions of life peculiar to each society. Frederick Tarr is a British artist who, not unlike Lewis, lives in Paris during the Edwardian period. Tarr, like Lewis, has no great fondness for Germans, although he is engaged to Bertha Lunken, a German art student. His need for her his largely physical, and once that need has been satisfied, he finds it inconvenient to have her around.

Bertha is a stereotypical German—that is, a German built on Lewis' personal, quite negative stereotype of Germans. Tarr wants to end his engagement because he finds Bertha tedious and uninteresting. His sexual attachment to her is also fading, a fact that he attributes to his devoting all of his creative energies and imagination to his art, leaving little for his sexual indulgences. Tarr clearly is plotting his break with Bertha in such a way that he will be perceived as taking the moral highroad. He will sacrifice his personal relationship for the greater good: his art.

Tarr goes to Bertha's flat, decorated with egregious kitsch that offends Tarr's artistic and tasteful soul. He tells her as gently as he can that marriage is not in their future. Bertha makes a prototypically bourgeois retreat into heaving sobs, reinforcing the Irish author Oscar Wilde's observation that "tears are the refuge of plain women but the ruin of pretty ones." Tarr leaves, feeling quite the cad, but he promises to see Bertha soon again.

Meanwhile, Otto Kreisler, a German artist living on a pittance that his father doles out fitfully, returns to Paris from Italy. Kreisler four years earlier shed one of his paramours, who promptly married his father, leaving Otto's inheritance diminished. The father, a bourgeois German businessman, disapproves of his son's artistic pursuits and wants him to return home and do something worthwhile—to wit, go into business. Kreisler's allowance is late, and when he arrives in Paris, he is destitute. He tries to borrow from a well-heeled friend who had helped him in the past, but this friend, Ernst Volker, has tired of him and has replaced him with Louis Soltyk, a Pole. Ernst knows from experience that Otto never repays his debts.

Otto goes to a café to eat and there meets Anastasya Vasek, to whom he is greatly attracted. He pours out his woes to her in a sequence that shows how Lewis views German sentimentality as a commingling of love and sorrow. He accepts an invitation to a dance that he knows Anastasya will attend, but before it occurs, he comes upon Anastasya and Soltyk in a cafe. He is insulting to Soltyk and through much of the rest of the book seeks Soltyk out in public so that he can insult and humiliate him, obviously setting the scene for a duel.

Meanwhile, Otto meets the spurned Bertha on the way to the dance and uses her to humiliate the other guests. He and Bertha kiss quite publicly. When this is reported to Tarr, he writes to tell Bertha that he is returning to London. The day after the dance, Otto's overdue allowance arrives with a command from his father that he return to Germany. Otto replies that he will kill himself in exactly one month. Tarr does not actually go to England but merely moves to another part of Paris so that he can work without interruption. When he finally sees Bertha and Otto together, he befriends Otto because he thinks it is ironically appropriate that these two exemplars of German sentimentality be paired. Tarr now finds that he is attracted to Anastasya and has deep aesthetic conversations with her.

Meanwhile, Tarr observes Otto's increasing aggressiveness toward Soltyk. Otto several times rushes up to Soltyk in public and slaps his face. A duel is inevitable. When the morning of this encounter finally comes, their seconds try to effect a compromise. Suddenly, Otto agrees to forget the duel if Soltyk will kiss him publicly. Soltyk leaps upon Otto, pummeling him, while the seconds engage in their own combat. As they seek to lead Soltyk away, he strikes out at Otto, who fires his pistol and kills him. Five days later, Otto is captured and jailed. He hangs himself in his cell, delivering on his promise of suicide.

Back in Paris, Tarr and Anastasya are having an affair as Tarr gradually ends his relationship with Bertha. When he learns, however, that Bertha is pregnant with Otto's child, he marries her out of pity. He continues to live with Anastasya. After two years, Bertha divorces Tarr to marry someone else. Tarr and Anastasya never marry, but Tarr fathers three children by another woman.

This novel, Lewis' first, is a satire on the decadence of the Edwardian era. Tarr's main function is to espouse Lewis' philosophy. Otto Kreisler emerges as a more fully developed character than Frederick Tarr. Realizing this, Lewis later admitted that perhaps he should have called the novel "Kreisler" rather than *Tarr*.

THE REVENGE FOR LOVE

First published: 1937
Type of work: Novel

This political satire views the political Left in Spain during its civil war and in London in the 1930's, making trenchant comments about politics and art.

The Revenge for Love is generally regarded as Lewis' most successful novel. Despite its sometimes stinging satire, the book has a warmth and gentleness that distinguishes it from Lewis' other writing, particularly his writing of the 1930's. The novel is arranged in seven parts; Lewis is slow but calculated in bringing together its various characters and situations. The writing is vivid. The novel's visual effects are meticulous and detailed.

The setting of the first section is Spain during its civil war. Percy Hardcaster, a Briton who is in Spain as a Communist organizer, is in prison waiting to be tried. A verdict against him will result in his execution. Rather than await the outcome, Percy, with the help of a Spanish double agent posing as a prison guard, escapes. The guard, Serafin, is shot and killed; Percy is injured and loses his leg.

The novel then shifts to London, where Lewis introduces a number of leftist intellectuals and artists. Among them are Victor Stamp, an Australian painter, and his wife, Margot. They are impoverished, and Victor is losing confidence in himself as an artist. In the next section, Jack Cruze, a tax consultant, is introduced, along with a successful young painter, Tristram Phipps, and his wife, Jill. Jack is interested in Tristram because he paints nudes. He quickly falls in love with Tristram's wife and one day, accidentally seeing her nude, is totally inflamed with passion. By the next section, Jack and Jill are having a torrid affair (one inevitably recalls what happened to Jack and Jill in the well-known nursery rhyme).

The fourth section of the book is pivotal. It involves a party at the home of Sean O'Hara, a gunrunner. At the party, Lewis juxtaposes armchair leftists and committed leftists who fight for their beliefs. Percy Hardcaster represents the latter element. Jill, as a representative of the former, articulates her views, which Percy denigrates. Jack beats Percy up for insulting Jill. In this section, Lewis shows clearly his suspicion of the leftist views among intellectuals in London during the early 1930's.

In the next section, Victor Stamp and Tristram Phipps, who cannot support themselves on their art, become art forgers in an art factory that turns out old masters to order. Lewis comments satirically on artistic integrity and how it can be compromised in a society in which artists cannot support themselves legitimately. He had written about this problem much earlier, addressing it in his early essays in *Blast* and the *Criterion.*

Ultimately, Victor is persuaded to go back to Spain with Percy to run guns that the leftist Spanish forces will use against the Fascists. In the book's final section, Victor and Margot are in the Basque country on the French/Spanish border. Margot has had dire premonitions of what the outcome will be, but she cannot dissuade Victor from running the guns until the last minute, when she frightens him by telling him that he is soon to be arrested. The two strike out to cross clandestinely into France. Meanwhile, Percy is captured by the Spanish Civil Guard and imprisoned.

In prison, he reads of how Margot and Victor wandered off in the rain and fell off a cliff to their deaths. Percy's tears are both for the loss of his friends and for the loss of ideals that he has held dear. *The Revenge for Love* is an anti-Communist Manifesto of sorts. It reflects Lewis' intellectual conservatism and explains to an extent his flirtations with Fascism, which, in his eyes, offered artists more than Communism could.

This novel differs from Lewis' other works in that it is compassionate and, at times, warm. The characters are well developed and exceptionally well balanced against each other. The dramatic tensions both in Lewis' characters and in his basic situations are sustained and assure a high level of reader interest.

SELF CONDEMNED

First published: 1954
Type of work: Novel

History professor René Harding leaves England in 1939 for Canada to wait for the war to end and in so doing comes to realize the difference between history and reality.

It is easy to read *Self Condemned* as an autobiographical novel, although to take it as point-by-point accurate autobiography would be a mistake. The book's protagonist, René Harding, and his wife, Hester, leave Britain for Canada in the year that World War II erupts and, like Lewis, settle around Toronto. Harding arrives in Canada with little notion of what he will do there, but soon he is employed at the University in Momaco, whose anti-British faculty members do not accept him and make him feel always the outsider.

The Hardings endure the cruel winters holed up in the Blundell Hotel, where the boring routine of their lives oppresses and depresses them. The news that they get from the radio is discomfiting, and the future seems tenuous at best. When the hotel burns down, the Hardings are further dislocated. Lewis writes of the fire as the Italian poet Dante Alighieri wrote of the tenth circle of Hell. Fire and ice intermix in the cold Canadian night as firefighters pour water into the inferno.

When the hotel's manager finds that the owner set fire to the building to collect the insurance, Mr. Martin, the owner, murders her to avoid detection. Shortly after the fire, Harding is invited to teach in the College of the Sacred Heart, which offers a more hospitable environment than he found in Momaco. The priests, eyeing him as a possible convert, treat him with warmth and deference.

If Harding feels disembodied in Canada, his wife feels even more alienated. She becomes hysterical at times, and Harding tries to ignore her, retreating into his work. Hester suffers a breakdown and ultimately throws herself in front of a lorry, which squashes her, but spares her head. In the morgue, Hester's head seems strangely dissociated from her body, a heavy-handed indication of Lewis' separation of emotion from intellect. In this image, intellect prevails. Although affected by her death, Harding views it as her final attempt to derail him from his professional pursuits, but he will not allow that to happen. Emotionally spent, he accepts a teaching position at an American university, where he functions successfully even though he is thoroughly disillusioned.

In part, Lewis is pointing in *Self Condemned* to the dislocations that war wreaks upon a populace. More than that, however, he is pitting history against life's daily realities, questioning perhaps the validity of history or at least cautioning readers not to put absolute faith in it. The interplay of intellect and emotion is evident throughout the book both overtly and symbolically. The interplay of fire and ice when the Blundell Hotel burns is a major part of this symbolism, which is—in this case, quite consciously—derived from Dante's the *Inferno*, the first canticle of *La divina commedia* (c. 1320; *The Divine Comedy*, 1802).

The Hardings are involved in a marriage that has become pointless and is strained nearly to the breaking point by the exile into which the couple is forced. This exile, however, is the glue that holds the union together. The Hardings are in a trap. The husband finds his escape from that trap when he ignores his wife's excesses of emotion. She, however, pursues a more active course and, by her suicide, tries to regain her control of René from the grave.

BLASTING AND BOMBARDIERING

First published: 1937
Type of work: Autobiography

Lewis recounts the effects that the war had on his life from 1914, when *Blast* was first issued, to 1926, when *The Art of Being Ruled* was published.

Perhaps *Blasting and Bombardiering* was an attempt at exorcism. Lewis was disenchanted with the role of the artist in society long before World War I erupted, but his war experiences deepened that disenchantment and added to it a cynicism that festered within him for much of the remainder of his life. The title of the book, of course, refers to Lewis' editorship of the avant-garde journal *Blast*, which, although suspended after two issues, made a significant artistic statement in its day, and to his training as a bombardier after he entered military service in 1916.

The book is divided into five sections, the first of which deals with the London literary scene as the war became a reality, focusing on the publication of *Blast*. The next two sections have to do with Lewis' entry into military service and with his service, first as a lieutenant in the Royal Artillery serving in France and later as a painter of war pictures attached to the Canadian army and stationed in London.

The next section deals with postwar England, a period when Lewis was semiretired, trying to find himself after the shock of the war. He was a dedicated womanizer and lived to a large extent on the patronage of various rich women with whom he had liaisons. The period from 1919 to 1926 was a fallow one for Lewis, although he was working regularly on his writing and published six important books between 1926 and 1929. These books were all in the formative stages during his semiretirement.

The final section focuses on Lewis' three closest literary associates: Ezra Pound, T. S. Eliot, and James Joyce. He regards Pound as brilliant and important for his influence on other writers, most notably Eliot. He discusses Pound less charitably in some of his other writing. Lewis thinks that Eliot was lackluster, with occasional moments of artistic brilliance. He considers Joyce idiosyncratic but extremely promising. His view of these three writers was tempered by the fact that war intervened in all of their lives, diverting them from their true courses, which would inevitably have led to a more classical art, to a detached literature.

Although *Blasting and Bombardiering* extends for nearly a decade beyond the end of World War I, the impact of that war is evident on every page. The central theme of the book has to do with the inroads that war (and by extension, philistine society) makes upon art and artists.

A valuable side benefit in this book is found in Lewis' thumbnail sketches of some of the intellectuals of his day, aside from those aforementioned. His comments about Nancy Cunard, Rebecca West, T. E. Lawrence, Augustus John, T. E. Hulme, Bertrand Russell, Alfred North Whitehead, William Butler Yeats, and others with whom he was closely involved as an artist and a writer are highly subjective and largely unsubstantiated, but they provide shrewd and sharp insights into these people.

Summary

Wyndham Lewis will likely be long remembered for his support of the Fascists in the late 1920's and early 1930's. His ultraconservative views during that time stemmed from his dislike of the Germans, who had plunged the world into World War I, and from his cynicism engendered by that conflict. Yet that is an oversimplification of a highly complicated personality whose cynicism cannot be laid to a single cause.

The fact remains that Lewis was prodigiously productive and that he had some of the keenest critical insights of his day. His own novels were well crafted. His essays, although often wrongheaded, were brilliant in presenting heterodox views of society. Lewis as a *provocateur* served a valuable function in his day, and his ideas continue to provoke contemporary readers.

Bibliography

Campbell, SueEllen. *The Enemy Opposite: The Outlaw Criticism of Wyndham Lewis.* Athens: Ohio University Press, 1988.

Jameson, Fredric. *Fables of Aggression: Wyndham Lewis, the Modernist as Fascist.* Berkeley: University of California Press, 1979.

Kenner, Hugh. *Wyndham Lewis.* Norfolk, Conn.: New Directions, 1954.

Kush, Thomas. *Wyndham Lewis's Pictorial Integer.* Ann Arbor, Mich.: UMI Research Press, 1981.

Materer, Timothy. *Wyndham Lewis: The Novelist.* Detroit: Wayne State University Press, 1976.

Meyers, Jeffrey. *The Enemy: A Biography of Wyndham Lewis.* London: Routledge & Kegan Paul, 1980.

_____, ed. *Wyndham Lewis: A Revaluation.* London: Athlone Press, 1980.

_____. *Wyndham Lewis.* London: Routledge & Kegan Paul, 1972.

Pritchard, William H. *Wyndham Lewis.* New York: Twayne, 1968.

Wagner, Geoffrey. *Wyndham Lewis: A Portrait of the Artist as the Enemy.* New Haven, Conn.: Yale University Press, 1957.

R. Baird Shuman

LI PO

Born: Central Asia
A.D. 701
Died: Tan Tu, Anhwei Province, China
A.D. 762

Principal Literary Achievement

Widely celebrated as one of China's greatest lyric poets of the T'ang Dynasty (A.D. 618-907), China's golden age of literature, Li Po is equally legendary for his bohemian life-style.

Biography

Though legends about Li Po abound, relatively little reliable biographical information about him has been preserved. Despite claiming an illustrious background, he, in fact, was born to an obscure family (the origins of which are impossible to trace, though it is variously thought to have been from Iran, Turkey, or Afghanistan) in A.D. 701, in Central Asia. Wherever his birthplace, early in his life his family moved to Szechwan, a mountainous province in southwest China known for its sizable foreign merchant community; perhaps in that fact lies a clue to his family's occupation. His undistinguished origins meant that in the capital, where prominent family and political connections were critical, he had to rely on his own innate wit and talent; although he did so to great success, he seems always to have felt himself to be the outsider who had to prove himself.

In approximately 725, Li Po left Szechwan, to which he never returned, and traveled for a few years, studying Taoist mysticism, one of his lifelong passions, as well as visiting noted poets, whose acquaintance he hoped could further his career. In 730, he settled down for a while and married the daughter of a minor provincial official of modest means. Evidence of Li's desire for illustrious connections, however, can be found in his declaration in a letter that he had married into a renowned noble family. This first wife eventually divorced him, and he married three more times; two of his wives died, and his fourth outlived him. His poetry suggests that he had at least one son and one daughter.

Within ten years of his first marriage, Li Po left home to wander again and to attempt to better his fortunes. He had a stroke of luck in 742, when Emperor Hsüan Tsung, an avid supporter of the arts, appointed him to a post at the Han-lin Academy in the capital city of Changan. Li found himself in eminent company: scholars, art-

ists, entertainers—all of whom were privy to the emperor's inner court. His job was to write documents for the emperor, as well as poems for special court occasions. One thing that he refused to do after coming to Changan was take the civil service examinations, which were considered imperative for success in the capital; his refusal is difficult to explain, and it cost him the respect of some important people in the capital.

Perhaps he was one of the world's earliest practitioners of a public-relations campaign, because he put considerable effort into promoting himself as both a poetic genius and a bon vivant. His time in the capital city and in the inner court circle provided numerous famous anecdotes of his freewheeling life with his friends and of his drunkenness. Indeed, legends about Li Po are much more numerous than facts. One tale that indicates his popularity with the emperor tells of Yang Kuei-fei, the emperor's favorite concubine, holding Li's inkwell for him while he wrote; another tells of an important palace eunuch being forced to kneel and remove the drunken poet's slippers for him. Yet another anecdote tells of the emperor himself seasoning Li Po's soup for him, but a less charming story tells of his drunkenly vomiting on the emperor's robes.

Still, he amused the emperor, who tolerated his indiscretions and lack of regard for authority and decorum, though one famous story tells of Emperor Hsüan Tsung putting him to the test. Once, when Li had been drinking all day, the emperor summoned him to the palace and insisted that he draft an important document, a duty that Li fulfilled even in his inebriated state. He had cultivated the public image of a cheerful, free-drinking poet who dashed off his works spontaneously rather than laboring over them, and he was able to prove his case in this instance. How much of Li Po's behavior was genuine and how much was a cultivated persona is hard to say. His nickname, "Banished Immortal," acknowledges both his poetic genius and his occasionally outlandish behavior, implying as it did that he was a demigod who had been exiled from heaven for misconduct.

Li's job was secure only as long as he held imperial favor, and in 744, he lost or left his position in the Academy. Stories vary as to whether he was dismissed following scandal or chose to resign, but he left Changan and wandered again, managing to make a living by his reputation as a popular poet and eccentric and by visiting old friends who held provincial posts. It was during his travels that he met fellow poet Tu Fu, a young unknown who admired and emulated the famous older poet. Later generations were to venerate them as the two greatest poets of the T'ang Dynasty, China's golden age of literature.

In 755, eleven years after Li Po had left Changan, a rebellion occurred, and Emperor Hsüan Tsung was forced to abdicate. Li once again gained court connections, this time in a minor position with Li Lin, prince of Yung, the sixteenth son of Emperor Hsüan Tsung. Though the prince was supposedly fighting rebel troops, he apparently had thoughts of starting a rebellion himself. When the prince's army was destroyed, and he was executed, Li fled but was captured and imprisoned as a traitor. Eventually released and pardoned, he resumed his wanderings for the last few years of his life and embraced fully the Taoist mysticism that he had studied as a younger man and in which he had had an abiding interest for most of his life. Once again, he hoped to find a place for himself in the government, but his hopes were not to be fulfilled, for he died in A.D. 762, in Tan Tu, Anhwei Province, China. The legend of his death is in keeping with his life: He is said to have drowned when, inebriated, he fell out of his boat while trying to embrace the reflection of the moon on the water.

Analysis

Although the T'ang Dynasty saw the introduction of several new poetic forms, Li Po was not an innovator. What he did accomplish was to raise tradition-bound lyric poetry to its pinnacle of beauty and power. Many of the approximately one thousand poems attributed to him continued the established verse forms and subjects of his predecessors. For example, he was apparently happiest with the ancient *shih*, a lyric form that employed a predominantly four-, five-, or seven-character (syllable) line, and the *yueh-fu*, ballads or folk songs with lines of irregular length. Even so, he occasionally ignored formal restrictions and wrote verse in irregular meter when it suited his purpose; some of his poems have as few as three or as many as ten or eleven characters. Critics believe that he was influenced in this usage by the popular music of his time.

Li Po's work cannot be understood apart from the tradition from which it sprang. Many aspects of Chinese poetry distinguish it from Western poetry. For instance, Chinese poetry relies very little on the most common poetic devices familiar to Western readers such as symbolism, figures of speech (metaphor and simile), and personification. There again, however, Li Po is unusual in occasionally personifying elements of nature.

Typically, Chinese poetry is spare and concentrated, implying and suggesting ideas through images rather than lavish description. (This feature of Chinese poetry has influenced modern Western poets, especially the Imagists.) Most often, these images are drawn from nature. Many of Li's subjects, too, were long established in Chinese poetry: the emperor's concubine hoping for her ruler's favor or, more commonly, lamenting the loss of it; the lonely wife longing for her husband, who is far away; friends celebrating their friendship or bidding farewell when parting; or a journey to visit a hermit, who turns out not to be at home. These subjects on which Li Po wrote were very familiar to his audience since they had appeared in Chinese poetry since the fifth century B.C., when Confucius supposedly collected and first recorded China's earliest poetry in the *Shih Ching* (c. 1066-541 B.C.; *Book of Songs*, 1937); that Li Po knew the *Book of Songs* by heart by the age of ten indicates its importance in Chinese culture. Li's reputation as one of the greatest poets of China stems, then, not from technical or thematic innovation, but from the great skill with which he managed to surprise his readers in presenting the unexpected within the familiar.

Li startled his readers by upsetting their assumptions that his poetry would follow fixed patterns of development. In a poem on the traditional topic of visiting a holy man in the mountains, for example, Li's reader would have expected him to establish the scene and the occasion, but instead he opens with the sound of a barking dog. Another of his poems begins with a wild cry of the poem's speaker. Repeatedly, he violated his readers' sense of decorum, and they loved him for it.

Another characteristic of Li's poetry is his playful wit, especially in his personification of natural elements, which goes far beyond a Taoist identification with nature. For example, he makes the moon his drinking companion, says that a star spoke to him, or claims that he and a mountain gaze long at each other without either becoming bored. Such humorous, fanciful images were most unusual in T'ang poetry and contributed to his readers' surprised delight.

Yet another distinctive aspect of Li's poetry is the dream vision. Such poems concern fantastic voyages, his own or the gods', through the cosmos, riding the tail of a comet, pulled by a phoenix, or flying on one's own power. He catches sight of the Queen of the Skies in the light of a rainbow, climbs a cloud ladder, sees fairies, and hears dragons roar—then awakens in bed, filled with longing.

Li Po is frequently compared to the European Romantics, whose lyric poetry and emphasis on the individual would seem to parallel his, and yet, for all that he did to promote his public image, his poetry itself contains little of biographical note. Thus, scholars have found it all but impossible to assign dates to his poems. Shortly after his death in 762, two editions of his work were in print: *Li Han-lin chi* and *Ts'ao-t'ang chi.*

Many English translations of his work exist; perhaps some of the most famous are those in *Cathay* (1915) by twentieth century American poet Ezra Pound, who did not know classical Chinese but worked from the notes of a translator, who had himself studied Li Po's works with a Japanese master. Thus, for all of their fame, they are more reflections of Pound's poetic genius than a faithful rendering of Li Po's originals. Because of the significant grammatical and syntactical differences between Chinese and English (nouns are neither singular nor plural but stand for the idea of the thing itself, verbs do not have subjects, verb tenses do not exist, for example), English translations of the same work can vary widely. Rhyme, substitution of words to preserve rhyme scheme, antiquarian diction or neologisms, contractions such as " 'twas"— all found in different translations of Li Po's poems—do not preserve the integrity of the original lines.

Li Po is the Chinese poet most widely known outside of China. Those only superficially acquainted with him sometimes think of him as the "bad boy" of Chinese poetry because of his popular reputation as a hard drinker who loved women and good times with his friends. It is true that he cultivated his reputation as a cheerful man who could never succumb to sorrow as long as there was a cup of wine to drink. To see him only in the light of that persona, however, is to miss the richness and complexity of his combination of established poetic forms and themes with his own humorous, sometimes mystical vision of the world.

IN THE TAI-T'IEN MOUNTAINS

Written: c. 718-720 (English translation, 1973)
Type of work: Poem

Wandering in the mountains in search of a reclusive holy man, the poet does not find him at home.

In his poem "In the Tai-t'ien Mountains, Failure to Find the Wise Man," Li Po addresses a topic very familiar to his Chinese audience. Many Taoist masters turned away from their society and lived simple, austere lives in the mountains, which the Chinese considered to be very spiritual places. While his topic may have been a conventional one, his presentation of it is somewhat unorthodox.

Li opens the poem with the sound of a dog barking, an indecorous beginning. His audience would have expected him, instead, to establish the occasion and set the scene; barking, if it appeared at all, would properly have come later in the poem. Typically, however, Li Po liked to startle his audience.

The poet moves from one sound to another—the bark is heard over the roaring of rushing water—and at last visual images appear: wet peach blossoms, deep woods, a deer. Ironically, the sound he could actually expect to hear is missing; at noon, he pauses in his journey and notices that no noon bell is struck.

The images leap forward as he climbs on through tall bamboo, green against a bright blue sky, to a waterfall, whose spray hangs in the air. There he expects to find the holy man, but no one knows where he has gone. The poet makes no direct statement about his feelings, and interpretations vary as to whether he is disappointed or content. The dreamily beautiful images have assumed an almost magical quality, so it is easy to believe that his is not merely a physical journey, but a spiritual quest that has not been in vain, whether or not he finds the hermit.

This poem brings together Li Po's fascination with the Taoist recluses and his affinity with the mountains as places charged with the supernatural, where he could experience a mystical union with nature. As different as this poem is from his drinking poems, each represents equally a true love of Li Po.

MARBLE STAIRS GRIEVANCE

Written: c. 740 (English translation, 1915)
Type of work: Poem

A palace lady waits hopefully for the emperor's visit, but as the night grows late she sadly realizes that he will not come.

Li Po's famous "Marble Stairs Grievance" is of that large body of Chinese poems that treat the subject of the palace lady, abandoned and forgotten by the emperor. The poems are always subdued but filled with longing and sadness. The poetry accurately reflected historical fact; many beautiful young girls were selected as the emperor's concubines, and to be chosen brought honor both to the young woman and to her family. Many grew old and lonely at the palace, however, rarely seeing the emperor but considered still in his service. A subcategory of this subject is that of the mocking treatment of the older palace lady, who still adorns herself with makeup and finery and waits for the emperor's visit.

In the first stanza, the dew that has formed on the marble stairs indicates, on a literal level, the lateness of the hour, thus the fact that the emperor is not coming; but the dew could also refer to tears on the lady's face. Her beauty is suggested by her clothing in the reference to her silk stockings and in the smoothness of her marble (sometimes translated as "jade") cheek. The fact that her stockings are now dew soaked underscores the poignance of her long—and fruitless—vigil.

In the second stanza, she sadly lowers the curtain and looks at the autumn moon through glittering crystals. Beaded curtains made of rock crystal were used in the palace, so the reference could be taken literally, but again, the suggestion is strong that the clear, glittering drops are her tears. The specific naming of an autumn moon intimates that she is no longer a young girl.

In a brief scene contained in a two-stanza poem, Li Po portrays the pathos of the cruel plight of the abandoned palace lady; without the attentions of her lord, her life is meaningless. Li conveys both her sorrow and the idea that she has waited and hoped many times—and will do so many more.

Summary

Contemporary readers often want a poet to enable them see the familiar world afresh, but Li Po's readers expected his work to reveal knowledge of ancient poetic traditions. He gave them what they wanted—and more. To the old familiar subjects and themes, he brought a fresh vision that charged his poetry with spontaneity. His unrestrained vitality gives a scattered, exuberant energy to many of his poems. The inebriation that is so often associated with the man and his work could serve as poetic metaphor; life and nature in his poetry come across as intoxicating.

Bibliography

Cooper, Arthur, trans. *Li Po and Tu Fu.* New York: Penguin Books, 1973.

Owen, Stephen. *The Great Age of Chinese Poetry.* New Haven, Conn.: Yale University Press, 1981.

Waley, Arthur. *The Poetry and Career of Li Po.* London: Allen & Unwin, 1950.

Watson, Burton. *Chinese Lyricism: Shih Poetry from the Second to the Twelfth Century.* New York: Columbia University Press, 1971.

——————. *The Columbia Book of Chinese Poetry: From Early Times to the Thirteenth Century.* New York: Columbia University Press, 1984.

Whincup, Greg, trans. *The Heart of Chinese Poetry.* Garden City, N.Y.: Anchor Press, 1987.

Yip, Wai-lim. *Ezra Pound's Cathay.* Princeton, N.J.: Princeton University Press, 1969.

Young, David, trans. *Five T'ang Poets: Wang Wei, Li Po, Tu Fu, Li Ho, Li Shang-yin.* Oberlin, Ohio: Oberlin College Press, 1990.

Linda Jordan Tucker

HUGH MacLENNAN

Born: Glace Bay, Nova Scotia, Canada
March 20, 1907
Died: Montreal, Quebec, Canada
November 7, 1990

Principal Literary Achievement

Recognized as Canada's outstanding man of letters of the mid-twentieth century, MacLennan expressed the Canadian national character in internationally respected novels and essays.

Biography

John Hugh MacLennan, the only son of dour Calvinist surgeon Samuel MacLennan and his vivacious, artistic wife, Katherine MacQuarrie MacLennan, was born in the mining town of Glace Bay on Cape Breton Island, Nova Scotia, on March 20, 1907. Though three generations of MacLennans had lived on Cape Breton, the doctor thought of himself as Scottish. Like the Scots in the homeland, he had aspirations of improvement through education. Consequently, in 1912-1913 he decided to take specialist training abroad, his family joining him in the summer, and at the beginning of World War I he moved to Halifax, where both he and Hugh would have more opportunities. There Hugh witnessed his father's departure to war and his return as an invalid. The boy also witnessed in 1917 the carnage wrought by the explosion of a TNT-laden ship in Halifax Harbor.

In accordance with his father's aspirations—indeed, demands—MacLennan studied the classics, in 1928 took an honors B.A. from Dalhausie University, played championship tennis, won a Rhodes Scholarship to Oxford, and took a B.A. from Oriel in 1932. While in Oxford, he also traveled considerably in Britain and Europe, observing firsthand the economic and political conditions that led to World War II. He also wrote poetry. Unable to find a publisher for it, a failure that he blamed on the Depression, MacLennan turned to fiction with Ernest Hemingway as his model.

Unable to find a job in 1932, because of the Depression and colonialism—the two classics positions available at Canadian universities went to Englishmen with no better qualifications than his—MacLennan followed his father's insistent advice and accepted a fellowship for a Ph.D. at Princeton. In 1935, Princeton awarded him the degree for a study, based on papyri, of the decline and fall of Oxyrhynchus, a Greek city in Egypt, in the third century. Princeton published the thesis.

Yet MacLennan was unable to find a publisher for the novel that he had written by 1935 and could not get a teaching position at a Canadian university. He thus became a schoolmaster at Lower Canada College (a private high school) in order to be able to marry and support Dorothy Duncan, an American whom he had met on the ship from England in 1932. Despite the demands of his teaching, MacLennan continued to write. When no publisher would take his second novel, MacLennan took the advice of his wife, also a writer, to create a Canadian consciousness, realistic Canadian characters, the Canadian scene in literature.

The next book, *Barometer Rising*, centered on the Halifax Explosion of 1917. Published in 1941, it was a popular and critical success. Deemed "a first novel of unusual quality" and "a landmark in Canadian writing," the novel fixed MacLennan in the category of "literary nationalist." The success of *Barometer Rising* contributed to his obtaining a Guggenheim Fellowship to work on a second novel about the French and English duality. That novel, *Two Solitudes* (1945), merited the Governor General's Award.

Although sales of his books never made him rich, the success of *Two Solitudes* enabled MacLennan to resign from Lower Canada College and to secure a summer home in North Hatley, Quebec. His next two books, the novel *The Precipice* (1948) and *Cross-Country* (1949), won Governor Generals' Awards, but Canadian critics panned *The Precipice* because its Canadian-American theme diluted MacLennan as a "distinctly Canadian novelist," and it did not sell well in Canada. During the early 1950's, then, to augment his finances, MacLennan accepted commissions for many magazine articles, and in 1951, the year that *Each Man's Son* was published, he took a part-time professorship in English at McGill University to get medical insurance for his wife, who had had a rheumatic heart from childhood. MacLennan found teaching congenial, he received even more recognition in the 1950's, and he published essays widely. Dorothy, however, died in 1957. The powerful novel of 1959, *The Watch That Ends the Night*, is the story of a woman with a weak heart but enormous spirit.

The Watch That Ends the Night was a great financial and critical success, and MacLennan in 1959 married a lovely old friend, Frances Walker. He published the essay collections *Seven Rivers of Canada* (1961, revised as *The Rivers of Canada*, 1974) and *Scotchman's Return and Other Essays* (1960). An influential teacher, he was made full professor at McGill in 1968, the year after the publication of *Return of the Sphinx* (1967), a novel, as the name might imply, about the cycles of history and generational conflict, demonstrated in the inflammatory French separatist movement in Quebec.

Although he continued to teach, to write essays and to work on his last novel, the 1970's were not golden years for MacLennan. *Two Solitudes* became a disastrous 1978 film. Separatist terrorism developed as, in *Return of the Sphinx*, he had said it would, and he, a symbol of English Canada, became a target for terrorist attack. Then scholars began a reassessment of his work. "It is time," said one, "to remove MacLennan from the pantheon"; "this is the man who prepared the way for everyone else, but, you know, Moses never enter the promised land," said another.

Nevertheless, in his seventies MacLennan completed *Voices in Time* (1980), a foreboding survey of the twentieth century and its future. In 1984, he looked to his roots in *On Being a Maritime Writer.* In the 1980's, scholars began a more balanced appraisal of the 1970's reassessment of his literary worth. Despite continuing personal misfortunes and his concern for the turbulence of the times, MacLennan wrote shortly before his death in Montreal on November 7, 1990, "I have really enjoyed my existence." *Maclean's,* the Canadian newsmagazine, concluded that "he was a fine man and a great writer, and we were lucky to have lived in a time and place that had him for its town crier."

Analysis

After a publisher had rejected one of MacLennan's first novels, suggesting that it needed a stronger sense of locale, he became an external force that directed the young writer's focus to the Canadian scene. When, in 1960, the great American editor and critic Edmund Wilson found in MacLennan's essays "a Canadian way of looking at things which had little in common with either the 'American' or the British colonial one and which has achieved a self-confident detachment in regard to the rest of the world," he set his seal on the reputation of MacLennan as a Canadian nationalist. Although it is true that his seven published novels are set in Canadian culture and that his heroes, like the author himself, come home again, it is also true that Mac-Lennan's world travels and his studies of classics and history in universities of three nations, as well as his Canadian heritage, have informed his thinking and his novels.

In his doctoral researches (1935), for instance, MacLennan found that the private enterprise responsible for Rome's greatness "was also responsible for the reduction of democratic communities to quasi-feudal serfdom." As early as *Two Solitudes,* Mac-Lennan warned against the dangers of uncontrolled capitalism. In his next novel, *The Precipice,* the same message appears as a denial of the value of the American Dream. Later, in 1960, MacLennan identified another element of the cycle of history. From a book by Gordon Rattray Taylor, MacLennan adapted the Freudian notion that "the extreme father-identifier, the 'patrist' is compelled by hidden psychological needs to crave authority," whereas the mother-identifier, the matrist, "hates conflict . . . is bored by power . . . tends toward democracy" and "softens by corruption any authoritarian institutions he has inherited." In history, matrist and patrist political systems alternate. Disturbed by the permissiveness of the 1960's and 1970's, MacLennan foresees in *Voices in Time* democratic freedom declining into chaos and ushering in a new authoritarianism as antidote.

All MacLennan's novels treat the conflicts of father and son not only because Mac-Lennan spent years coming to terms with his own stern father but also because Mac-Lennan knows his Freud and his Sophocles. Scholar Alec Lucas points out numerous Oedipus motifs in the novels: "heroes with physical defects," "separation from the father; the search for a father during which . . . [the son] discovers himself," "kindly foster-parents, and sexual attraction to a member of one's own family or a maternal female." In MacLennan's first three novels, *Barometer Rising, Two Solitudes,* and

The Precipice, the rebellious sons never come to terms with their fathers or their fathers' sexuality. In *Each Man's Son*, however, the middle-aged son gives up the ghost of his father, and in *The Watch That Ends the Night*, MacLennan turns Dr. Jerome Martell, a parallel to his own father, into a Christ figure. By 1980, MacLennan himself has turned into a father, critical of the permissive younger generation; but his author figure, childless John Wellfleet, in *Voices in Time* becomes the kindly teaching father to the children of the future.

MacLennan scholar T. D. MacLulich says that MacLennan's historical study leaves him uncertain as to whether society's course is determined by forces beyond human control. The play of human will against externally determined destiny is also the subject of Sophocles' great Oedipus tragedies, which MacLennan loved. The thinker who grew up with a Calvinist father and who came to manhood during the Great Depression might well be inclined to see the external as determiner. Yet critics who fault MacLennan for the use of external determiners are unwise. Such events as the Halifax Harbor explosion in *Barometer Rising*, which frees Neil Macrae from a disgrace (also externally caused by a false accuser), are actual determiners in real life; and it is his reaction to the suffering caused by the explosion that frees Neil from the desire for revenge. Yet the lesson of tragedy and of life is that the noble individual must struggle against determinism or, unable to prevail, accept fate with dignity and self-control. MacLennan and his heroes do one or the other; they are never craven.

The great myth of the struggle of life—of will against determinism—is that of Odysseus. That myth recurs in all the novels. Like Odysseus, Neil Macrae in *Barometer Rising* comes home unknown to Halifax from World War I, wounded and disgraced, to reclaim his identity and his place in society, to take vengeance on his enemy, and to restore his house. Neil and his faithful Penny and their son are reunited in seasoned happiness like that of Odysseus, Penelope, and Telemachus. In *Each Man's Son*, structured like the *Odyssey* (c. 800 B.C.) with counterpointed scenes at home and in the world, Archie MacNeil, a boxer, lacks Odysseus' cunning to survive the exploitation of prizefighting, and his wife, Mollie, lacks the strength to resist her suitor. On his return, Archie kills Mollie and her lover and dies, but "Telemachus" (the son) survives to live with Dr. Ainslie, a Calvinist Mentor at last grown wise. In *The Watch That Ends the Night*, Dr. Jerome Mantrell, like Odysseus an "oddly pure sensualist so many experimenting women had desired," returns from war and wandering to bring Catherine, his dying former wife, and her husband, George, to terms with their past, to enable them to affirm her remaining life and accept her death. This affirmation of life and death is a major theme of the *Odyssey*. Scholar George Woodcock calls the *Odyssey* "the product of a people in the process of becoming aware of itself . . . [appropriate] to illuminate" the rise of a "Canadian national consciousness." It is also a myth of communication with the world. MacLennan's novels and his Canada are part of the world.

TWO SOLITUDES

First published: 1945
Type of work: Novel

The lives of three generations of two Canadian families are bound up in the conflict between French-Canadian and Anglais ideas and aims for Canada.

A Galsworthian family saga, which of course includes intergenerational conflicts, *Bildungsroman*, and love stories, *Two Solitudes* presents the bipartite consciousness for "European" Canada and urges reconciliation through reciprocal understanding: "Love consists in this," says the epigraph from the German poet Rainer Maria Rilke, "that two solitudes protect, and touch, and greet each other." In the account of the older generation from 1917 to 1921, Athanase Tallard, member of Parliament and seigneur of the agricultural community of St. Marc, represents the French tradition, Catholic, communal, "bound in sacred trust to the soil"—although he is critical of the Church, advocates scientific education, and has taken as his second wife a sensuous Irish Catholic girl. Typical Anglais are represented by the self-made capitalist Huntley McQueen, and by Janet Methuen, who has married into an old moneyed English family of Montreal, one with manners but very little noblesse oblige. Janet's father, John Yardley, a retired sea captain who buys a farm in St. Marc, is the sort who should help bring about conciliation. Honorable, humane, exuberant, attuned to nature, Captain Yardley earns acceptance in the community. The parish priest, Father Beaubien, who opposes Yardley and Athanase, embodies the Church's antiassimilationist policy. In the interest of controlled progress, Athanase collaborates with McQueen to set up industry in St. Marc. When he loses his place in his own community and can no longer be useful to McQueen, the tycoon bankrupts him. Yet it is Marius, the son of Athanase and his ascetic, sanctimonious first wife—Marius, "sexually puritanical, politically ambitious, a tool in the hands of the Church and the fledgling separatist movement," ultimately a failure—who destroys his father in the French Catholic community.

Paul Tallard, the son of Athanase and his Irish second wife, Kathleen, is the focus of the episodic account of the next generation. Educated in French and English, humanely and scientifically, living as little lord of the country manor and then in urban poverty in Montreal, studying at university and then traveling the world for five years (1934 to 1939), Paul would seem ideal for developing the unified Canadian consciousness in the world, and so he is. In Athens, the cradle of his civilization, he thinks that "in spite of all the things he had done and the places he had seen, he [is] essentially unchanged: a Canadian, half French and half English, still trying to be himself and stand on his own feet." In 1939, Paul goes home to write—for Paul is an incipient writer—about "naturally vital people" in Canadian society, and to marry Heather

Methuen. The daughter of Janet Methuen and granddaughter of Captain Yardley, Heather has denied the mercenary values of her mother and has sought breadth and independence by studying art in the United States. Like Paul, she is faithful to Canada. Like her grandfather, she is full of joy. Though theirs is a romance of individuals, their marriage points the way toward national reconciliation.

The novel ends with declaration of war against Germany. Paul will volunteer, his first act as a unified Canadian being the defense of the civilization of which both the French and the English are a part. Among the French and English Canadians, Mac-Lennan concludes, "there woke . . . the felt knowledge that together they had fought and survived. . . . The country took the first . . . steps toward becoming herself," alone but in touch with a world of nations.

VOICES IN TIME

First published: 1980
Type of work: Novel

In the twenty-first century, an aged survivor of political and physical cataclysm tries to recover and record historical knowledge as a help to the renewal of civilization.

Voices in Time is at once a futuristic and a historical novel. When André Gervais, one of a new generation stirring in the 2030's, born after "the Great Fear," "the Destructions," and the establishment of the repressive, simplistic Third Bureaucracy, discovers buried records of a Wellfleet family in Metro (once Montreal), John Wellfleet, a seventy-five-year-old "inoperative" in the new society, organizes his family's experiences into a model of what went wrong in the twentieth century. Since John Wellfleet tries to recount the stories of his family members in their own voices, his resulting book is structured as a montage written in a variety of styles.

Central to the novel is the elegant voice of Conrad Dehmel, John Wellfleet's stepfather. The son of a German naval officer bound utterly to pride, discipline, and duty and a gentle, war-loathing mother, Conrad develops liberal values. Studying history in England in the 1930's, he falls in love with Hannah Erlich, a German Jew. Both return to Germany right before World War II. As part of a plan to save Hannah and her psychologist father from extermination, Conrad joins the Gestapo, but the plan fails; Hannah and his own family die under the Nazis, their fates determined by Adolf Hitler's horrible misuse of power. Tortured terribly, Conrad survives and emigrates.

The second major voice—one of late twentieth century vulgarity—is that of John's older cousin, Timothy Wellfleet. Like Conrad, he is the son of a military man, a man who, however, never disciplined his son, Timothy becomes a representative member of late twentieth century society. First an advertising agent, he later becomes a radical-chic television interviewer, the kind of "media" newsman who belittles his guest from established society and makes himself the star of the show. When Timothy sympathetically features terrorist separatists whose kidnapping and murder trigger the government crackdowns of Canada's October Crisis (1970), his producer, a Jew who is also his mistress, accuses him of encouraging terrorism. She leaves him and his program.

Timothy and Conrad's stories come together when Conrad, a respected history professor who feels duty-bound to warn North Americans that the young generation's loss of confidence in civilization makes conditions right for an upsurge of fascism, appears on Timothy's program. Using garbled information from a Marxist-terrorist source, Timothy accuses Conrad of his Gestapo connections and of responsibility for Hannah's death. A Holocaust survivor, having mistakenly identified him from television as a Nazi torturer, kills Conrad, then, seeing his mistake, kills himself. Undisciplined Timothy's banal misuse of banal power has wrought horrible results.

In the book that he edits, John Wellfleet and his voices suggest a pattern of history: After Germany's defeat in World War I and its suffering in the Depression, Hitler appealed to the Germans' need for an authority figure, a superego to approve their doing anything to recover their pride. In late twentieth century North America, undisciplined young people and their permissive elders also were demoralized; they, too, felt the need for authority and discipline that they could not give themselves. According to MacLennan's apocalyptic story, an authoritarian regime (the Second Bureaucracy) did follow a time of license and terrorism (the Great Fear), but its strength was not real: Its uncontrolled war computers caused the Destructions. In the Third Bureaucracy, there is hope in the cycle of history: André Gervais, his colleagues, and his children may restore civilization; John Wellfleet's history book may guide them. MacLennan may have hoped that the warning of his novel might forestall the destruction that he prophesies.

Summary

Critics of Hugh MacLennan's novels deplore his conservative techniques: his didacticism, his allegorizing the stories of individuals, his heavy use of local color, his oversimplified and moralistic characterization, his describing rather than evoking, his use of external circumstance, his basically chronological narration, his prudish and clichéd accounts of sex. (Defenders counter that his "reconstructive reporting" of historical events is superb and commend his development of counterpoint, memory, and montage narration.) Future assessments will probably praise his capturing, as he said, "the conflict . . . between the human spirit of Everyman and Everyman's human condition"—Everyman, of course, wearing twentieth century Canadian garb.

Bibliography

Cameron, Elspeth. *Hugh MacLennan: A Writer's Life.* Toronto: University of Toronto Press, 1981.

Jones, Joseph, and Johanna Jones. *Canadian Fiction.* Boston: Twayne, 1981.
MacLulich, T. D. *Hugh MacLennan.* Boston: Twayne, 1983.
Mandel, Eli. *The Family Romance.* Winnipeg: Turnstone Press, 1986.
New, William H. *A History of Canadian Literature.* New York: New Amsterdam, 1989.
Woodcock, George. "A Nation's Odyssey." In *Odysseus Ever Returning.* Toronto: McClelland & Stewart, 1970.

Pat Ingle Gillis

THOMAS MANN

Born: Lübeck, Germany
June 6, 1875
Died: Zurich, Switzerland
August 12, 1955

Principal Literary Achievement

Mann is generally regarded as the finest German prose writer of the twentieth century and the greatest German literary figure since Johann Wolfgang von Goethe.

Biography

Thomas Mann was born in Lübeck, Germany, on June 6, 1875. He was the son of Johann Heinrich Mann, a wealthy businessman, and Julia da Silva-Bruhns, a mother of Brazilian origin; the Mann family was very much like that described in the author's novel *Buddenbrooks: Verfall einer Familie* (1901; English translation, 1924). Thomas was not the only person in his family with literary talent. His older brother, Heinrich, was an important novelist in his own right, and for a time his works were better known than those of Thomas. Mann's father died in 1891, and the family's fortune declined rapidly afterward. Thomas attended the University of Munich and was briefly an insurance agent before settling down into his career as a full-time author.

Mann's first publication was a collection of short stories, *Der Kleine Herr Friedemann* (1898; *Little Herr Friedemann*, 1928), and it met with general critical acclaim. Three years later, the novel *Buddenbrooks* firmly established Mann as an important author with an international reputation.

In 1905, Mann married Katja Pringsheim, the daughter of a wealthy Jewish banking family. Because of this marriage and the large sales of his books, Mann became independently wealthy. Together, Thomas and Katja Mann had six children. One of their children, Klaus, became an important author in his own right and is best known for his novel *Mephisto* (1936), which details events concerning his sister's unhappy marriage to the famous actor and Nazi collaborator Gustav Gründgens.

The 1920's were particularly fruitful years for Mann. In 1924, he published his novel *Der Zauberberg* (1924; *The Magic Mountain*, 1927), and five years later he received the Nobel Prize in Literature. The Mann family lived in Munich until 1933, when the Nazis came to power. Abhorring the policies of the new regime, Mann

became an outspoken proponent of liberal democracy. He was publicly denounced by the new government, and by a large number of creative artists who were sympathetic to the Nazi regime, after the publication of his essay "Leiden und Grösse Richard Wagners" ("Sufferings and Greatness of Richard Wagner"). Fearing for the safety of his family, Mann emigrated, first to Switzerland and then to the United States. During his years of exile, Mann continued to write prolifically. In 1944, he became a U.S. citizen, and during World War II he made radio broadcasts to Germany imploring German citizens to resist the Nazi government.

Mann wrote some of his greatest works in exile, including the tetralogy *Joseph und seine Brüder* (1933-1943; *Joseph and His Brothers*, 1933-1944) and his masterpiece, *Doktor Faustus: Das Leben des deutschen Tonsetzers Adrian Leverkühn, erzählt von einem Freunde* (1947; *Doctor Faustus: The Life of the German Composer Adrian Leverkühn as Told by a Friend*, 1948). In 1952, he returned to Europe and settled in Switzerland. Mann died in Zurich, Switzerland, on August 12, 1955.

Mann's works have been the subject of literally thousands of scholarly articles and monographs. His novels and stories have been adapted for television, film, stage, and opera. His reputation and popularity remain supreme over those of all other German writers of the twentieth century. In his own way, Mann has come to dominate and symbolize his era as Goethe dominated the late eighteenth and early nineteenth centuries.

Analysis

In a creative life as prolific and varied as Mann's, it is very difficult to enumerate one or several overall themes that permeate his literary output. One general theme is the search for spiritual meaning in one's life, which is necessarily concerned with banal details of business, family relations, and everyday activities. The dichotomy between spirit (*Geist*) and life (*Leben*) in Mann's work has an authentic ring inasmuch as Mann himself was both a member of the upper bourgeoisie and a creative artist of the highest caliber. This concern with the spiritual dimension of life led Mann to investigate the philosophical and religious thought not only of German civilization but also of the Greek, ancient Hebrew, and Oriental cultures. In his novella *Der Tod in Venedig* (1911; *Death in Venice*, 1925), Mann examined the influence of the Apollonian-Dionysian dichotomy of ancient Greece and the effect it had upon the story's protagonist, Gustav von Aschenbach. In the tetralogy of novels *Joseph and his Brothers*, the biblical story of Joseph and his return from the pit into which he was cast by his brothers is utilized as a metaphor for human redemption. In the novella *Die vertauschten Köpfe: Eine indische Legende* (1940; *The Transposed Heads: A Legend of India*, 1941), the Eastern concept of reincarnation and its consequences are examined in great detail.

For Mann, the internal psychological life of a character was generally at odds with the external events and situations in which the character was found. The conflict between the real life of a character and his or her ideal psychological yearnings (in German this is termed *Zerrissenheit*) motivated much of Mann's writing. In *Buddenbrooks*, for example, the mundane, bourgeois existence and its attendant business and civic duties of Thomas Buddenbrooks, the scion of a wealthy Lübeck family of merchants, are at odds with Thomas' spiritual yearnings and repressed artistic proclivities; they eventually manifest themselves in Thomas' wife (who is a brilliant violinist) and their child Hanno, who suffers a tragic death from typhoid fever at an early age.

Also of great significance in Mann's works is the idea of decadence, the feeling that past standards are being obviated in the present. This idea occurs on personal, artistic, and cultural levels. For Mann the spiritual and/or physical decadence of an individual is often analogous to the decline of individual artistic creativity or a general decadence of the culture at large. A common device utilized by Mann is to allow physical disease to symbolize spiritual degradation. This depiction is seen to greatest effect in the novel *Doctor Faustus*, in which the syphilis suffered by the protagonist, composer Adrian Leverkühn, serves as the symbol of his spiritual and creative decline, which in turn serves as the symbol of the decline of German civilization into the barbarities of the Nazi regime.

Mann's prose style is lofty and elegiac, a beautiful embodiment of the finest prose attainable in high German. He is given to philosophical discourse, oftentimes of a very complicated nature, which displays the tremendous influence of the German philosophers George Wilhelm Friedrich Hegel and Friedrich Wilhelm Nietzsche. Yet simultaneously present in Mann's prose is a pervasive ironic quality, at times verging on the comic. When close scrutiny is given to the statements made by Mann's most serious characters, it is often revealed that they are contradicting themselves or coming to illogical conclusions.

Mann was also a master of descriptive detail of both the physical settings of his novels and the psychological states of his characters. He was an astute observer of human nature and manners, and in this regard, he compares most favorably with the American novelist Henry James. Mann was a man of great culture and learning, as evidenced by the range and depth of subject matter presented in his works. A common theme in his novels is the role of music in German culture, particularly the music of the German opera composer Richard Wagner.

Mann's novels are permeated by direct and paraphrased quotations from other literary works, philosophical and historical treatises, the popular press, and other sources. His novels assume on the part of their readership a general understanding of the history of Western civilization and its cultural monuments. In this regard, Mann, who carried the traditions of the nineteenth century novel into the twentieth century, was very much a modernist writer. In his own way, the myriad references to external events and sources found in his novels follow a general pattern established by such modernist literary figures as James Joyce, Ezra Pound, and T. S. Eliot. Mann's technique of putting all of these external references and literary symbols into a unified structure is referred to most commonly as the montage, a term that is derived from the montage techniques of the visual arts and the editing techniques of cinema. The montage technique is probably seen to greatest effect in *Doctor Faustus*. Another technique used by Mann is the leitmotif, the use of a continually recurring phrase, image, symbol, or idea throughout a literary work. The idea of the leitmotif was taken by Mann from the musical works of Richard Wagner, whose lengthy operas were unified by the use of short, recurring melodies.

THE MAGIC MOUNTAIN

First published: *Der Zauberberg*, 1924 (English translation, 1927)
Type of work: Novel

On the eve of World War I, a young man visits a relative at a tuberculosis sanatorium, stays there for seven years before recovering his physical and spiritual health, and then leaves to fight in the war.

The Magic Mountain is essentially a *Bildungsroman*, the story of the education and spiritual development of a single character. The individual in this case is Hans Castorp, a young engineer who, before assuming his position in a shipbuilding firm, decides to go to a sanatorium to visit his cousin Joachim, a soldier who is recovering from tuberculosis. At the sanatorium, a spot is detected on one of Castorp's lungs, and he decides to stay for a few weeks to take some treatments. Weeks stretch into months, and Castorp remains at the sanatorium long after Joachim has gone. In fact, Castorp stays for a total of seven years. The disease that is really afflicting Castorp, however, is a spiritual malaise. Castorp encounters a wide range of characters at the sanatorium, each of whom has an effect on him. Shortly before the end of his stay, Castorp finds himself hallucinating while hiking after a severe snowstorm. This hallucination serves as a catalyst for Castorp's decision to reenter the world, which he does by volunteering for military service in World War I. The impression is left with the reader that Castorp's reintegration into the world is ambivalent at best.

The Magic Mountain shows to great effect Mann's use of physical disease as a metaphor for spiritual malaise. At its very worst, Castorp's tuberculosis is a mild case. His decision to stay at the sanatorium is, in reality, a flight from the duties and mundanities of the world. The existence that Castorp leads at the sanatorium is one of contemplation, not unlike the existence of a monk at a monastery. Castorp's struggle is entirely of an internal nature. He is well-to-do and lives in a world of comfortable, if remote, luxury.

The internal struggle in Castorp's mind is exemplified in the dialectical relationship between Herr Settembrini and Herr Naphta, the two most intellectual patients at the sanatorium. Herr Settembrini represents reason, while Naphta symbolizes the will-to-power of the suprarational philosophy of Friedrich Wilhelm Nietzsche. Naphta's eventual suicide, like the hallucination in the snowstorm, is a vivid jolt to the comfortable existence to which Castorp has become accustomed.

Another image that motivates the novel is the idea of a physical ascent (the action of Castorp ascending to the sanatorium on top of a mountain), symbolizing the attainment of wisdom or spiritual awareness. That Castorp's struggle to ascend the mountain of self-realization has been an internal struggle, rather than a battle with external forces, is best exemplified by Mann in the final page of the novel, likening Castorp's time at the sanatorium to a dream. As in all dreams, no one interpretation may be universally valid, and, therefore, the destiny of Hans Castorp, as he descends from the mountain to return to full participation in the world, is left open to debate.

The Magic Mountain also exemplifies the author's preoccupation with music. In this regard, the novel serves as an important link between his earlier short stories that deal with or refer to music and his later masterwork *Doctor Faustus* (1947). In *The Magic Mountain*, however, musical performances have a redemptive quality. Toward the end of Castorp's stay at the sanatorium, a new Victrola has been added to the amenities of the establishment, and Castorp avails himself of this new device on an almost daily basis. In one memorable section of chapter 7 titled "Fullness of Harmony," Castorp listens to five musical selections: the last two scenes from Giuseppe Verdi's *Aïda*, Claude Debussy's *Prélude à l'après-midi d'un faune* (*Prelude to the Afternoon of a Faun*), the second act of Georges Bizet's *Carmen*, Franz Schubert's "Lindenbaum," and Valentine's aria from Charles-François Gounod's *Faust*. These five musical selections have obvious metaphorical value in the novel. Death by suffocation in *Aïda* has a certain morbid appropriateness in a novel whose main characters are suffering from tuberculosis. The dreamlike quality of Debussy's *Prelude to the Afternoon of a Faun* approximates the dreamlike existence of Castorp and his fellow patients, who must of necessity emphasize their mental, rather than physical, existence. *Carmen* represents the dangers of passion, dangers that constantly threaten the sanatorium's inhabitants. The Schubert song (from the composer's song cycle *Winterreise* (winter journey) evokes the memory of Castorp's own "winter's journey" and its resulting hallucinations. Valentine's aria represents the acceptance of duty and death and is, in many ways, a foreboding of death.

These five musical selections, therefore, operate collectively as a summation of the novel's main thematic ideas. Yet the selection from Gounod's *Faust* functions not only as part of a recapitulation but also as a foretelling of future events. Valentine's dedication to duty, even in the face of death, is a metaphor for the premature departure from the sanatorium by Castorp's soldier-cousin Joachim. Likewise, Valentine's aria presages Castorp's departure from the sanatorium and his joining the military at the outbreak of World War I. Valentine's aria is also played on the Victrola later during the séance, in which the spirit of the now-dead "Joachim" appears. This episode demonstrates the perfection of Mann's literary technique. The leitmotif, montage, and frequent use of extended metaphors combine in such a way as to bring about an unprecedented complexity of meaning to the novel.

DOCTOR FAUSTUS

First published: *Docktor Faustus*, 1947 (English translation, 1948)
Type of work: Novel

A German avant-garde composer, whose personal life parallels the events of German society up to the end of World War II, creates influential musical compositions, contracts syphilis, and eventually dies of the disease.

Doctor Faustus is arguably one of the most significant novels of the twentieth century in any language. Acclaimed as a masterpiece at the time of its original publication, *Doctor Faustus* has been the subject of hundreds of scholarly articles and books.

The story centers on the life and career of Adrian Leverkühn, a preternaturally gifted man who is born into the Germany of the Second Reich in the generation following the Franco-Prussian War (1870-1871). The novel follows Leverkühn's life and career until his death in 1943. Leverkühn is born into a provincial middle-class farming family. His parents are conventional, but his father does harbor some eccentric scientific interests. During his childhood, Leverkühn becomes lifelong best friends with Serenus Zeitblom, who serves as the novel's putative narrator. Originally attracted to both mathematics and music, Leverkühn goes to college to study theology, a course of study that he eventually abandons in favor of music. Leverkühn's prowess as a composer advances rapidly, but it is not until after he contracts syphilis from a prostitute (his only sexual experience) that his music becomes totally original and groundbreaking. As the syphilis proceeds to destroy Leverkühn's physical and mental states, his creativity as a composer increases. After having achieved the first fruits of international success, Leverkühn suffers a complete nervous and mental breakdown and spends the last ten years of his life as an invalid.

The most significant aspect of the novel is the author's use of the Faust legend, the age-old story of a man who sells his soul to the Devil in exchange for wealth, power, and sexual prowess. Although the only overtly similar situation in the novel to the traditional Faust story is the imaginary dialogue between Leverkühn and the Devil, which occurs in chapter 25, the Faust legend is a very powerful presence in Mann's novel. Central to the Faust legend is the contract, the quid pro quo, between the Devil and Faust. The Faustian contract for Leverkühn involves his contracting syphilis from a prostitute. At the price of the loss of his physical and mental health, the syphilis unleashes untold powers of creativity within Leverkühn. The syphilis from which he suffers is, in turn, a symbol of the "disease" of extreme nationalism and ethnic chauvinism that eventually led the Germans to embrace Adolf Hitler and the Nazis. In both cases—Leverkühn's contraction of syphilis and the coming to power of Hitler—Mann makes it clear that the parties involved have entered into their "agreements" by their own volition, just as the original Dr. Faust entered into his demonic pact of his own free will. Significantly, Leverkühn's final composition of his creative career is a cantata titled "The Lamentations of Dr. Faustus."

As in *The Magic Mountain*, Mann uses physical disease as a symbol for spiritual and cultural decline. In the nineteenth and early twentieth centuries, syphilis was an incurable disease with a mortality rate approaching one hundred percent. Its symptoms could be mitigated and temporarily halted, but the disease was inevitable in its effects until the discovery of penicillin. Therefore, the selection of syphilis as a symptom of spiritual and cultural decline was significant because the disease was irreversible. Mann uses syphilis symbolically to suggest the inevitability of the decline of German civilization.

Mann uses Leverkühn's life to parallel events occurring simultaneously in German politics and society. Leverkühn's lifetime roughly approximates that of Hitler, the implication of which is that the same historical forces that brought the Nazis to the fore had a similar effect on Leverkühn's art. Leverkühn's final physical and mental collapse occurs in 1933, the year in which the Nazis came to power in Germany. Leverkühn dies in 1943, a year in which the war in Europe turned decidedly against the Axis Powers, leading to their eventual defeat.

The selection of a composer as the symbol of Germany's moral and cultural decline is significant in that music is generally regarded as the most German of the arts. One composer, Richard Wagner, held a particular fascination for both Mann and Hitler. Wagner's operas based on Teutonic myths were a great enthusiasm of Hitler, as were Wagner's anti-Semitic racial views, as expressed in the composer's book-length diatribe, *Das Judentum in der Musik* (1869; Jewry in music). Mann had an ambivalent attitude toward Wagner; he greatly admired the composer's music but was repelled by the man himself. It was Mann's essay "The Sufferings and Greatness of Richard Wagner" that led to Mann's public denunciation and eventual exile to America. In a real sense, then, music and politics were intricately related in the nightmare of events occurring in Nazi Germany.

Adrian Leverkühn's *daimon*, the catalyst whose function it is to see that the protagonist's fate is fulfilled, appears in many guises, but perhaps never more significantly than in the being of Wendell Kretzschmar, the American expatriate music master and Leverkühn's only real teacher of composition. Kretzschmar's significance as a *daimon* extends not only to Leverkühn's choice of a career as a composer—it is Kretzschmar who ultimately supplies Adrian with the justification to abandon theological studies and return to music—but also to the course that Adrian's musical career will follow.

Adrian's years of theological study at the University of Halle cause him to be influenced by several versions of his *daimon*. Professor Kolonat Nonnenmacher instructs Leverkühn in Pythagorean philosophy and reinforces Adrian's long-held fascination with an ordered cosmos, particularly one susceptible to mathematical reduction. Nonnenmacher's lectures also deal with Aristotelian philosophy and stress the philosopher's views on the inherent drive to the fulfillment of organic forms—in other words, the urge toward the unfolding of destiny. These lectures have a profound impact on Leverkühn, who comes to the realization that his personal destiny is not necessarily of his own making.

Adrian's *daimon* finds a different and more subtle version in the form of Ehrenfried Kumpf, Mann's caricature of Martin Luther. Kumpf's theology rejects humanism and reason and embraces a rather lusty appreciation of life, including its sensual pleasures, of which music is but one facet. Although Kumpf is a minor figure in the novel, his influence is long-lasting on Adrian, who adopts the former's archaic German phraseology and syntax and who eventually abandons the rationality and "coldness" of theology for the "warmth" of music.

Of all Adrian's professors at Halle, none leaves a more permanent impression and is more overtly a manifestation of Leverkühn's *daimon* than Eberhard Schleppfuss, the mysterious theologian whose very difficult lectures combine the tenets of Christianity with a blatant Manichaeanism. Schleppfuss views evil as a necessary concomitant to good and posits a sinister interpretation of the nature of creativity.

Leverkühn's involvement with music is made permanent, however, only after the liaison with the prostitute Esmeralda, which, interestingly enough, occurs after Adrian has witnessed the Austrian premiere of Richard Strauss's opera *Salome* (based on Oscar Wilde's visionary Decadent drama). This liaison is a curious phenomenon in that neither lust nor intellectual curiosity appears to be its root cause. In many ways, Adrian is as irresistibly drawn to the prostitute Esmeralda as the symbolic butterfly *hetaera esmeralda* of chapter 2 is susceptible to visual or olfactory stimuli. There is a certain inevitability in both cases in which moral laws and the individual will are transcended by reflex actions firmly based in the instinctive domain. Additionally, Adrian's brief sexual encounter permits the appearance in rapid succession of two other manifestations of his *daimon*, namely Dr. Erasmi and Dr. Zimbalist, both of whom are thwarted from treating Adrian's syphilis in its incipient stage.

Adrian's fall is akin to the fall of Adam; both are terrible yet necessary for the evolution of the human condition. One can no more imagine a Christian view of history without Adam's transgression than a continuation of musical evolution beyond Wagner without the imposition of a seminal figure such as Leverkühn. The connection between Adrian and Adam is further strengthened by the fact that one of Leverkühn's first mature works is a setting of William Blake's poem "A Poison Tree," with its references to the poisoned fruit and the serpent who despoils an altar. In the end, however, as Mann always makes clear in his writings, untempered creativity ultimately consumes its creator. All knowledge, all fruits of artistic genius carry with them a terrible price in the imaginary world of Mann's fiction.

TONIO KRÖGER

First published: 1903 (English translation, 1914)
Type of work: Novella

A young German author experiences and comes to terms with the difference between his artistic temperament and the healthy, yet sterile, bourgeois society.

Tonio Kröger is one of Mann's best stories and was the author's favorite work, understandable inasmuch as many of the details of the story are autobiographical in nature. The protagonist is the scion of a very respectable upper-middle-class family. The father is a north German patrician, while the mother (Consuelo) is of southern European origin. This dichotomy is apparent not only in the unusual combination of names of the protagonist but also in the inability of Tonio to resolve the conflict between his artistic nature and the expectations of bourgeois society.

The quintessence of the bourgeois world is symbolized by Hans Hansen, Tonio's best friend, and Ingeborg Holm, the object of Tonio's unrequited love. Hans excels at everything that is expected of the son of a respectable family—school, sports, social activities—while Tonio's accomplishments, other than those pertaining to his artistic ambitions, are lackluster and indifferent.

Tonio's father dies, his mother marries an Italian musician, and Tonio leaves his northern German hometown to live in the south. While he is in southern Europe, his health declines, but his artistry increases. His first publications meet with critical and popular acclaim, and for the first time in his life he experiences the success that had so eluded him in the past.

Some time later, Tonio is living in Munich and runs into his friend, the painter Lisaveta Ivanovna. After a lengthy and heated discussion, Lisaveta declares Tonio to be a failed bourgeois. At the end of the summer, Tonio decides to take a vacation in north Germany and Denmark, in essence retracing his bourgeois youth. He arrives at his resort in Denmark and has a pleasant, uneventful stay, until one day near the end of his sojourn. Hans and Ingeborg appear at the resort to attend a dance. The couple do not recognize Tonio, but he recognizes them. While he is watching the couple dancing, Tonio reminisces about the dancing lessons that the three of them took when they were little. His confidence and spirit restored, Tonio writes to Lisaveta and says that in the future his writing will be concerned with his love of the ordinary, uncomplicated lives of his north German compatriots, who were really the inspiration for his art in the first place.

Once again, one sees the stress that Mann places on the idea of a dichotomy existing between the "healthy" bourgeois world and the "diseased" world of the artist. This dichotomy also has a geographical dimension for Mann: Northern Europe is "healthy," safely bourgeois, and stable; southern Europe, however, is mysterious and "diseased," but it is also the source of artistic creativity.

One important literary device utilized by Mann in *Tonio Kröger* is the leitmotif. For example, whenever Tonio's mother is mentioned, she is described with the same phrase: "who played the piano and the mandolin so enchantingly." *Tonio Kröger* is an extremely important work in Mann's literary output in that he developed many of the techniques and themes that he would perfect in his later major novels.

DEATH IN VENICE

First published: *Der Tod in Venedig*, 1912 (English translation, 1925)
Type of work: Novella

A famous writer suffers from an emotional crisis while on vacation in Venice, becomes infatuated with a young boy, and dies of cholera.

Death in Venice is one of the greatest novellas of the twentieth century and has been adapted for film (1971, directed by Luchino Visconti) and opera (1973, with music by Benjamin Britten and libretto by Myfanwy Piper). In this story, Mann further develops many of the ideas that he had so successfully explored in *Tonio Kröger*.

The story is centered on Gustav von Aschenbach, a famous writer who has come to Venice for a vacation. Aschenbach is suffering from fatigue and world-weariness, the result of intense literary efforts and an incipient emotional crisis. When Aschenbach arrives at his hotel in Venice, he notices a Polish family that is also on vacation, in particular, a young boy named Tadzio. Aschenbach's serenity is disrupted by his emotional response to the boy's youthful beauty and athletic grace. Wherever Aschenbach goes, he manages to run into Tadzio and his family. He begins to think of the boy as a character from Greek mythology. Rather than admit his ambivalent feelings toward Tadzio, Aschenbach makes plans to leave Venice, partly because the city is beginning to suffer from a deadly cholera epidemic that is being covered up by civil authorities worried about the loss of tourist revenues. When Aschenbach arrives at the railway station to leave, he discovers that his luggage has been sent ahead to the wrong destination. Aschenbach goes back to his hotel and once again follows Tadzio and his family around various Venetian locations. Disquieting dreams plague Aschenbach, who imagines that Tadzio is a participant in Dionysian revels. One day, after most of the guests have departed the hotel, Aschenbach goes to the beach, where he sees Tadzio and his family. Feeling weaker and weaker, Aschenbach dies of cholera.

Death in Venice brings to the fore the major themes that were to dominate Mann's later writings, particularly the tension involved in the mind's struggle between self-control and reckless, emotional irrationality. Aschenbach is the paradigm of the objective thinker, a man whose mental processes are under such fine control that he appears to be lacking any true emotion or sentimentality. The floodgates of emotion are released in Aschenbach only after he views Tadzio. Yet Aschenbach's turmoil is entirely internal in nature; Tadzio is the catalyst by which the strings of mental self-control within Aschenbach's mind are released. Aschenbach, in fact, never speaks to Tadzio, and it is suggested that Tadzio and his family are completely unaware of Aschenbach's presence.

The internal emotional struggle Aschenbach is undergoing is represented by Mann in classical terms. Mann uses the ancient Greek gods Apollo (god of reason, knowledge, and the arts) and Dionysus (god of sensuality, drunkenness, and boundless creativity) to represent the dichotomy between reason and irrationality. The Apollonian side of Aschenbach is present during his waking hours, when he can use his finely developed powers of self-control to subdue his attraction for Tadzio; while he is asleep, however, the Dionysian aspect of Aschenbach's psyche is released, and his imagination runs rampant with emotional speculation about Tadzio.

Another classical aspect of the story is the seeming inevitability of its outcome, an end that is rooted in the protagonist's destiny, much like the role that destiny and fate played in the classical dramas of ancient Greece. Wherever Aschenbach goes, he runs into Tadzio; when Aschenbach tries to leave Venice, his luggage is accidentally shipped to the wrong destination. It is unclear whether Aschenbach is being controlled by forces beyond his control or whether he is subconsciously creating these "accidents" so as to prevent his leaving Tadzio. In the end, however, the side of Aschenbach's psyche that served him so well in his career as a successful author (Apollonian self-control, health, northern geographical location, and bourgeois normality) succumbs to the mysterious inner workings of the id (Dionysian abandon, disease, southern geographical location, repressed homosexuality).

Summary

Thomas Mann's prose works exemplify the problems faced by humankind in the twentieth century: the loss of community, the decline of personal and cultural standards, and the reaction of the individual to both totalitarian governments and conventional society. Although Mann's prose style stemmed from the traditions of the nineteenth century, it embraced the innovations of the modernists. His works also display the influence of the other arts, in particular, music, which served not only as a source of thematic material but also as a repository of formal procedures, such as the leitmotif. Mann's works are extraordinarily complex and densely filled with metaphors and other types of allusions; however, they remain popular and accessible to readers at large.

Bibliography

Bergsten, Gunilla. *Thomas Mann's "Doctor Faustus": The Sources and Structure of the Novel.* Translated by Krishna Winston. Chicago: University of Chicago Press, 1969.

Bloom, Harold, ed. *Thomas Mann.* New York: Chelsea House, 1986.

Carnegy, Patrick. *Faust as Musician: A Study of Thomas Mann's Novel "Doctor Faus-*

tus." London: Chatto & Windus, 1973.

Ezergailis, Inta M., comp. *Critical Essays on Thomas Mann.* Boston: G. K. Hall, 1988.

Hatfield, Henry. *Thomas Mann.* Rev. ed. New York: New Directions, 1962.

Heller, Erich. *The Ironic German: A Study of Thomas Mann.* Boston: Little, Brown, 1958.

Hollingdale, R. J. *Thomas Mann: A Critical Study.* Lewisburg: Bucknell University Press, 1971.

Jonas, Klaus W., and Ilsedore B. Jonas. *Thomas Mann Studies: A Biography of Criticism.* Vol. 3. Philadelphia: University of Pennsylvania Press, 1967.

Reed, T. J. *Thomas Mann: The Uses of Tradition.* Oxford, England: Clarendon Press, 1974.

Wolf, Ernest M. *Magnum Opus: Studies in the Narrative Fiction of Thomas Mann.* New York: Peter Lang, 1989.

William E. Grim

KATHERINE MANSFIELD

Born: Wellington, New Zealand
October 14, 1888
Died: Fontainebleau, France
January 9, 1923

Principal Literary Achievement

Mansfield broke conventions and chiefly used precise images and pointed dialogue to reveal her characters' shifting emotional states.

Biography

Katherine Mansfield was born Kathleen Mansfield Beauchamp in Wellington, New Zealand, on October 14, 1888. During her life she used many names: her family called her "Kass," and she took "Katherine Mansfield" as her name in 1910. Her father, Harold Beauchamp, was a businessman who rose to become chairman of the Bank of New Zealand. He was knighted in 1923.

In 1903, the Beauchamps sailed for London, where Kass enrolled at Queen's College, a school for young women. She remained at Queen's until 1906, reading authors such as the Irish novelist and playwright Oscar Wilde and the Norwegian dramatist Henrik Ibsen. She played the cello and published several stories in the college magazine. After her parents insisted that she come back to Wellington in 1906, she published her first stories in a newspaper. In 1908, when she was nineteen, she left New Zealand for London, never to return.

Her next decade was characterized by personal problems and artistic growth. She was sexually attracted both to women and to men. At Queen's College, she met Ida Baker, who would become her friend and lifelong companion. After she returned to London, she fell in love with a violinist named Garnet Trowell, whom she had met in New Zealand. Then on March 2, 1909, she abruptly married a man she hardly knew, George C. Bowden, and just as abruptly left him. At her mother's insistence, she traveled to Germany, where she suffered a miscarriage. The Bowdens were not divorced until April, 1918.

In Germany she met the Polish translator Floryan Sobieniowski. In the opinion of her biographer Claire Tomalin, it was his fault that she became infected with venereal disease. Mansfield would suffer from many medical problems for the rest of her short life: rheumatic symptoms, pleurisy, and eventually tuberculosis. Most of them probably were the result of this infection. Back in London, Mansfield met the editor

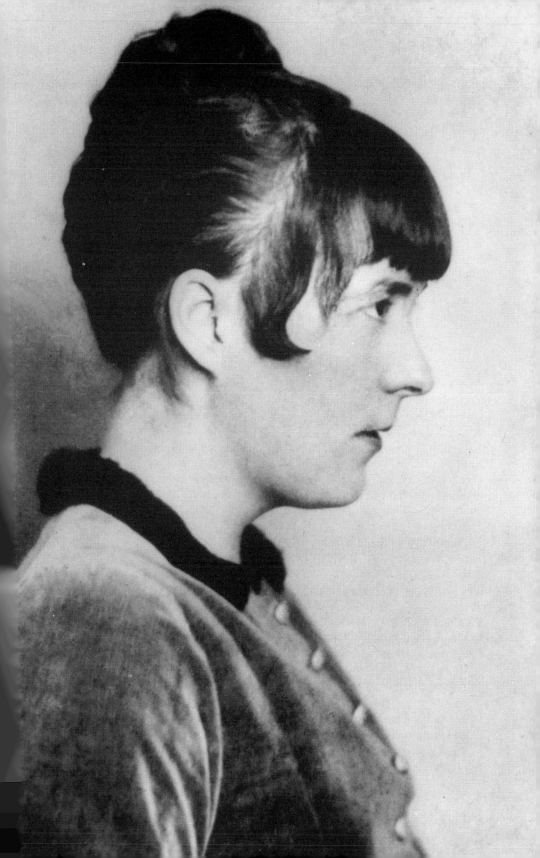

and literary critic John Middleton Murry. They were married on May 3, 1918. Their relationship was stormy, but it endured until her death. After Mansfield died, Murry edited her stories, letters, and journals. Meanwhile, World War I had begun. Her brother, a soldier with the British army, was killed in France. His death and her own worsening health may have strongly influenced her stories.

Mansfield and Murry knew many famous writers and artists, particularly those who gathered at Garsington, the country estate of the famous hostess Lady Ottoline Morrell. There Mansfield met the biographer Lytton Strachey, the novelist Aldous Huxley, the economist John Maynard Keynes, and the American poet T. S. Eliot. She and the novelist and feminist Virginia Woolf had an off-and-on friendship and professional association. Mansfield had a serious relationship with the mathematician, pacifist, and philosopher Bertrand Russell. The Murrys' closest friendship was with novelist D. H. Lawrence and his wife, Frieda; the character Gudrun in Lawrence's *Women in Love* (1920) is said to be based on Mansfield. Both Woolf and Lawrence were influenced in their writings by Mansfield; both made negative remarks about her before her death.

When she was in Germany, she read stories by the Russian author Anton Chekhov. His influence has been seen in some of the bitter stories with German settings she collected in her first book, *In a German Pension* (1911). For the next seven years, Mansfield experimented with many styles and published stories in journals such as *New Age*, *Rhythm*, and *The Blue Review*. Her first truly great story, "Prelude," was published as a booklet in July, 1918, by Virginia and Leonard Woolf's Hogarth Press.

Mansfield's health continued to get worse. From the time she learned she had tuberculosis, in 1917, she spent most of each year outside England. Accompanied by Murry or Baker, she traveled to France, Switzerland, and Italy, trying to fight off her disease. In 1922, her search led her to a rest home near Paris. She seems to have been moderately happy there until her death on January 9, 1923, in Fontainebleau, France.

During her last five years, Mansfield wrote most of the stories for which she is best remembered. They were usually published in journals such as *Athenaeum*, *Arts and Letters*, *London Mercury*, and *Sphere*. Many were then compiled in *Bliss and Other Stories* (1920) and *The Garden Party and Other Stories* (1922). She also wrote poems, literary criticism, fragments of plays, and the beginning of a novel.

Analysis

Mansfield once described in a letter two of the things that compelled her to write. One is the "joy" she felt when, in "some perfectly blissful way," she is "at peace." At that time, she said, "something delicate and lovely seems to open before my eyes, like a flower without thought of a frost." Everywhere in her work she communicates the exhilarating delicacy of the world's beauty: "A heavy dew had fallen. The grass was blue. Big drops hung on the bushes and just did not fall."

Her second motive is almost the opposite: "Not hate or destruction . . . but an extremely deep sense of hopelessness, of everything doomed to disaster, almost willfully, stupidly." She summed up this second motive as "a cry against corruption . . .

in the widest sense of the word." Her story "Je Ne Parle Pas Français" is such a cry. The central character is an amiable young Frenchman who seems to be a sympathetic friend to a young Englishman and his intended bride. The friend, however, reveals himself as a depraved, heartless hustler. More frightening is the central character of "The Fly." He is a businessman who grieves when he thinks about his son who was killed in World War I. He appears to be an unpleasant man when he treats an old employee badly, but readers do not understand the full horror of the story until he sadistically tortures and kills a fly that has landed in his ink pot.

Not all of the hopelessness expressed in Mansfield's stories is so rooted in corruption. Mansfield continually shows the yearnings, complexities, and misunderstandings of love; men and women spar at cross-purposes. Sometimes they fail to love because they are timid. Sometimes one person rejects another because he or she simply has more important goals to pursue. Sometimes the rejected person is sick or old. In one story, appropriately titled "Psychology," two artists, a male and a female, are so painfully conscious of the ebb and flow of their relationship that it eventually fails. Finally, in some stories, individual yearnings are complicated by sexual confusions with homoerotic overtones.

Society, according to Mansfield, is corrupt and destructive. She is brilliant when she renders the vapid conversation of fashionable, artistic figures. They prattle on about the latest fashions or recite silly poems, while ignoring the drama of real feelings that is going on around them and destroying the lives of people better than they. She is equally brilliant in portraying the banalities of more common people. Even when her characters mean well, many of them cannot say anything that makes a difference.

Not all corruption involves blame. Mansfield's work expresses the idea that life itself seems corrupt when one realizes how many people are failures. Failure is most vividly apparent in the life of a lonely person, often a woman, playing a guitar with no one to hear, looking out a hotel window, writing a letter, noticing the happiness of lovers or reflecting on what has gone wrong with her own relationships. Often in Mansfield's stories, the reader senses the ultimate in corruption: the ceaseless erosions of time and forgetfulness. The natural world itself is not always consoling. Its beauty is sometimes frightening and ominous. Its power, especially the power of the sea, can be indifferent.

Mansfield's style is economical; she has edited her prose so that there is seldom an unnecessary or insignificant word. Yet although she is noted for her precise descriptions, her exact meanings are not always easily understood. Her tone is complex; she mixes witty satire with shattering emotional reversals. Moreover, because she uses dialogue and indirect speech extensively and does not often seem to speak directly in her own voice, the reader is not always sure what to believe.

The action of her stories does not surge powerfully forward. People talk and think; they do not ride horses or shoot rifles. Their lives do not move toward climaxes that reveal something definite. Often her stories are designed, by means of quick changes in time and by surprise turns, to lead the reader to epiphanies, unexpected moments of illumination. It is vital for readers to understand that Mansfield does not conceal a hidden "message" in her stories. If a story appears to point in many directions, not all of which are logically consistent, that is the way Mansfield feels the whole truth is most honestly communicated. In this she resembles Chekhov.

Mansfield's descriptive passages repay careful attention, for they are always significant. Her descriptions are always more than a mere record of what New Zealand or England was like. For example, in the short story "At the Bay" a young girl visits an empty house and finds, among other things, only "a lump of gritty yellow soap in one corner of the kitchen window sill." That is not a very pretty picture. It suggests that the girl is unhappy to leave her home because it has been reduced to such ugly things. Mansfield has provided details that a girl would notice and that suggest what the girl is feeling. In this technique, she is among the innovators of her day. During the years she was writing, new poets such as T. S. Eliot tried to provide not statements about emotions but concrete details that would evoke a desired emotional response in the reader—a literary device called an objective correlative. Similarly, Mansfield does not usually state what her characters feel. She presents details that will make the reader feel what they feel.

Sometimes, however, at very important moments, Mansfield's details become even more suggestive or symbolic. The sea is used to suggest the power of time. A girl's party hat in a room with a corpse suggests frivolity. Often, Mansfield builds trees into symbols. Both the pear tree in "Bliss" and the aloe tree in "Prelude" must be considered both as natural details and as symbols. What they symbolize is not simply an arbitrary idea such as hope or death. Each tree is different, and what it symbolizes can be understood only as each story is read.

As noted above, Mansfield's finest stories are also characterized by epiphanies. That term, popularized by the Irish novelist James Joyce, refers to a sudden revelation triggered by an ordinary experience. In Mansfield's stories, epiphanies happen to characters, but readers can also experience epiphanies when they are led to an unexpected moment, as when they realize that a silent, wretched little girl has remembered, not how a snobbish woman has hurt her, but that she has seen a marvelous tiny lamp in a doll's house.

MISS BRILL

First published: 1920
Type of work: Short story

The happiness of a middle-aged woman sitting in a park is shattered by a young couple's unfeeling remarks.

"Miss Brill" brings to life one of Mansfield's many lonely women, and the reader lives through this story in the main character's mind without the author's making any obvious comment. As the story opens, it is a Sunday afternoon in the autumn; a chill is in the air. In her room, Miss Brill, a lonely English teacher, prepares to go as usual to the Public Gardens in what appears to be a French city. She happily unpacks the fur she will wear for the first time this season, a piece that includes the head of a small animal, perhaps a fox. Miss Brill strikes the reader as imaginative, for she pretends she hears what the dead animal is thinking after being in storage for many months. She then feels a tinge of sadness. In her introductory paragraph, Mansfield's details evoke the fragility of Miss Brill's happiness.

At the Gardens, Miss Brill listens to the band play and watches the people. That is her idea of bliss. Though she yearns to talk to them, she must be content to listen. An old couple disappoints her, for they are silent; last week she heard a memorable conversation about eyeglasses—memorable to her, but trivial to the reader. Then Miss Brill takes her first step away from the superficiality of the afternoon. She reflects that most of the people she sees at the Gardens are old and strange. She hopes for their happiness.

In a surprise ending typical of the author, Mansfield then includes two very short paragraphs. The first points beyond the gardens to the sky and sea, as if to suggest that there is a wider world than what the reader has experienced so far. The second brings the reader back to the banality of the park, as it reproduces the sound of the band.

Miss Brill's experience deepens. She does not simply listen; she imagines what the people she sees are saying. Mansfield employs dramatic irony when she hints that the woman who Miss Brill thinks is innocently chatting is actually a prostitute. Then Miss Brill stumbles on a kind of truth: They are all acting in a play. She (Miss Brill) is in the play too, with a role that she plays every week. Miss Brill has turned her understanding of how drama underlies public events into a consolation for her state. Even so, she knows all people are not happy. She has a vision of them all singing together.

Mansfield has artfully brought the reader to sympathize with Miss Brill as her love flows out to all she sees. Then comes a shock. A young couple, rich and in love, sit down on the end of her bench. They wonder aloud why she is sitting there, wonder who would possibly want her company, and compare her prized fur to a fried fish.

The reader has lived through the story within Miss Brill's mind. Now Mansfield backs away and asks the reader to imagine what this shock is like. Miss Brill silently goes back to her lonely room. She says nothing. When she puts her prized fur piece away in its box, she imagines she hears a cry. Her imagination has projected her own sorrow. The dead, unfashionable fox has become a symbol to her of her own life, and a symbol to the reader as well.

"Miss Brill" is a typical Mansfield story in that it has little action. It dwells in the mind of a lonely person, as she deepens her understanding and receives a shock. The reader is drawn into sympathy with the brave, sad, central character.

BLISS

First published: 1918
Type of work: Short story

After Bertha, a young wife, thinks that she has found a loving friend at a party, she discovers that her friend is being intimate with her (Bertha's) husband.

"Bliss" begins with Bertha, a young wealthy woman married to Harry Young, in a state of bliss. As usual, Mansfield can evoke the wonders of being alive. The spring afternoon is brilliant, the fruit has arrived for her to arrange, her lovely baby seems happy with her nanny, some sophisticated friends are coming to dinner, and her house looks beautiful. Bertha sees herself in the mirror, and she thinks that something wonderful is about to happen.

Things are not quite so nice as they seem. Once again, the details tell the story. The nanny bosses Bertha around. Bertha herself is a bit childish. Harry will be late; when he does arrive, he makes an abrasive remark. One guest, Miss Fulton, is mysterious, as are some cats prowling around in the garden. A tree, however, bodes well, a tree described with Mansfield's customary evocativeness. Bertha sees "the lovely pear tree with its wide open blossoms as a symbol of her own life."

The guests arrive, and Mansfield shows her ability to satirize the social world of poets and painters. One guest wears a dress that shows a procession of monkeys; married couples call each other by silly names; a languid homosexual playwright has had a bad experience with his taxi driver. Harry, Bertha's down-to-earth husband, forms a contrast, as does the cool Miss Fulton, who arrives dressed all in silver.

Up until now, the story's action has seemed haphazard, and the reader has been given few clues as to what may happen. Then Mansfield delivers her surprise, a series of events that may have shocked her original readers. Bertha touches Miss Fulton's arm and feels a "fire of bliss"; a look passes between them. Through the inane dinner conversation, Bertha wonders at her experience. She waits for "a sign" from Miss Fulton with little idea of what such a sign would mean.

Its meaning soon becomes more clear. Miss Fulton seems to give a sign, and they go to the garden and gaze at the pear tree that Bertha views as a symbol of her openness and vulnerability. What exactly does it suggest now? No matter what, to Bertha the women achieve a perfect, wordless understanding. Again Mansfield is ambiguous. What have they understood? Something feminine? Something about desire? Has Miss Fulton really participated in this experience, or is Bertha imagining their communion, their epiphany?

Mansfield has more surprises. As the guests prepare to leave, Bertha's feelings take a new twist: "For the first time in her life Bertha Young desired her husband." Not many writers can dramatize so effectively how a young women's homoerotic feelings could so quickly shift to heterosexual ones. Then Bertha's bliss is shattered. She glimpses Miss Fulton and her husband intimately whispering together, arranging for a rendezvous. Bertha is left alone, wondering what will become of her life. Mansfield does not ask the reader to draw a conclusion. Is he or she to understand that Bertha is trapped in an evil world? That her happy, childish life is over? Or that she is a free adult at last?

AT THE BAY

First published: 1922
Type of work: Short story

Many members of a family live through a day in which they face the realities of sex, love, indifference, failure and death.

Mansfield set two longer short stories in her native New Zealand: "Prelude" and "At the Bay." In both, she drew extensively upon details of her own extended family and employed an unusual structure peculiarly her own.

"At the Bay" is composed of thirteen short episodes in which a number of lives intertwine. Readers are set down in an unidentified place among unidentified characters. Soon it becomes clear that the story takes place in a settlement of families living in separate houses at the side of a bay. What is known of Mansfield's life makes readers assume that this is Wellington Bay in New Zealand, but they must guess at the characters' relationships. That the reader must work to discover these things is part of the story, a result of Mansfield's narrative technique. Most of the characters are relatives of Kezia, who most resembles a young Katherine Mansfield. They are Kezia, a young girl, about seven years old; Stanley Burnell, her father; Linda Burnell, her mother; Isabel, her older sister; Lottie, her younger sister; her baby brother; aunt Beryl, Linda's sister; Uncle Jonathan Trout, and Pip and Rags, his sons; Mrs. Fairfield, Kezia's grandmother, Linda and Beryl's mother; Alice, a servant; Mrs. Stubbs, Alice's friend; and Mr. and Mrs. Harry Kember.

Each episode is separate. They are not usually joined by obvious transitions, but the reader gradually senses that "At the Bay" has a kind of unity. The same characters appear and unexpectedly reappear. The story lasts for a complete day, from early morning until late at night. Most important, the characters live in a web of delicate interrelationships, some of which satisfy, some of which do not. The life of almost every character shows a variation on a central theme: To live is to yearn for something more and only occasionally to be calm and happy. Characters yearn most strongly for what is seldom possible. Each must face moments in which his or her hopes are thwarted.

The first and last episodes frame the story with descriptions of nature. Both provide descriptions of the bay, the sea and the waves, and the plants and the buildings on the shoreline. The first episode sets the scene as a peaceful but vibrant place that waits for what the day will bring. At the beginning, the only moving beings are some sheep, a sheep dog, and a shepherd. They enter and leave. In the very brief last episode, no living thing appears. The concluding episode is more obviously symbolic.

The day opens with Stanley Burnell jumping into the bay for an invigorating swim. He is the most masculine force in the story, a competitive man who proudly thinks that he is the first in the water. Stanley finds, however, that another man, Jonathan Trout, has beaten him to it. Trout is as good a swimmer as Stanley, more imaginative and less impatient. No wonder Stanley is irritated and leaves. Trout muses on the encounter: Poor Stanley makes work out of pleasure, he thinks. The episode ends with a suggestion that Trout is in poor health. Mansfield begins her story with its only adult males, each of whom is severely limited.

Mansfield is at her best in evoking many different lives at the same time. Episode three depicts the Burnell household while Stanley gets ready to leave for work. Stanley is the center of attention. He questions, accuses, blusters, and irritably orders everybody about. The man of the house is leaving for work, and everyone must know it. Just as he leaves, he notes that his sister-in-law Beryl, though attentive, has her mind elsewhere.

The reader has suspected all along that Beryl has some private secret. The other women have their secrets as well: The child Kezia has her own way of eating porridge, Isabel is consciously full of virtue, Mrs. Fairfield privately responds to the beauty of the sun's illuminations, Linda's mind is miles away, and Alice is critical of men in general. Beryl believes that the women have a kind of communion after Stanley is gone—the wonderful day will be theirs. Her mother and sister do not seem to share this feeling so ecstatically.

Succeeding episodes show the various strands of the story belonging to the children, the servant Alice, Mrs. Fairfield, Beryl, and Linda. By constructing her narrative in parallel stories, Mansfield insists on the separateness of the individual minds and on the problems they have in communicating. By having characters cross from strand to strand and by showing parallels in their lives, Mansfield implies that people's lives have many things in common.

The following exchange, involving children, illustrates the beginning of power struggles based on gender. As usual on a fine morning, the Burnell girls go to the beach, where they play with their male cousins, the Trouts. Later, they regroup for a childish card game. The girls bicker; the whole group is dominated by Pip, the oldest Trout boy. In another scene, sexual tensions are the point of Alice's visit to Mrs. Stubbs, a storekeeper, who frightens Alice by saying that she prefers being without a man. A third exchange describes how Kezia confronts death when she spends her siesta with her grandmother. Mrs. Fairfield has the wisdom of age; though her heart still aches for her dead son, she is resigned to the fact that he is dead. When Mrs. Fairfield tells the girl of this, Kezia rebels. Kezia *will* not die, and she demands a promise that her grandmother will not die either.

Linda is Mansfield's most enigmatic figure. She strikes everyone as listless, vague, and detached. She seems to be past yearning, much as her mother was. The reader often lives in her private thoughts, though she touches the lives of three males. With Jonathan, her brother-in-law, she listens sympathetically though distantly to his complaints about his weakness and his fate. Her attitude toward Stanley is more complex. She remembers transferring her affections from her adored father to Stanley—loyal, loving, tongue-tied, uncomplicated, sincere Stanley. She loves him but resents having to support his ego as one would that of a big child. Her listlessness appears to be the result of her children. She dreads having more and does not love the ones she has. Then, in a moment in the middle of the story, she looks down at her baby boy. For a moment, she may love him. The moment is over, and she is alone again.

Beryl is younger than Linda, in years and in experience. (Perhaps the sisters and their mother show three stages in women's lives.) The young Beryl is secretive with Stanley, impatient with Kezia at breakfast, and vibrant with hope in the morning. Her crisis begins when she meets the ominous Mrs. Harry Kember at the beach. Mrs. Kember is married to an extremely handsome man ten years her junior. She is rich. Her body is long and narrow. She smokes and plays bridge. She talks like a man. When Beryl disrobes before putting on her bathing suit, Mrs. Harry Kember teases her about her beauty. Beryl is startled and feels "poisoned," but she is fascinated as well.

That night when everyone else is asleep, the aroused Beryl imagines a perfect lover. As she blissfully fantasizes, she hears a noise outside her window. It is Harry Kember himself. Although she is persuaded to come outside, she is terrified and revolted when she sees the smile on his face, a kind of smile she has never seen before. When she breaks from his embrace, he is puzzled and angry. Beryl, like Linda, and before that her mother, finds that sexual love is not what she had imagined.

THE GARDEN PARTY

First published: 1922
Type of work: Short story

Laura enjoys a garden party, even though a man next door has died. She then visits his grieving widow, sees his corpse, and is greatly moved.

"The Garden Party" may be Mansfield's most famous story. It is exceptional and typical at the same time. Laura, a vibrant young woman, is the central character. The story also depicts a worldly older woman (Laura's mother), a sophisticated social gathering (the party itself), some moderately dense males, and a disturbing event to which they all react differently. The action of the story, more conventionally straightforward than that of "At the Bay," is also typical of Mansfield. It leads both Laura and the reader to an epiphany—an enigmatic moment of revelation that, in this story, is comic and overwhelming at the same time.

Unlike "At the Bay," where Mansfield took us into many minds, we live through this story in only one. Laura appears to be about sixteen, a young woman on the edge of adulthood. Not only do we hear her talk, we listen in on her thoughts. She is a bit afraid of the men who put up the tent for the party but enjoys hearing their good-natured banter. We sense her joy at being alive when she reacts ecstatically to the spots of light the sun makes on an inkpot. Mansfield brings the reader close to Laura in another typical way. Even the opening description of the day and the flowers seem to be in a character's mind, not the storyteller's. To many readers, that mind soon becomes Laura's.

The opening scenes all suggest a wealthy, normal, and happy family. Laura appears to supervise the tent, but is not allowed to decide where it should be placed. Her sisters strike sophisticated poses; one sings a gruesome song and flashes a big smile. Laura's mother protests that she will leave the arrangements to her children but organizes the party anyway, providing expensive flowers, a band, and dainty sandwiches. As usual, Mansfield suggests moments of happiness with telling details and evocative descriptions.

Then comes the news that turns Laura's day around: A man has been killed in an accident, a man who lived in a lower-class cottage almost next to their home. Laura's instinctive reaction is that the party must be stopped, since the man's family might hear the band playing. Her sisters and her mother argue with her. She does not change her mind until she sees herself in a mirror—a lovely girl with a spectacular black hat trimmed with gold daisies—and until her brother Laurie compliments her. The party goes ahead, a typically exciting, shallow Mansfield party. Guests compliment Laura, especially on her hat. When the party is over, her mother tries to make amends by filling a basket with party leftovers and sending Laura with it to the dead man's cottage.

The journey at dusk is frightening. Laura walks into a different world, a lower-class world of grieving, ill-dressed, unsophisticated people. At the dead man's house, she gives the widow her basket. She is led against her wishes to the bedroom where the corpse has been laid out. Laura, however, is not horrified, but sees the corpse as merely sleeping. She sees death as something calm and even beautiful, something far removed from her silly afternoon. "Forgive my hat," she says. She has had an epiphany. Her reply is woefully inadequate, but the reader has been shown a character's moment of understanding and growth. The reader has had an epiphany as well, though it is not the same as Laura's.

The story ends ambiguously. Laura heads home and meets her brother. She tries to say something but cannot find the words. She thinks he understands, but whether he does is left unclear. As usual, Mansfield does not push her case too far.

Summary

In her short stories, Katherine Mansfield exemplifies innovative literary techniques that have influenced many later short-story writers. Her stories do not depend upon showing a chain of actions or upon explanations by the author. Rather, they dramatize webs of personal thoughts and interrelationships and evoke these relationships in descriptive, suggestive, and even symbolic details. Her stories often lead the reader to moments of revelation. Her themes are those of her time and were also taken up by later writers: joy in beauty, yearnings for happiness (particularly by women), disappointment, callousness, and cruelty.

Bibliography

Alpers, Antony. *The Life of Katherine Mansfield.* New York: Viking Press, 1980.

Berkman, Sylvia. *Katherine Mansfield: A Critical Study.* New Haven, Conn.: Yale University Press, 1951.

Hankin, C. A. *Katherine Mansfield and Her Confessional Stories.* New York: St. Martin's Press, 1983.

Hanson, Clare, and Andrew Gurr. *Katherine Mansfield.* New York: St. Martin's Press, 1981.

Kobler, J. F. *Katherine Mansfield: A Study of the Short Fiction.* Boston: Twayne, 1990.

Mansfield, Katherine. *The Stories of Katherine Mansfield.* Edited by Anthony Alpers. Auckland, New Zealand: Oxford University Press, 1984.

Nathan, Rhoda B. *Katherine Mansfield.* New York: Continuum, 1988.

Tomalin, Claire. *Katherine Mansfield: A Secret Life.* New York: Alfred A. Knopf, 1987.

George Soule

CHRISTOPHER MARLOWE

Born: Canterbury, England
February 6, 1564
Died: Deptford, England
May 30, 1593

Principal Literary Achievement

The Elizabethan playwright and poet Marlowe is considered the founder of English tragedy and of dramatic blank verse.

Biography

Christopher Marlowe was born in Canterbury, England, on February 6, 1564, the eldest son of a shoemaker. He was baptized exactly two months before William Shakespeare was baptized at Stratford—a significant detail, as Marlowe exercised an enormous influence on Shakespeare and is generally believed to be the rival poet of Shakespeare's sonnets.

As a pupil at the King's School, Canterbury, Marlowe was elected a "Queen's scholar." He entered Corpus Christi College, Cambridge, in 1580 and was again awarded a scholarship. In 1584, he earned his B.A. degree and entered into graduate study of divinity in preparation for taking holy orders. Just before Marlowe was to receive his M.A., the university proposed to withhold the degree. The decision was based on rumors that, after spending time at the seminary for exiled English Catholics in Reims, France, Marlowe meant to take Catholic Holy Orders. The seminary was a hotbed of Catholic insurrection against Elizabeth I's Protestant rule. Marlowe was awarded his M.A. only after the exceptional intervention of the Privy Council, which dealt with matters of national security. Records imply that Marlowe may have gone to Reims as an intelligence agent in the employ of Elizabeth's secretary of state, Sir Francis Walsingham.

Marlowe left Cambridge for London in 1587 without taking holy orders. Literature, not divinity, preoccupied him. Among works believed to date from his Cambridge years are *Elegies* (1595-1600), a translation of Ovid's *Amores* (before A.D. 8), *Pharsalia* (1600), a translation of Lucan's *Pharsalia* (first century A.D.), a play, *The Tragedy of Dido, Queene of Carthage* (1586-1587), and *Tamburlaine the Great, Part I* (c. 1587). Some scholars add to this list his epic poem *Hero and Leander*, though it was not published until after his death, in 1598.

Marlowe's rise to fame as a playwright was rapid. The opening performance of

Tamburlaine the Great, Part I was enthusiastically received. With its ruthless conquering hero and vivid pageantry, the play tapped the popular mood of feverish excitement at the prospect of war with Spain, and Marlowe quickly followed up with
Tamburlaine the Great, Part II (1587). Few plays were more imitated, satirized, and
joked about in print than the *Tamburlaine* plays.

The *Tragicall History of D. Faustus* (first quarto edition, 1604; hereinafter referred
to as *Doctor Faustus*) was produced in 1588. It gripped the imagination of the play-
going public, with frequent performances into the Jacobean Age. *The Famous Tragedy of the Rich Jew of Malta* (1589; first quarto edition, 1633) was also a theatrical
success. In 1592, Marlowe offered a new play, *The Troublesome Raigne and Lamentable Death of Edward the Second*, to the Earl of Pembroke's players. All of his other
plays were performed by the Lord Admiral's men. A minor play, *The Massacre at
Paris*, was produced in 1593.

Marlowe's personal life did not run as smoothly as his career. His impetuous and
rebellious character frequently led him into trouble. In 1589, he was arrested and
briefly imprisoned, then pardoned, as a result of his involvement in a fight in which a
man died. Less than three years later, a constable sought the protection of the law
against Marlowe.

In 1593, his heterodox opinions brought him into serious danger with the authorities. He was sharing living quarters with dramatist Thomas Kyd when Privy Council
agents searched Kyd's papers and discovered a treatise containing "vile heretical conceits denying the deity of Jesus Christ our Saviour." Under torture, Kyd disclaimed
the paper, saying it was Marlowe's. Kyd was not alone in charging Marlowe with free
thinking. More evidence came from Richard Baines, one of Walsingham's ex-
intelligence agents. Baines testified to Marlowe's "damnable Judgment of Religion,
and scorn of God's word." According to Baines, Marlowe doubted the historical truth
of the Bible and held that "the first beginning of Religioun was only to keep men in
awe." Baines added that "almost into every company he cometh he persuades men to
atheism, willing them not to be afraid of bugbears and hobgoblins."

Marlowe's works reinforced charges of religious skepticism, containing as they did
attacks on all major religions. In 1588, the year after the first performances of the
Tamburlaine plays, Marlowe's Cambridge senior Robert Greene accused the playwright of "daring God out of heaven with that atheist Tamburlaine." To complicate
the issue, on the evidence of *Doctor Faustus*, Marlowe was well versed in the lore of
witchcraft: Shakespeare suggests in Sonnet 86 that he dabbled in it.

Privy Council suspicions against Marlowe were fueled by the company that he
kept. Among his friends were Sir Walter Ralegh, famous for his so-called School of
Atheism, and astronomer Thomas Harriot, labeled an atheist. (Both might more accurately be described as deists.) Marlowe was arrested on May 20, 1593. He was instructed to report daily to the Privy Council while they deliberated, yet he was never
to face the consequences of his nonconformism. On May 30, Marlowe spent the day
at an inn in Deptford, England, with companions of his friend Sir Thomas Walsingham. At the end of the day, a dispute about the bill arose between Marlowe and

Ingram Frizer, Walsingham's business agent, who had, it seemed, invited him. Marlowe, in a fit of anger, drew Frizer's dagger and cut him over the head. Frizer retrieved his dagger and stabbed Marlowe above his right eye. Marlowe died instantly. Frizer was later pardoned as having acted in self-defense.

Analysis

Marlowe is often called the father of English tragedy because *Tamburlaine the Great* was the first tragedy to combine a grand concept, a strong central character capable of carrying the action of the play, and suitably heightened verse style. The extent of the revolution in drama that Marlowe initiated cannot be understood without considering his contribution to English verse. The poetry of *Tamburlaine the Great* was a kind never before heard on the English stage, with passages of exultant magnificence and lyrical sweetness. Its power was attributable largely to Marlowe's discovery of true blank verse style. Previous dramatists had experimented with an unrhymed decasyllabic line with five iambic feet (each foot having a weak stress followed by a strong one). Consider as an example these lines from an earlier play, Thomas Norton and Thomas Sackville's *Gorboduc* (1561; also published as *The Tragedy of Ferrex and Porrex*): "Your lasting age shall be their longer stay,/ For cares of kings, that rule as you have ruled." Each line has five pairs of two syllables, each pair consisting of a weak stress followed by a strong one (the iambic foot); the strong stresses are uniform in weight; and this iambic rhythm is never varied. The result is tiresomely repetitive.

Marlowe had a sufficiently sensitive ear to perceive that, though the norm of blank verse should be this regular iambic rhythm, and though the audience's awareness of that norm should not be lost, in fact few lines should conform to that pattern. The strong stresses per line should be fewer than five; the line should be broken into four, three, even two groups of sounds, separated by a minuscule pause; moreover, different kinds of feet other than the iamb should be introduced. In applying these discoveries, Marlowe exploited the flexibility and expressiveness of blank verse and cleared the way for other poets such as Shakespeare, John Milton, and William Wordsworth. Compare the *Gorboduc* lines with the following passage from *Doctor Faustus*: "Was this the face that launch'd a thousand ships?/ And burnt the topless towers of Ilium?/ Sweet Helen, make me immortal with a kiss." The first line is regular, with five iambic feet and five stresses. The second is regular in rhythm but has only four strong stresses, and the line falls into three sound groups. The third, however, diverges completely from the regular meter, beginning with a foot of two strong stresses and having a foot of two weak and one strong stress ("me immor-") in the middle. Such changes in the basic rhythm emphasize emotionally charged words and phrases, increasing the expressive power and enlivening the listener's attention.

Marlowe was an innovator also in his choice of themes. Religious skepticism recurs throughout the plays. *Tamburlaine the Great* challenged both Christian and Moslem faiths; *The Famous Tragedy of the Rich Jew of Malta* confounded Christianity and Judaism alike. Marlowe's questioning of humanity's place in the universe reached its height in *Doctor Faustus*, an agonized cry of defiance against an orthodoxy represented as chaining humankind's unquenchable thirst for knowledge. One cannot, however, assume that Marlowe was atheistical in the modern sense of materialistic. If there is anything of Marlowe in the solemn speech given to Orcanes in *Part II*, act 2 of *Tamburlaine the Great*, one may infer that the dramatist accepted the existence of a nondenominational supreme intelligence.

At the core of Marlowe's heterodoxy was his fascination with humanity's aspirant spirit and illimitable mind—a theme that did not fit easily into contemporary Christian thought. Marlowe's heroes are self-made, fired by a sense of their own power and greatness, in strong contrast to Shakespeare's, with their orthodox assumption of the privileges and honor due to noble birth.

Marlowe's treatment of this theme became more complex over the years. Faustus shares with the earlier hero Tamburlaine aspirations for worldly power at any cost. Both plays display the immense power of the individual to unleash massive forces for good or ill. Yet Faustus' odyssey, unlike Tamburlaine's, is intellectual rather than physical, internal rather than external. Whereas *Tamburlaine the Great* was a play of action and show, *Doctor Faustus* is a play of ideas—hence, perhaps, its more enduring fascination. Tamburlaine's approach to life is never seriously challenged, whereas the obstacles placed in Faustus' path form the premise of the play.

Marlowe's other major plays contain views as controversial as those in *Doctor Faustus*, for different reasons. The action of *The Troublesome Raigne and Lamentable Death of Edward the Second*, remarkable for the time, revolves around a homosexual relationship between Edward II and his favorite minion, Gaveston. Marlowe, who according to Baines said that "all they that loue not Tobacco & Boies were fooles," often treated the subject of homosexuality sympathetically. *The Famous Tragedy of the Rich Jew of Malta* also adopts an unorthodox standpoint, this time in public matters: The play is a cynical commentary on the corruption and greed of social and political life, after the theories of Italian political philosopher Niccolò Machiavelli.

TAMBURLAINE THE GREAT

First produced: *Part I*, c. 1587 (first published, 1590); *Part II*, 1587 (first published, 1590)

Type of work: Plays

In *Part I*, the Scythian shepherd Tamburlaine conquers many Eastern countries, becomes King of Persia, and marries the Soldan of Egypt's daughter Zenocrate; in *Part II*, Tamburlaine continues his conquests, Zenocrate dies, and Tamburlaine slays his cowardly son and finally dies.

When *Tamburlaine the Great* burst upon the Elizabethan stage in 1587, it took audiences by storm. The most popular tragedy of the time had been Kyd's *The Span-*

ish Tragedy (c. 1585-1589), which featured a strong dramatic sense but unmemorable verse. *Tamburlaine the Great*, in contrast, was written in poetry of the scope and magnificence that moved Shakespeare to write of "the proud full sail of [Marlowe's] great verse" (Sonnet 86).

Vital to the play's success was the figure of Tamburlaine. The prologue introduces him in lines that were to become famous: "Threatening the world with high astounding terms,/ And scourging kingdoms with his conquering sword." Tamburlaine's power comes from his limitless self-concept, not from his birth, which was that of a humble shepherd. In Marlowe's world, a person's worth is measured by his or her actions. Thus Tamburlaine declares, "I am a lord, for so my deeds shall prove—/ And yet a shepherd by my parentage." His thoughts, he says, are coequal with the clouds, and his aspiration is immortality such as the gods enjoy. Indeed, he claims to gain his authority to terrorize the world from Jove himself, whose scourge he is.

As for the traditional enemies of the aspirant—Death and Fortune—the plays contain frequent references to Tamburlaine's mastery over them, as in the passage in *Part I*, act 1, where he claims that he has bound the Fates in iron chains and turns Fortune's wheel with his own hand. He appears to have assumed the role of Fate in condemning the virgins of Damascus to death for their failure to surrender before he symbolically decked his tents in black: His Customs, he says, are "as peremptory/ As wrathful planets, death, or destiny."

Such assertions are hubristic in the extreme and, in a Christian context, would merit a downfall such as Faustus'. Tamburlaine, however, moves freely in a non-Christian setting. His death, when it comes, occurs through illness. He is never punished for his past exploits; rather, he is lionized by all save his enemies. "Nature," he says, ". . . doth teach us all to have aspiring minds"; our souls are ever "climbing after knowledge infinite." Compare this blithe celebration of the illimitable mind with the Chorus' fearful and bitter epilogue to *Doctor Faustus* lamenting the tragic fate of inquiring minds who are tempted to explore forbidden knowledge.

Christianity makes a brief appearance in *Part II* in the unsympathetic character of Sigismund, a Christian king. Sigismund makes a treaty with the Moslem king Orcanes only to be persuaded to break it on the grounds that oaths made with heathen are not binding. When Orcanes defeats the treacherous force of Sigismund, he wonders whether his victory was attributable to his invocation of Christ's wrath on the enemy or to Mahomet's favor. The skeptical Gazellus pointedly suggests that the cause lies in neither prophet, but in the fortunes of war. Marlowe's casual dismissal of Christ and Mahomet as a couple of rival prophets is indicative of his skeptical attitude toward all religions and their claims to a monopoly on truth.

The taste of the theatergoing public has changed since the Elizabethan Age, and modern audiences may view the bloody acts of ruthless tyrants with less enthusiasm. The negative sides of Tamburlaine's character—his cruelty, vengefulness, and extraordinary amount of machismo—may put him in danger of losing the audience's sympathy altogether. Scenes that spring to mind are, in part 1, his slaughter of the virgins of Damascus after the town's surrender and his inhuman treatment of Bajazeth. *Part II* depicts his self-indulgent act of burning the town where Zenocrate dies; his deliberately cutting his arm to show his sons that a wound is nothing, and his insistence that they wash their hands in the blood; his slaying of his son for cowardice; and his harnessing of the captured kings in his chariot.

Yet evidence exists that the Elizabethan response to Tamburlaine's overweening arrogance was not without a certain tongue-in-cheek humor. Tamburlaine's words to the harnessed kings as they draw his chariot onstage—"Holla, ye pamper'd jades of Asia!"—apparently brought the Elizabethan house down, since the line was the subject of jokes and was imitated and satirized in the works of different authors for years to come.

Tamburlaine the Great's appeal has diminished also because of its lack of inner dramatic conflict. Even its external conflicts—the battles—lack any threat to Tamburlaine's invincible status. The play's appeal to the modern mind more often lies in its grand images and breathtaking poetry. Take, as an example, Tamburlaine's glorious hymn to his own boundless spirit in act 4 of *Part II*. Delivered just before he stabs his son, it exemplifies the vast cosmic images that sustain the heightened effect of the plays.

Lines memorable for their loveliness abound. Some examples are Callapine's description of the Grecian virgins, "As fair as was Pygmalion's ivory girl,/ Or lovely Io metamorphosèd," and Tamburlaine's speech to the dying Zenocrate punctuated by its lyrical refrain. The part of Tamburlaine's soliloquy in act 5 of *Part I* dealing with poetry's attempts to capture the essence of beauty has attained the status of a set piece.

DOCTOR FAUSTUS

First produced: c. 1588 (first published, 1604)
Type of work: Play

A brilliant scholar sells his soul to the Devil in return for forbidden knowledge and worldly power.

Marlowe's last play, *Doctor Faustus*, is generally considered his greatest. The play shares certain elements with its ancestor, the medieval morality play: the opposing admonishments of good and bad angels; the characters of Lucifer and Mephostophilis; and the appearance of the Seven Deadly Sins. Yet it breaks with tradition in two important respects: in the sympathy evoked for the straying hero, and in the questions raised against the cosmic order of conventional Christian doctrine.

Faustus pursues his grand aspirations in what Marlowe portrays as a repressive climate of Christian orthodoxy, which, in designating certain knowledge as forbidden, blocks fulfillment of his desires and effectively becomes his antagonist. The play opens with Faustus in his study. He has plumbed the depths of all disciplines and found them unfulfilling. He will settle for no less than a dominion that "Stretcheth as far as doth the mind of man"—a world of physical beauty, sensual delight, and power over life and objects. He decides his best hope is necromancy, an art forbidden by Christian doctrine.

Thus, the scene is set for Faustus' tragic decline. Planted in the text, even from the beginning, are warnings of the terrible fate awaiting Faustus. A master of dramatic irony, Marlowe has these warnings go unheeded by his hero while they build an uneasy tension in the audience's awareness. An example is Faustus' remark on his own great powers in conjuring up Mephostophilis. Only a few lines later, it is revealed that Mephostophilis has come more out of his own and Lucifer's self-interest than in deference to Faustus' wishes. Similarly, when Mephostophilis tells Faustus that Lucifer was thrown from Heaven for aspiring pride and insolence, the audience recognizes that Faustus exhibits the same faults and may meet the same fate. There is ambivalence, too, in Faustus' repeated exhortation to himself to be resolute in his damnable course of action. The word, used more often in connection with Christian virtue, gains an ironic weight, rendering *Doctor Faustus* a negative version of *The Pilgrim's Progress* (1678, 1684).

Counterbalanced against this carefully crafted tragic inevitability is the hope that Faustus *will* repent and save himself. Marlowe keeps the conflict in Faustus' soul active until the end. In the moving soliloquies, Faustus' initial confidence in his pact with Lucifer alternates with regret and determination to turn back to God. Despair however, prevails. In his second soliloquy, Faustus is turned back from repentance by his sense of God's indifference to him and his own indifference to God: Faustus serves only his own appetite. In one profoundly moving scene, Faustus announces, "I do repent" only to have Mephostophilis threaten him with having his flesh torn into pieces for disobedience to Lucifer. Faustus effects a hasty turnabout of meaning in an ironic echo of his previous phrase: "I do repent I e'er offended him."

Yet just as God failed Faustus in his aspirations, so does Lucifer. Disillusionment follows rapidly on his pact. Faustus asks for a wife; but marriage is a sacrament, so Mephostophilis cannot provide one. When Faustus questions him about astronomy, Mephostophilis tells him nothing the scholar Wagner could not have told him. Although the Chorus reveals that Faustus attains fame for his learning, his achievements are superficial and empty in comparison with his grandiose intentions at the outset. He humiliates the pope (a typically Marlovian scenario), avenges some petty wrongs done to him by Benvolio by attaching antlers to his head, and entertains the duke and duchess of Vanholt with insubstantial illusions. At the play's start, no area of knowledge is large enough for Faustus' overweening sense of self; toward the end, fear and despair have so diminished him that he wants only dissolution and oblivion: "O soul, be chang'd into little water drops,/ And fall into the ocean, ne'er be found."

In spite of the intellectual nature of the play's premise, it contains scenes of a striking visual immediacy. The first entrance of Mephostophilis, too ugly for Faustus' taste, and the appearance of Helen of Troy are examples. Often, scenes of horror are not directly represented on stage, but chillingly evoked in words. Faustus' blood congeals as he attempts to sign his soul away to the Devil; a Latin inscription meaning "Fly, O man!" appears on his arm. That the audience is told this by Faustus rather than seeing it for itself lets it experience the terror through his awareness. Similarly, a chill of fear is produced by Faustus' words to the Scholars: "Ay, pray for me, pray for me; and, what noise soever ye hear, come not unto me, for nothing can rescue me." The image is as powerful in its understatement as the explicit horror of the final scene, where devils drag Faustus off to Hell.

Marlowe's verse reached its full emotional power in *Doctor Faustus*. Faustus' soliloquy beginning "Ah, Faustus,/ Now hast thou but one bare hour to live" is an example of the emotional intensity of which Marlowe was capable. Faustus' request that the spheres of Heaven cease their motion to give him time to repent is heartrending because of its very impossibility. Desperation is conveyed in the rapid and diminishing series of time extensions that he demands. His violent reversals of mood—from calling on God to anguish at being dragged downward by devils, from the vision of Christ's blood streaming in the firmament to the pain of Lucifer's tortures—move the audience with him from despair to hope. His spiritual agony is summarized in the evocative and poignant line, "O lente lente currite noctis equi" ("Slowly run, O horses of night").

The traditional morality play affirmed Christian virtue and faith and condemned the vices of those who strayed from the path. *Doctor Faustus* offers no such comfortable framework. It does not offer a reassuring affirmation of Christian faith or a straightforward condemnation of Faustus. Instead, it presents a disturbing challenge to the cosmic order as defined by Christian orthodoxy. Listeners are invited "Only to wonder at unlawful things,/ whose deepness doth entice such forward wits/ To practise more than heavenly power permits."

The question with which the play ends is whether the tragedy of Faustus is individual, the tragedy of one man's fall from grace, or universal, the tragedy of Everyman in a system of belief that offers no place or path for the growth of the illimitable human spirit.

HERO AND LEANDER

First published: 1598
Type of work: Poem

Leander falls in love with Hero, who lives on the opposite side of the Hellespont, and tries to seduce her.

Marlowe left *Hero and Leander* unfinished at his death. It was completed by dramatist George Chapman in very different style and published by him the following year. (This analysis deals only with the part of the poem that Marlowe wrote, the first two sestiads.)

Hero and Leander is the most famous example of a favorite Elizabethan genre, the brief epic. It circulated in manuscript for some years before publication. During this time, it was certainly read by William Shakespeare, whose poem of the same genre *Venus and Adonis* (1593) was influenced by it, and whose plays contain strong echoes of its lines. The brief epic was a poem on an erotic and mythological subject, often drawn from Ovid's *Metamorphoses* (c. A.D. 8). *Hero and Leander* is Ovidian in character, though the story actually comes from a later version of the myth by Musaeus. Most adaptors of Ovidian subjects indulged in a high degree of moralizing, a factor dispensed with by Marlowe.

Hero and Leander is an exuberantly sensuous poem enlivened by an irrepressible comic spirit. Having fallen in love with the beautiful Hero, Leander wastes no time in attempting to bed her. He uses the commonplace arguments of Renaissance naturalism: Since virginity has no material reality and is imperceptible to the senses, it is no thing—and therefore nothing to preserve or anything of which to be proud. Such specious logic is meant to be enjoyed as flights of wit and audacity, and would only be taken at face value by someone of Hero's naïveté. Leander's devious sophistry is pointed out in lines whose rhymes anticipate George Gordon, Lord Byron's *Don Juan* (1819-1824, 1826): "At last, like to a bold sharp sophister,/ With cheerful hope he thus accosted her." Also enlisted into the argument is a theme shared by Shakespeare's *Venus and Adonis* and his sonnets, the sterility and waste of youth and beauty's keeping its gifts to itself in the virginal state.

In spite of Leander's sophistication in the art of persuasion, in the art of love he is an innocent. In a passage of comic understatement, he toys with Hero "as a brother with his sister," "Supposing nothing else was to be done"—"yet he suspected/ Some amorous rites or other were neglected." Hero is able to deflect Leander's inept advances and greets the morning still intact. Leander returns home, and the narrator's ironic comment on his encounter with his father sustains the comic detachment: "His secret flame apparently was seen,/ Leander's father knew where he had been." Mock-heroic images also contribute to the poem's comic tone, as in the passage in sestiad 2 likening Leander's attempt to touch the reluctant Hero's breasts—exaggeratedly described as a globe "By which love sails to regions full of bliss"—to a siege. She "did as a soldier stout/ Defend the fort, and keep the foeman out."

Another comic episode shows Leander, determined to see his love, swimming the Hellespont to reach her home. He is nearly frustrated in his aim by the sea god Neptune's taking a fancy to him. Neptune mistakes Leander for Jove's page Ganymede and, in a scene of intense homoeroticism as funny as it is sensuous, tries to seduce the unwitting young man. Leander, at cross-purposes with Neptune, protests that he is no woman. The worldly-wise Neptune smiles at his innocence. It is not the first homoerotic element in the poem: Leander's feminine beauty is described in unusually intimate detail, from the point of view of the male narrator and of other male admirers.

The imagery of the poem creates a world of intoxicating sensuality. Leander's beauty exceeds that of Narcissus, who fell in love with his own reflection in a pool. Hero worships Venus at a temple sumptuously described; about her neck, she wears chains of pebble-stone that shine like diamonds.

THE PASSIONATE SHEPHERD TO HIS LOVE

First published: 1599
Type of work: Poem

This work is one of the best-known Elizabethan lyrics and was endlessly imitated, parodied, and answered well into the seventeenth century.

"The Passionate Shepherd to His Love," comprising six stanzas of four lines each, is an intellectual's vision of pastoral life, in a tradition going back to the Roman poets Theocritus and Vergil. Its undoubted emotional power hinges on its yearning evocation of an idyll that never was and can never be. The wistful invitation of the poet to his love to live with him in this impossibly perfect place evokes the pathos of unfulfilled desire and longing.

The work is rich with images chosen to delight the senses. There is the visual feast of the pastoral landscape and of the belt with coral clasps and amber studs, the soft touch of the gown made from wool pulled from lambs, the sounds of the birds singing melodious madrigals and of the shepherds' songs, the smell of the beds of roses and of the thousand fragrant posies.

The regular rhyme scheme, of two pairs of rhyming couplets per stanza, the smooth iambic rhythm, and the use of alliteration add to the songlike quality of the poem, and indeed, an adapted version of one of its stanzas appears as a song in Shakespeare's *The Merry Wives of Windsor* (1597; revised, c. 1600-1601).

Summary

Christopher Marlowe was a brilliant innovator and an intellectual nonconformist, with much to tell and much to question about power, desire, sensuality, greed, and suffering. His poetic images, vast in scale and cosmic in conception, as well as his larger-than-life characters of grand aspirations and prodigious sensual appetites, inspired critic Harry Levin to dub Marlowe "the overreacher." No better word could be chosen to characterize the magnificence, the vehemence, and the violent egotism that give his genius such an intensely personal stamp.

Bibliography

Bevington, David M. *From Mankind to Marlowe: Growth of Structure in the Popular Drama of Tudor England.* Cambridge, Mass.: Harvard University Press, 1962.

Ellis-Fermor, Una M. *Christopher Marlowe.* London: Methuen, 1927.

Empson, William. *Faustus and the Censor: The English Faust-Book and Marlowe's "Dr. Faustus."* New York: Basil Blackwell, 1987.

Farnham, Willard, ed. *Twentieth Century Interpretations of Doctor Faustus.* Englewood Cliffs, N.J.: Prentice-Hall, 1969.

Hotson, J. Leslie. *The Death of Christopher Marlowe.* Cambridge, Mass.: Harvard University Press, 1925.

Leech, Clifford, ed. *Marlowe: A Collection of Critical Essays.* Englewood Cliffs, N.J.: Prentice-Hall, 1964.

Levin, Harry. *The Overreacher.* London: Faber & Faber, 1952.

Morris, Brian, ed. *Christopher Marlowe.* London: Ernest Benn, 1968.

Pinciss, Gerald. *Christopher Marlowe.* New York: Frederick Ungar, 1975.

Claire Robinson

ANDREW MARVELL

Born: Winestead-in-Holderness, England
March 31, 1621
Died: London, England
August 18, 1678

Principal Literary Achievement
Marvell's work, which embodies the best qualities of Metaphysical poetry, is marked by a distinctive ability to present and resolve seemingly irreconcilable opposites, a trait that allows him to examine complex situations and issues with great depth and sensitivity.

Biography
Andrew Marvell was born in Winestead-in-Holderness on March 31, 1621. His father, Andrew Marvell, was a local vicar, and in 1624 the family moved to Hull, where Marvell's father had been appointed lecturer at Holy Trinity Church. Marvell was educated at Hull Grammar School, and in 1633 he left Hull for Trinity College, Cambridge. At Cambridge, Marvell read widely; his studies included the works of Roman poets such as Horace and Juvenal, which would influence Marvell's own later poems. In 1637, his first verses, in Latin and Greek, were published. During this year, he also experienced a brief conversion to Roman Catholicism and ran away from Cambridge to London. His father, however, found him and forced him to return to the university. He received his B.A. and left Cambridge after his father's death in 1641. For the next several years, Marvell traveled extensively, visiting Holland, France, Italy, and Spain. In Rome, he visited the English Catholic priest and poetaster, Richard Flecknoe, who was to become the subject of satirical poems by both Marvell and, later, John Dryden. Although few details are known about Marvell's life during the 1640's, it appears that his lengthy travels abroad kept him from taking any direct part in the bloody and divisive English Civil War.

In 1650, Marvell took a position as tutor to Mary Fairfax, the young daughter of Lord Thomas Fairfax, a Parliamentary general who resigned from military service in June of that year. Marvell lived for two years with the Fairfax family in their home, Nun Appleton House, in Yorkshire. It was during this time that Marvell is thought to have written much of his finest lyric poetry, including a lengthy poem celebrating the virtues of the Fairfax home and its master. John Milton, a friend and mentor, recommended Marvell for an appointment as Latin secretary to the Council of State, but

A. MARVELL.

the post was not awarded to Marvell until four years later. In the meantime, Marvell was appointed tutor to William Dutton, who would later become a ward of Oliver Cromwell, the English soldier and statesman. During Cromwell's years as lord protector, Marvell wrote many poems in praise of Cromwell and his government, including "An Horatian Ode upon Cromwell's Return from Ireland" (commonly known as "An Horatian Ode"), *The First Anniversary of the Government Under His Highness the Lord Protector*, and *A Poem upon the Death of His Late Highness the Lord Protector*. Despite Marvell's admiration for Cromwell, both as a man and as a political force, and his enjoyment of Cromwell's favor, however, Marvell was not a fanatical partisan or a Puritan zealot, and he seems to have weathered the Restoration of the monarchy without difficulty. Marvell was instrumental in protecting Milton, who had been a vocal anti-Royalist, from retribution under the restored monarchy.

Marvell was elected to Parliament as a representative for Hull in 1659. He remained a member of Parliament for the rest of his life, a span of nearly twenty years. During his tenure in Parliament, he continued to travel widely, accompanying the earl of Carlisle on a tour of Russia, Sweden, and Denmark, returning to England in 1665. Though Marvell is little remembered today as a politician, he was in his day an active and conscientious supporter of his constituents' interests, as his numerous letters to the mayor and aldermen of Hull show. After the Restoration, Marvell was sometimes outspoken in his criticism of Charles II's government, and in 1667 he wrote "Last Instructions to a Painter," a poem satirizing various politicians and political affairs of the day, particularly the conduct of the 1667 naval campaign against the Dutch. He also gained some notoriety as a political pamphleteer, most notably for his two-part *The Rehearsal Transpros'd* (1672-1673), a clarion call for religious tolerance in the face of a campaign for religious conformity being waged by Samuel Parker, a Church of England divine. In the early 1670's, it was feared that Charles II was conspiring with the Catholic Louis XIV of France to curtail the religious and political freedom of his subjects; in reaction, Marvell, operating under an assumed name, took part in a clandestine, pro-Protestant campaign designed to influence English foreign policy and compel Charles and the English forces to conclude hostilities with the Dutch. When Marvell died on August 18, 1678, in London as a result of a physician's mistreatment of a fever, it was rumored that he was the victim of a political murder.

During Marvell's life, few of his poems were published, and he was known in his day primarily for his pamphlets and a few verse and prose satires. In 1681, three years after his death, a collection that included many of his lyrical pastoral poems was published from papers brought forward by his housekeeper, Mary Palmer, who claimed to be his wife. Although these poems enjoyed some popularity at their publication, Marvell remained relatively unknown as a poet until his "rediscovery" by later writers such as Charles Lamb and Alfred, Lord Tennyson, in the nineteenth century and T. S. Eliot in the twentieth.

Analysis

Marvell is a poet attracted by complexity and paradox and is reluctant to oversimplify the themes and experiences that he explores in his poems, be they pastoral lyrics or overtly political works. His best poems frequently display an ambiguity and irony that is not a mere stylistic device, but rather a reflection of Marvell's penchant for seeing many sides of an ostensibly simple situation. In addition, Marvell was artistically influenced by other Metaphysical poets such as John Donne, who avoided hackneyed poetic conventions and used clever, convoluted logic and incongruous imagery to bring fresh perspectives to bear on traditional poetic subjects such as love and death.

The term "Metaphysical poet" is not one with which Marvell would have been familiar. Although it was first used by Dryden in criticizing Donne for his use of far-fetched, extravagant metaphors and abstract logic in poems dealing with emotional subjects, it gained a nonpejorative status and wider currency as a result of Eliot's seminal 1921 essay "The Metaphysical Poets." Eliot's essay praises the Metaphysical poets (including Marvell) for their harmonious uniting of reason and emotion. Some qualities of Metaphysical poetry that Marvell shares are a logical and analytical strain in dealing with emotional subjects, the use of extended, incongruous metaphors, or "conceits," that link dissimilar images, a fondness for puns and paradox, and, occasionally, a deliberate roughness or unevenness of meter designed to add vigor to the lines.

"The Definition of Love" illustrates some of these qualities. In it, Marvell explores the paradox of an unrequited love that by its very impossibility achieves perfection. Marvell inverts traditional poetic images, referring to "Magnanimous Despair" and "feeble Hope." Like Donne, who compared his love to a compass, Marvell employs mapmaking imagery to describe the separation from his lover. He and his beloved are like "the distant Poles," around whom the entire world turns. He speaks of love in terms of oblique angles and infinite parallel lines that can never meet, and he invokes the oxymoronic image of a planisphere (literally a flat sphere, a term used to describe two-dimensional representation of the globe) to illustrate the impossibility of their union. He "defines" his love by these images of impossibility.

Many of Marvell's earlier poems deal with the subject of retirement or withdrawal from public life to a life of private contemplation. Indeed, many critics divide Marvell's work into two bodies; his early poems in praise of the contemplative life, and his later poems that address more explicitly political subjects and advocate engagement in public, political life. Many of his poems praising retirement employ imagery of gardens and green woods, a trait that has led to his being called "the green poet" or "the garden poet" for his pastoral works.

"The Garden" exemplifies this type of poem. In it, Marvell wavers between whimsy and melancholy as he describes the joys of solitude in a lush, green garden. The garden is the home of "Fair Quiet" and "Innocence," far from the "busy companies of men." Paradoxically, the lack of human company results in a higher form of civilization: "Society is all but rude,/ To this delicious solitude." In arguing that solitude in the garden is superior to love, he inverts romantic images from classical mythology, claiming that Apollo was rewarded, rather than thwarted, when Daphne, his romantic quarry, was metamorphosed into a tree; likewise, he suggests that Pan pursued Syrinx "Not as a nymph, but for a reed." In typical fashion, however, Marvell subtly qualifies the paradisiacal scene, suggesting that the garden may not be as perfect as the speaker describes. The speaker stumbles over fruits and vines and says "Ensnared with flowers, I fall on grass," recalling Adam's fall in Eden. As the speaker withdraws further and further into inward contemplation in the garden, his thoughts destructively begin "Annihilating all that's made/ To a green thought in a green shade." Marvell moves this vaguely unhealthy solipsism into hubris as the self-absorbed speaker criticizes the Divine plan, saying "Two paradises 'twere in one/ To live in paradise alone." As in many of Marvell's poems, the meaning rests on the reader's interpretation of the tone. Despite the subtly qualifying negative imagery, the garden is portrayed throughout as beautiful and peaceful. Marvell appears neither to embrace wholeheartedly nor to reject entirely retirement in the garden, and his equivocal lyrics seem to suggest an ideal of balance between total withdrawal and engagement in society.

Marvell explores the issue of pastoral retirement versus engagement in worldly affairs in other poems such as "The Nymph Complaining for the Death of her Fawn," which offers the garden as a fragile refuge from violent society, "The Emigrants in the Bermudas," which posits the necessity of escape from corrupt society in order to achieve spiritual perfection, and the several "Mower" poems, which depict meadows and gardens as wholesome retreats from unhappy social relations. The subject receives its fullest treatment in the lengthy "Upon Appleton House." As in "The Garden," the positive values of retirement are expounded through garden imagery. In this work, however, Marvell is more openly ambivalent about the virtues of retirement. The poem celebrates the character, home, and family of his employer, Lord Fairfax. Fairfax embodies all the positive qualities that Marvell sees as springing from a life of retirement and contemplation. Marvell suggests, however, that Fairfax has a responsibility to bestow the benefits of his virtue on society by taking active part in the politics of the day. Unlike "The Garden," "Upon Appleton House" does not ignore the political and social exigencies of the day; Fairfax cannot live in a kind of horticultural vacuum. Instead, Fairfax must cultivate and cherish the values nurtured in retirement but use them in the service of society. That is achieved metaphorically through the marriage of Fairfax's daughter Mary, as she takes the values of Appleton House out into the wider world.

"Upon Appleton House" can be considered a bridge to Marvell's later poems advocating active engagement in society and politics. Marvell recognized that the extraordinary times in which he lived required individuals of integrity and ability to take an active role in the conduct of the state. As Marvell himself became increasingly involved in public life, his work was likewise concerned more and more with political topics. Among his politicized writings are several poems praising Cromwell, satires such as "Last Instructions to a Painter," which severely criticized English policies and politicians, and a number of political pamphlets.

TO HIS COY MISTRESS

First published: 1681
Type of work: Poem

The swift passage of time and its attendant decay is a compelling reason to enjoy life's pleasures in the present, but it may also be as strong an argument for religiously motivated abstinence.

"To His Coy Mistress" is a witty exploration of the traditional *carpe diem* theme, and it can be read on several levels. On the surface, it functions extremely effectively as a lover's argument in favor of pursuing pleasure. The speaker begins by assuring his lady that, "Had we but world enough, and time," he would be well content to love her at a slow pace, devoting thousands of years to adoring each part of her. Time in this stanza is an agent of growth, as the speaker assures his beloved, "My vegetable love should grow/ Vaster than empires, and more slow." The initial stanza moves at a leisurely metrical pace as the speaker uses extravagant and playful images to persuade the lady of his devotion and his wish that he could love her with the slow thoroughness that she deserves.

In the second stanza, the speaker shifts to images of swiftly passing time to impress upon his love that they in fact do not have the leisure to love at this slow rate. "At my back I always hear/ Time's wingèd chariot hurrying near," he says. Now time is destructive, and the meter moves rapidly. The speaker resorts to images of decay that are at once whimsical and frightening as he attempts to convince the beloved of the need to consummate their love in the present. Though images of death and decay are not unusual in *carpe diem* lyrics, Marvell's images are particularly graphic and alarming: "in thy marble vault . . ./ worms shall try/ That long-preserved virginity:/ And your quaint honour turn to dust." The speaker employs dark humor as he ironically comments, "The grave's a fine and private place,/ But none, I think, do there embrace."

The third stanza exhorts the beloved to action. While they are still young, able, and desirable, he urges, they should "sport" while they may, and "Rather at once our time devour,/ Than languish in his slow-chapped power." By seizing the initiative and enthusiastically embracing life and pleasure, they can win a victory over destructive Time: "Thus, though we cannot make our sun/ Stand still, yet we will make him run."

As always, though, Marvell is aware of an equally compelling counterpoint to his argument, and he chooses ambiguous imagery to communicate it subtly. In the first stanza, Marvell uses explicitly religious terminology to describe the enormous length of time that he would like to devote to the wooing of his lady: "I would/ Love you ten years before the flood:/ And you should, if you please, refuse/ Till the conversion of Jews" (it was a traditional belief that the Jews would convert to Christianity at the end of the world). Marvell thus evokes a specifically divine or eternal time frame, with overtones of judgment (the Flood was divine punishment for the human race's corruption) and salvation.

Similarly, the following stanzas are studded with religious references. Marvell conjures up an image of the "Deserts of vast eternity" that lie before the lovers, an image that may spur his beloved to action in this life but may just as well remind her of her eternal afterlife. He argues that time will turn her honor to "dust" and his lust to "ashes," suggesting the terminology of the Christian burial service. He refers to the way (in reality or perhaps merely in his hopes) that her "willing soul transpires/ At every pore with instant fires." Conjoining images of souls and fires cannot help but suggest hellfire and eternal damnation.

The final stanza, in which he urges action, presents a problematic vision of love. He compares himself and his lover to sportive animals, specifically "amorous birds of prey," an odd image to use in attempting to win his lady. The love that he describes seems rough and violent: He suggests that they "devour" their time and says, "Let us . . ./ Tear our pleasures with rough strife/ Thorough the iron grates of life" ("thorough" here means "through"). The lines have a rather strange and unromantic ring and qualify the speaker's ostensibly enthusiastic description of love. Love as described in this stanza is not conventionally sweet and sentimental but rather vaguely dangerous and threatening; beneath the surface, Marvell seems to be issuing a warning as much as an exhortation.

More than a love poem, "To His Coy Mistress" is a meditation on time and death. Marvell dramatizes the questions: What are the implications of physicality and mortality? In using time most wisely, should one focus on this life or the afterlife? Marvell avoids a simple, conventional answer, and the poem works well as an argument for either view.

AN HORATIAN ODE

First published: 1681
Type of work: Poem

Cromwell, the hero and prime mover of the English Civil War, which led to the overthrow of King Charles I, is celebrated as a valorous man of action, but Marvell warns that his exercise of power must be tempered with prudence and restraint.

Like "To His Coy Mistress," "An Horatian Ode" operates on several levels. On the surface, it is a conventional celebratory ode about a military and political hero, praising his exploits and virtues. One can infer from Marvell's other laudatory poems about Oliver Cromwell that the poet genuinely admired the lord protector; the tone of the poem is not openly ironic. Woven into the praise, however, or hidden behind it, are subtle signs indicating an equivocal attitude toward Cromwell and his achievements.

Cromwell is depicted as a larger-than-life figure, a conqueror who is almost as much a force of nature as a man; Marvell compares him to "three-forked lightning" and calls him a "greater spirit." He is likened to a scourge of God, sweeping away corruption. " 'Tis madness to resist or blame/ The force of angry heaven's flame." He is a conqueror on a par with "Caesar" and "Hannibal." Yet intermingled with this praise for Cromwell is a sense of regret at the destruction of ancient institutions. The effect of Cromwell's revolution has been "to ruin the great work of time," in other words, society and government as it had been. Marvell calls Cromwell an instrument of fate and power rather than one of righteousness when he says "Though justice against fate complain,/ And plead the ancient rights in vain:/ . . . those do hold or break/ As men are strong or weak."

Of course, the greatest institution that Cromwell succeeded in destroying was the monarchy. Marvell treats the scene of King Charles I's execution with great sensitivity and sympathy. The king is likened to an "actor" playing his final scene on a stagelike scaffold, while all around "the armèd bands/ Did clap their bloody hands." Marvell praises the dignity and courage of the king: "He nothing common did or mean/ Upon that memorable scene . . . / Nor called the gods with vulgar spite/ To vindicate his helpless right." In describing the king's execution, Marvell seems more concerned with the human drama than with the political circumstances surrounding the event; the king is not a tyrant or an enemy, but an admirably brave prisoner.

Beyond this open ambivalence are more indirect qualifications to the praise of Cromwell. The whole poem is rife with puns and double meanings, from the opening lines describing Cromwell's supporters as "forward" (either "eager" or "presumptuous"—or both) to the sly description of Cromwell's progress from farmer to conqueror and statesman. Before his emergence as a public figure, Marvell says, Cromwell labored in his "private gardens . . . / As if his highest plot/ To plant the bergamot." The pun on "plot" is apparent, but the choice of "bergamot" is interesting. A bergamot is a fruit tree whose etymological name means "prince's pear"; the reference is perhaps a swipe at Cromwell's aspirations to rule.

A kind of resolution, or at least an acknowledgment, of the tensions established by his equivocal praise is achieved toward the end of the poem when Marvell openly expresses his concerns about Cromwell's rule. Though he praises Cromwell for being responsive to the wishes of the people, having "his sword and spoils ungirt,/ To lay them at the public's skirt," he offers an explicit warning, both to Cromwell and to the people, about the exercise of absolute power and the possible necessity of further bloodshed to uphold it: "The same arts that did gain/ A power, must it maintain."

Summary

Andrew Marvell's poetry offers a clear, distinctive reflection of both the events and the issues of his time, and of his own unique and penetrating mind. With wit and intelligence, he offers novel perspectives on poetical commonplaces from love to virtue (both individual and social) to death. By treating the conventional in a highly unconventional way, Marvell is able to reveal an astonishing complexity to his subjects, what Eliot calls "a recognition, implicit in the expression of every experience, of other kinds of experience which are possible." Marvell's conclusions are never forced or obvious; he subtly manipulates language and tone to hint at rather than clearly delineate his views and invites the reader to draw his own conclusions.

Marvell's work incorporates the best features not only of Metaphysical poetry but of all poetry: His depiction of individual consciousness is worthy of the Romantic poets, and his vivid treatment of public events and themes is equally adept and incisive. His harmonious blending of reason and passion as he treats the inner world and the outer world with equal ease assures him of a lasting and prominent place in the literary canon.

Bibliography

Berthoff, Anne E. *The Resolved Soul: A Study of Marvell's Major Poems.* Princeton, N.J.: Princeton University Press, 1970.

Colie, Rosalie L. *"My Ecchoing Song": Marvell's Poetry of Criticism.* Princeton, N.J.: Princeton University Press, 1970.

Craze, Michael. *The Life and Lyrics of Andrew Marvell.* London: Macmillan, 1979.

Donno, Elizabeth Story. *Andrew Marvell: The Critical Heritage.* Boston: Routledge & Kegan Paul, 1978.

Hunt, John Dixon. *Andrew Marvell: His Life and Writings.* Ithaca, N.Y.: Cornell University Press, 1978.

Lord, George de Forest, ed. *Andrew Marvell: A Collection of Critical Essays.* Englewood Cliffs, N.J.: Prentice-Hall, 1968.

Rees, Christine. *The Judgment of Marvell.* New York: Pinter Publishers, 1989.

Catherine Swanson

MATSUO BASHŌ

Born: Ueno, Iga Province, Japan
1644
Died: Ōsaka, Japan
October 12, 1694

Principal Literary Achievement

Although Bashō did not originate the *haiku*, he is credited with perfecting forms earlier made popular by such masters as Matsunaga Teitoku and Nishiyama Sōin.

Biography

Matsuo Bashō, poet, essayist, critic, and writer of travel journals, was born Matsuo Kinsaku in Ueno, in the Iga Province in the western part of Honshu, the largest of the Japanese islands, in 1644. His father, Matsuo Yozaemon, is thought to have been a low-ranking samurai, and Bashō entered the service of Tōdō Yoshitada with the idea of following in that tradition. His master enjoyed writing *haikai*, or linked verse; thus, Bashō became interested in this form of poetry and began to write poems under the name of Sōbō. The earliest of his surviving verses, largely humorous and with clever wordplay, date from 1662. In 1666, his master died unexpectedly, and Bashō resigned his service, abandoning his hope of becoming a samurai, and began to travel. He continued to write *haikai* and published a collection of poems in 1672.

Also in 1672, Bashō moved to Edo (now Tokyo) where he gradually developed a literary reputation. Most of the early poems are of little literary value but are historically important. He acquired a large number of students, and this enabled Bashō to publish a collection of poems by twenty of these students.

Before the end of 1692, Bashō moved into a small hut in the Fukugawa district of Edo and began calling himself Bashō ("banana hut") because of the association that people made between the poet and the banana trees planted near his hut. He studied Zen Buddhism for a time; some believe that Bashō, although now comfortable and fairly well known, was not spiritually at peace with himself during this period of his life. His poems changed in both style and form, suggesting that he wished to break down convention and add variety to his work.

In the fall of 1684, Bashō began the first of four famous journeys. While he continued to write *haiku*, these travels also provided the opportunity to write travel journals, a type of writing well known in Japan. The first trip extended from Edo west-

ward to Ueno, his hometown area; he then moved on to Nagoya, Nara, Ōgaki, and Kyōto before returning to Edo the following summer. This journey resulted in the production of five volumes of linked verse by a team of poets, as well as the travel journal *Nozarashi kikō* (1698; *The Records of a Weather-Exposed Skeleton*, 1959). The journal, though uneven in quality, has a serious theme: the search for freedom from self-doubt. This journey seems to have been helpful in finding that freedom.

The next journey, of about ten months, retraced his first one only until he arrived in Ueno; there he continued to Suma and Akashi, on the Inland Sea, and then on to Sarashina in the Japan Alps. In addition to *haiku* inspired by the trip, Bashō wrote two more poetic diaries, *Oi no kobumi* (1709; *Manuscript in My Knapsack*, 1962), which covers the journey as far as Akashi, and *Sarashina kiko* (1704; *A Visit to Sarashina Village*, 1957), which describes his travels through the mountains to Sarashina. The first volume sounds almost didactic, as if he were teaching a lesson.

Having had a successful second journey, Bashō headed north on his next venture. This trip was a long period of 156 days and about fifteen hundred miles of travel through some of Japan's less developed areas. He left in the late spring of 1689, traveling through a number of cities that he had not visited before, and concluded his journey at Ōgaki. This journey was also a significant one in his literary career. He composed some of his best poetry, developed the principle of *sabi*, a nonemotional kind of loneliness associated with beauty, and produced one of the greatest of the Japanese poetic diaries, *Oku no hosomichi* (1694; *The Narrow Road to the Deep North*, 1933).

Following this northern trip, Bashō spent about two years in the Kyoto area, where he produced some of his most mature work, before returning to Edo in the winter of 1691. He had some heavy responsibilities during this period and became quite depressed. In 1694, however, he set out again on a westward journey during the summer, but while he was in Ōsaka, he developed a serious stomach condition, from which he died on October 12, 1694.

Analysis

The works of Bashō represent a high point in the history of Japanese poetics. He is chiefly known as a writer of the *haiku*, a tiny poem that, unless irregular, contains seventeen syllables in three lines of five, seven, and five syllables each. Actually, in Bashō's lifetime, the term *haiku* had not yet come into use. *Haiku* comes from the blending of *haikai*, or linked verse, and *hokku*, the starting verse of a *haikai*. Over time, the *hai-* of *haikai* was combined with the *-ku* of *hokku* to form *haiku*. Thus, the opening verse of a group of linked verses came to standing independently as a poem.

In addition to his mastery of the *haiku* and of travel diaries, he was also an excellent teacher of verse writing. His poetic ideas were never recorded as a poetic theory, and some of them are very difficult to comprehend. Some of the most important of these ideas were those of the poetic spirit, *sabi*, *shiori*, slenderness, inspiration, fragrance, reverberation, reflection, plainness, and highness. Actually, the concept of the poetic spirit is central, and the rest could almost be considered various aspects of the poetic spirit. This poetic spirit can be categorized into a style that has both qualities transcending time and place and a quality that is rooted in the taste of the times.

Bashō's poetic spirit is the source of all art and goes back to the source of the universe. It is something of a return to a beautiful nature whose creation and appreciation differentiate the civilized and the uncivilized. The two major aspects of Bashō's poetic spirit are a high spiritual attainment, on the one hand, and a mundane enjoyment of pleasure in the modern world, on the other. The goal of enlightenment is at the center of spiritual attainment, while enjoyment of the world includes such ideas as plainness and lightness.

Some of the values that contribute to attaining enlightenment include *sabi*, *shiori*, and slenderness. *Sabi* connotes a kind of objective, nonemotional loneliness, not grief or sorrow, which is an emotional trait. Bashō's kind of loneliness is enjoyable and is associated with impersonal nature, not human life. It has been said that Bashō found *sabi* in this *haiku*:

> Under the blossoms
> Two aged watchmen,
> With their white heads together.

Shiori, unlike *sabi*, which manifests the poet's attitude toward life, derives loneliness from the structure of the poem itself. *Shiori* can mean "to be flexible" or "to drop" or "wither." Both meanings seem to apply in Bashō's usage. Thus, a poem with *shiori* may have several layers or meaning open to several interpretations while at the same time creating an atmosphere of loneliness. Bashō found *shiori* in the following *haiku*:

> The Ten Dumplings
> Have become smaller, too—
> The autumn wind.

Also important to an analysis of the *haiku* are the concepts of the "cutting word," *kireji*, and the "season-word," *kigo*. The cutting word often follows the subject, but a verb is missing, forcing the reader to supply one; this omission results in a kind of ambiguity that is vague and impersonal. *Kigo*, the season-word, is a part of the traditional rule that a *haiku* must contain a word associated with a particular season, for according to Bashō, each poem must present an atmosphere of nature, which, of course, is seasonal. Fall is the season mentioned in this translation of one of Bashō's poems:

> On the Stone Mountain
> It is whiter than the stones:
> Autumnal wind.

Slenderness can perhaps be explained best by imagining the mind as being so slender that it is able to pierce and enter any kind of object and reach and touch its innermost life. Bashō used as an example of a poem with slenderness one of his own:

The salted sea bream's
Gums are chilly, too,
At the fish shop.

With this mental slenderness, not actual physical touch, the poet feels the chilliness in this objective, impersonal poem.

Another term necessary to an understanding of some of Bashō's haiku is synesthesia, the process of describing one of the senses in terms of another. Thus, the fragrance of peach blossoms may be described as being whiter than that of daffodils; a duck's cry is white, the autumn wind is whiter than the rocks of Ishiyama (which are noted for being white). Using these surprising comparisons seems to imply an interrelatedness of all things; the descriptions are not made for their shock effect, but rather because they employ the essence of the natural, simple, even primitive, in nature.

Later in his life, Bashō developed the idea of lightness, by which he seems to have meant a kind of beauty that is always plain, simple, ordinary. On one occasion, Bashō illustrated the concept by comparing vegetable soup (light) and duck stew (heavy, dark). It is a beauty that is unsophisticated, simple, and delicate rather than sophisticated, ornate, and heavy in any way. Thus, this concept of lightness does not indicate lightness in the sense of frivolousness or lack of substance, although humor may not be missing. For the unenlightened Buddhist who views life as constant suffering, detachment from the cares of the world enables one to see the humor of things, that is, to take a "lighthearted" attitude toward things, to smile in a world full of grief.

For Bashō, then, the essential element for a successful *haiku* is complete impersonality, the ability to view things as nature does, devoid of emotion. His success in perfecting the *haiku* form resulted in his enjoying a reputation that few other Japanese poets have enjoyed. His influence is so pervasive that no poet after him could write a *haiku* without an awareness of that influence. Nor has that influence stopped on the shores of Japan: The writing of *haiku* is international, even attempted in Western languages.

ON A WITHERED BRANCH

First published: "Kareeda ni," between 1673 and 1680 (Makoto Ueda's
English translation, 1970)
Type of work: Poem

The small black body of a crow on a dead tree limb is contrasted with the dull darkness of an autumn night.

"On a withered branch" is a well-known *haiku* written by Bashō during the developing stage of his career. During this period, from 1673 to 1680, he often used the technique of the surprising comparison. Coming fairly early in his career, the poem also contains elements characteristic of some earlier work in which the poem was intended to amuse with puns, or play on words. Both in identifying wordplay and in counting syllables, English translations can rarely render the poem satisfactorily. One must see the Japanese version to understand some of the important elements of the *haiku*:

Kareeda ni	On a withered branch
Karasu no tomari keri	A Crow is perched—
Aki no kure	Autumn evening.

Kareeda, translated as "withered," is understood to be a "dead" branch, thus providing a contrast with the living bird perched upon it. The word *karasu* ("crow") is the same as the transitive verb form *karasu*, meaning "to cause to wither" or "to kill," thus showing some wordplay typical of Bashō's early work. *Tomari* ("perched") signifies stopping or staying, as a temporary stopover at a hotel. *Keri* is an example of the "cutting word"; a literal translation would be simply "crow's perch." There is no word for "is." Thus, the *keri* leaves the relationship of the perched crow to the poem's next line vague and impersonal. The autumn nightfall is simply juxtaposed with the preceding concept, allowing readers to make their own connections. The Japanese lines follow a 5-9-5 pattern rather than the typical 5-7-5: ka-re-e-da-ni, ka-ra-su-no-to-ma-ri-ke-ri, and a-ki-no-ku-re.

The image of the small (relative to a tree) living crow, with shiny black feathers, perched on the dead tree limb, provides an interesting contrast with the dull darkness of nightfall on an autumn evening. The darkness of the night is of a very different order of blackness from that of the bird. Another convention of the *haiku*, the "season-word," is provided by the reference to autumn. Autumn, also the "fall" of the year, suggests the dying period of the year, even as the tree limb is a dead one.

Altogether, the images come together to evoke a certain kind of loneliness as the outline of the crow is viewed against the background of the immense universe.

THE SEA DARKENS

First published: "Umi kurete," c. 1685 (Makoto Ueda's English translation, 1970)
Type of work: Poem

As night approaches, the call of a wild duck is interpreted in terms of color rather than sound.

"The sea darkens" belongs to a period of Bashō's career in which he was searching for his unique identity as a poet. Most critics agree that he reached at this stage a peak level in the composition of *haiku*. To see how the poem distributes the seventeen syllables among the lines in a 5-5-7 (irregular) pattern, it is necessary to look at the Japanese words:

5	Umi kurete	The sea darkens
5	Kamo no koe	The cries of the wild ducks
7	Homokani shiroshi	Are faintly white.

Bashō wrote this *haiku* on the first of his four long journeys. The poem, written on a day spent on the seacoast, appeared in a travel journal of that trip, *Nozarashi kikō* (1698; *The Records of a Weather-Exposed Skeleton*, 1959), in 1698.

Bashō uses synesthesia as a significant convention in this poem. Synesthesia refers to one sense being described in terms of another. Thus, the sound of the duck is described as being a color, white. The cosmic loneliness, or stillness, amid the approaching darkness is broken by the sounds of the ducks flying overhead and is interpreted as "seeing white," so to speak, rather than as "hearing sound." Thus, a vision of the ultimate interrelatedness of all things and events in the universe is captured in this tiny poem.

OLD POND

First published: "Furuike ya," between 1686 and 1691 (W. G. Aston's English translation, 1899)
Type of work: Poem

A frog leaping into an old pond provides a contrast between the small finite and the vast infinite.

"Old Pond" is possibly the best known *haiku* in English translation. Written sometime between 1686 and 1681, it is a product of the poet's peak period. During this time, a number of the poems focused on the manifestation of *sabi*, that objective, nonemotional loneliness so difficult to define clearly in English, or in Japanese, for that matter.

This *haiku* follows the classical pattern of a 5-7-5 arrangement of the seventeen syllables in three lines:

5	Furuike ya	Old pond:
7	Kawazu tobikomu	frog jumps in
5	Mizu no oto	water-sound.

A number of translations have been made of this famous haiku. W. G. Aston's rendition is perhaps among those closest to the actual Japanese wording, and it exemplifies the notion of juxtaposing images without using connecting words.

The colon at the end of the first line denotes the *ya*, or the "cutting word" that separates the subject from the rest of the poem, leaving the reader to make an appropriate association between the elements. The first image here is an ancient, ageless, primeval natural phenomenon, the pond. Possibly for centuries it has existed in stillness—infinite, timeless. In an instant, that quiet is broken by the intrusion of the splash of a small, living (and hence recent, immediate) object. This contrast elicits the accepting, perhaps welcomed, feeling of loneliness as the two elements make contact. Harold G. Henderson provides a Zen interpretation by attributing symbolism to the frog's leap: The jump into the pond symbolizes a sudden leap to *satori*, or spiritual enlightenment.

Summary

Matsuo Bashō is credited with perfecting the *haikai* form, following the lead of such masters as Matsunaga Teitoku and Nishiyama Sōin. It would be largely the efforts of Masaoka Shiki to establish formally the independence of the *hokku*, the opening verse of the *haikai* (linked verse), to form the term *haiku*.

While Bashō never wrote a theory of poetry, his poetic ideas focused on several elements that include, in particular, the concept of the poetic spirit, which is manifested in such qualities as *sabi* (loneliness); *shiori*, a loneliness produced out of the poem's structure, manifested in great flexibility in meaning; slenderness, inspiration, fragrance, plainness, and lightness. *Haiku* need not be logical in its internal structure, but it must be objective and impersonal. Understanding the feelings of the ordinary individual in everyday life was of great importance to Bashō, and this belief is echoed in the subject matter of the *haiku*. Bashō may have anticipated the difficulty that some readers would have understanding some of his *haiku* when he commented that if they could not understand them naturally, they would have trouble understanding them at all.

Bibliography

Aitken, Robert. *A Zen Wave: Bashō's Haiku and Zen*. New York: Weatherhill, 1979.

Campbell, Liberty. *To a Far Province with Bashō*. Pittsburgh: J. Pohl Associates, 1983.

Henderson, Harold G. *An Introduction to Haiku: An Anthology of Poems and Poets from Bashō to Shiki*. Garden City, N.Y.: Doubleday, 1958.

Keene, Donald. *Landscapes and Portraits: Appreciations of Japanese Culture*. Tokyo: Kodansha, 1971.

Miner, Earl. *Japanese Linked Poetry: An Account with Translations of Renga and Haikai Sequences*. Princeton, N.J.: Princeton University Press, 1979.

Sato, Hiroaki. *One Hundred Frogs: From Renga to Haiku to English*. New York: Weatherhill, 1983.

Ueda, Makoto. *Literary and Art Theories in Japan*. Cleveland: The Press of Western Reserve University, 1967.

_____. *Matsuo Bashō*. New York: Twayne, 1970.

_____. *Matsuo Bashō*. Tokyo: Kodansha, 1983.

_____. *Zeami, Bashō, Yeats, Pound: A Study in Japanese and English Poetics.* The Hague: Mouton, 1965.

Victoria Price

W. SOMERSET MAUGHAM

Born: Paris, France
    January 25, 1874
Died: Saint-Jean-Cap-Ferrat, France
    December 16, 1965

Principal Literary Achievement
A prolific novelist, short-story writer, and playwright, Maugham, who wrote unabashedly for popular audiences, was a skilled craftsman and satirist.

Biography

William Somerset Maugham was born in the British Embassy in Paris, France, on January 25, 1874, and was therefore a British subject. French was his first language, however, and he spent much of his life in France. His father, Robert Ormond Maugham, an attorney whose firm, Maugham and Sewell, was located in Paris, was married to Edith Mary Snell Maugham, twenty-one years his junior.

Willie, as Maugham was familiarly called, was the family's fourth son and was reared virtually as an only child. He was six years younger than his next youngest brother Henry Neville, who, with the other two brothers, Frederic Herbert (born in 1866) and Charles Ormond (born in 1865), was sent to the Dover School in England before Willie knew them well.

When Maugham was eight, his mother, suffering from tuberculosis, died a week after bearing another son, who also died. Two and a half years later, Robert Maugham succumbed to cancer, leaving Maugham an orphan. The boy was sent to England to live with his uncle, a stolid, humorless clergyman, in Kent. He attended the junior annex of King's School in Canterbury until he was sixteen. Leaving King's School in 1891, Maugham spent an academic year in Germany, where he enrolled in Heidelberg University to study philosophy and literature. It was there that he had his first homosexual encounters and began to act on the sexual impulses that would help define his life.

Enrolling as a medical student at St. Thomas's Hospital in London in 1892, he received the medical degree in 1897, the year in which his first novel, *Liza of Lambeth* (1897), based on his hospital experiences, was published. England was still gripped by Victorian prudery. In 1895, Oscar Wilde was convicted under the Sexual Offenses Act of 1867 of having sexual liaisons with Alfred Lord Douglas and was sentenced to a prison term. This conviction sent a chill through the homosexual world and caused

the homosexual minority, including Maugham, to become more repressed than ever before.

With the publication of *Liza of Lambeth*, Maugham abandoned his medical career to pursue writing. For the next six years, during which he traveled extensively in Spain and Italy, his writing received little notice. His books, which included *The Making of a Saint* (1898), *Orientations* (1899), *The Hero* (1901), *Mrs. Craddock* (1902), *The Merry-Go-Round* (1904), *The Land of the Blessed Virgin* (1905) (also known as *Andalusia*, 1920), *The Bishop's Apron* (1906), *The Explorer* (1907), and *The Magician* (1908), attracted small audiences but are meaningful because they affirm the fact that Maugham never stopped writing. His first really successful novel was the autobiographical *Of Human Bondage* (1915).

Maugham's first play, *A Man of Honour*, was performed in 1903. In 1907, his play *Lady Frederick* had its premiere at the Royal Court Theatre, and a year later, Maugham had three other plays—*Jack Straw*, *Mrs. Dot*, and *The Explorer*—running in London.

In 1906, Maugham began an affair with Sue (Ethelwyn Sylvia) Jones that lasted for almost eight years. When she declined to marry him, he began a liaison with Syrie Wellcome that culminated in his marrying her in 1916. She divorced him in 1927; they had one daughter, Lisa, born in 1915.

During the first year of World War I, Maugham served in a British ambulance unit in France. At about the time *Of Human Bondage* was published, he was moved to Military Intelligence in Geneva. During 1916, he and Gerald Haxton, whom he had met during his service in the ambulance unit and whom he called the most significant male love of his life, traveled to the South Seas, where Maugham first saw Paul Gauguin's paintings and found the germ of his novel *The Moon and Sixpence* (1919).

After the publication of *The Moon and Sixpence*, Maugham returned to the South Seas and embarked on several years of world travel. Now that his writing was reaching extensive audiences, his literary future seemed assured. The year after Maugham was divorced from Syrie, he purchased Villa Mauresque at Saint-Jean-Cap-Ferrat in southern France, near Nice. Except for the six years he lived in the United States during World War II, Maugham spent the rest of his life at Villa Mauresque, although he traveled abroad for about half of every year.

After settling into his new estate, Maugham wrote *Cakes and Ale* (1930), generally considered his most successful novel. In 1933, he stopped writing for the theater and concentrated on novels, short stories, and autobiographical works, producing some thirty books between 1928 and his death in 1965. The most noted of these were *The Summing Up* (1938), *Strictly Personal* (1941), *The Razor's Edge* (1944), and *A Writer's Notebook* (1949). During the 1940's, Maugham, working intermittently in Hollywood, spent his winters in South Carolina and his summers at Edgartown on Cape Cod. *The Razor's Edge* was made into a successful film, and the well-received film *Quartet* (1949), based on four of his short stories, was followed by *Trio* (1950) and *Encore* (1951).

Maugham never recovered fully from his mother's death in 1882, and he frequently dissolved into tears when he thought or spoke about her. He was deeply shaken as well by the death in 1944 of Gerald Haxton, his lifelong friend who had served as his secretary. In 1945, Alan Searle, with whom Maugham had had a love affair that began at about the time Syrie divorced him, became his secretary and continued in that capacity until the writer's demise. Searle handled most of the details of Maugham's day-to-day existence and was sufficiently comforting to him that in 1962 Maugham adopted Searle legally, in part to prevent his daughter and other members of his family from being appointed guardians.

On December 10, 1965, Maugham fell and cut his head. He was taken to a hospital in Nice, his condition became grave, and on December 15 he slipped into a coma. Shortly after midnight, in the early hours of December 16, Alan Searle loaded Maugham into an ambulance and returned him to Villa Mauresque in Saint-Jean-Cap-Ferrat, to die. Death came within the next hour.

Analysis

Somerset Maugham never claimed to be a deep intellectual, a writer in whose work future generations of critics would reveal deep, arcane meaning. Rather, he considered himself a storyteller whose stated objective was to entertain. Perhaps in billing himself thus, Maugham sold himself short. Although a few academic critics—most notably Richard A. Cordell, who wrote seriously about Maugham's work produced from the 1930's until after Maugham's death—paid him more than condescending attention, most have scored his work. Some, like Brigid Brophy, Michael Levey, and Charles Osborne, wrote viciously about him, saying in *Fifty Works of English and American Literature We Could Do Without* (1968) that Maugham worked always "at the frontiers of his meagre imagination" and contending that the talent he possessed was not enough "to sustain one's interest in his narrative." Despite such vitriolic expressions of derision from various quarters, Maugham's writing delighted an enthusiastic reading public for half a century.

That Maugham wrote with a conscious artistry and with remarkably even craftsmanship is undeniable. His reputation suffered in his time from various accusations that had little to do with his artistic achievement, notably his homosexual life-style, his seeming indifference to his daughter, his seeming misogyny, and his supposed anti-Semitism. Ted Morgan, one of his posthumous biographers, fueled anti-Maugham sentiments in his biography, *Maugham* (1980). Morgan demonstrates homophobia and a self-righteous misunderstanding of the role that homosexuality and male friendships played in the author's life. Robert Calder's *Willie: The Life of W. Somerset Maugham* (1989) sets right many of the misapprehensions set forth in Morgan's book, which, although thoroughly researched and well written, proceeds from such a biased point of view as to be frequently misleading.

Maugham is at his best when he writes from his own experience. His most celebrated work, *Of Human Bondage*, is consistently autobiographical. *Liza of Lambeth* grew out of situations Maugham encountered as a medical student. Much of his work focuses on the role of artists in society and on the sacrifices they make for the sake of art. In *The Moon and Sixpence*, for example, Maugham writes about Charles Strickland, a stolid, socially correct British businessman with the requisite wife and children. He secretly yearns to be a painter. Strickland finally leaves his secure life, goes to Paris, and paints. His wife, thinking that he has left her for another woman, follows him, believing she can win him back. When she learns, however, that the mistress with whom she is competing is art, she has to admit defeat. She returns to England and Strickland goes off to the South Seas, much as the painter Paul Gaugin had done, there to live the remainder of his life painting the lustrous scenes of his land of heart's desire.

Maugham certainly had experienced the emotions he attributes to Charles Strickland. In his mid-forties, he was married to a woman with whom he had a child out of wedlock. He also had a homosexual lover and was obsessed by a burning desire to travel as much as he could. He was a successful writer who had a distinct plan for the remainder of his creative life, but that plan was not really consistent with the life he found himself living.

Maugham knew that the life of an artist, no matter how successful, is always a precarious one. He had lived through Oscar Wilde's disgrace and had seen this notable playwright and salon dandy ruined both personally and financially by his conviction for committing homosexual acts. Over and above this, Maugham was never sure of the love of other people. Had not his mother, who loved him dearly, abandoned him by dying when he was eight years old?

Maugham's stories often focus on artists struggling to be artists, as in his notable short story "The Alien Corn," in which the protagonist, George, refuses to stand for Parliament because he wants to be a pianist. Philip Carey, the protagonist in *Of Human Bondage*, faces the struggle of justifying himself as the artist he needs to be.

Perhaps Maugham's incredible and steady productivity was part of his daily struggle to justify himself. Nuances in much of his writing suggest this, and a letter from Maugham to the French scholar Paul Dottin written on October 23, 1927, clearly outlines what Maugham hoped to accomplish artistically in the next decade. He was beginning to have a sense of his own mortality—he would turn sixty-five in 1939—and he outlined for Dottin his literary plans for the years before he reached that age.

He told Dottin that he hoped to write three short stories to accompany the three others that came to constitute *Six Stories Written in the First Person Singular* (1931); a novel set in the Malay, which became *The Narrow Corner* (1932); another book of short stories that did not materialize; a book set in Spain, which became *Don Fernando* (1935); a book of Malay stories, resulting in *Ah King* (1933); a picaresque English novel, *Cakes and Ale* (1930); and a final volume written to assess his work and life, *The Summing Up* (1938). Few authors have made such long-range, systematic plans; the few who have have not adhered to them as doggedly as Maugham did.

Maugham did not foresee, apparently, that by 1938 he would write four more books other than those on his outline: *Ashenden: Or, The British Agent* (1928), *The Gentleman in the Parlour* (1930), *Cosmopolitans* (1936), and *Theatre* (1937). He also failed to realize that he would live for twenty-seven years after the publication of *The Summing Up* and would produce a score of books in those years.

Maugham surmises in *The Summing Up* that his position in literary history is not likely to be a secure one. He notes that few serious critics have analyzed his work and that "clever young men who write about fiction" do not include him in their considerations. Despite such expressions, Maugham's stock rose considerably in his later years and has gained even more ground since his death. Two major bibliographies, one of his writing and one of Maugham criticism, appeared in the early 1970's. At least ten scholarly books about him have been published since 1970, and scholarly articles about him continue to appear in recognized journals.

OF HUMAN BONDAGE

First published: 1915
Type of work: Novel

Philip Carey, after the loss of his mother, undergoes a difficult education that leads to his accepting life as a compromise.

Of Human Bondage, published when Maugham had just ended his fourth decade, was a highly polished, considerably more mature book than its unpublished antecedent, "The Artistic Temperament of Steven Carey," written during a sojourn in Spain and unpublished first because Maugham did not want it published at once, and later because no publisher would accept it. Any disappointment that ensued from that book's rejection was well assuaged over the succeeding years when Maugham—now a mature writer with considerable experience in writing plays, short stories, and novels—returned to the manuscript around 1911 and began to rewrite it, this time renaming the protagonist Philip Carey. The result was *Of Human Bondage*, probably Maugham's best-known novel and certainly among his two or three most artistically successful ones. The philosophical scope of this book far exceeds that of the earlier version, presumably because Maugham had now matured into middle age.

By this time he realized that he did his best writing when he wrote about his own experience. Also by this time, he had experienced considerable success as a playwright and was able to apply to his prose writing some of the techniques he had learned as a dramatist, thereby bringing greater dramatic tension into his fiction.

Philip Carey's story, with certain artistic alterations, is Maugham's own story. The novel opens when the young Philip is informed of his mother's death. The boy went to his mother's closet, just as young Willie did, and wrapped his arms around as many of her dresses as possible, burying his face in them, inhaling the lingering vestiges of his mother's perfume. Like Maugham, Philip is soon sent to England to live with his uncle, a vicar, and his Aunt Louisa. Philip differs from Willie in that he has a club foot, but this touch is simply a substitution for Willie's affliction: stuttering. The young Maugham stuttered badly, particularly after the death of his parents, and suffered from this problem throughout his life. As Philip was abused by the students and masters of the school he attended at Tercanberry, so was Maugham ridiculed for his stuttering by his masters and fellow students at King's School.

Through Philip, Maugham broaches the question of his own loss of religious faith. Young Philip hears that if one prays fervently enough, all one's prayers will be answered. When he puts this guarantee to the test by praying as fervently as he can that his club foot will be made whole, his prayers are not answered. This disappointment unleashes a doubt that finally causes Philip to reject the religion in which he has been reared.

Now, no longer willing to tolerate the brutality of his school masters, Philip goes to Heidelberg to study. It is there, in his close association with two intelligent friends and his immersion in the study of philosophy, that Philip disabuses himself of the notion that there is a God. He finds this revelation liberating. On his return to England, he meets Gertrude, his aunt's German friend, and with her has his first sexual experience.

Philip is expected to be practical and to become self-supporting. He tries accounting but finds it unbearable. Reminiscent of Strickland in *The Moon and Sixpence*, Philip flees to Paris, where he studies art for two years, only to conclude that his talent is insufficient to justify further study.

Needing to find a way to support himself, Philip returns to England and, although his uncle opposes it, becomes a medical student at St. Thomas's Hospital, there meeting Mildred Rogers, a waitress at a nearby restaurant. He has an affair with her, but it ends when Mildred runs off with someone else. Then Mildred returns and announces that she is pregnant. Philip takes her in, imposing upon himself one of the bondages referred to in the book's title. Mildred, like Sue Jones in Maugham's own life, is less interested in him than he is in her.

When Mildred returns to stay with Philip, however, he has just met Norah Nesbitt, who is more interested in him than he is in her. As soon as Mildred leaves again, Philip seeks out Norah only to find that she has now made plans to marry someone else. Mildred, now a streetwalker, returns yet again, and Philip takes her in, but they obviously have no future together, and Mildred finally leaves for good.

When Philip's old Parisian friend, Cronshaw, dies, Philip recalls Cronshaw's comment that the meaning of life can be found in a Persian rug. He muses that life has no inherent pattern, that it is up to each individual to find a pattern and impose it upon life.

Finally, almost by default, Philip falls into an affair with Sally, the daughter of his friends, the Athelnys. After a scare that Sally might be pregnant proves to be groundless, Philip decides that he wants to marry her even though he does not love her. He needs the pattern that such a marriage will provide, just as Maugham apparently sought a similar pattern in his abortive marriage to Syrie Wellcome.

A major theme that emerges from *Of Human Bondage* is the futility of human relationships. Humans, having only themselves to depend upon, make compromise after compromise searching for the patterns that give order to their lives. Maugham's agnosticism and some of his cynicism about humanity are important elements in this novel.

THE RAZOR'S EDGE

First published: 1944
Type of work: Novel

Larry Darrell, an enigmatic young man, is involved in a spiritual quest that intrigues and mystifies those around him.

The Razor's Edge is quite similar to T. S. Eliot's *The Cocktail Party* (1949). Celia Copplestone is a uniquely spiritual person surrounded by a group of people who have no notion of what she is about. Larry Darrell is the fiancé of Isabel, the niece of Elliott Templeton, who invites Mr. Maugham (referred to hereafter as *Mr. Maugham* to distinguish the character from author W. Somerset Maugham), who is visiting in Chicago, to dinner. Templeton is an old friend of Mr. Maugham, who that evening meets Templeton's niece Isabel, her mother Sophie (a friend of the family), and Gray, who eventually will marry Isabel.

Darrell, having just returned from the war, lives very much in his own world, surrounding himself with an invisible carapace that outsiders quickly realize they cannot penetrate. The air of mystery that surrounds Larry intrigues Mr. Maugham, who is impressed and curious to know more about him.

Soon Mr. Maugham learns that Larry has postponed his impending marriage to Isabel to go abroad, first to Paris and then to the East in an attempt to find the meaning of life, much as Celia Copplestone goes off to Kinkanja to seek her destiny. Further into the novel, Mr. Maugham also learns that Larry has come face-to-face with death in the war and that one of his close friends died saving him. A sensitive person, Larry has to find answers before he can get on with his life.

Throughout the rest of the novel, Maugham carries his readers with him, involving them intimately in Larry's quest but sharing with them, both as the author and as a character in his own novel, an inability to reach the spiritual pinnacle that Larry finally achieves. Although the novel is about Larry Darrell, readers learn little about him. He reveals little of himself and, in chapter 6, when the author records a conversation that Mr. Maugham had with Larry, he begins the chapter by telling his readers that they can skip it without losing the thread of the story. He goes on to say that had he not had this conversation, he would not have written *The Razor's Edge*.

It is a novel of spiritual quest, much as *The Moon and Sixpence* and *Cakes and Ale* were. *The Razor's Edge*, however, is more mystical than those novels. When he was working on this book, Maugham himself was on a quest that led him to consult his friend Christopher Isherwood and Isherwood's guru, Swami Prabhavananda, to find the precise meaning of a passage in the *Katha Upanishad* (c. 1000 B.C.), that was, indeed, rendered "the razor's edge" or "the edge of the razor." The razor, in this *Upanishad*, represents a narrow, painful path. Swami Prabhavananda equated it with enlightenment. He pointed out that some translations suggest that the path is difficult to cross, whereas the real problem is that of discovering how to walk upon the razor's edge. The Eastern mysticism in this novel represents a turning for Maugham and reminds one of *The Cocktail Party* and of E. M. Forster's *A Passage to India* (1924), a book Maugham did not particularly admire.

The particular skill Maugham demonstrates in this book is his ability to engage his readers in a mysterious quest in which he and his readers are both participants, all of them functioning on an equal basis. This device of engagement is unique and, in this case, highly successful, although it is a device that puts an author at risk because it could easily veer out of control. That Maugham could control it masterfully is evidence of an artistic advancement in a writer who was entering the eighth decade of his life. The amazing thing about Larry is that, once having achieved his spiritual quest, he can return to New York City—perhaps to support himself as a taxicab driver—and rise above the materialism and corruption in what was then the world's largest city. Maugham allows Larry to shape the pattern in his Persian rug much as Maugham had been trying to do.

RAIN

First published: 1921
Type of work: Short story

The Reverend Mr. Davidson sets out to reform the beautiful prostitute Sadie Thompson, but, overcome by his repressed desires, finally rapes her.

Originally titled "Sadie Thompson," "Rain" was the second story in Maugham's collection, *The Trembling of a Leaf* (1921). Clearly his most famous short story, in 1925 it was turned into a highly successful drama, adapted by John Colton and Clarence Randolph, that ran for 648 performances on Broadway. The story is a finely tuned satire in which Maugham depicts the hypocrisy of conventional morality in devastating terms. He found his material for "Rain" on a trip he took with Gerald Haxton in 1916. The two sailed from San Francisco, first to Hawaii, then, aboard the *Sonoma*, to Pago Pago in Samoa. Among the passengers on board was a Miss Thompson, a prostitute from Honolulu who had, as it turned out, fled Hawaii after a police raid on the establishment in which she worked. She hoped that she could ply her trade in Western Samoa.

Using Miss Thompson's actual last name and giving her the first name "Sadie," Maugham wove an exceptionally well-balanced story involving two couples, Dr. and Mrs. McPhail and the Reverend Mr. and Mrs. Davidson, who became fast friends on a long, transpacific journey. They share a condescending attitude toward their fellow passengers, particularly those not traveling in first class. Dr. McPhail, a medical doctor, is about forty.

When the *Sonoma* is quarantined in Pago Pago, the McPhails and the Davidsons are housed, with their fellow passengers, in a hotel. They soon become aware of Sadie Thompson's presence because boisterous laughing and loud music come from her room. Davidson decides that it is his duty to reform the unregenerate Sadie, and he goes about his task with a missionary zeal of which the two women approve but that Dr. McPhail views with some suspicion, despite his admiration for the clergy-man, who, unlike the retiring and timid doctor, is stout-hearted, self-assured, and stalwart.

Throwing himself fully into the moral challenge before him, Davidson, a trem-bling mass of repressed desire, finally rapes Sadie. The aftermath of this assault is an uncontrollable guilt that results in the clergyman's committing suicide. As the story ends, music and laughter drift in from Sadie's room. Sadie can be heard complaining that all men are beasts.

In this story, Maugham is in total control, balancing his characters against each other with an admirable precision. McPhail is the moderate. His wife is in the David-sons' camp, and the Davidsons, of course, know what righteousness is and are deter-mined to make everyone righteous whether they desire salvation or not. The ironies in the story contribute to a tightly constructed plot that, on a philosophical level, turns out to be quite profound.

This story, more than anything else Maugham wrote, is an encomium to those who hover around the bottom of the social ladder, people such as Liza in *Liza of Lambeth* or Mildred in *Of Human Bondage*. Perhaps as he developed the character of David-son, Maugham thought back to the days when he lived with his cleric uncle in Whit-stable or when he bore the taunts of his self-righteous masters at King's School.

THE ALIEN CORN

First published: 1931
Type of work: Short story

A Jewish youth rejoices in his ethnicity. Refusing to stand for Parliament, he goes to Germany to study music, then, realizing his mediocrity, commits suicide.

"The Alien Corn" is included in Maugham's short-story collection *Six Stories Writ-ten in the First Person Singular* (1931), and is a telling story in terms of what it reveals about the author's values and concerns. It has echoes in it of the Fannie Price incident in *Of Human Bondage*. The story was adapted for film in 1949 as one of the four parts of *Quartet* (1949).

The story has to do with a Jewish family trying hard not to appear Jewish. Sir Adolphus Bland, who calls himself Freddy and whose name was originally Alphonse Bleikogel, is the nephew of Ferdy Rabenstein, a flamboyant patron of the arts. Freddy owns a period mansion in Sussex and has acquired the trappings of elegance. His son, George, is the apple of his eye.

George, unlike his younger brother, does not look Jewish, but ironically, he does not want to pass as a Gentile and cherishes his Jewish heritage. His brother, who does not want to appear Jewish, looks Jewish. George has just finished his studies at Oxford, and it is assumed that he will return to Sussex and live the life of a gentleman, standing for election to Parliament in a race he would likely win.

George, however, wants to be a concert pianist and announces that he plans to go to Munich to study music. He quarrels animatedly with his father over dinner and finally, breaking down in tears, moves the rest of the family to tears.

George's grandmother, the sister of Ferdy, volunteers to give George five pounds a week to enable him to study music as he wishes. She will finance him for two years, but if, at the end of that period, he is not judged excellent, he will return to Sussex and, in accordance with his father's wishes, stand for Parliament. Thus subsidized, George goes to Germany and studies for the agreed-upon period. When his time there expires, he is judged, like Fanny Price, not to have exceptional ability, and it is evident that he will have to return home. Rather than do that, he kills himself.

The theme of this story—the struggling artist—is one to which Maugham returned several times during his lifetime. In *Of Human Bondage*, Philip Carey goes to Paris to study art and is, like George and Fanny, found wanting. He lives with this defeat and accepts compromises that enable him to live. In *The Moon and Sixpence*, Charles Strickland goes to Paris to study art and succeeds, but the price he pays is exile and the loss of his family. Maugham, who long feared that he was a mediocre writer, as many statements in *The Summing Up* reveal, had only one desire in life: to write. He was certainly familiar with the uncertainties and insecurities he wrote about in "The Alien Corn."

Some critics have accused Maugham of anti-Semitism and have read such a bias into "The Alien Corn." This story obviously considers the problems of Jews who try to fit into mainstream society and who, in doing so, deny their heritage. Maugham, however, is reporting a common social phenomenon and, in this story, does so objectively and amiably.

Summary

W. Somerset Maugham was a highly competent dramatist who succeeded best in his fiction after he had learned to apply the devices he had used successfully in drama to other genres. His novels prior to *Of Human Bondage* lacked the dramatic tension and thematic intensity of such works as that autobiographical novel and of such later novels as *The Moon and Sixpence*, *Cakes and Ale*, and *The Razor's Edge*. If sophisticated literary scholars found his work disappointing, the general readers whom he defined as his audience read his novels and short stories with considerable appreciation and enthusiasm. In their eyes, he was a highly successful author who entertained them genially and who, in novels like those mentioned in the preceding paragraph, caused them to think.

Bibliography

Burt, Forrest D. *W. Somerset Maugham*. Boston: Twayne, 1985.

Calder, Robert. *W. Somerset Maugham and the Quest for Freedom*. London: Heinemann, 1972.

——————. *Willie: The Life of W. Somerset Maugham*. London: Heinemann, 1989.

Cordell, Richard A. *Somerset Maugham; a Writer for All Seasons: A Biographical and Critical Study*. 2d ed. Bloomington: Indiana University Press, 1969.

Maugham, Robin. *Somerset and All the Maughams*. New York: New American Library, 1966.

Maugham, W. Somerset. *The Summing Up*. London: Heinemann, 1938.

Morgan, Ted. *Maugham*. New York: Simon & Schuster, 1980.

Sanders, Charles, ed. *W. Somerset Maugham: An Annotated Bibliography of the Writings About Him*. DeKalb: Northern Illinois University Press, 1970.

Stott, Raymond Toole. *A Bibliography of the Works of W. Somerset Maugham*. London: Kaye & Ward, 1973.

R. Baird Shuman

GUY DE MAUPASSANT

Born: Château de Miromesnil, near Dieppe, France
August 5, 1850
Died: Passy, France
July 6, 1893

Principal Literary Achievement

Maupassant helped move the short-story form away from the primitive folk-tale to modern psychological realism in the early twentieth century.

Biography

Born on August 5, 1850, in the imposing Château de Miromesnil, near Dieppe, France, Henri-René-Albert-Guy de Maupassant was the first son of Laure Le Poittevin and Gustave de Maupassant. Although both parents were from fairly well-to-do families, they were only renting the château where Guy de Maupassant was born. According to biographers, he probably was born in a small house nearby but was immediately taken to the château so his birth announcements would look more impressive. When the boy was eleven, his parents were legally separated, and he spent most of his youth with his mother, who became a powerful influence on his life.

As a member of the upper middle class, Maupassant was enrolled at a school suitable for him, a small seminary near Rouen. The place, however, was not to the boy's liking, and he purposely got himself expelled before completing school. After returning home to his mother, he fell under the tutelage of his uncle Alfred and a friend of the family who was later to become his most famous and important influence, the writer Gustave Flaubert.

When he was eighteen, Maupassant tried to complete his education by enrolling at Lycée de Rouen, but his law studies were disrupted soon after by his enlistment in the Franco-Prussian War. As a result of his military experience, he was able to get a position after the war as a clerk in the Naval Ministry in Paris, where his primary job was the supervision of printing supplies. Yet his real ambition was to be a writer, and under the guidance of Flaubert he began publishing his poetry and stories in a number of small journals. His work was also encouraged by his membership in an informal group of writers who met at Flaubert's house and included Émile Zola, Alphonse Daudet, and Ivan Turgenev. His first story to appear in a published book was in a collection of stories by various writers, including Zola; it is a story that remains one of his best, "Boule de suif," translated "Roly-Poly" or "Ball of Fat." Because the

1274

story received so much praise from Flaubert, Maupassant was encouraged to quit his government job and spend all of his time writing. He soon realized that his special skill lay in the area of the *conte*, or short story, a form that was highly popular at the time in newspapers and magazines. Like his American counterpart O. Henry, and his Russian counterpart Anton Chekhov, Maupassant learned to master the short-story form by writing anecdotal sketches and articles for newspapers.

Maupassant's first collection of short stories was published in 1881, taking its title from the longest story in the collection, "La Maison Tellier," translated as "Madame Tellier's House" or "Madame Tellier's Establishment." The book was a commercial success and made Maupassant's name so well known that his work was soon solicited by many additional newspapers and magazines. In the following twelve years, Maupassant published twelve collections of short stories, six novels, and two plays. Of the 250 short stories that he published during his relatively brief career, Maupassant is probably best known for such ironic-ending stories as "La Parure" ("The Necklace") and "La Ficelle" ("A Piece of String"), although at the time that his stories were published he received the most attention for what was called his unwholesome naturalistic presentation of peasant characters and street people. In addition to his anecdotal, surprise-ending tales and his realistic stories of the lower class, Maupassant also mastered the mystery tale, a form that he helped to bring out of the nineteenth century and into the modern era by making what was previously presented as supernatural events the result of hallucinatory experiences of obsessed narrators.

The years 1883 and 1884 were high-water marks in Maupassant's career, for during this period he published his first novel, *Une Vie* (1883; *A Woman's Life*, 1888), and his most famous short story, "The Necklace"—a story so well known that it has become synonymous for many readers with the short-story form as a genre. By this time, however, Maupassant had already contracted the disease of syphilis, which was to take his life. In an era before the discovery of penicillin, there was little that the medical profession could do for him except to watch helplessly as he showed increasing signs of mental disintegration.

After 1890, Maupassant was unable to continue his writing, for his eyesight began to fail, he suffered from severe migraine headaches, his memory faded, and he suffered from delusions. He tried futilely to recuperate through a sea voyage and a stay on the Riviera, but in 1892 he attempted to kill himself and had to be taken to a sanatorium in a straitjacket. On July 6, 1893, a month short of his forty-third birthday, Maupassant died, in Passy, France.

Analysis

Maupassant occupies an ambiguous place in the history of modern literature. On the one hand, his short fiction has been disparaged as, at its best, mere trickery, and at its worst, probable pornography. O. Henry, who was highly influenced by Maupassant, bridled at comparisons with Maupassant, saying he did not wish to be compared with a "filthy writer." On the other hand, the Russian short-story writer Isaac Babel gladly acknowledged his debt to Maupassant by devoting one of his best short stories to him, acknowledging that Maupassant knew the power of a period put in just the right place. At the end of the nineteenth century, only Chekhov loomed larger than Maupassant as a powerful influence on the short-story form. In fact, British short-story writer A. E. Coppard once said that if he ever edited a collection of stories, it would be an easy job, for half would be by Chekhov and half by Maupassant.

In the range of short-fiction subtypes, it is obvious that Maupassant's work falls on the side of the patterned anecdote, while Chekhov's work is more impressionistic and lyrical. Whereas Chekhov's stylized realism has influenced such twentieth century writers as Sherwood Anderson, Ernest Hemingway, and Raymond Carver, Maupassant has influenced the work of such short-story masters as Eudora Welty, Flannery O'Connor, and Bernard Malamud. Maupassant falls somewhere in between writers such as Turgenev and Chekhov, who are admired for their lyricism and realism, and writers such a Ambrose Bierce and O. Henry, who are scorned for what are called narrative tricks. On the one hand, he had the ability, like Chekhov, to focus in a highly perceptive way on a small group of characters in a meaningful and revealing situation; on the other hand, like Bierce, he was able to create tight little ironic masterpieces that depend, as all short stories do, on the impact of a luminous ending. Maupassant perfected the technique originated by Edgar Allan Poe, and continued by modern short-story writers as seemingly diverse as Hemingway and Malamud, of creating a fictional realm in which everyday reality takes on a hallucinatory effect and hallucination assumes the concreteness of the physical world. It is unfortunate that, like his predecessor Poe, his life-style often receives more attention than his work.

MADAME TELLIER'S HOUSE

First published: "La Maison Tellier," 1881 (English translation, 1903)
Type of work: Short story

A group of prostitutes attend the First Communion of the Madame's niece in a small French village and are welcomed as if they are fine ladies.

"Madame Tellier's House" (sometimes translated as "Madame Tellier's Excursion") is often called Maupassant's masterpiece, although it is not as generally well known as his ironic-ending story "La Parure" ("The Necklace") or his psychological thriller "Le Horla ("The Horla"). Written while he was still under the influence of his mentor Gustave Flaubert, the story is unlike his later works in that it depends more on realistic detail and detached comic tone than on anecdote and narrative irony. The story begins with a brief portrait of Madame Tellier, who, although she keeps a house of prostitution, is herself quite virtuous. The girls in the house are described as the epitome of each feminine type so that each customer might find the realization of his ideal: the countrygirl blond, the mysterious Jewess, the plump "ball of fat," and two others representing the classic French and the classic Spanish woman.

The central event of the story is a simple one. The Madame is invited to the First Communion of her little niece, and since she cannot leave her frequently quarreling girls alone, she closes the brothel and takes them all to the country with her. The arrival of the prostitutes in the small town is a classic comic scene as they march down the street in their flashy elegance while the townspeople peek out their windows in amazement. It is the scene in the church during the communion, however, that constitutes the center of the story. Remembering their own communions, the prostitutes begin to cry. Soon, throughout the church, wives, mothers, and sisters are struck by a pervasive sympathy, and everyone begins to cry. Something superhuman pervades the church, a "powerful breath of an invisible and all-powerful being." It is as though the Holy Spirit has visited the occupants of the modest country church, a "species of madness" that passes over the people like a gust of wind. Thus, a more general communion than that of the niece is effected, and all are united in harmony and peace.

At the end of the story, the prostitutes return to Madame Tellier's house and to their lives there, not with a sense of guilt but with a sense of having had a holiday that makes it possible for them to return to work refreshed and rested. The quarrels that formerly plagued the house no longer exist, for a true sisterhood is affirmed. Only Maupassant could carry off such a potentially sentimental situation as the whores crying in church about their lost innocence and not have it lapse into banal sentimentality. It is his genuine identification with the prostitutes, his refusal to reduce them to objects of either pity or ridicule, and his consequent elevation of them, with no hint of sarcasm, to the rank of true ladies that makes the story a masterpiece of comic realism.

THE NECKLACE

First published: "La Parure," 1884 (English translation, 1903)
Type of work: Short story

A young woman loses a borrowed necklace, works for ten years to pay for it, and then discovers that it was made of paste.

What makes Maupassant's famous story "The Necklace" so popular is not merely the ironic shock that the reader feels at the end when Madame Loisel discovers that she has worked long and hard to pay for a worthless bit of paste, but rather the more pervasive irony that underlies the entire story and makes it a classic exploration on the difference between surface flash and hidden value.

The story begins with a pretty young girl who thinks she is really a lady, and who feels that she needs only the external trappings of her true status. Although she is married to a simple clerk, she acts as though she has fallen from her proper station; she feels that she was born for luxuries but must endure poverty. Determined to make the best of an opportunity when she and her husband are invited to an elegant party, she borrows a necklace from an acquaintance to impress those not easily impressed and, like Cinderella at the ball, has all of her desires fulfilled as she is transported into the fairy-tale world about which she has dreamed. All of this comes crashing down to reality, however, when she reaches home and discovers that the necklace is missing. Her husband exhausts his meager inheritance and then borrows the rest, mortgaging their life away to buy a replacement for the necklace.

Now that Madame Loisel knows true poverty, she shows herself to be made of something more valuable than her petty desires for surface flash have suggested. With heroism and pride, she shoulders her responsibility with her husband and for ten years does brutal manual labor until she has paid for the necklace. When the reader discovers that the necklace was made of paste, it is a momentary shock; on closer reflection, this final knowledge proves to be anticlimactic, for one realizes that the story is about deeper ironies. What was taken to be real is found to be false. What looked rich on the outside is actually very poor. Yet Madame Loisel, who has looked poor on the outside, turns out to be genuine inside. "The Necklace" is a classic example of the tight ironic structure of the short story in which the unified tone dominates every single word.

THE HORLA

First published: "Le Horla," 1887 ("The Horla," 1890)
Type of work: Short story

A man slowly goes mad as he is seemingly possessed by an occult external force.

"The Horla," a story almost as famous as "The Necklace," is often considered the first sign of the syphilis-caused madness that eventually led to Maupassant's death. As a story of psychological horror, however, it is actually the pinnacle of several stories of madness with which Maupassant had experimented previously. The predominant mode of these stories is not the manifestation of the ghostly supernatural in the traditional sense; rather, the focus is on some mysterious dimension of reality that exists beyond what the human senses can perceive.

Told by means of diary entries, the story charts the protagonist's growing awareness of his own madness, as well as his understanding of the process whereby the external world is displaced by psychic projections. The narrator begins considering the mystery of the invisible, the weakness of the senses to perceive all that is in the world, and the theory that if there were other senses, one could discover many more things about the reality that surrounds human life. Another predominant Maupassant theme here is that of apprehension, a sense of some imminent danger, a presentiment of something yet to come. This apprehension, which the narrator calls a disease, is accompanied by nightmares, a sense of some external force suffocating him while he sleeps, and the conviction that there is something following him.

This sense of something existing outside the self but not visible to the ordinary senses is pushed even further when the narrator begins to believe that there are actual creatures who exist in this invisible dimension. This conviction is then developed into an idea that, when the mind is asleep, an alien being takes control of the body and makes it obey. All of these ideas lead easily into the concept of mesmerism or hypnotism; under hypnosis, it seems as if an alien being has control of an individual's actions, of which, upon awakening, he or she has no awareness. Although the narrator doubts his sanity, he also feels that he is in complete possession of all of his faculties, and he becomes even more convinced that an invisible creature is making him do things that his own mind does not direct him to do. Thus, he finally believes that there are Invisible Ones in the world, creatures who have always existed and who have haunted humankind even though they cannot be seen.

The final event that persuades him of the external, as opposed to the psychological, existence of the creatures is a newspaper article about an epidemic of madness in Brazil, in which people seem possessed by vampire-like creatures that feed on them during sleep. He remembers a Brazilian ship that sailed past his window and believes that one of the creatures has jumped ship to possess him. Now he knows that the reign of humanity on earth is over and that the forces of the Horla, which humankind has always feared—forces called spirits, jinn, fairies, hobgoblins, witches, devils, and imps—will enslave the world.

Finally, he "sees" the creature in the mirror when its presence blurs his own image by coming between him and the mirror. He decides to destroy the creature by locking it in his room and burning his house to the ground. As he watches the house burn and realizes that his servants are burning too, he wonders if indeed the Horla is dead, for he considers that it cannot, like a human being, be prematurely destroyed. His final thought is that, since the Horla is not dead, he will have to kill himself; the story ends with that decision.

What makes "The Horla" distinctive is the increasing need of the narrator to account for his madness as being caused by something external to himself. Such a desire is Maupassant's way of universalizing the story, for he well knew that human beings have always tried to embody their most basic desires and fears in some external but invisible presence. "The Horla" is a masterpiece of hallucinatory horror because it focuses so powerfully on that process of mistaking inner reality for outer reality, which is indeed the very basis of hallucination.

Summary

Guy de Maupassant had as much to do with the development of the short-story genre in the late nineteenth century as Anton Chekhov did, albeit in somewhat different ways. Yet because such stories as "The Necklace" are so deceptively simple and seem trivial, Maupassant's experiment with the form has often been ignored. Not until the short story itself receives the recognition that it deserves as a respectable literary genre will Maupassant receive the recognition that he deserves for his contribution to the perfection of the form.

Bibliography

Ignotus, Paul. *The Paradox of Maupassant.* London: University of London Press, 1966.

Lerner, Michael G. *Maupassant.* New York: George Braziller, 1975.

Steegmuller, Francis. *A Lion in the Path.* New York: Random House, 1949.

Sullivan, Edward. *Maupassant the Novelist.* Princeton, N.J.: Princeton University Press, 1953.

_____. *Maupassant: The Short Stories.* Great Neck, N.Y.: Barron's Education Series, 1962.

Wallace, A. H. *Guy de Maupassant.* New York: Twayne, 1973.

Charles E. May

CZESŁAW MIŁOSZ

Born: Šeteiniai, Lithuania
June 30, 1911

Principal Literary Achievement

Miłosz is a Nobel Prize-winning poet whose work captures both the depths to which human beings have fallen in the twentieth century and the heights to which they continue to aspire.

Biography

Czesław Miłosz was born on June 30, 1911, in Šeteiniai, a small village near Wilno (now Vilnius) in Lithuania to Aleksandr and Weronika (née Kunat) Miłosz, Polish-speaking descendants of Lithuanian gentry. In his autobiography, *Rodzinna Europa* (1958; *Native Realm: A Search for Self-Definition*, 1968), Miłosz reports that his first memories are of exile: Like thousands of other refugees, his family fled Lithuania for Russia when the Germans invaded at the beginning of World War I. After the war, Miłosz's family returned to a rural Lithuania that he describes as steeped in religion, superstition, and nature in his lyrical second novel *Dolina Issy* (1955; *The Issa Valley*, 1981).

Miłosz attended Zygmunt August High School and King Stefan Batory University in Wilno—a city that he often recalls in his poetry—and was a founding member of the poetry group Zagary and its literary magazine. In 1931, he traveled to Paris, where he met the French poet Oscar de L. Milosz, a distant relative whose work and mystical temperament were a major influence on the young Czesław's own intellectual development. In 1933, Miłosz published his first book, *Poemat o czasie zastygłym* (a poem on frozen time). In 1934, he earned a law degree, won an award from the Polish Writers' Union, and received a fellowship that allowed him to spend another year in Paris.

When Miłosz returned to Wilno, he worked at its Polish radio station and published his second book of poems, *Trzy zimy* (1936; three winters). In 1937, he moved to Warsaw, where he joined a group of poets known as the catastrophists because of their apocalyptic view of the future of Europe and Western civilization. In 1939, the catastrophists' worst nightmares were realized when Germany again invaded Poland and the Nazis quickly occupied Warsaw. During the occupation, Miłosz was an active member of the Polish Resistance and a major contributor to the city's elaborate underground culture. He edited *Pieśń niepodlegla* (1942; invincible song), a mim-

eographed anthology of resistance poetry, translated Jacques Maritain's *À travers le désastre* (1941), an attack against French collaboration with the Germans, and wrote poems such as "The World: A Naive Poem" and *The Voices of Poor People*, which were published by the underground presses and passed from hand to hand in the desolated city. When the Communists took power in postwar Poland, a volume of his collected poems, *Ocalenie* (1945; rescue), was one of the first books published by the new government.

As a prominent anti-Nazi, resistance figure, and poet, Miłosz's support was eagerly sought by the new regime. At first, he gave it: Between 1946 and 1950, he served as a Polish cultural attaché to Washington and Paris. In 1951, however, he broke with the government and became an exile in Paris. At a time when most French intellectuals were still enamored of Joseph Stalin and the Soviet Union, Miłosz courageously spoke the unwelcome truth about intellectual life in the East in the essays published as *Zniewolony umysł* (1953; *The Captive Mind* 1953)—a book that the critic Irving Howe has described as a "central text in the modern effort to understand totalitarianism." In the same year, Miłosz's first novel was published in French as *La Prise du pouvoir* (1953; *The Seizure of Power*, 1955), and awarded the prestigious Prix Littéraire Européen.

In 1960, Miłosz accepted a position as a professor of Slavic languages at the University of California at Berkeley and moved to the United States—his final exile—where he continued to live and work. Since 1960, his books have included an anthology of *Postwar Polish Poetry* (1965); *The History of Polish Literature* (1969; numerous books of poetry in Polish, published in *Miasto bez imienia* (1969); *Selected Poems*, 1973), *Bells in Winter* (1978), *The Separate Notebooks* (1984), *Nieobjęta ziemia* (1984; *Unattainable Earth*, 1986), *The Collected Poems, 1931-1987* (1988), and *Provinces* (1991); and three collections of essays, *Emperor of the Earth: Modes of Eccentric Vision* (1977), *Widzenia nad zatoką San Francisco* (1969; *Views from San Francisco Bay*, 1982), and *Ziemia Ulro* (1977; *The Land of Ulro*, 1984). In 1978 Miłosz was awarded the Neustadt International Prize for Literature by the University of Oklahoma. In 1980, he was awarded the Nobel Prize in Literature by the Swedish Academy.

Analysis

In the West, Miłosz observes in *Świadectwo poezji* (1983; *The Witness of Poetry*, 1983), "the separation of art and the public has been an accomplished fact" since the time of Charles Baudelaire. Yet "in Central and Eastern Europe," he wrote thirty years earlier in *The Captive Mind*, "a poet does not merely arrange words in beautiful order. Tradition demands that he be a 'bard,' that his songs linger on many lips, that he speak in his poems of subjects of interest to all the citizens." Czesław Miłosz has himself been such a bard.

For thirty years after Miłosz went into exile in 1951, none of his books was officially published in Communist Poland. Yet during the years that he was an "unperson"—a poet whose name could not be mentioned in print and whose writings had to be circulated in underground samizdat editions and tape recordings—he became Poland's unofficial poet laureate. When Solidarity first emerged and a monument was erected in 1981 to the memory of the Polish workers slain in the Gdansk food strikes of 1970, the words on its base were quite naturally taken from one of his poems: "You who wronged a simple man . . ./ Do not feel safe. The poet remembers/ You can kill one, but another is born./ The words are written down, the deed, the date." When the first officially sanctioned edition of his collected poetry since the war was published in Poland in the same year, two hundred thousand copies sold out within a month.

"The poet remembers. . . ." To Miłosz and his Polish readers, that is more than merely a warning or a promise. It is a definition of vocation. What Miłosz has done in each of his books is, above all, to remember: to keep his and his era's past alive in the present through the power of his words. Because those words have been written mostly in Polish, Miłosz can be read in the United States only in translation. He has always understood this predicament. "The abyss for me was exile," he wrote in *The Captive Mind* shortly after emigrating to the West. "My mother tongue, work in my mother tongue, is for me the most important thing in life." When he finally broke with his country, he says in *The Captive Mind*, he fully expected the consequences to be not merely exile but "sterility and inaction."

"Wrong Honorable Professor Miłosz," he writes sardonically of himself in the poem "A Magic Mountain," "Who wrote poems in some unheard-of tongue./ Who will count them anyway." In one section of the cycle "From the Rising of the Sun," he summarizes his situation with even greater irony and wit. "Oh yes," he writes, "not all of me shall die, there will remain/ An item in the fourteenth volume of an encyclopedia/ Next to a hundred Millers and Mickey Mouse." Nevertheless, Miłosz has remained faithful to both his native language and his Eastern European sense of the poet's vocation. "Whatever I hold in my hand, a stylus, reed, quill or a ballpoint," he announces in the opening section of the same cycle, "Wherever I may be . . . / I attend to matters I have been charged with in the provinces."

Memory has always been his Muse, he declares in the early poem "Magpiety." In his Nobel lecture (1981), he explains why. "Perhaps our most precious acquisition is . . . respect and gratitude for certain things which protect people from internal disintegration and from yielding to tyranny," he writes. Paramount among those things is memory. Yet, he goes on to say, "our planet that gets smaller every year, with its fantastic proliferation of mass media, is witnessing a process that escapes definition, characterized by a refusal to remember." Under these circumstances, he insists, the poet's role must be to see and to describe. Yet " 'To see' means not only to have before one's eyes. It may also mean to preserve in memory. 'To see and to describe' may also mean to reconstruct in imagination."

The reader of Miłosz's poetry is immediately struck by this effort "to reconstruct in imagination," to make memories live again through description. Poem after poem is built of powerful and recurrent images of his Lithuanian boyhood, his World War II youth, and his California émigré adulthood. The poems vary in tone, of course—

many strive to make affirmations in the face of the historical tragedies that he has seen in his long life. The strongest and most memorable poems, however, are those in which he recalls the war years and their aftermath with a survivor's painful guilt.

DEDICATION

First published: 1945 (English translation, 1973)
Type of work: Poem

This keynote poem is one of the first expressions of Miłosz's lifelong commitment to understand and testify to the history and experience of his Europe.

"Dedication," written soon after the occupation and destruction of Warsaw, is an homage to those who died from one who survived. In it, Miłosz acknowledges the difficulty of speaking about the unspeakable, reveals his guilt at having lived to tell the story of those years, and dedicates himself to writing poetry that will grapple with history and memory.

It begins by directly addressing those to whom it is dedicated—"You whom I could not save/ Listen to me"—as if the poet sees them before him and must speak to give their spirits rest. He then confesses his own lack of skill and expresses his decision to abandon the aesthetic of complexity that characterized his prewar writing: "Try to understand this simple speech as I would be ashamed of another./ I swear there is in me no wizardry of words." In the second stanza, he tries to understand why he survived and fails. All he can say is that, somehow, "What strengthened me, for you was lethal." He then recalls the excitement of the prewar years, when the catastrophists and other talented young people, now dead, faced anxiety with energy and art. "You mixed up farewell to an epoch with the beginning of a new one./ Inspiration of hatred with lyrical beauty,/ Blind force with accomplished shape."

The third stanza links the dead with the destroyed city, nearly burned to the ground by the Germans while the Soviet army watched from the opposite bank of the Vistula River. "Here is the valley of shallow Polish rivers. And an immense bridge/ Going into white fog. Here is a broken city." The white fog literally describes the smoldering city; but it also suggests that what lay on the far side of the bridge—the Soviet Army, doing nothing to help—was shrouded in silence in Communist Poland, where official dogma whitewashed the Soviets and made them the city's saviors.

In the fourth stanza, the elegiac tone of the first three stanzas is replaced by an angrier, tougher voice, a voice that seems to rebuke the poet himself, while insisting that after this destruction poetry can never be the same. "What is poetry which does not save/ Nations or people?" the poet asks. He then quickly and absolutely answers his own question: "A connivance with official lies,/ A song of drunkards whose throats will be cut in a moment,/ Readings for sophomore girls." The poet clearly speaks from bitter experience. Only now does he see what poetry must be and do. Moreover, while he does not condemn totally his own earlier efforts in a different poetic vein, he strongly feels the need to move beyond them. "That I wanted good poetry without knowing it,/ That I discovered, late, its salutary aim,/ In this and only this I find salvation," he says. That "late" is a profound self-indictment that echoes throughout the remainder of Miłosz's career—an indictment to which he pleads guilty and of which he will never quite exonerate himself.

In the final, haunting stanza, the young poet who wanted to escape the provinces for the cosmopolitan worlds of Paris and Warsaw (see his 1980 poem, "Bypassing Rue Descartes") finds himself returning to his roots, as he compares the book that he is dedicating with the village ceremonies of his childhood in Lithuania. "They used to pour millet on graves or poppy seeds," he recalls. "To feed the dead who would come disguised as birds./ I put this book here for you, who once lived/ So that you should visit us no more." It proves to be a vain hope. In the other poems in his first postwar book, and in many of the poems that will follow, Miłosz is drawn back, again and again, to these same memories of the war and its dead.

IN MILAN

First published: 1962 (English translation, 1973)
Type of work: Poem

This poem reveals the conflict that Miłosz has always felt between his commitment to writing a poetry of history and memory and his attraction to an art celebrating beauty and the senses.

"In Milan," which was written in France in 1955 but first published in his 1962 collection *Król Popiel i inne wiersze* ("King Popiel and other poems"), expresses the conflict that Miłosz has faced as an artist throughout his career. As "Dedication" shows, he feels compelled to use his art to bear witness to his time. Yet he has always felt an equally strong attraction to embracing the beauty of existence and the pleasures of the senses, to transcending his experience of history through mysticism, nature, and art. These two impulses are apparent in the mix of poems that he has chosen to include in each of his collections; and occasionally, as "In Milan," they become the subject of the poems themselves.

The poem begins with two brief stanzas. The first recalls a time, years ago, when the impulse to celebrate the beauty of life led the poet to write poems on Italy. The second recounts a charge made by a friend as they walked at night through a piazza: that Miłosz's art was "too politicized." The third, longest stanza records Miłosz's reply—a response that is both deeply felt and tinged with regret.

He would love to write poems about the beauty of the world, Miłosz says: "I am for the moon amid the vineyards . . . I am for the cypresses at dawn." He could "compose, right now, a song/ on the taste of peaches, on September in Europe." In fact, "I would like to gobble up/ All existing flowers, to eat all the colors./ I have been devouring this world in vain/ For forty years, a thousand would not be enough." He would desperately like to be "a poet of the five senses"—because those senses are so powerful, because it would be easy to lose oneself in their pleasures—but "That's why I don't allow myself to become one." Because "Thought has less weight than the word lemon," it needs a poet to express it, to defend it, to insist on its importance.

In this poem, Miłosz manages to have it both ways. In a poem of ideas, which regretfully insists on his commitment to ideas in poetry, he creates an occasion that allows him to write exactly the kind of poem that he claims he must not allow himself to write: a poem full of beauty, emotion, and sensuous imagery.

Summary

"Have I fulfilled anything, have I been of use to anyone?" Czesław Miłosz asks in "From the Rising of the Sun." The self-doubt seems genuine and is still evident in an extraordinary later poem such as "Far Away," published when he was eighty. Yet while Miłosz cannot stop asking himself these questions, his readers certainly may. He has created a body of poetry and prose that serves as an eloquent testament to the human spirit struggling with the extremes of twentieth century experience. In that—in his poetic witness—Miłosz has, indeed, been "of use" to everyone fortunate enough to have discovered his work.

Bibliography

Atlas, James. "Poet, Exile, Laureate." *The New York Times*, October 10, 1980, p. A10.

Bayley, John. "Return of the Native." *The New York Review of Books* 28 (June 25, 1981): 29-33.

Carnecka, Ewa, and Aleksander Fiut. *Conversations with Czeslaw Miłosz.* Translated by Richard Lourie, San Diego, Calif.: Harcourt Brace Jovanovich, 1987.

Filkins, Peter. "The Poetry and Anti-Poetry of Czeslaw Miłosz." *The Iowa Review* 19 (Spring/Summer, 1989): 188-209.

Hoffman, Eva. "The Poet of the Polish Diaspora." *The New York Times Magazine*, January 17, 1982, p. 29.

World Literature Today 52 (Summer, 1978). Special issue on Miłosz.

Woroszylksi, Wiktor. "Miłosz in Polish Eyes." *The New Republic* 84 (May 23, 1981): 28-31.

Bernard F. Rodgers, Jr.

JOHN MILTON

Born: London, England
December 9, 1608
Died: London, England
November 8, 1674

Principal Literary Achievement

Milton, author of the last and greatest epic poem in English, *Paradise Lost*, is generally considered to be second only to William Shakespeare as the greatest English poet.

Biography

John Milton was born in Bread Street, Cheapside, London, England, on December 9, 1608. His father, John Milton, was a very successful scrivener, one who copied legal documents and performed some of the services associated with banking and finance. His mother's name was Sara Jeffrey Milton. Though the younger Milton was never rich, his father made enough money to guarantee his son's financial independence throughout the great poet's lifetime. Milton was a precocious child, demonstrating a particular facility with ancient and modern languages. By the time he was graduated from college, Milton read, spoke, and wrote Latin nearly as well as he did English and was competent in Greek, Hebrew, French, and Italian. From approximately the age of nine to twelve, Milton was tutored at home, and from the age of twelve to sixteen he walked about three blocks to attend St. Paul's School at the famous London cathedral.

Milton started college in 1625, a few months after turning sixteen, attending Christ's College, Cambridge, where he earned the nickname "the lady of Christ's" because he took meticulous care of his appearance, had delicate features, and disdained many of the masculine activities, such as drinking and visiting brothels, that occupied many of his schoolmates. He may have been "rusticated," or suspended from school, briefly, in 1626, because of a conflict with one of his teachers, but he returned to earn his B.A. in 1629 and his M.A. in 1632. Initially, Milton had planned to be a minister, but as a Puritan, or radical Protestant, he came to believe that the Anglican church was too much like the Catholic church and decided to dedicate his life to poetry instead. While in school, Milton began writing poetry, mostly in Latin, and in December, 1629, just after his twenty-first birthday, he wrote, in English, "On the Morning of Christ's Nativity," which in effect signaled his great promise as a poet.

In the early 1630's, Milton's family moved to Horton, Buckinghamshire, seventeen miles west of London, where Milton's father retired to a country estate. After leaving Cambridge in 1632, Milton lived with his family for six years (usually called the Horton period). During this time, he read voraciously, attempting to complete his education by reading everything that was written in the languages that he had mastered. While at Cambridge and during the years of the Horton period, Milton wrote many of the early works that helped to make him famous during his lifetime—the twin "mood" poems "L'Allegro" and "Il Penseroso," the masque, or play, *Comus* (1634; *A Masque Presented at Ludlow Castle 1634 on Michaelmas Night*, 1637), the pastoral elegy "Lycidas," and several of his familiar sonnets, such as "How Soon Hath Time." Some poems, such as "Lycidas," were published under very particular circumstances and can be easily dated, but most of Milton's early poems circulated in manuscript well before they were formally published for the first time in his collected poems of 1645.

In August of 1638, at the age of twenty-nine, Milton set out on his Grand Tour, a trip on the European Continent that most educated men undertook in Milton's day to complete their studies and to polish them as gentlemen. Milton traveled mostly in Italy, where he met many important people, including the great astronomer Galileo. He returned home somewhat prematurely in August of 1639 because England was nearing its momentous civil war.

The English Civil War, which began in 1642, was caused by a power struggle between the monarchy and Parliament. In 1625, Charles I had taken over the throne from his father, James I, and by 1629 had dissolved Parliament in an attempt to govern autocratically. Parliament, however, insisted on a more representative form of government, and years of political infighting culminated in armed conflict in August of 1642. In 1647, the king's forces were defeated, and the king was taken prisoner. Then, in an act unprecedented in English history, Charles was executed on January 30, 1649. This began the period of the Puritan Commonwealth, ultimately headed by Oliver Cromwell. These historical events are important in Milton's life because after his return from Italy he published relatively little poetry between "Lycidas" in 1638 and *Paradise Lost* (1667, 1674). Milton spent twenty years writing prose in support of various personal and political causes; most of this prose is only read now by highly specialized scholars.

Of the approximately twenty prose works that Milton published between 1641 and 1660, the two most widely known are *Of Education* and *Areopagitica*, both published in 1644. The first outlined an ideal system of education, and the second argued against censorship, with the latter now considered one of the world's most important defenses of freedom of the press. In fact, Milton's *Areopagitica* helped inspire the writing of the United States Constitution's Bill of Rights.

Between 1643 and 1645, four of Milton's prose works argued for more liberal divorce laws, presumably because of the crisis of his first marriage. In June of 1642, at the age of thirty-three, Milton had married the first of his three wives, seventeen-year-old Mary Powell. Within six weeks of the marriage, she left him, returned to her father's home in Oxford, England, and did not rejoin Milton until 1645. Her motives are still not entirely clear—she may have been responding to family or political pressures, but the passion of Milton's divorce tracts indicated considerable marital discord. In 1643, *The Doctrine and Discipline of Divorce*, the first of Milton's four divorce tracts, made him quite infamous, and he was often portrayed throughout his life as "Milton the Divorcer," a sexual libertine, because of his liberal opinions on divorce. After returning to her husband, Mary Powell gave birth to four children and died in 1652 after giving birth to their last. In 1656, Milton married his second wife, twenty-eight-year-old Katherine Woodcock, who also died giving birth two years later. This death probably inspired one of Milton's greatest sonnets, "Methought I Saw My Late Espousèd Saint," though some contend that the poem refers to Mary Powell. In 1663, he married Elizabeth Minshull, who outlived him. The divorce pamphlets made Milton infamous, but the prose works that caused Milton the most controversy in his lifetime were the four that he wrote between 1649 and 1654 to justify the execution of Charles I. Almost as soon as Charles was executed, there was a backlash of negative sentiment all over Europe, as well as England, and Milton came to be known as the defender of regicide as well as of divorce.

In the 1650's, then, Milton's life was anything but happy. Scorned in many quarters for his views on divorce and the regicide, embroiled in politics rather than fulfilling his calling as a great national poet, suffering from the death of two wives, Milton also went totally blind early in 1652. Modern ophthalmic research generally agrees that Milton's blindness was caused by glaucoma, but the more romantic theory is that it was caused by years of reading and writing by low candlelight. Whatever the cause, Milton's blindness was a great burden for one who by then was planning to write the next verse epic to rival the great epics of Homer, Vergil, and Dante Alighieri. In Milton's most widely known sonnet, "When I Consider How My Light Is Spent," Milton describes this anxiety but ends the poem with an assertion of calm faith that God will use his talents as He sees fit.

Ironically, Milton's blindness probably helped save his life when the Commonwealth collapsed and the Monarchy was restored. When Cromwell died in 1658, his son Richard was not able to maintain power. Parliament invited Charles II, the son of Charles I, to return from exile in France, and the Restoration of the Monarchy took place in May of 1660. Many of those involved in the execution of Charles I were then executed themselves, but Milton was spared in spite of his active and public role in the justification of the regicide. Yet he was severely punished, despite being relatively old at fifty-one, being totally blind, and possessing a considerable literary reputation. Besides a short period of imprisonment, he lost his government position as secretary for foreign tongues (Latin secretary), paid a fine, and suffered the confiscation of most of his property. The playwright Sir William D'Avenant and the poet Andrew Marvell (who had been his assistant as Latin secretary) may have helped Milton earn clemency by speaking in his behalf.

After 1660, Milton returned to writing poetry and published his three major poems, *Paradise Lost*, *Paradise Regained*, and the classical tragedy *Samson Agonistes*, the last two printed in one volume in 1671. The precise dating and even the sequence in which Milton wrote these works is still a matter of scholarly conjecture, but after his blindness he wrote with the help of an amanuensis, someone who served as a secretary to record, usually every morning, what Milton dictated while composing the verses in his head. Sometimes Milton's daughters served in this capacity, sometimes paid assistants. Milton published additional prose works in these last years of his life, most notably *The History of Britain* (1670). He also completed the monumental Latin work *De Doctrina Christiana*, a systematic exposition of Christian doctrine, which attempted to bring the Old and New Testaments into harmony. Although willed to one of his secretaries, the manuscript disappeared and remained unpublished until 1825. Milton died on November 8, 1674, in London, one month short of his sixty-sixth birthday, from complications arising from gout.

Analysis

Milton is not "easy reading" for the modern student of literature. Extremely well-schooled in the Bible, the Greek and Latin classics, and the learning of his own time, Milton frequently alludes to materials that were common knowledge for his educated seventeenth century audience but that are usually simply arcane footnotes for today's readers. The modern reader also confronts vocabulary no longer in use, highly figurative language, and a convoluted syntax influenced by Milton's lifelong study of Latin. Yet the effort is always worth the trouble; the modern reader who becomes more comfortable with Milton's style discovers a majesty and delicacy of expression in both verse and prose that can be found in few other authors. In act 2, scene 2, of William Shakespeare's *Antony and Cleopatra* (c. 1606-1607), Antony's friend, Enobarbus, says of Cleopatra, "age cannot wither her, nor custom stale her infinite variety." The same can be said of Milton and his literary achievements.

Like Shakespeare, Milton remains a literary giant hundreds of years after his death because he completely mastered the wide variety of literary forms that he attempted. On the one hand, Milton perfected the fourteen-line Italian sonnet, which demanded poetic significance in a brief form. On the other hand, he was the last poet in English to rise to the level of Homer, Vergil, and Dante in the epic poem, his massive and flawlessly sustained blank verse of *Paradise Lost* covering twelve books and more than ten thousand lines. Between these two extremes, Milton wrote "Lycidas," which the critic Marjorie Hope Nicholson calls "the most perfect long short poem in the English language"; *Samson Agonistes*, which might be the last great classical (and Christian) verse tragedy; and the "brief epic" sequel to *Paradise Lost*, *Paradise Regained*.

In some cases, even Milton's minor verse has survived the passage of time. For example, in 1631, at the age of twenty-two, Milton joined many of his fellow Cambridge students in commemorating the death of Thomas Hobson, the eccentric university "carrier," who drove a coach carrying students and mail between Cambridge and London for sixty-seven years until his death in 1630. In two poems titled "On the University Carrier," Milton adopts a witty style very different from the "grand style" associated with his major works, yet he manages a poetic depth and genuine pathos astounding for so slight an occasion.

The "infinite variety" of Milton's work refers as well to the evocative power of the single line, even the single phrase or word. The poetic force of the emotionally charged and intellectually rich details in all of his poems is sometimes hard for beginning students to see, given the difficult context of Milton's poetry; however, focusing on some of the more familiar examples of this quality can lead the patient and industrious student to many other examples. For example, at the end of "Methought I Saw My Late Espousèd Saint," the blind Milton wakes from the dream in which he "sees" her: "But O, as to embrace me she inclined,/ I waked, she fled, and day brought back my night." The rich, evocative quality in the words "day" and "night" suggests both his grief for Katherine and the crushing burden of his blindness. In his dream, Milton imagines actually seeing Katherine for the first time, since he had married her after the onset of his blindness; but as the literal day returns, he experiences both a literal and a figurative night, on the one hand unable again to see, and on the other tormented by his sense of loss and loneliness. "Night" can also suggest the political difficulties that Milton was experiencing in a declining puritan government. Throughout Milton's works, the student will find such rich details that reward continued study and revisitation.

Finally, the ageless appeal of Milton's works comes from his effective treatment of some of the most significant themes that literature can offer. From *Comus* to *Samson Agonistes* and *Paradise Regained*, Milton is investigating the nature of good and evil, the nature of temptation, and the power of reason, patience, and faith to create a meaningful human existence. Milton's dominant Christian theme beginning with *Comus* concerns his concept of Providence and the idea that God's destiny for humans mysteriously includes freedom of choice. At the end of *Paradise Lost*, Adam and Eve learn that obeying Providence provides them with "a Paradise within thee, happier far." Yet Milton's works can be read either within the boundaries of Christianity, as Milton intended them, or in a more secular way, as many twentieth century critics have chosen to do. As early as 1900, the critic Sir Walter Raleigh could admire *Paradise Lost* even though he considered it "a monument to dead ideas." A more secular reading of the poem finds great pathos in the image of human beings struggling to make sense of a world where death, pain, unhappiness, and failure are daily reminders of a less-than-perfect existence. Milton is essentially attempting to explain the presence of evil in a world that he believes is completely in the control of a benevolent, supernatural deity. Yet his Christian explanation can be secularized and remain very much the same: Evil in the world exists because of the failure of human choice, the refusal to follow reason—the best available guide for human conduct. Finally, however, Milton survives as a great poet of hope, celebrating the power of learning, patience, faith, and endurance. The final scene in *Paradise Lost*, of Adam and Eve forever banished from the perfection of Eden but conquering their despair and fear to face an unknown, new world, is as powerful an image as any in literature.

LYCIDAS

First published: 1638
Type of work: Poem

In the form of a pastoral elegy, Milton mourns the death of a fellow Cambridge student, Edward King, who drowned in the Irish Sea in 1637.

The nominal subject of "Lycidas" is the death of Edward King, a fellow student one year behind Milton at Cambridge, who died when his boat capsized in the Irish Sea on August 10, 1637. In a commemorative volume of poems, Milton saw an opportunity to test his poetic skill and comment on those whom he considered to be the corrupt clergy in his day. He chose the form of pastoral elegy, wherein a shepherd laments the death of a fellow shepherd, because the pastoral elegy was a classic type of poem rooted in Greek and Roman literature that allowed for the presentation of allegorical meaning. As the poet speaks of an idyllic rural life of shepherds, it is understood that he can be talking about contemporary life and universal truths at the same time. Milton uses a traditional pastoral name, Lycidas, to refer to King, and he employs a number of other pastoral conventions.

It is customary to see "Lycidas" as a poem in three parts, opening with a conventional pastoral lament for the premature death of the friend, portrayed as a fellow shepherd. The surviving shepherd has a responsibility to commemorate the friend in song, so he asks the Muses to inspire the song/poem he has now undertaken. This invocation is followed by another convention of the pastoral elegy, the accusation that protective forces (in this case, the pastoral nature deities) failed to prevent the death. In a poem filled with associative leaps, Milton moves at this point to a complaint about being an artist in an unappreciative world. Even Calliope, the muse of epic poetry, was not able to save from destruction her own son, the poet Orpheus, when the mob, or "rout," disapproved. It is clear, continues the speaker, that the poet's task in this world is a thankless one. Why then does the poet persist? The pursuit of fame is the most obvious answer, but fame can be denied by premature death, as was the case with Lycidas. The final answer to this line of questioning, provided by Phoebus Apollo, the god of poetic inspiration, is that "Fame is no plant that grows on mortal soil." True fame is winning the salvation of Jove (or God). With this consolation, the first section of the poem ends.

In the second section of the poem, Milton criticizes the church government of his day, much as he would in his antiepiscopal prose tracts of the early 1640's. To lead into and allegorize this criticism, Milton begins the section by having his shepherd-poet call forth Triton, spokesman for Neptune, the god of the sea, who explains that Neptune, the sea, was not responsible for Lycidas' death. Triton reports that the sea and winds were calm that day; the drowning was caused by the defective ship in which

Lycidas was sailing, "that fatal and perfidious bark,/ Built in th' eclipse." Allegorically, this ship is the Church, and Saint Peter, the founder of the Christian Church and the keeper of the keys to Heaven, arrives to deliver a stern rebuke. Peter says that Lycidas was far superior to those who dominated the Church in Milton's day, those who do not care about their congregations or flocks: "the hungry sheep look up, and are not fed." Yet Peter warns that proper punishment awaits these negligent leaders: "that two-handed engine at the door/ Stands ready to smite once, and smite no more." Exactly to what Milton intends this "two-handed engine" to refer is hotly debated—it is one of the famous "cruxes" of Milton scholarship—but it is clear at least that the punishment will be severe and final.

The last section is far less angry and more clearly pastoral in its setting. The valleys come and bring flowers to spread on the waters of the river Alpheus in memory of Lycidas' passing. In the final consolation, the poet tells his fellow shepherds to stop their weeping because Lycidas is not really dead. Just as the sun sinks in the west but rises again every morning in the east, Lycidas is rising in Heaven. From this point, Lycidas will be the protective deity of all those who sail the Irish Sea. The lament now done, the shepherd poet, having sung since morning, watches the sun sink below the bay, rises, and departs: "tomorrow to fresh woods, and pastures new."

Milton's poem has survived as great art because it is much more than a memorial for a dead friend or even an attack on seventeenth century clergy. Milton transcends these immediate purposes and creates a hauntingly evocative testimony to the fragility of human life. It is a poem about the fear of premature death, a fear that Milton felt keenly, given his great aspirations to become a national poet and his slow progress toward the great epic poem that would fulfill his aspirations. "Lycidas" is a poem that faces the fears of premature death and overcomes them because it is also a poem about rebirth, specifically a Christian rebirth, but also a more abstract rebirth that can give hope to all people, hope that life can be meaningful in the face of corruption, apparent chance, and disappointment. What began in part as a formal exercise, an attempt to demonstrate skill in a classic poetical form, became one of the world's greatest poems, a personal expression of fear and anger balanced with a final affirmation of faith in cosmic order.

PARADISE LOST

First published: 1667, 1674
Type of work: Epic poem

After being cast out of Heaven, Satan leaves Hell, travels to the newly created world, and succeeds in tempting Adam and Eve to sin against God.

In the tradition of the epic poem, *Paradise Lost* begins *in medias res*, in the middle of the story, showing in the first two of twelve books how Satan and his followers gathered their forces on the burning lake of Hell and sought out the newly created race of humans on Earth. (The revolt and resulting war in Heaven that preceded this action and earned the devils their place in Hell is reported in books 5 and 6.)

In book 3, God observes Satan traveling toward Earth, predicts the fall of human beings, and asks for someone to ransom them. Christ, the Son, accepts. In book 4, Adam and Eve are introduced, as Satan lies hidden in the Garden of Eden. Satan appears in Eve's dream, encouraging her to taste of the forbidden Tree of Knowledge, and in book 5 God sends the angel Raphael to warn Adam and Eve of their danger. Raphael begins the story of Lucifer's revolt in Heaven, which he completes in book 6, and in book 7 Raphael tells of how God responded to Satan's revolt by creating a new world, the Earth, and a new race in Adam and Eve. In book 8, Adam describes to Raphael his and Eve's creation, and Raphael delivers his final warning and departs. Book 9 tells the story of Satan's successful temptation of Eve, the eating of the fruit of the Tree of Knowledge, and the resulting discord between Adam and Eve. In book 10, Christ passes judgment on Adam and Eve, and Sin and Death build a bridge from the gates of Hell to Earth as Satan is returning to Hell. At the end of book 10, Adam and Eve resolve their discord and petition God for forgiveness, which is granted in book 11 as God sends the archangel Michael to give Adam a vision of the future for humans. In book 12, after the vision of Christ's sacrifice and redemption of the human race, Adam and Eve are expelled from Eden.

This brief synopsis, of course, does not communicate the grandeur and emotional intensity of Milton's great poem. Milton begins *Paradise Lost* with two captivating books set in Hell and featuring Lucifer, or Satan, who rallies his defeated forces and vows eternal war on God before journeying toward Earth to destroy Adam and Eve. In Hell, Satan has a kind of heroic splendor, and such apparent grandeur led English Romantic poets such as William Blake and Percy Bysshe Shelley to identify with Satan as a tragic rebel and to proclaim that Milton subconsciously admired Satan. Although Milton's subconscious mind must forever remain a mystery, this interpretation is very dubious, and generations of readers misled by Blake and his followers should read the poem more carefully. Milton began his epic with this larger-than-life portrait of Satan in order to provide God (who will obviously win) with a worthy adversary. Yet Satan's pseudo-heroic size is severely diminished in all of his appearances outside the first two books, and by the end of the poem Satan is not at all prominent, the heroic focus having shifted to the figure of Christ and the tragic focus having shifted to Adam and Eve. By the end of the poem, Satan is defeated and overshadowed by the larger themes of redemption and human responsibility.

One of the main causes of this Romantic distortion of *Paradise Lost* is the contrast between the first two books and book 3, where God the Father delivers theological lectures and clears Himself of blame for the Fall that He foretells but does not predestine. Compared to Hell and Satan, the figures of God and Christ the Son discoursing in Heaven seem dull, at least to most twentieth century readers. It is almost with relief at the end of book 3 that the reader finds Milton returning to the description of Satan, who nears the Earth and passes through what is called the Paradise of Fools.

Only when the reader meets Adam and Eve is there a narrative interest to compete with Satan's pseudoheroic stature, but the success of Milton's poem comes from the fact that the two human characters, who finally become much more interesting even than the diabolical Satan, are domestic rather than heroic figures. Gradually, Adam and Eve become characterized as much by their conflict with each other as by their conflict with Satan. In what are now seen as strikingly sexist characterizations, Milton describes Adam as "for contemplation . . . and valor formed" while Eve is formed "for softness . . . and sweet attractive grace." Yet the love between them is so convincingly real that even Satan is jealous as he watches "these two/ Imparadised in one another's arms." When Eve falls to Satan's temptations in book 9, she is attempting to rise toward Adam's supposedly superior status, and when Adam accepts sin and death with her, knowing the consequences, he does so out of "uxoriousness," or excessive love for and submission to a wife. The immediate consequence is domestic bickering, each blaming the other for what has happened. Then Eve initiates a reconciliation, Adam suggests praying for forgiveness, and the poem ends with the first married couple walking "hand in hand" out of Paradise.

This rich quality of domestic tragedy has helped make *Paradise Lost* significant and powerful for twentieth century readers. It also may have had some effect on the creation of the modern novel. It can be argued that eighteenth century writers, overwhelmed by Milton's achievement in *Paradise Lost*, were too intimidated to attempt again the epic scope in poetic form. Since no one was going to be able to surpass Milton in verse, the artistic impulse to work with epic size shifted to prose, and the novel was born in the eighteenth century with Daniel Defoe, Samuel Richardson, and Henry Fielding. Certainly by shifting the epic subject from the traditional subjects of war and valor to marriage, *Paradise Lost* elevated domestic subject matter for centuries to come.

AREOPAGITICA

First published: 1644
Type of work: Essay

Milton addresses the English Parliament and urges it to protect the freedom of the press by not permitting the licensing, or censorship, of books.

Areopagitica is the most famous of Milton's prose works because it has outlasted the circumstances of its original publication. On June 14, 1643, the English Parliament passed a law called the Licensing Order, which required that all books be approved by an official censor before publication, and on November 23, 1644, Milton wrote *Areopagitica*, pleading for the repeal of the law. His arguments were not successful—official censorship of books in England lasted until the nineteenth century—but *Areopagitica* has long been an inspiration for those demanding a free press. In fact, its arguments against censorship are nearly as fresh and convincing today as they were in the middle of the seventeenth century.

Milton realized how difficult it would be to change Parliament's opinion, so he marshaled his argument with great subtlety. His title alludes to a famous speech by the Greek educator Isocrates, and Milton uses a classical argumentative structure and many techniques of classical rhetoric that would have commanded respect from his seventeenth century audience. Yet the modern reader, unaware of classical rhetoric, can still marvel at the cleverness and logic that Milton uses to persuade his contemporary lawmakers. He begins by praising Parliament for its defense of liberty in the past. He then offers a historical review of censorship, pointing out that freedom of the press was highly valued in ancient Greece and Rome. Milton traces the tradition of tyrannical censorship to the Roman Catholic Council of Trent and the Spanish Inquisition, both of which found few champions among the members of the English Protestant Parliament. As Milton points out, the Roman Catholic church was a traditional enemy of the freedom-loving Parliament.

Milton's next tactic is to disarm the argument that censorship serves society by destroying bad books. In a world where good and evil are often intermingled and difficult to discern, the reading of all books—good and bad—contributes to the human attempt to understand and pursue Truth. God gave human beings Reason as a reliable guide, and judgment is the exercise of Reason; true Christian virtue rests in facing trials and choosing wisely. In one of the most famous passages from *Areopagitica*, Milton says,

> He that can apprehend and consider vice with all her baits and seeming pleasures, and yet abstain, and yet distinguish, and yet prefer that which is truly better, he is the true warfaring Christian. I cannot praise a fugitive and cloistered virtue, unexercised and unbreathed. . . . That which purifies us is trial and trial is by what is contrary.

Milton then shows that external restraint is futile in the attempt to make human beings good. The temptations to evil are infinite, and to protect humans from all harm, the number of censors would have to be infinite as well. Even if censorship were limited to books, too many censors would be required for the great number of books to be examined, and the work of reading so many bad books would be tedious drudgery. Those best qualified to judge would be disinclined for this work, and censorship would fall to ignorant and less qualified men.

Milton's final points are that censorship will discourage intellectual activity, impede the pursuit of Truth, undermine the nation's respect for scholars, and cast doubt on the ability of ordinary persons to think for themselves. Furthermore, censorship will limit the pursuit of new truths since its activity is by nature conservative; only accepted truths would ever pass examination. Yet truth is never stagnant and never simply accepted uncritically from an external authority. Human beings come to know Truth from constant testing and discussion, a process that can be tolerated because

Truth is so powerful: "And though all the winds of doctrine were let loose to play upon the earth, so Truth be in the field. . . . Let her and Falsehood grapple; who ever knew Truth put to the worse, in a free and open encounter?"

In the face of such eloquence, there is only one disappointment in *Areopagitica*: Milton is not willing to give the same freedom from censorship to books espousing Roman Catholicism. Milton, most Puritans, and many Englishmen saw Catholicism as tyrannical, even evil. In his journey to Italy, Milton had seen a Catholic government imprison Galileo for asserting that the earth was not the center of the universe. In England, on November 5, 1605, the Roman Catholic conspirator Guy Fawkes had come dangerously close to blowing up the king, his ministers, and Parliament with twenty barrels of gunpowder (the Gunpowder Plot). It stands to reason that a lawful society cannot tolerate what would destroy it, and the radically Protestant Milton saw Roman Catholicism as a serious threat to social order: "I mean not tolerated Popery, and open superstition, which as it extirpates all religions and civil supremacies, so itself should be extirpate, provided first that all charitable and compassionate means be used to win and regain the weak and the misled."

In spite of this flaw in Milton's argument, *Areopagitica* remains one of the most eloquent defenses of an essential social freedom and therefore an invaluable document in the history of Western society.

Summary

If John Milton had written only *Paradise Lost*, he would still be considered one of the world's greatest poets; but, like Shakespeare, Milton graced nearly everything he touched, from delicate Italian sonnets, such as "Methought I Saw My Late Espousèd Saint," to the sonorous majesty of his great verse tragedy, *Samson Agonistes*. Milton wrote the greatest pastoral elegy ever written, "Lycidas," and one of the greatest defenses of a free press, *Areopagitica*. Shakespeare is almost universally appealing to the twentieth century because his work seems less learned and doctrinaire than Milton's, but after becoming well acquainted with Milton, the modern reader will find universal meaning, poetic grace, and emotional intensity second only to that found in Shakespeare.

Bibliography

Hanford, James H., and J. G. Taaffe. *A Milton Handbook*. 5th ed. New York: Appleton-Century-Crofts, 1970.

Hunter, William B., Jr., ed. *A Milton Encyclopedia*. 9 vols. Lewisburg, Pa.: Bucknell University Press, 1978-1980.

Hill, Christopher. *Milton and the English Revolution*. London: Faber & Faber, 1977.

Klemp, P. J. *The Essential Milton: An Annotated Bibliography of Major Modern Studies*. Boston: G. K. Hall, 1989.

Lewis, C. S. *A Preface to "Paradise Lost."* London: Oxford University Press, 1942.

Nicholson, Marjorie Hope. *John Milton: A Reader's Guide to His Poetry*. New York:

Farrar, Straus & Giroux, 1963.

Parker, William Riley. *Milton: A Biography*. 2 vols. Oxford, England: Clarendon Press, 1968.

Ralegh, Sir Walter. *Milton*. London: Edward Arnold, 1900.

Waldock, A. J. A. *"Paradise Lost" and Its Critics*. Cambridge, England: Cambridge University Press, 1947.

Terry Nienhuis

YUKIO MISHIMA

Born: Tokyo, Japan
January 14, 1925
Died: Tokyo, Japan
November 25, 1970

Principal Literary Achievement

Japan's best-known writer after World War II, Mishima blended patriotism, sex, and death into a series of fictional works that chronicle Japan's rise to a modern nation, while lamenting the loss of traditional values and morality.

Biography

Yukio Mishima, whose name at birth was Kimitake Hiraoka, was born in Tokyo, Japan, on January 14, 1925, to a family descended from samurai nobility. His father was Azusa Hiraoka; his mother, Shizue Hashi Hiraoka. Kimitake, who took the name Yukio Mishima when he began to write in 1941, was a frail child who, perhaps because of his lack of physical prowess, became enamored at an early age with the warriors of feudal Japan who followed *bushido* as a code of conduct. *Bushido*, which means "way of the warrior," stressed self-sacrifice, indifference to pain, control of both mind and body, and loyalty to the Japanese emperor. Mishima came to live and die by this code. Reared largely by his grandparents during his early years, he was enrolled in 1931 at the Gakushuin (Peers' School), advancing in 1937 to the middle school and in 1942 to the senior school. During this time, Mishima began to distinguish himself in literature. His first long work, *Hanazakari no mori* (1944; the forest in full bloom), was published in the school magazine when he was thirteen and later, in 1944, as a book. In fact, he was graduated first in his class from the Gakushuin in 1944 and was awarded a silver watch by Emperor Hirohito.

Coming to maturity in the 1930's and 1940's, during Japan's imperialist wars with China and the United States, Mishima was kept out of military service by poor health. Instead of dying nobly as a warrior in combat, he was assigned by the War Ministry to work in an airplane factory. After the war, he returned to his schooling, this time to Tokyo University, where he studied law, but writing was becoming more and more compelling. He discontinued his studies in 1947 to work for Japan's Ministry of Finance and quit that job the following year to write full-time. His first mature publication, *Kamen no kokuhaku* (1949; *Confessions of a Mask*, 1958), appeared in 1949 and was an immense success.

Discontented with his frail body and fragile health, he began to lift weights in the mid-1950's and to practice martial arts such as samurai swordsmanship and kendo, the Japanese art of fencing with bamboo swords. By his mid-thirties, Mishima was an astonishingly handsome and muscular man, a perfect embodiment of the young, bronzed manhood that he came to celebrate in such works as *Hagakure nyūmon* (1967; *The Way of the Samurai*, 1977) and *Taiyō to tetsu* (1968; *Sun and Steel*, 1970). Yet he was a man of many contradictions. Although he married and had children, Mishima retained his strongest sexual feelings for men. An intensely private man, he was a public performer as both a stage and a motion-picture actor—he played the leading role in a film version of "Yūkoku" ("Patriotism"), one of his own stories— and he entered into public debates with left-wing college students. A fervent nationalist, Mishima lived on the outskirts of Tokyo in a Western-style home and collected British antiques.

During the 1950's and 1960's, Mishima wrote prolifically, publishing novels, short stories, essays, and plays. He published more than 250 books in Japan during his lifetime, and the collected edition of his works in Japanese runs thirty-six volumes. Novels such as *Kinjiki* (1951) and *Higyō* (1953; combined with *Kinjiki* as *Forbidden Colors*, 1968), a controversial account of homosexuality in Tokyo; *Shiosai* (1954; *The Sound of Waves*, 1956); *Kinkakuji* (1956; *The Temple of the Golden Pavilion*, 1959); and *Utage no ato* (1960; *After the Banquet*, 1963), a novel of Japanese political life, earned for him an international reputation as Japan's greatest contemporary novelist. He came to the United States three times and traveled to many foreign cities. His revival of *Nō* plays, the classical drama of Japan, was a great success not only in Japan but also all over the world (several one-act plays were staged in New York late in 1960). In addition, he wrote many popular Japanese detective novels and commercial books.

In 1967, Mishima formed what came to be considered his own private army, the Tate No Kai, or Shield Society. This group of student warriors trained at Japanese army bases and swore to restore the prestige of a defeated Japan, raising it to its old imperial glory. Mishima and his Shield Society were never taken seriously by their own compatriots, and Mishima's right-wing politics seemed strident and out of date in a rapidly developing, prosperous Japan.

Increasingly frustrated in effecting his imperialist views, Mishima and four of his young followers entered the Tokyo headquarters of Japan's Eastern Ground Self-Defense Forces on November 25, 1970. They took its commander hostage, and Mishima, dressed in full Shield Society uniform and wearing a samurai headband, proceeded to address the troops below from a balcony but received only heckling in return. Finally, he shouted, "Long live the emperor!" and went back inside. There, he stripped to the waist, knelt on the floor, and began the rite of *seppuku*, the ancient ritual suicide whereby a warrior performs self-disembowelment. After plunging a knife into his left side and cutting open his stomach, Mishima lowered his head, and a young follower standing behind him decapitated him with one stroke of his sword. Mishima's suicide shocked the world. He died at the age of forty-five, on the very date that he had given his publisher the final pages of his last masterpiece, *Hōjō no umi* (1969-1971; *The Sea of Fertility: A Cycle of Four Novels*, 1972-1974). His art and his life came to an end within hours of one another and with a single act.

Analysis

When the war ended in 1945, the code that Mishima glorified ended with it. Japan was no longer a muscular military nation whose young warriors died for the glory of the emperor. The emperor, in fact, was forced to renounce his claims to deity after the war, and a new constitution was adopted that stripped the emperor of all power, abolished the military, and ended the nation's foreign influence. Mishima increasingly came to deplore the new Japan that developed between 1945 and 1970. Although the nation was swiftly becoming a prosperous industrial giant, Mishima felt that it was crass, materialistic, and vulgar, a nation that had forsaken its glorious traditions of the past, lost its spiritual focus, and betrayed the proud young warriors who had died for it during the war.

Mishima's writings reflect the changing historical period. His last great work, a series of four novels called *The Sea of Fertility*, give a panoramic view of Japan from 1913 to the 1970's, moving from romance and idealism to opportunism and decay. The Japan of the final novels is one of Coca-Cola signs and litter, cruelty and sexual perversion. Yet Mishima is far from a gloomy writer. His work abounds in the Japanese love of flora, fauna, and natural surroundings, and there is in his writing a deep sensuality and spirituality. Not a particularly religious man, Mishima nonetheless has a deep reverence for things and a sense of the heartbreaking loveliness of mortal and fleeting life. Mizoguchi, the young monk in *The Temple of the Golden Pavilion*, one of Mishima's best novels, can achieve freedom only by destroying the ideal beauty of Kinkakuji (the Golden Temple), a fifteenth century Zen temple. The greatest beauty is a beauty that does not last.

While Mishima is quintessentially Japanese in many of his values and sensibilities, he is also a very Western author. Among his favorite writers were Thomas Mann, Marcel Proust, Fyodor Dostoevski, and the classic Greek dramatists. Like Mann, the German author of *Buddenbrooks: Verfall einer Familie* (1901; English translation, 1924), and Proust, who wrote the epic *À la recherche du temps perdu* (1913-1927; *Remembrance of Things Past*, 1922-1931, 1981), Mishima is concerned with the tragic implications of a developing commercial world and the destruction of art, spirit, and morality. Like Russian novelist Dostoevski, Mishima explores inner dualities of good and evil, mind and body, reality and imagination. He has been compared to Ernest Hemingway in his masculine code of violence, to Edgar Allan Poe in his coupling of love and death, and to Walt Whitman in his masculine eroticism. Mishima felt at home with all of these writers.

It is his peculiar eroticism that many readers find repellent. Mishima, like the boy in *Confessions of a Mask*, finds sexual arousal and beauty in the sight of bloody young males dying in agony, and in the thought of young men, such as the kamikaze pilots of World War II, plunging gloriously to their death in suicide attacks. One of his most difficult works, "Patriotism," is the story of a young military officer and his wife who, after making passionate love to one another, commit ritual *seppuku* in gory and nauseating detail. As if in preparation for his own death, Mishima directed a film version of the story and played the role of the young officer.

It is too easy to see in all of this simply the mind of a sadomasochistic deviate. The contradictory pulls of Eros and Thanatos, love and death, are strong within each individual, and for Mishima, death had a greater attraction than life, as it does for many saints and martyrs. In espousing an eroticism that many find repellent, he is to be applauded for his courage. Mishima looked into his own heart and stated what he found there with honesty, candor, and conviction. The same is true for his unpopular political views. While his politics seemed antiquated and slightly ridiculous even to his fellow Japanese, his beliefs were nonetheless intelligently formulated and passionately held. Further, he had the courage of his convictions; Mishima was willing to die for what he believed.

What is most important about Mishima, however, is his artistry. His books are rich in background and historical detail, his descriptions of Japanese life are accurately observed and beautifully described, and his characters are sharply focused and often memorable. He has a remarkable eye for the quirky and eccentric behavior of individuals, and he is a candid explorer of the human soul, often taking readers where few other writers have gone. Finally, he is a deeply personal writer who bravely faced the worst in himself, transforming these private insights into public works of art. Mishima transforms his readers as well, making them see and feel in new and unsettling ways. That is the mark of a major writer.

CONFESSIONS OF A MASK

First published: *Kamen no kokuhaku,* 1949 (English translation, 1958)
Type of work: Novel

Growing up in Japan in the 1930's and 1940's, a young boy discovers the contradictions and confusions within his nature, the reality behind the mask that he wears for the world around him.

Confessions of a Mask has been compared to James Joyce's *A Portrait of the Artist as a Young Man* (1916) and D. H. Lawrence's *Sons and Lovers* (1913). Like those novels, Mishima's work is a *Bildungsroman,* the story of a young man's growth to maturity. Yet while Joyce and Lawrence emphasize the struggle of a boy to achieve a conventional, heterosexual manhood, Mishima emphasizes the seemingly aberrant desires of his young protagonist, whose struggle is to face his feelings honestly and openly.

The confession begins with the narrator's earliest memories, almost all of them connected with either sex or death. Almost dying at the age of four of autointoxication

(Mishima himself suffered from this chronic illness), he remembers at the same time the image of a young man carrying buckets of excrement and becomes strangely aroused by his handsome face and close-fitting trousers. The image associates sex and filth, just as the boy's later arousal by marching soldiers combines beauty and death. These dualities occur throughout the novel, as do masks and false appearances. Captivated by a picture book illustration of a knight holding a sword aloft on a white horse, the boy is later shocked to find out that it is the picture of a woman, Joan of Arc, not of a man. Like the boy, the knight's sex is masked and is not what it appears to be. A later book illustration, that of Saint Sebastian, whose body was pierced by arrows, arouses him even further. Finding exquisite beauty in the saint's white flesh dripping blood, the boy finds sexual arousal in agonizing masculine death.

The narrator's first strong sexual feelings are for a young tough named Omi, a fellow student at school. Omi is the opposite of the frail, thin, unhealthy narrator. Omi is physically strong, mentally weak, and, being older than the other boys, sexually mature. The narrator falls in love with him, desires him carnally, and longs to see his naked body, a desire that is fulfilled one day in gym class. Omi's beautiful nakedness, however, fails to satisfy the boy's longing. It merely makes him feel jealous, ashamed of his own comparative ugliness.

The boy soon learns to mask his true feelings, pretending to desire the opposite sex and to anticipate sexual fulfillment with women. Yet he has no adolescent fantasies about women (though he does for young sailors and soldiers on the streets) and only achieves sexual satisfaction through masturbation. At the age of twenty, he begins to see the sister of a schoolmate, a girl named Sonoko, and it is even expected that he will become engaged to her. He tries to convince himself that he is deeply in love with Sonoko: They exchange love letters and photographs, hold hands, and eventually kiss. Still, the young man has no sensation of pleasure, no sexual arousal. Finally, in order to discover if he is a "normal" male, he goes to a prostitute but is unable to have sexual intercourse with her.

By the end of the novel, he has ended his relationship with Sonoko, who then marries someone else. In the final scene, he meets Sonoko, now a married woman, in a chance encounter, and she hints that she still loves him, is even willing to have an extramarital affair with him. Yet as she tells him this in a tawdry Japanese dancehall, he glances at a nearby table at a young male, a gang tough who has removed his shirt and is flexing his muscles. Burning with sexual desire, the protagonist knows what his destiny will be. He can wear a mask no longer.

THE SEA OF FERTILITY

First published: *Hōjō no umi*, 1969-1971 (English translation, 1972-1974);
includes *Hara no yuki*, 1969 (*Spring Snow*, 1972); *Homba*,
1969 (*Runaway Horses*, 1973); *Akatsuki no tera*, 1970 (*The
Temple of Dawn*, 1973); *Tennin gosui*, 1971 (*The Decay of
the Angel*, 1974)

Type of work: Novels

Widely recognized as Mishima's masterpiece, this series of four novels offers
a sweeping view of modern Japan, chronicling the nation's changing values from
1913 to 1970.

The Sea of Fertility: A Cycle of Four Novels is a tetralogy whose title is taken
from a name on the surface of the moon. It suggests both the fertile sea of earthly
life and the arid sea of the cosmic moon—being and nothingness. Mishima said that
he put everything he knew about life into these four novels; the very last words of the
final book were written and submitted to his publisher on the day that he died.

Spring Snow is Mishima's version of *Romeo and Juliet* (c. 1595-1596). A story
of star-crossed lovers, Kiyo Matsugae and Satoko Ayakura, the novel is romantic,
poignant, and tragic. As the title suggests, spring is the season of love, while snow
is the cold, life-covering element of death, and this novel combines the two. Satoko,
the daughter of a nobleman, is engaged by imperial decree to a prince of the court,
while Kiyo, also from a noble family, is a student at Peers' School who falls in love
with her. By doing so, however, he challenges the emperor himself. The lovers meet
secretly, love passionately, and take terrible risks. Emotionally weak and immature,
Kiyo tries to distance himself from Satoko, who becomes pregnant, gets an abortion,
and, in disgrace, isolates herself in a nunnery. Kiyo, guilty and desperately ill, comes
daily to see the cloistered Satoko and eventually dies for love.

Two minor characters in *Spring Snow* figure prominently in the second novel of
the cycle, *Runaway Horses*. Before Kiyo dies, he tells his school friend, Shigekuni
Honda, of a dream in which he sees his friend Honda again, beneath a waterfall.
Another minor character, Kiyo's tutor, Shikeyuki Iinuma, also reappears in the second novel, which takes place some eighteen years after Kiyo's death. Honda, now an
associate judge in the Osaka Court of Appeals, meets Isao Iinuma, son of Kiyo's
tutor, who is now headmaster of his own academy. When Honda sees the boy bathing
beneath a waterfall near the shrine, he notices three small moles on the left side of
the boy's breast—the same three moles that Kiyo had. He concludes that the boy is
Kiyo reincarnated, the incarnation of Kiyo's earlier dream.

Whereas Kiyo was a romantic dreamer, Isao is a political idealist who wants to
purify the corrupt Japanese government of Westernized financiers and restore the em-

pire's former glory. Using as his model The League of the Divine Wind, a group of student rebels who tried to overthrow the Japanese government in 1873, Isao forms his own student rebel group, whose members pledge to assassinate the most prominent financiers in Japan and to kill themselves by *seppuku* if their plan fails. The assassination plan indeed fails, and the rebel students are imprisoned. Honda, convinced that Isao is the reincarnation of his old friend Kiyo, resigns from the court and becomes defense counsel for the students, who are given their freedom and treated as patriotic heroes. Isao, however, more in love with romantic death than political reform, carries out his plans of assassination by killing a financier named Kurahara and then taking his own life by *seppuku*.

Reincarnation, something in which Mishima did not personally believe, also plays a part in the final two novels of the tetralogy. In *Runaway Horses*, Kiyo/Isao has a dream in which he becomes a woman. In *The Temple of Dawn*, he becomes that woman, a Thai princess named Ying Chan; later, in *The Decay of the Angel*, he will reappear as a boy named Toru. In both novels, Honda is again the central controlling sensibility through whose eyes are seen Kiyo's various incarnations.

Both *The Temple of Dawn* and *The Decay of the Angel* emphasize the decay of the final book's title. From the earlier two novels of romantic passion and patriotic sacrifice, readers descend to a world of ugliness, corruption, and death. In *The Temple of Dawn*, Thailand is a place of drizzling rain and fragmented images, India a nation of beggers, lepers, and public crematoriums, and Japan a defeated nation of bombed-out ruins and perverted sexuality. Honda has become materially wealthy but physically and morally impoverished. Trapped in a sterile marriage, he is reduced to peeping at the sexual activity of others through holes in walls and behind bushes. Ying Chan, the object of Honda's sexual fantasies, turns out to be a lesbian and dies from a snakebite after returning to Thailand. There is equal sterility in *The Decay of the Angel*. Honda, now seventy-six years old, dreams of angels; going to Udo Beach, where a mythical angel supposedly descended in the fourteenth century, he finds a shore littered with Coca-Cola bottles, food cans, plastic bags, and garbage. Meeting Toru, a young signalman who has the distinctive three-mole marking on his breast, Honda adopts the sixteen-year-old, but Toru turns out to be evil incarnate, a destroyer of human life and spirit, a malevolent genius who ends up blind, helpless, and isolated.

Mishima's four novels move from spring, youth, and love to old age, senility, and death, from the romantic idealism of early twentieth century Japan to a crass, decaying, and valueless society of the 1970's. Like his principal character Judge Honda, who serenely looks forward to death at the end of the tetralogy, Mishima himself saw at the end of his life only an empty garden, no memories, nothing.

Summary

Yukio Mishima has been compared to the American author Hemingway in his masculine code of violence and death, to the British author Lawrence in his mystical sense of primitive impulses, to the French author André Gide in his candid treatment of homosexuality, and to the great Japanese writers of the past.

Yet Mishima is always uniquely himself. His way of combining beauty and death, his peculiar eroticism, and his conservative political and social views make him unlike any other author, and while he often repels his readers, he just as often fascinates them. While every age produces very good writers, it produces very few geniuses. Mishima was such a rarity—a writer of genius.

Bibliography

Miller, Henry. *Reflections on the Death of Mishima*. Santa Barbara, Calif.: Capra Press, 1972.

Miyoshi, Masao. *Accomplices of Silence: The Modern Japanese Novel*. Berkeley: University of California Press, 1974.

Nathan, John. *Mishima: A Biography*. Boston: Little, Brown, 1974.

Petersen, Gwenn Boardman. *The Moon in the Water: Understanding Tanizaki, Kawabata, and Mishima*. Honolulu: University Press of Hawaii, 1979.

Scott-Stokes, Henry. *The Life and Death of Yukio Mishima*. New York: Farrar, Straus & Giroux, 1974.

Wolfe, Peter. *Yukio Mishima*. New York: Frederick Ungar, 1989.

Yourcenar, Marguerite. *Mishima: A Vision of the Void*. Translated by Albert Manguel. New York: Farrar, Straus & Giroux, 1986.

Kenneth Seib

MOLIÈRE

Born: Paris, France
January 15, 1622 (baptized)
Died: Paris, France
February 17, 1673

Principal Literary Achievement
By adding realistic characterization and penetrating social criticism to conventional farce, Molière produced a new type of French comedy and earned a reputation as France's finest comic playwright.

Biography
Jean-Baptiste Poquelin was born in Paris, France. Although his date of birth is not known, he was baptized on January 15, 1622. Jean-Baptiste was the oldest child of Marie Cressé Poquelin and Jean Poquelin, a prosperous upholsterer who was connected with the court. The boy was educated at the Jesuit College of Clermont, then studied law, becoming a notary in 1641. Meanwhile, his father had arranged for Jean-Baptiste to inherit the court office, which he himself had purchased from his brother. The young man's future seemed assured.

Jean-Baptiste, however, had fallen under the spell of the theater, in the person of the actress Madeleine Béjart, whose parents were neighbors of the Poquelin family. With Madeleine, her brother Joseph, her sister Geneviève, and nine other actors, Jean-Baptiste, or Molière, as he now called himself, founded the *Illustre Théâtre* and began to present plays. Molière's action was much more than a change of profession; in his day, actors and actresses were considered disreputable, even, according to many in the Roman Catholic church, destined for eternal damnation. Therefore, when Molière became an actor, he lost his social standing, his security, and seemingly his future.

The new troupe did not prosper in Paris. After being imprisoned for debt, Molière, now the manager, decided to take his company on a tour of the provinces. Little more is known about Molière's life during the next thirteen years except the names of some of the towns and cities where the company appeared. Evidently, at this time Molière polished his skills as an actor, alternating in leading roles and, incidentally, excelling in comedy. Molière also began to write for his troupe. At first, he produced short farcical sketches; by 1655, however, his first full-length comedy had been presented. Three years later, Molière believed that his company was ready once again to

Engraved by J. Pofselwhite.

MOLIERE.

try its luck in Paris, where the court of Louis XIV was the center not only of political power but of French culture, as well.

In Paris, Molière's company became the *troupe de Monsieur* (Monsieur's troupe). The name signified that it was under the protection, or sponsorship, of the king's oldest brother, who, according to long-standing tradition, was called simply *Monsieur.* On October 24, 1658, at the Louvre, Molière's troupe appeared before King Louis XIV, his brother, and the rest of the court, presenting a tragedy by Pierre Corneille and a farce by Molière himself. Although the tragedy was not well received, the king was particularly enthusiastic about Molière's play, and as a result, he granted the troupe permission to perform at the *salle du Petit-Bourbon*, or the Petit-Bourbon Theater, which initially was shared with an Italian company but later was assigned solely to the *troupe de Monsieur.*

On November 18, 1659, the company produced *Les Précieuses ridicules* (*The Affected Young Ladies*, 1732). It was Molière's first comedy of manners. In it, he satirized the pedantry and the folly, the affectations and the snobbishness, that were characteristic of Parisian society, and especially of those women who aspired to higher social standing. The play was the troupe's greatest financial success to that point. In 1660, Molière first appeared as a character named "Sganarelle," playing the part of the bourgeois husband in a delightful comedy called *Sganarelle: Ou, Le Cocu imaginaire* (*Sganarelle*, 1748). Later, perhaps thinking that it brought him good luck, Molière used the name of Sganarelle for quite different characters in other comedies. He always insisted on playing the "Sganarelle" role himself. Interestingly, all the plays in which some "Sganarelle" appeared happened to be successful.

Although, as manager, Molière could make such decisions about casting and production, he had no power to prevent his jealous rivals from injuring him and his company, in one way or another. In 1661, they managed to have a court official obtain approval for a new colonnade; oddly, the new construction necessitated the demolition of Molière's theater. Unwilling to countermand the orders of his official, the king instead arranged for Molière's troupe to be moved to the *Palais-Royal Théâtre*, where they were to remain for the rest of Molière's lifetime. There, they continued to present plays by various writers, regularly introducing new works by Molière, some of which were highly successful and some of which were failures. One of the latter was the first play produced in the Palais Royal, a heroic comedy. The second play presented after the move, however, *L'École des maris* (1661; *The School for Husbands*, 1732), in which Molière played another Sganarelle, was very popular. The play was based on a work by the Roman writer Terence, in which the playwright contrasted two kinds of education, harsh and permissive. Molière decided to examine this issue in regard to girls, not boys. The side of harshness in his play is represented by the foolish Sganarelle, who has kept his ward in strict seclusion, intending eventually to make her his wife. In contrast, there is another guardian, Ariste, who has put no limits on the girl's sister. As the play proceeds, Sganarelle's rebellious ward manages to trick her guardian into helping her marry her young lover.

The story of the older man and the young woman was repeated over and over again in Molière's plays; it was also relevant to his own life. In 1662, the forty-year-old Molière married the actress Armande Béjart, who was probably the sister of his friend and former mistress Madeleine Béjart. Armande was a spoiled girl of twenty. Her hardheartedness and infidelity are reflected in many of Molière's plays, such as *L'École des femmes* (1662; *The School for Wives*, 1732). It is a mark of Molière's capacity for artistic detachment that, although he makes fun of coquettes like Armande in such plays, he also satirizes older men like himself, who marry young women and then suffer the torments of jealousy.

In the last decade of his life, Molière was troubled by domestic unhappiness and besieged by his personal and professional enemies. In addition, he had contracted tuberculosis, and, in the vain hope of a cure, he found himself forced to rely upon the medical profession, which, it is obvious from his plays, he deeply distrusted. Despite these personal difficulties, it was during this period that the playwright produced his greatest comedies.

In Paris, on February 17, 1673, even though he was ill, Molière insisted on appearing in the title role of *Le Malade imaginaire* (*The Imaginary Invalid*, 1732), which is, ironically, the story of a man who merely thinks himself to be unwell. Shortly after finishing the performance, Molière collapsed and died. Because he had not received the final rites of the Church, the clergy, never his friends, found an excuse to refuse him burial in consecrated ground; however, after the intervention of the king, Molière was buried in Saint-Joseph's cemetery in Paris.

Analysis

Molière's art derived from two sources. The first was the French farce, a story of trickery, punctuated with physical action, which had delighted simple audiences during the Middle Ages and continued to please more sophisticated audiences in Molière's own century. The second was the *commedia dell'arte*, which had originated in Italy and had only recently been introduced to France. These were plays with set situations but with improvised dialogue, presented by actors in masks, who represented character types. In developing his own kind of comedy, Molière depended for his plots on farce, with its elaborate schemes of deception, mistaken identity, disguise, and misdirection. The *commedia dell'arte*, however, suggested possibilities for stylization in production and even in dialogue. Furthermore, the characters who are the targets of Molière's satire, for example, the miser, the greedy doctor, the jealous husband, and the coquette, are based on the stock characters of the *commedia dell'arte*. What Molière did with these characters was to individualize them and to place them in the society of his own time, while still retaining in them the outlines of the universal types that they represented.

Molière's comedies are structured like the old French farces, which first identified the person to be deceived, then played a number of tricks on him, and finally exposed and humiliated him. At the beginning of the play, Molière establishes some obsession in the gull, which justifies his being embarrassed or thwarted, and similarly, he gives enough good qualities and appropriate goals to his tricksters so that at the end of the play, when they win, the audience is delighted. An example of such a gull would be Sganarelle in *The School for Husbands*. Because he is obsessed with his distrust of women, he deserves to be tricked. The ward and her young lover are attractive, their love is appealing, and their goal is to marry each other. Obviously, the audience identifies with them as they try to outwit the tyrannical Sganarelle and is delighted when they succeed.

In most comedies, as in this one, the tricksters are the disempowered, the servants or slaves instead of their masters, the young instead of the old, and women instead of men. It is for this reason that one does not disapprove of the lies and deception to which such characters must resort, for, after all, a person without power must triumph over the powerful by wit alone.

In neoclassical comedy, there is also a *raisonneur*, or a man of reason, who speaks for the author, while also reflecting the dominant intellectual tendencies of his time. In the speeches of Molière's *raisonneurs*, the audience would recognize Aristotle's theory of the Golden Mean, which in most cases placed virtue in a middle place between two extremes, for example, praising financial prudence as being neither extravagance nor miserliness. The obsessions of Molière's gulls would be examples of these extremes, where neither reason nor virtue dwells. The *raisonneur* would exemplify the ideal of the age, the *honnête homme*, the moderate, polite, honest gentleman, who is both rational and good.

If Molière's plays were nothing more than a dramatization of the advantages of moderation, however, they would be amusing but hardly memorable. Molière's best comedies not only warn of the consequences of obsession; they are also reminders that, by nature, human beings are obsessive creatures, and that although obsession may lead to embarrassment or even to tragedy, it is also obsession, not bland moderation, that creates lovers and saints. It has been suggested that Molière's plays reflect his own realization that two selves were at war within his own nature. One of the selves stressed the advantages of moderation; the other was at the mercy of his own emotions. Thus, Molière could see how foolish the lovesick older man might be, but he himself was tormented by his own love for his young, faithless wife; similarly, he could understand the need for discretion, but he could not deny his own idealism, and he castigated hypocrites wherever he found them, thus risking his career and even his freedom. Molière's best comedies do justice not only to the prudent plan for life that is the playwright's official stance, as voiced by his *raisonneur*, but also to the idealism, the passion for justice, and even the illusions whose loss, if perhaps necessary for survival, gives a tragic dimension to human existence.

THE SCHOOL FOR WIVES

First produced: *L'École des femmes*, 1662 (first published, 1663; English translation, 1732)

Type of work: Play

An older man discovers that he cannot manipulate a young woman as if she were a mere object.

The first scene of *The School for Wives* establishes the pattern of the drama. Arnolphe is the man in power, the guardian and virtual jailer of his young ward Agnès, whom he has kept in seclusion and in ignorance so that she will make him a virtuous wife. He refuses to listen to his friend Chrysalde, the *raisonneur*, who warns him against carrying out his plans. It soon becomes clear that Arnolphe deserves to be thwarted, not only because of his treatment of Agnès but also because he has other unappealing qualities. He is ill-natured, a man who spreads vicious gossip about husbands whose wives have cuckolded them; he is also a social climber, who has changed his name to "Monsieur Delafield" in order to pretend that he is an aristocrat.

This change of name makes possible a confusion of identity central to the plot. Because he is unaware of the name change, young Horace, the son of Arnolphe's friend Oronte, is soon innocently confiding in Arnolphe himself about the progress of his love affair with a girl whom he knows only as the ward of a Monsieur Delafied.

Although at first it seems that Arnolphe will be able to outwit the lovers, actually his advantage is very slight, because he discovers their encounters only after they have occurred. In scene after scene, Horace tells Arnolphe how his preventive measures have only served to benefit the young lovers. For example, when, in obedience to her guardian, Agnès threw a brick at Horace, she attached a love letter to it. Later, when Arnolphe set a trap for Horace, in the commotion, Agnès managed to escape from the house where her uncle had been keeping her a prisoner.

In their first conversation, Chrysalde warned Arnolphe that merely keeping Agnès ignorant would not keep her virtuous; in fact, he argued that a well-educated, rational woman would be better able to deal with her world than one who was too innocent to suspect wrongdoing. Certainly, the conversations that Agnès has with her guardian support Chrysalde's position. It is fortunate that Horace is honorable, for Agnès easily concludes that anything that brings her such pleasure as Horace's embrace could not possibly be wrong. Yet even if Agnès is too innocent to be skeptical about such delights, she is not stupid. It does not take her long to realize that the book about women's duties, which Arnolphe gives her to read, is biased; every maxim in it is intended to persuade women that they exist only for the pleasure of men. Not surprisingly, she prefers Horace's romantic devotion to Arnolphe's obvious distrust of women. Furthermore, Agnès is manifestly unwilling to remain passive, the mere ball of wax that Arnolphe boasts that he can mold as he wishes. Just as Chrysalde warned it would, Arnolphe's plan for producing a faithful wife fails, as it deserves to fail, because it is based on his own overwhelming egotism.

Agnès, however, does live in a hierarchical society, where women's freedom is extremely restricted. Therefore, in order to bring the lovers together, Molière must turn to fate or coincidence. In the final act of the play, Oronte appears with his long-absent friend Enrique. The two men have agreed on a marriage between Horace and the daughter of Enrique, whose identity has long been kept secret, but who in actuality is Agnès herself. Thus, Arnolphe loses his intended wife, and the lovers are married with the blessing of their parents.

There are a number of themes in this play. Obviously, one of them concerns the status of women. Molière is proving that men will be happier with women who are educated, respected, and trusted than with those who are deliberately kept in ignorance. Another is the theme of irrational obsession, as embodied in the character of Arnolphe. Essentially, Arnolphe's nastiness toward unfortunate husbands, his tyranny over Agnès, and his snobbishness, as reflected in the assumed title, are all aspects of a single character flaw, the fact that Arnolphe has no sense of himself, but only a consciousness of externals. That is the point of Chrysalde's long speech in act 4, where he attempts to persuade Arnolphe that he has misdefined honor, thinking of it as reputation, when it should be internal integrity. That is, of course, the ideal of the *honnête homme*. Chrysalde then says that he is not advocating the kind of tolerance that rejects all moral values; that would be the other extreme, not the Golden Mean. Instead, he is insisting on the middle way of the prudent man, who, unlike Arnolphe, finds his security not in the conduct or the opinions of others but in himself.

The very fact that *The School for Wives* was so successful inevitably brought bitter criticisms of the play from Molière's rivals. In order to answer them, he wrote a one-act sketch, meant to accompany the play whenever it was performed. *La Critique de "L'École des Femmes"* (*The Critique of "The School for Wives,"* 1957) was first presented on June 1, 1663. It is an interesting commentary on Molière's art. For example, he describes his characters as realistic but defends himself against the charge of personal ridicule by arguing that his satire is universal. To those who object to his double entendres, Molière responds that sexual suggestions come from the reader, not the writer. *The Critique of "The School for Wives"* makes it clear that Molière was not only an inspired dramatist but also an extremely careful craftsman, who took his work very seriously.

TARTUFFE

First produced: 1664 (first published, 1669; English translation, 1732)
Type of work: Play

A decent but gullible man is nearly ruined by the machinations of a religious hypocrite.

With *Tartuffe: Ou, L'Imposteur*, Molière moved further away from the simple structure derived from French farce. In this play, there is again a middle-aged man, Orgon, who can be tricked because of his obsession. Yet, although the trickster, Tartuffe, is a person outside the power structure, in this case he is a vicious hypocrite, who must be stripped of his power over Orgon if poetic justice is to prevail. Therefore, there is another pair of tricksters, Orgon's wife, Elmire, and his servant Dorine, who must set things right and aid the usual young lovers.

The structure of this play is also unusual in that the title character does not appear until the third act. In the first two acts, the characters voice their opinions of Tartuffe, this mysterious, seemingly pious man whom Orgon, the head of a prosperous Parisian household, has taken into his home as an honored guest. Except for Madame Pernelle, Orgon's mother, the family members are unanimous in voicing their dislike of the man. Orgon's young wife, Elmire, her stepson Damis, her stepdaughter Mariane, and her brother Cléante, the *raisonneur*, as well as the impertinent servant Dorine, all see Tartuffe for the hypocrite that he is.

After this preparation has been made, Orgon enters, and Molière begins to substantiate the fact that he is indeed besotted by this stranger. In a hilarious dialogue, Dorine attempts to report on the family, only to be answered over and over again by Orgon's anxious inquiry, "And Tartuffe?" followed by a heartfelt "poor fellow." Since Tartuffe's activities involve gluttonous eating and a good deal of sleeping, Orgon's concern about the man is ridiculous. The fact that Orgon's infatuation could have serious results is soon made clear, when he reveals his plan to make Tartuffe a member of the family by giving him his daughter in marriage. It is at this point that Elmire and Dorine begin to formulate plans to deceive the deceiver by attacking his own weaknesses.

Tartuffe's susceptibility to lust is revealed as soon as he makes his long-awaited entrance in the third act, when he begs Dorine to cover her bosom, so as not to tempt him to sin. Elmire's plan seems foolproof: She will lead him to make his designs upon her explicit and then threaten to tell Orgon unless Tartuffe relinquishes his claims on Mariane. The plan fails, however, and Tartuffe plays upon Orgon's emotions so skillfully that he manages to get Damis disinherited and himself made Orgon's heir. Now both of Orgon's children are powerless, and, of course, the *raisonneur* is still being ignored. Somehow, Elmire and Dorine must expose Tartuffe's perfidy so that even Orgon cannot deny it. They do have an ally, Tartuffe's own weakness.

Actors, directors, and critics agree that the nature of that weakness is the central issue of *Tartuffe*. There is no doubt that Tartuffe is bent on having his way with Elmire. Yet even in the scenes where he attempts to seduce her, he can be seen as dominated by the desire for power. Whether his later arrogance is the result of his humiliation by Elmire or merely his true nature, Tartuffe viciously seeks to deprive his former patron of his property, his freedom, perhaps even of his life, and he is stopped only by the intervention of the godlike King, who Molière says cannot be deceived.

This graceful compliment was not only politic but also probably expressed Molière's gratitude to Louis XIV, who had supported the playwright through his various attempts to stage this play. For some time, Molière had been suspect in the eyes of an influential party at court, which considered itself as the guardian of public morals. This group managed to have two versions of *Tartuffe* suppressed, first in 1664, then in 1667. Only after Louis XIV obtained the opinion of a theologian who was too prominent to be refuted was the final version of *Tartuffe* presented. Within its first year, it was performed fifty-five times. It has continued to be one of Molière's most popular plays, and it is considered one of his greatest masterpieces.

THE WOULD-BE GENTLEMAN

First produced: *Le Bourgeois Gentilhomme*, 1670 (first published, 1671; English translation, 1675)
Type of work: Play

A commoner who wishes to climb the social ladder becomes an easy dupe.

Even during his final decade, when he was producing comedies as complex and thought provoking as *Tartuffe*, Molière sometimes wrote works that were much more like French farce in their simplicity and lightheartedness. *The Would-Be Gentleman* is such a play.

The gull in this comedy-ballet is M. Jourdain, a commoner who has inherited some money and now wishes to become something that he is not, a gentleman. Like so many of Molière's obsessed characters, Jourdain defines what a person is in terms of externals. In contrast, his practical wife, Madame Jourdain, sees clearly what he is, what she is, and where they belong in society. Perhaps because this play takes place among the bourgeoisie, not among the gentry, there is no *honnête homme* in it to serve as the voice of reason. Instead, the function of the *raisonneur* is filled by Madame Jourdain herself, who, along with the servant Nicole, points out the merits of moderation.

As far as structure is concerned, *The Would-Be Gentleman* consists of a series of episodes, each one act long, which are brightened by songs and separated by interludes of dance. In each episode, tricksters take advantage of M. Jourdain's social ambitions. In the first act, a musician and a dancing master are instructing him; in the second, they are joined by a fencing teacher, and finally by a master of philosophy, who astonishes M. Jourdain by convincing him that he has been talking prose all of his life. M. Jourdain's willingness to be duped is illustrated when he sees his new coat, made with the flowers upside down; all his tailor has to say is that this is the fashion of the gentry, and once again M. Jourdain denies his reason and accepts the coat. If he can be so easily fooled by tradespeople, the would-be gentleman is no match at all for an impecunious nobleman. For some time, Count Dorante has been "borrowing" money from M. Jourdain. Now he has plans to maximize his profits, by persuading his victim that the aristocratic Dorimène might become his mistress, if only M. Jourdain will send enough magnificent gifts to her.

Throughout all of these incidents, the audience remains delighted but disengaged, sympathetic only with the sensible wife who, like all *raisonneurs*, is certain to be ignored. When the happiness of two young lovers is threatened because of M. Jourdain's social ambitions, however, it is time for a trickster of a different kind. As so often in these comedies, this turns out to be the thwarted young man. Because he is not a nobleman, Cléonte has been refused the hand of M. Jourdain's daughter. In a wonderful fifth act, Cléonte takes advantage of M. Jourdain's reliance on appearances. Dressed as the Grand Turk and speaking in gibberish, he wins his lady, and the play ends with several marriages, including that of Dorante to Dorimène, and, of course, the final ballet.

It is obvious that, except for the use of a woman as *raisonneur*, *The Would-Be Gentleman* is much like Molière's simpler early plays. Because it avoids the dark possibilities of plays such as *Tartuffe* and satirizes the pretentious bourgeoisie for an audience that considered itself vastly superior to it, *The Would-Be Gentleman* produced no controversy at court. It is interesting that Louis XIV pronounced it his favorite of Molière's works. The play has continued to delight later audiences even as it once pleased Molière's king.

THE MISANTHROPE

First produced: 1666 (first published, 1667; English translation, 1709)
Type of work: Play

An idealist who insists on being honest finds that he cannot survive in society.

Although in some of Molière's plays the protagonist is deceived because he is both egotistical and foolish, in more thoughtful works, such as *Tartuffe* and *Le Misanthrope* (*The Misanthrope*), it is an excess of virtue that makes him vulnerable. In *Tartuffe*, Orgon was obsessed by religion; in *The Misanthrope*, Alceste is obsessed by honesty.

The Misanthrope begins with a conventional opening dialogue between the central character, Alceste, and his friend, the easygoing Philinte, who is the *raisonneur*. In this scene, Alceste states his determination to speak nothing but the truth, and the horrified Philinte vainly attempts to warn him of the consequences. In society, Philinte points out, a little dishonesty is essential. Otherwise, there would be open warfare. Alceste, however, is adamant. The scenes that follow trace the consequences of his resolution, from the failure of a lawsuit to the loss of his beloved Célimène.

It is Célimène who is Alceste's one irrationality. Ironically, he is in love with the most deceitful woman at court. As far as the play is concerned, Célimène fulfills the function of the trickster. Her only motivation, however, is a selfish one: She lies so as to accumulate as many admirers as possible. Obviously, she is, in her own way, as obsessive as Alceste, without the excuse of virtue. Therefore, it is not surprising that she is finally exposed through some carelessness about letters. Nevertheless, she dashes Alceste's hopes; she would agree to marry him, she says, but not at the cost of leaving society, as the disillusioned Alceste has resolved to do. She would rather replace the lovers who have abandoned her than spend her youth in a desert.

Although Alceste loses Célimène forever, there is another match at the end of *The Misanthrope*, which actually materializes through Alceste's own insensitivity. Throughout the play, the gentle, rational Éliante has shown no interest in Philinte, who loves her and who sees in her the social but virtuous female counterpart of himself. Unfortunately, Éliante is as irrationally in love with Alceste as Alceste is with Célimène. Unlike Alceste, however, who always makes excuses for Célimène, Éliante can see the unpleasant truth about someone whom she loves. After Alceste has been rejected by Célimène, he churlishly offers to marry Éliante, making it quite clear that she is his second choice. At that moment, Éliante realizes that Alceste is less than a perfect person. Although honest, he is insensitive and inconsiderate. Without a second thought, Éliante rejects him, and, suddenly aware of the virtues of her friend, the devoted Philinte, she accepts his proposal of marriage.

With so slight a plot, *The Misanthrope* depends for its interest on characterization and on theme. Molière's contemporaries recognized in his characters most of the types present in aristocratic society, for example, dilettantes such as Oronte, empty-headed fops such as Acaste and Clitandre, and hypocritical prudes such as Arsinoé. Through Célimène's admittedly catty descriptions, Molière includes other character types who do not actually appear on stage, the incessant talker, the dramatically mysterious man, the name-dropper, the tediously dull woman, and the equally boring egotist. The result is a comprehensive view of a society that obviously deserved to be satirized.

As to Molière's own attitude toward that society, critics continue to disagree. Although Philinte and Éliante obviously represent good sense and moderation, some argue that Molière identifies more closely with Alceste. There is good reason for Philinte to remain loyal to his friend, who, unlike most of the other courtiers, takes life seriously. As a satirist, Molière could hardly do less.

Summary

From the plots and character types familiar to his audience, Molière developed modern comedy. His plays vary from simple to complex, from farce and comedy-ballet to comedy of manners and what might be termed comedy of character. Whatever their nature, they play beautifully. The words, the situations, and the scenes are as funny to twentieth century audiences as they were in Molière's time. Furthermore, in the plays that are considered Molière's masterpieces, such as *Tartuffe* and *The Misanthrope*, audiences find something more than humor, a realistic view of the world as the home of fools, along with a belief that good will ordinarily triumph over evil, but only by the narrowest margin.

Bibliography

Chapman, Percy Addison. *The Spirit of Molière: An Interpretation.* Edited by Jean-Albert Bédé. Princeton, N.J.: Princeton University Press, 1940.

Gossman, Lionel. *Men and Masks: A Study of Molière.* Baltimore: Johns Hopkins University Press, 1963.

Guicharnaud, Jacques, ed. *Molière: A Collection of Critical Essays.* Englewood Cliffs, N.J.: Prentice-Hall, 1964.

Howarth, W. D., and Merlin Thomas, eds. *Molière: Stage and Study.* Oxford, England: Clarendon Press, 1973.

Mander, Gertrud. *Molière.* Translated by Diana Stone Peters. New York: Frederick Ungar, 1973.

Moore, Will G. *Molière: A New Criticism.* Oxford, England: Clarendon Press, 1949.

Rosemary M. Canfield Reisman

MICHEL DE MONTAIGNE

Born: Château de Montaigne, France
February 28, 1533
Died: Château de Montaigne, France
September 13, 1592

Principal Literary Achievement

Montaigne, in *The Essays*, created a new literary form, the personal essay, which writers elsewhere would develop into a major literary genre.

Biography

Michel Eyquem de Montaigne was born to wealthy parents, Pierre Eyquem and Antoinette de Louppes, in the family château in southwestern France on February 28, 1533. From childhood, he was taught to speak Latin even before his own native language, for his German tutor knew no French and instructed his pupil exclusively in the language of antiquity. Consequently, during his first ten years, Montaigne knew little French at all. From classical languages, however, he learned clarity of expression and thought, and his writings are enriched by references to Roman history, mythology, and authors such as Cicero, Vergil, and Seneca.

Montaigne's training in classical languages and literature was also an indication of his century. The rapid spread of Greek and Roman classics and the newly revived humanistic learning of the Renaissance was no more than a quarter of a century old in France when he was born, and it was not unusual for children such as Michel to learn Latin. Earlier, however, the Latin that he was taught would have been church Latin, but Montaigne learned the secular Latin of the great poets and orators of the past. Montaigne went on to become one of the principal proponents of this classical learning, called the New Philosophy, and its insistence upon the individual as the measure of all things and upon a healthy skepticism in the pursuit of truth. Montaigne, in fact, took as his motto, "Que sais-je?" ("What do I know?"), reflecting his rejection of authority, his tolerance for all ideas, and his restless and searching mind.

Montaigne's father, a wealthy merchant, sent his son to the Collège de Guyenne in Bordeaux from 1539 to 1546 and later to the University of Bordeaux to study philosophy. Later still, in 1559, Montaigne studied law at the University of Toulouse. In 1557, his father was elected mayor of Bordeaux, leaving his post as counselor in the parliament of Bordeaux and passing it on to his son. Montaigne served as counselor until 1570, during a time of great religious and political upheaval in France. A series of

civil wars between Catholics and Protestants (who acquired the derisive name Huguenots) divided the country, culminating in 1572 with the ambush slaying of twenty thousand Huguenots on St. Bartholomew's Day (August 24).

One of Montaigne's fellow counselors on the Bordeaux parliament was Étienne de La Boétie, a gifted poet, dedicated humanist, and distinguished civil servant, and the two men developed a close friendship. La Boétie died suddenly in 1563, at the young age of thirty-two, and his death was one of the great losses of Montaigne's life. Montaigne's essays are filled with references to friends and friendship, and years after La Boétie's death Montaigne noted in his diaries his still painful recollections of his friend.

In 1565, Montaigne married Françoise de la Chassaigne, the daughter of a fellow counselor. They had six daughters, only one of whom, Léonore, survived infancy. The marriage itself seems to have been a reasonably happy one, but the subject is much debated by Montaigne scholars. The *Essais* (1580, 1588, 1595; *The Essays*, 1603) are full of acerbic comments about wives and marriage, and in his essay "De la diversion" ("Of Diversion"), Montaigne admits that he made himself fall in love to distract himself from the overpowering grief of La Boétie's death. In another essay, he insists that a good marriage—and there may not be one, according to Montaigne—is based not on love but on friendship. Whether of love or of friendship, his marriage lasted twenty-seven years.

When his father died in 1570, Montaigne retired to the family estate that he inherited. There he spent the greater part of his time writing and thinking in the tower-library of his château. For his career as a civil servant, he was ordained in 1571 into the Order of St. Michael, and King Charles IX gave him the title Gentleman of the King's Chamber. Mainly, though, he led the secluded life of a philosopher-author, and in March of 1580 the first edition of *The Essays* appeared for the amusement of a few friends and relatives.

After nine years of self-imposed exile to write a book, Montaigne set out on a seventeen-month journey to Italy via Switzerland and Germany. In part, the trip was intended to relieve the intense pain of a kidney stone, an illness that had killed his father, and Montaigne took curative waters and treatment at various foreign spas. While he was away, his fellow citizens of Bordeaux nominated and elected him as mayor in 1581, a post that he held until 1585, at which time he resigned and left Bordeaux when the plague broke out. Montaigne and his family wandered from place to place for six months, returning home around the end of 1586.

For the remainder of his life, Montaigne lived a life of retirement and seclusion, and he continued to write. A second edition of *The Essays* appeared in 1588 with some additions, and a final version came out in 1595 that included three books of essays and was almost twice as long as the 1580 book. It is this volume, the work of a fully mature mind, that stands as Montaigne's final monument. He died in his family château on September 13, 1592, and was buried in a small church in Bordeaux. Three centuries later, in 1886, his remains were placed in the entrance hall of the building of the Faculties of Theology, Science, and Letters of the University of Bordeaux.

They remain there to this day, appropriately secluded in a place of books and learning, the two principal passions of Montaigne's life.

Analysis

The word "essay," a familiar literary term today, was coined by Montaigne, but the word had a meaning that is different from its modern meaning. Essay derives from the Latin word *exagium*, a weighing, and from the French word *essai*, a trial or test. Montaigne's writings were weighings of himself and his beliefs, in the same way that one would weigh, or "assay," precious ore to determine its worth. They are equally a test of his judgments, a testing of ideas and random thoughts, an attempt to assess himself and his experiences at various points of his life. The subject of his essays, as he says in many places, is always himself, and his task as an author is to see himself as accurately as he can, to be truthful about what he believes.

Montaigne, however, never thought that his own life and thoughts would hold fascination for centuries of readers. What, then, has attracted readers to Montaigne over the centuries? First, there is his common sense and universality. He is attractive to readers precisely because he is so much like them, so much so that, in fact, his thoughts often seem commonplace. Second, preceding Sigmund Freud, Montaigne had a strong sense of the divisions within the human psyche, the conflict of humanity against itself, and the inability of human reason to solve all of humankind's problems. What Montaigne seeks is what one would today call "the integrated personality," a unified sense of being and an orderly view of life. Finally, readers appreciate Montaigne's clarity of thought and expression, his confessional style, and his mordant wit—all qualities found in the best contemporary essayists such as Joan Didion, Andy Rooney, and Tom Wolfe.

Exactly how to categorize Montaigne's thought, however, is not an easy task. He has been called a hedonist, a skeptic, a stoic, and even an existentialist, but none of these seems fully adequate. He is a hedonist in his love of life and enjoyment of sensual pleasures, but in essays such as "De la moderation" ("Of Moderation"), he warns that a person can become a slave to his or her senses. His essays on idleness, lying, cruelty, cowardice, vanity, and drunkenness testify to his skeptical view of humankind's innate goodness, but these are equally balanced by essays on constancy, friendship, virtue, repentance, and moderation. Montaigne's stoicism is clear in his thoughts on death, and he titles one of his essays "Que philosopher c'est apprendre à mourir" ("To Philosophize Is to Learn to Die"), but he also emphasizes the enjoyment of this life. Finally, like the existentialists of the twentieth century, Montaigne sees life in a continual flux, making the attainment of absolute truth impossible. Yet if the absurdity of the human condition prevents people from having true knowledge, they can at least know themselves in their perpetually changing condition.

Perhaps the best term for Montaigne is one suggested by Donald Frame, Professor Emeritus of French at Columbia University. Montaigne is an "apprehensive humanist," a lover of reason and books, and a student of human custom and behavior, who is uneasy about the human condition. While the mass of humans may be ignorant, stupid, lazy, and lustful, they can still accomplish occasional great things. Life is paradox and contradiction—composed, Montaigne says, of contrary things—and one must learn to accept human contrariness.

Finally, Montaigne's use of paradox and irony, balanced phrase and metaphor are masterful, and no one has written in the French language with greater elegance and grace. *The Essays* are stylishly written reflections upon the oppositions of humanity and God, good and evil, action and inaction, faith and reason. If Montaigne reaches no conclusions, his journey consists of fascinating intellectual twists and turns; and if he continually asks, "What do I know?" he always does so with wit, modesty, and candor.

OF CANNIBALS

First published: "Des cannibales," 1580 (English translation, 1603)
Type of work: Essay

What people call barbarism is merely vanity and ignorance on their part, for the behavior of "civilized" people surpasses the barbarism of supposedly "uncivilized" people in every way.

Montaigne's age was one of adventure and exploration, and many travelers returned to Europe with tales of strange and fascinating people elsewhere. During a French expedition to South America in 1557, the explorer Villegaignon encountered a tribe of cannibals in what was then called "Antarctic France" but what is now called Brazil. Some of them returned with the crew. Montaigne not only met one of these cannibals at Rouen in 1562 but also employed a servant who had spent a dozen years living among them in their native land.

From this firsthand knowledge, Montaigne in "Of Cannibals" reverses the egocentric European belief in the superiority of Western culture. Not simple, ignorant, and barbarous as some would insist, cannibals live in harmony with nature, employ useful and virtuous skills, and enjoy a perfect religious life and governmental system. Instead, it is the European who has bastardized nature and her works, while the so-called savage lives in a state of purity. Much like American author Herman Melville, who later chronicled his life among the cannibals in *Typee: A Peep at Polynesian Life* (1846), Montaigne sees more barbarous behavior among his immediate neighbors.

As evidence, Montaigne cites everything from language usage to architecture. The cannibals have, he says, no words for lying, treachery, dissimulation, avarice, envy, and other vices. They have no slaves, no distinctions between rich and poor, and no mania for owning things. They live in a land of plenty, eat only one meal a day, and spend the whole day dancing. Their religious and ethical beliefs are admirably simple. They believe in the immortality of the soul, in a kind of heaven and hell, and in divine prophecy. They have, in fact, tribal prophets who, if they fail to prophesy correctly, are immediately put to the sword, a swift justice that Montaigne does not condemn, for false prophets should be severely punished. As for their priests, they daily preach only two virtues: love and courage.

In wars with nations beyond their territory, the cannibals know neither fear nor cowardice even though their battles often end in bloodshed. Each man brings back the head of an enemy as a trophy and hangs it over the entrance of his dwelling. The enemy prisoners brought back are slain and eaten, not for nourishment but for revenge. Such behavior has earned for them the name "savages," but Montaigne sees more savagery in the European practices of torturing or burning alive—and, what is worse, doing it in the name of religion. While the cannibals clearly violate rules of reasonable behavior, Montaigne concludes, the Europeans surpass them in every kind of barbarity and cruelty.

There is little doubt that Montaigne romanticizes "the noble savage" in his essay, as authors were to do for centuries afterward, but he is one of the first great thinkers to question the Eurocentric view of human behavior, the notion that the standard for human behavior is white, Christian, and European. While it is doubtless true that he idealizes the life of Brazilian tribal peoples, nonetheless he sees the dignity, nobility, intelligence, and harmony of their lives. He forces the readers to confront themselves and their own social behavior; as Montaigne notes, there is such a distance in character between the cannibals and his audience that either the cannibals are savages or his readers are. Montaigne tries hard throughout his essay to find fault with the cannibals' behavior and way of life but can offer only one, slightly humorous, observation: They do not wear trousers.

APOLOGY FOR RAYMOND SEBOND

First published: "Apologie de Raimond Sebond," 1580 (English translation, 1603)

Type of work: Essay

People are incapable of true knowledge, for they exist in an eternal flux while truth is immutable and unchanging.

Raymond Sebond was a fifteenth century Spaniard who taught philosophy and theology at the University of Toulouse, dying there in 1436. His book *Natural Theology* was published posthumously in 1484 and was a popular success in France. It argues for the truths of Christianity on the basis of the natural world—the book of nature— and Sebond claims that God is in evidence in the Creation more than in theology or Scripture.

The "Apology for Raymond Sebond" is three times as long as any other essay that Montaigne wrote, and it is by far his most puzzling work. Supposedly a defense of Sebond's Christian doctrine, the essay has been seen as an attack on authoritarian religion and a covert undermining of Christian faith. Less than one-tenth of the essay defends Sebond's ideas at all. Primarily, the work argues the impotence of human reason and humanity's inability to determine truth, set as a counterargument to a group of Sebond's critics.

Montaigne begins with the first objection to Sebond's theology—that the divine can be conceived only by faith, not by human intelligence. Montaigne admits that faith is more apt to solve the mysteries of religion than reason, yet humans seem improperly suited to divine faith. Humankind's often immoral behavior testifies to the inability of faith alone to raise it above itself. Faith must be accompanied by ideas and reasonings in order to set humanity on the road to knowledge, to make it capable of the grace of God.

It is at this point that Montaigne addresses the issue of human knowledge, the heart of the essay, and his reflections reveal a deep despair about the human condition, an undercurrent of pessimism found in such other Renaissance works as William Shakespeare's *Hamlet* (c. 1600-1601) and John Donne's sermons and devotions. Humankind is a puny and miserable creature, swollen with vanity, who calls itself master of the universe while unable even to master its own passions and weaknesses. Viewing itself as the equal of God, it is actually no better than an animal. "When I play with my cat," Montaigne says, "who knows if I am not a pastime to her more than she is to me?" Citing the Renaissance notion of the Great Chain of Being, an orderly universe in which each thing is in its properly fixed place, Montaigne insists that there is a natural order that constrains and limits humanity's vain ambitions to become a god, and that people must be forced to accept the barriers of this order.

If people are made in God's image, then God is, like them, an animal. If He is an animal, He has a body, and if He has a body, He is also subject to corruption. On the other hand, if God has no body, He has no soul, for the soul exists only in the body. This paradox is unthinkable to Montaigne. Similarly, if a person has a divine soul that knows all things, it would at least know itself, if nothing more than its outward body. Yet Montaigne sees medical doctors everywhere disputing even simple matters of human anatomy, and for all its science, arts, and learning, humanity knows very little about itself. Therefore, Montaigne concludes, the human mind can never penetrate the dark recesses of hidden truth. Learning consists of nothing more than an infinite confusion of opinions, and people are in agreement about nothing. They can never know truth.

The ultimate truth is knowledge of God, and at the end of the essay, Montaigne more or less returns to Sebond, adding a few paragraphs stating that humankind is nothing without God and that God must lend a helping hand if humans are to attain knowledge of Him. By then, however, it is too late. Montaigne has raised profound questions about humankind, God, and human knowledge, and his candid reasoning has led him (and the reader) to unsettling conclusions.

Summary

Michel de Montaigne's place in the history of world literature has been secure for more than four hundred years. He is not only the father of the modern essay form but also a writer of singular artistry who has been admired down through the centuries by such noted authors as Lord Byron, Gustave Flaubert, Thomas Carlyle, Ralph Waldo Emerson, Virginia Woolf, André Gide, T. S. Eliot, and many others. His epigrammatic style makes him an often-quoted author, while the clarity of diction, the balanced phrasing, and the proper words in proper order make his statements ring with truth and stay in the mind.

"Free association artistically controlled—this is the paradoxical secret of Montaigne's best essays," said British novelist and essayist Aldous Huxley. "One damned thing after another—but in a sequence that in some almost miraculous way develops a central theme and relates it to the rest of human experience." Perhaps the American essayist Emerson summarized him best: Montaigne is "never dull, never insincere, and has the genius to make the reader care for all that he cares for."

Bibliography

Bloom, Harold, ed. *Michel de Montaigne.* New York: Chelsea House, 1987.

_____, ed. *Montaigne's Essays.* New York: Chelsea House, 1987.

Burke, Peter. *Montaigne.* New York: Oxford University Press, 1981.

Emerson, Ralph Waldo. "Montaigne: Or, The Skeptic." In *Representative Men: Seven Lectures.* Boston: Philips, Sampson, 1850.

Frame, Donald. *Montaigne: A Biography.* New York: Harcourt, Brace & World, 1965.

_____. *Montaigne's Discovery of Man: The Humanization of a Humanist.* New York: Columbia University Press, 1955.

Friedrich, Hugo. *Montaigne.* Translated by Robert Rovini. Paris: Gallimard, 1968.

Regosin, Richard L. *The Matter of My Book: Montaigne's "Essais" as the Book of the Self.* Berkeley: University of California Press, 1977.

Starobinski, Jean. *Montaigne in Motion.* Chicago: University of Chicago Press, 1985.

Tetel, Marcel. *Montaigne.* Rev. ed. Boston: Twayne, 1990.

Kenneth Seib

FARLEY MOWAT

Born: Belleville, Ontario, Canada
May 12, 1921

Principal Literary Achievement

One of Canada's foremost authors, Mowat is primarily concerned with nature, environmental issues, the ethics of modern life, and governments that seemingly have no regard for tradition.

Biography

Farley McGill Mowat was born in Belleville, Ontario, on May 12, 1921, to Angus McGill and Helen E. Thomson Mowat. After completing his public school education in Ontario, he joined the Canadian army in 1939, rising to the rank of captain in the infantry and serving overseas during World War II. In 1945, Mowat returned to Canada and received his B.A. from the University of Toronto in 1949. That year, he married Frances Elizabeth Thornhill, with whom he had two children, Robert Alexander and David Peter; the marriage ended in divorce, and Mowat married Claire Angel Wheeler in 1961. He and his wife settled in Port Hope, Ontario.

The author of more than two dozen books ranging from autobiography to children's literature, Mowat began his writing career as a result of his conflict with his employer, the Canadian government. After returning from military service, he accepted a job as a biological researcher for the Dominion Wildlife Service in the Barren Grounds of northern Canada to observe what effects the wolves had on the caribou herds. While there, Mowat also became friends with a small Eskimo tribe, the Ihalmiut, who call themselves the People of the Deer because the caribou provides them with food, clothing, and shelter. In response to what Mowat perceived to be the Canadian government's negligent attitude toward these people, he began a crusade to help them preserve their heritage, a campaign that not only failed but also cost him his job. Mowat's first book, *People of the Deer* (1952; revised, 1975), chronicles his experiences, and its sequel, *The Desperate People* (1959; revised, 1975), describes the Ihalmiut's defeat. Both books were later revised and reissued to temper what some critics saw as misrepresentations of natural and social history. In 1954, *People of the Deer* won the Anisfield-Wolfe Award for contribution to interracial relations.

People of the Deer begins Mowat's career-long engagement with issues relating to the far north country of Canada; he views himself as more of a storyteller than a

1331

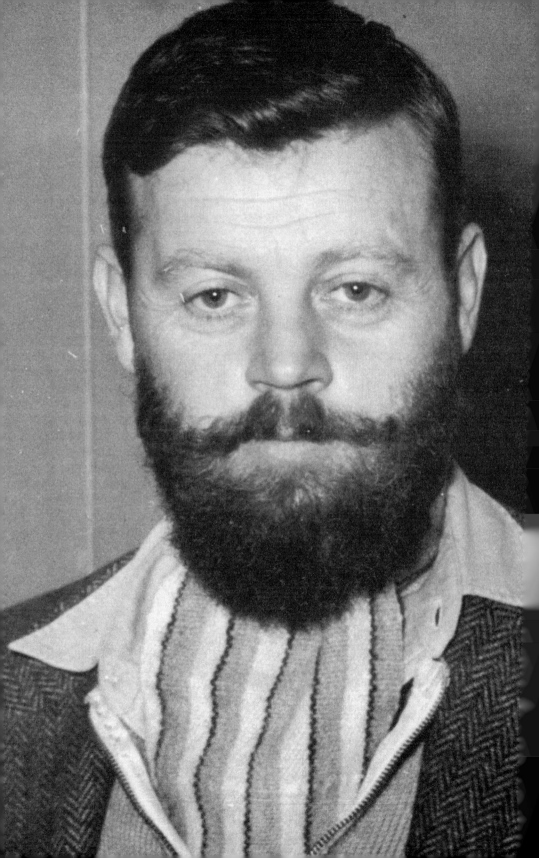

naturalist, despite what he considers to be misguided attempts to categorize him as such. Mowat seeks to explore the complicated relationships between species: wolf and humankind, caribou and Eskimo, and the hunter and the hunted.

A summer spent in Churchill, Manitoba, with his uncle, western Canadian ornithologist Frank Farley, first introduced the author to the beauties of the Canadian north country; this tundra world is a place to which Mowat returns again and again in his writing. Besides *People of the Deer* and *The Desperate People*, Mowat pursues this interest in what is referred to as The Top of the World Trilogy: *Ordeal by Ice* (1960), *The Polar Passion* (1967), and *Tundra* (1973), in which he presents intimate glimpses of the explorers who faced the challenge of arctic exploration, drawing heavily from the explorers' journals to create his story. In *Canada North* (1967), Mowat wrote the text for the photographic volume that was published in conjunction with the Canadian Centennial project. *Sibir: My Discovery of Siberia* (1970; published in the United States as *The Siberians*, 1970) recounts Mowat's experiences on his 1966 and 1969 visits to Siberian communities in the Soviet Union. *Snow Walker* (1975) contains short stories and sketches of the people of the north country as they fight a harsh natural environment and the encroachments of modern technology.

Mowat lived for many years in Newfoundland, and his work reflects his connectedness to that region. In the 1950's, Mowat worked on two books about the maritime salvage industry: *The Grey Seas Under* (1959) and *The Serpent's Coil* (1961), both of which look at people in contact and often in conflict with their natural surroundings. Yet in 1967 he left his home at Burgeo, Newfoundland, after becoming embroiled in a bitter and unsuccessful fight with local residents and government bureaucrats to save a trapped whale; his experiences resulted in *A Whale for the Killing* (1972).

While much of Mowat's work reflects his personal interests broadened to include a more global perspective, a fair amount of his writings is also autobiographical: *Never Cry Wolf* (1963) tells of his first job as a wildlife researcher; *The Boat Who Wouldn't Float* (1968), which won the Leacock Medal and was named to *L'Étoile de la Mer*'s honors list, describes his 1967 adventures sailing along the Newfoundland and Maritime Provinces' coastlines; *The Dog Who Wouldn't Be* (1957), which won the Canadian Women's Clubs Award, and *Owls in the Family* (1961), which won both the Hans Christian Andersen International Award and the Boys' Clubs of America Junior Book Award, tell of pets that he had as a child; *And No Birds Sang* (1979) describes his experience of what he labels "The Worm That Never Dies," the terror of war; and *My Discovery of America* (1985) recounts his exclusion from the United States in 1984 as a result of being labeled an undesirable.

Mowat's work in the 1980's has received high praise as well as popular attention: *Sea of Slaughter* (1984) is his account of the decimation of the wildlife populations off the northeastern coast of North America; *Woman in the Mists: The Story of Dian Fossey and the Mountain Gorillas of Africa* (1987) is Mowat's biography of the American naturalist murdered in 1985 after her vigorous attempts to preserve the wild gorillas in Rwanda, Central Africa. Three of Mowat's books have been made into films: a television production of *A Whale for the Killing* in 1981, the movie version of *Never Cry Wolf*, released in 1983, and *Gorillas in the Mist*, the film version of *Woman in the Mists*, in 1988.

Mowat has received many honors, including the President's Medal, University of Western Ontario, 1952, for best Canadian short story of 1952; the National Association of Independent Schools Award, for juvenile books, 1963; the Hans Christian Andersen Honours List for juvenile books, 1965; the Canadian Centennial Medal, 1967; doctor of literature, Laurentian University, 1970; Vicky Metcalf Award, 1970; Mark Twain Award, 1971; doctor of law from Lethbridge University, 1973, the University of Toronto, 1973, and the University of Prince Edward Island, 1979; Curran Award, 1977, for "contributions to understanding wolves"; Queen Elizabeth II Jubilee Medal, 1978; Knight of Mark Twain, 1980; Officer, Order of Canada, 1981; and doctor of literature, University of Victoria, 1982, and Lakehead University, 1986.

Analysis

In a 1987 interview, Mowat characterized himself as someone

> interested in writing about wildlife, but that's secondary. I am basically a storyteller. . . . [I]t's my life. . . . [M]ore and more I'm being categorized as a nature writer. That's nonsense. I'm not a nature writer. I write about life on this planet, and that includes human life and nonhuman life. I'm concerned about what's happening to all forms of life.

For Mowat, nature provides the arena in which to explore the interconnectedness of all life and to assert the legitimacy of the many ways of living on this planet. The primary targets of his work are bureaucracy, technology, and cultural imperialism and the ways in which industrialized societies have arrogantly ignored the needs and rights of the other inhabitants of the globe, including those inhabitants that are not human.

Mowat's strong personality reverberates throughout his work, a style that has been labeled "subjective non-fiction" by one of his critics. He does not shrink from confrontation or from assigning blame where he thinks it lies, as in the case of the Canadian government in *People of the Deer*. This pugnaciousness often earns for him criticism or, as in the case of the events that prompted him to write about the Ihalmiuts, the loss of his job. Pleasing the powers that be has never been one of Mowat's concerns, however; he instead is determined to make his views known and, by doing so, to raise public awareness and effect change.

The Canadian North Country and the tundra provide Mowat with ample opportunity to accomplish both goals. *The Siberians*, for example, is his account of two trips that he made to the Soviet Union, visiting remote settlements where people lead a self-contained and self-respecting way of life. In the case of both the Siberians and the Ihalmiut Eskimo, in *People of the Deer*, Mowat finds people who tread softly on the earth, who are in tune with rather than up in arms against nature. These people do not destroy for the sake of the hunt; rather, he says, "they kill to eat, to keep themselves going, but they don't kill for fun, they don't kill for greed, they don't kill from any of the motivations that we have." Mowat repeatedly looks at the Canadian wilderness and sees it as a staging ground for exploitation and neglect, for human arrogance and greed, and for disregard for a more widely focused ecological balance and harmony. His examination of the early polar explorers in *Ordeal by Ice* and *The Polar Passion* clearly demonstrates the futility of battling against nature, which always wins.

Mowat's angry reverence for nature and his accusatory stance against arrogant technological aggression on the part of the Canadian government may be seen in such books as *Never Cry Wolf* and *A Whale for the Killing.* He and others have pointed out the irony in the Canadian government's disregard of his findings concerning the tundra wolves. In *A Whale for the Killing*, Mowat could not convince his neighbors that a trapped whale had a right to be freed rather than tortured, and he used the creature's story to explore the wholesale slaughter of sea creatures and the negligence of the Canadian government. *Sea of Slaughter* represents a broader consideration of the issues that Mowat raised in the previous two books and clearly demonstrates his anger at the senseless injuries that people inflict on other species. Mowat makes a strong case against the exploitation of both the land- and the sea-dwelling animals along the Atlantic seaboard from Cape Cod to Labrador. To strengthen the impact of *Sea of Slaughter*, he offers a historical account of the area beginning in the sixteenth century, clearly demonstrating the frightening and unnecessary changes that humans have caused as they pillaged both land and sea: pollution, overhunting, destruction of habitat and food sources, poaching, and government-sanctioned cullings of seal and other animals.

Mowat sees himself as a rebel and seems to relish the opportunity that his confrontations with government and other representatives of the establishment such as business and industry afford him for driving his message home. He sometimes uses wry humor to make his points, as in *My Discovery of America* (1985), in which he describes his attempts to discover why he had been denied permission to enter the United States on a speaking tour in 1984. Mowat speculates that he had been accused of anti-American sentiments; his pugnacious attitude surfaces in his refusal to come to the United States despite that country's Immigration and Naturalization Service having belatedly granted him admission, refusing because the U.S. government has yet to apologize for its mistake.

NEVER CRY WOLF

First published: 1963
Type of work: Natural history and autobiography

The wolves of the arctic wilderness are not the fierce predators that their detractors have accused them of being.

Never Cry Wolf recounts Mowat's experiences as a biologist/naturalist sent by the Canadian government to study a group of wolves in the Canadian tundra of the far north. It had always been assumed that the wolves were a threat to other wildlife populations and, by extension, to domestic herds because they needlessly destroyed large numbers of animals. Mowat's experiences living in the midst of the tundra, the wolves, and the caribou herd stand in direct contradiction to the Canadian government's assumption that the wolves were to blame for the decline in those caribou populations. As Mowat was to discover, however, his findings were not information that government bureaucrats wanted to hear. Unlike the Canadian government, which did nothing to alter its negative treatment of the wolves, when *Never Cry Wolf* was translated into Russian, the Soviet government banned the slaughter of wolves, animals that it had previously considered dangerous predators.

Never Cry Wolf is as much about the way in which humans misperceive the behavior of other species as it is about the true behavior of the wolves that Mowat observed. The story brings the social dynamics of this wolf population to light, animals representing a complex family network, one making little impact on the ecosystem in which it lives. As well as these two issues, Mowat gives readers a humorous and revealing look at himself as he changes his mind about the "threats" that these animals pose, not only to the greater population but also to himself as the lone observer living in close proximity to them on the tundra. The book achieves its power because it is both a global treatment of what might be called species imperialism and shortsightedness on the part of humans and a "local" portrait of one wolf group and the one human who must live in and adapt to their world, a place that is oftentimes harsh and unpredictable.

In order to see his wolves, whom he names George and Angeline, Mowat clearly had to learn to think like a wolf, to see the world as wolves see it, to hear what they hear, and to respond to what matters to them. Sometimes the results are comical, as when Mowat resorts to marking out his territory in the same way as George had done, with urine. The book describes wolves, and their observer, going about the day-to-day business of surviving, and it is this act of making do in a stubbornly hostile environment that gives the book its power and allows Mowat to invest the wolves with great dignity. He concludes that wolves take from nature only what they need—principally field mice and a few ailing caribou; the lesson that his observations teach is obvious, but one that the Canadian government did not heed: The wolves have as much right to be where they are and do what they are doing as any other species.

Never Cry Wolf was adapted into a successful motion picture of the same name starring Charles Martin Smith in 1983.

A WHALE FOR THE KILLING

First published: 1972
Type of work: Natural history and autobiography

A man stands up to the people of his hometown in an attempt to save a stranded fin whale.

A Whale for the Killing presents a time when Mowat was forced to stand up to the people among whom he had chosen to live, people whom he had admired for their rugged individualism, their tenacity in the face of nature's harshness, and their refusal to give in to adversity. In his attempts to force the townspeople of Burgeo, Newfoundland, to rescue a stranded eighty-ton fin whale, he learns that not everyone has the same reverence for nature as he and his wife and that the Canadian government is less concerned about protecting its natural heritage than it is about public relations.

This autobiographical narrative goes beyond recounting the erosion of the friendships that Mowat and his wife had established over many years in Burgeo; it also becomes a means by which Mowat can offer insight into the destruction brought about over time by the whaling industry. Interwoven in his account of the whale's inhumane treatment and slow death are sections that explore the decimation of the North American North Atlantic fishing grounds and that give vivid accounts of the slaughter of whales, animals that in earlier times ranged the ocean in vast pods. The behavior of the people of Burgeo—tormenting the whale with speedboats and shooting endless rounds of ammunition into its body, inflicting wounds that would eventually make it prey to infection and great suffering—parallels the rapacious nature of the whaling industry. Mowat's book thus works on two levels: as a local story and as an account of humankind's wanton destruction of anything and everything for its own use, without giving thought to the balances that might be upset in the process.

A Whale for the Killing presents what Mowat perceives to be a direct relationship between the destruction of the normal natural balance in nature and the rise of technologically "superior" industrial cultures. The connection that once existed between humankind and the rest of the animal kingdom is broken; the reverence once felt for other beasts is replaced by vicious sport and selfish destruction. Yet while Mowat blames the villagers of Burgeo, he accuses the Canadian government and the global scientific community for failing to come to the aid of the whale, an animal that could have been saved. The tensions that he depicts between the people doing what they please and a greater "good" are interesting because these people have been predisposed by their culture to behave as they do toward the fin whale. Thus, Mowat's demanding that they cease their behavior is, in effect, asking that they deny the culture in which they have managed to live. His ultimate response to the incidents—the torture and death of the whale and Mowat's neighbors' growing hostility and denunciation—is to leave the place that he had formerly considered the embodiment of rugged virtue.

Summary

Farley Mowat maintains a deep interest in the interrelationship between the human species and the other creatures with whom it shares the earth. His interests range from correct use for the land to appropriate interactions between humans and other species to bureaucratic and technological arrogance. Sometimes Mowat makes his point through what some people categorize as young persons' fiction—stories about animals; other times, he does so by interweaving current events and natural and social history.

In his work, Mowat demands that readers view themselves from the perspective of the global village, a setting that includes all species and the rights of all animals and all peoples. Although he denies that he writes natural history, his work is certainly natural history in its broadest context: considerations of the interconnectedness of events, peoples, and creatures. He asks that his readers look critically at the many dangerous ways in which industrial, technological cultures are changing and damaging the complex balance of lives on the earth. Although Mowat characteristically focuses much of his attention on the far northern regions of his native Canada, his work carries many more far-reaching implications.

Bibliography

Davison, Peter. "Mowat Country: An Introduction." In *The World of Farley Mowat: A Selection from His Works*. Toronto: McClelland & Stewart, 1980.

Egoff, Sheila. *The Republic of Childhood: A Critical Guide to Canadian Children's Literature in English*. Toronto: Oxford University Press, 1967.

Lucas, Alec. *Farley Mowat*. Toronto: McClelland & Stewart, 1976.

Rotert, Richard. "Farley Mowat in the Wilderness." In *Triumphs of the Spirit in Children's Literature*, edited by Francelia Butler and Richard Rotert. Hamden, Conn.: Shoestring Press, 1986.

Thompson, Eric. "Farley Mowat." In *Canadian Writers, 1920-1959*. Vol. 68 in *Dictionary of Literary Biography*. Edited by William H. New. Detroit: Gale Research, 1988.

Melissa E. Barth

ALICE MUNRO

Born: Wingham, Ontario, Canada
July 10, 1931

Principal Literary Achievement

Munro, with her sharply detailed settings and her fully realized characters, contributed to the resurgence of the popularity of the short story.

Biography

Born on July 10, 1931, in rural southwest Ontario, Canada, in the region east of Lake Huron, Alice Munro and her younger brother and sister were the children of Robert Eric Laidlaw, a farmer, and Anne Chamney Laidlaw, a former elementary school teacher turned homemaker. The family always seemed to be struggling financially. With the failure of his fox-farming business in 1948, Munro's father became a night watchman in a local foundry and began raising turkeys in 1952. In 1943, when Munro was twelve, her mother began a long decline because of Parkinson's disease, which led to her death sixteen years later.

Although her mother hoped that her daughter would escape their hometown of Wingham, Ontario, Munro's future was expected to be that of a farmer's wife. From the age of nine, however, she wanted to be an author. At fifteen she started writing, spending her school lunch hour composing stories while her classmates, who lived closer to the school, went home to eat. She finished a novel—a romantic, Gothic work—that later was stored in her father's basement and eventually thrown out by her stepmother.

In 1949, she received a scholarship that enabled her to attend the University of Western Ontario in London, Ontario, where she majored in journalism, a more explainable choice, she thought, than writing. While an undergraduate, she published her first story, "The Dimensions of a Shadow," in a university journal and sold another to CBC (Canadian Broadcasting Corporation) Radio. On December 29, 1951, she married James Munro, left the university, and moved to Vancouver, British Columbia. During the twelve years they lived in Vancouver, she tended to the needs of her two daughters, Sheila and Jenny, and cared for the family home. Writing but discarding much of what she wrote, she did sell a few stories each year to small journals such as the *Canadian Forum*, *Mayfair*, *Montrealer*, and *Queen's Quarterly*. In 1963, the family moved to Victoria, British Columbia, where Alice and her husband opened a bookstore, Munro's Books. Their third daughter was born in 1966.

In 1968, at thirty-seven, Alice Munro published her first collection of short stories, *Dance of the Happy Shades.* For these stories Munro drew on the familiar. The characters share traits with her, her family, and their neighbors. The setting—the small towns of southwest Ontario—was the landscape of her childhood. For this volume she received the Governor-General's Award (1969), the most prestigious literary prize in Canada. Its publication in 1973 in the United States brought her a wider audience.

Munro's next book, *Lives of Girls and Women* (1971), her first novel, is set in the fictional Ontario town of Jubilee and follows the development of Del Jordan as she comes to terms with her parents, with sex, and with her desire to become a writer. This, Munro's most autobiographical work, received the Canadian Booksellers Association International Book Year Award (1972) and was chosen as an alternate Book-of-the-Month Club selection in Canada and in the United States. In 1973, one section of the book was adapted for the television series *CBC Performance* with Munro's seventeen-year-old daughter Jenny playing the lead.

In 1972, with her marriage over, Munro returned to London, Ontario, with her two youngest daughters, intending to make writing her career. In 1974, she accepted a one-year position as writer-in-residence at the University of Western Ontario. This position was one she would fill over the years in numerous universities, including one in Queensland, Australia. In 1976, with her divorce final, she married Gerald Fremlin, a geographer and retired cartographer. They began living in the house of his birth in Clinton, Ontario, a small town twenty miles from Wingham.

In 1974, she published *Something I've Been Meaning to Tell You: Thirteen Stories.* Unlike her first two books, which concern the experience of growing up, this collection focuses on the problems of adulthood. In 1978, she published *Who Do You Think You Are?*, which was retitled *The Beggar Maid: Stories of Flo and Rose* (1979) for publication in the United States. This collection, a series of linked stories focused on the protagonist Rose, resembles a novel. As the collection went to press, Munro insisted on and paid for substantial changes. She deleted three stories that were later published in *The Moons of Jupiter* (1982), rewrote three others, and added one so that the entire volume concentrated on Rose.

In the 1970's, Munro was gaining recognition as a major writer. In 1978, she was awarded the Canada-Australia Literary Prize, was a runner-up for England's Booker Prize, and was awarded her second Governor-General's Award for *Who Do You Think You Are?* Her scripts were being accepted by the CBC. Her stories were appearing in major magazines, including *The New Yorker, The Atlantic Monthly, Ms., McCall's, The Canadian Forum: A Monthly Journal of Opinion and the Arts,* and *Redbook.*

Consistent with her practice of publishing a collection of short stories every three or four years, *The Moons of Jupiter* appeared in 1982, with *The Progress of Love,* which appeared in 1986, earning for Munro her third Governor-General's Award. *Friend of My Youth* arrived in 1990. The later stories, while bleaker and darker than the earlier ones, nevertheless portray characters, usually middle-aged women, who are survivors and who approach the future with hope.

Analysis

Munro is one of Canada's major writers and one of the best short-story writers anywhere. While she tried novel writing with her *Lives of Girls and Women*, her preferred form is the short story. She argues that a novel implies a continuity that is not mirrored in the lives of real people, who seem to move disjointedly from one experience to another. With the short story she can focus on the "intense . . . moments of experience" that constitute a life. Other than her first novel, she has published collections of short stories.

The majority of Munro's stories are set in Canada, often in southwest Ontario, now sometimes called "Munro Country," the region of her childhood. Her hometown of Wingham, Ontario, becames Hanratty in *Who Do You Think You Are?*, Dalgleish in *The Moons of Jupiter*, or Jubilee in *Lives of Girls and Women*. The rural countryside, the poverty-stricken small towns, the farms, and the salt mines are well documented, as is the Canadian climate, which can be bleak, dark, and foreboding with its bitter cold, its snowstorms, and its ice. Even though some stories might be set in Victoria or Toronto, generally the protagonist has moved to the city and still retains some provincialism. Similarly with the stories set in Australia or Scotland, the protagonist is Canadian and comes into these new environments with Canadian eyes. In all Munro's stories, the reader gets a clear sense of place whether the story is set in the Canada of today, of a hundred years ago, or of somewhere in between. In many cases the past and the present are juxtaposed so that there is a sense in which the past, though distant, is always present.

Just as Munro writes of the places that she knows, she also writes of familiar people. Her works, like those of many other writers, are autobiographically based, so much so that her hometown paper, the Wingham *Advance-Times*, once complained: "Sadly enough Wingham people have never had a chance to enjoy the excellence of her writing ability because we have repeatedly been made the butt of soured and cruel introspection on the part of a gifted writer." Munro would deny the accusation. On the copyright page of her most autobiographical book, *Lives of Girls and Women*, she included, "This novel is autobiographical in form but not in fact. My family, neighbors and friends did not serve as models." Yet there is no mistaking the similarities of characters and events in her stories with those in her life. Her mother died from a slow, debilitating disease, as does the narrator's mother in "Ottawa Valley," the last story in *Something I've Been Meaning to Tell You*. Her father's turkey farm serves as the setting for "Turkey Season" in *The Moons of Jupiter*. She and her first husband had many of the same differences in background as the protagonist and her husband in the stories in *Who Do You Think You Are?* Much of her life finds its way into her fiction, but that does not mean the fiction should be read as a documentary. Instead Munro takes these experiences and rearranges them, filtering them through her imagination and forging them into stories of sensitivity.

The majority of Munro's stories feature either girls or adult women as the central figures. The young girls, such as Rose in *Who Do You Think You Are?*, are slated to escape their impoverished beginnings primarily because they are sensitive and observant. Other stories chronicle the lives of ordinary, lower-middle-class women who have married young, have realized that life should be more than accommodating a husband and caring for children, and have left the safety of their homes to explore life's possibilities. They go back to school, find a career, and form new relationships. The stories focus on moments in their lives in which the past has been discarded, the present is being confronted, and the future is uncertain. These women, though faced with strong evidence of the fragility of male-female relationships, seek lovers. As the narrator in "Hard Luck Stories" in *The Moons of Jupiter* explains, "There's the intelligent sort of love that makes an intelligent choice. That's the kind you're supposed to get married on. Then there's the kind that's anything but intelligent, that's like a possession. And that's the one, that's the one, everybody really values. That's the one nobody wants to have missed out on." Similarly, Munro's women willingly take risks in order to find that second type of love. The relationships might not last, but the women survive, wounded, perhaps, but intact.

Munro explores the intricacy of personal relationships, examining the ties that bind people together. She does not interpret the lives of her characters as much as involve the reader in the complexity of their lives, creating an unsentimental drama out of the personal experiences of her ordinary characters. As she suggests, "A story is a spell, rather than a narrative." She examines the mother-daughter relationship from the perspective of the daughter in the stories of *Who Do You Think You Are?*, which range from the daughter being punished as a child in "Royal Beatings" to her committing her old, and increasingly senile, stepmother to the county home in "Spelling." In "Moons of Jupiter" in the collection of the same name, the narrator is both parent and daughter. She is parent to her adult daughters, who have dismissed her from their lives, and is daughter to her hospitalized father, who has a serious, and soon fatal, heart condition. There are stories about the relationships of friends, such as that of Georgia and Maya in "Differently" from the collection *Friend of My Youth*, who share confidences about their marriages and their dreams; the sharing of a lover shatters their friendship. There are also stories about husbands and wives and lovers. Margot in "Wigtime," also in *Friend of My Youth*, deals with her husband's affair with a teenage girl by extracting from him a promise of a new house in exchange for her silence. The stories are about the hopes, dreams, disappointments, and betrayals that constitute personal relationships. Munro explores what the narrator in "The Stone in the Field" in *The Moons of Jupiter* calls "the pain of human contact."

For Munro the truth can be suggested but never known completely. She relates her stories as though she and her reader are slowly discovering, or at least nearing, the truth. Her stories offer conflicting or multiple interpretations of the same situation. Sometimes the different versions result from the passage of time. Her stories, shifting effortlessly between the past and the present, suggest not only that the past influences the present but also that the present colors the interpretation of the past. Sometimes the same event might be viewed differently by several characters. For example, in the title story of *Friend of my Youth*, the narrator's mother believes that the life of Flora, who had twice been denied the love of the same man, was one of noble self-sacrifice, but as the narrator says, "I had my own ideas about Flora's story. . . . My Flora would be as black as hers was white. . . . What made Flora evil in my story was just what made her admirable in my mothers's—her turning away from sex." In a Munro story, certainty is approachable but never reached.

Munro is praised for her craft in fashioning her stories. Her details are realistic: A few carefully chosen words create precise images and often suggest an entire life. Her characters are recognizable as people one meets at work, at a party, or in a store. Her structuring of the narrative suggests the texture of real life with all of its doubts and uncertainties. She is a highly skilled writer whose stories are thought-provoking as well as entertaining.

HALF A GRAPEFRUIT

First published: 1978
Type of work: Short story

This work portrays a young girl who experiences self-discovery and comes to terms with her stepmother and her dying father.

"Half a Grapefruit" was first published in *Redbook*, then in the collection *Who Do You Think You Are?* (1978) in Canada, and the following year in the United States with the volume being retitled *The Beggar Maid: Stories of Flo and Rose*. It was thought that readers in the United States would not be familiar with the implication of the title's question: a criticism of aiming above one's origins. That is precisely one of the issues that "Half a Grapefruit" explores.

Even though the stories in *Who Do You Think You Are?* are each complete and self-contained, they can be read as a *Bildungsroman*, chronicling the development of Rose as she grows up in poverty, spends a few years at a university, experiences marriage, rearing a family, and divorce, and finally reaches a measure of success as an actress and university professor. The stories are arranged chronologically, but each story is a blend of the past and the present. Thus, even though "Half a Grapefruit" focuses on Rose's high school days, it concludes with a reference to Rose coming back to her hometown to make arrangements at a nursing home for her stepmother.

Rose, on her way to her high school, crosses the bridge that marks the boundary between her impoverished side of town, West Hanratty, and the more prosperous Hanratty. The only one from her West Hanratty grade-school class to attend high school, she keenly feels the difference between herself and the students from Hanratty. When the students are asked about their breakfasts, Rose lies, responding with "Half a grapefruit" rather than "tea and porridge"—which would have marked her as a country girl. Her presumption is recognized, however, and for weeks and even years, she hears, or imagines, people calling softly after her, "half a grapefruit." It is the schoolmate's equivalent of "Who do you think you are?"

Just who is Rose? She is not like her crass stepmother, Flo, who encourages the tales Rose brings home from school about lost Kotex or about one girl's sexual encounters under a dark porch. Rose does not tell Flo about her own uncertainties or her dreams. Flo responds with tales about herself working in a glove factory at the age of fourteen. Nor is Rose entirely like her father. They share a love of books, but she lacks his discipline and ability to work with his hands. Worse, she is a "disgrace" to him because her bookish tendency does not correspond to her gender; in his eyes a woman "should be naive intellectually, childlike, contemptuous of maps and long words and anything in books, full of charming jumbled notions, superstitions, traditional beliefs. 'Women's minds are different,' " he tells Rose.

Rose will eventually leave this harsh life but will have to endure the taunts and insults of her classmates, her stepmother, her father, and the townspeople to do so. Insulating herself, she becomes an observer and a limited participant. She watches the decline of her father's health with the detachment of a stranger; she is able to verbalize the word "cancer" when no other family member can. Yet she can never entirely leave her childhood behind. Before her father's final trip to the hospital, "[S]he understood that he would never be with her more than at the present moment. The surprise to come was that he wouldn't be with her less." The past is always part of the present.

BARDON BUS

First published: 1982
Type of work: Short story

The narrator, a middle-aged woman, is struggling to loosen herself from the grip of a broken love affair.

"Bardon Bus" appears in *The Moons of Jupiter* (1982), a collection of eleven stories, all of which focus on "intense . . . moments" in the lives of the female protagonists, most of them middle aged. The opening of the story sets the tone for what follows. Had the narrator been an old maid in another generation, she would have perhaps saved a letter and dreamed about an affair while continuing to milk the cows and scour the tin pails. She would have fantasized about surrendering herself completely to a lover who perhaps was a soldier or "a farmer down the road with a rough-tongued wife and a crowd of children" or a preacher. Yet though she is of a later generation, and though her actions reflect that, her obsessions are the same.

The narrator, writing a book on the history of a wealthy family, is staying in Toronto at a friend's apartment. As part of her research on the family, she recently spent a few weeks in Australia, where she met an anthropologist whom she had known slightly in Vancouver when she was a married college student. She, now divorced, and he, traveling without his third wife, embark on an affair that, because of the imposed brevity, seems "perfect." On returning to Canada, however, she becomes obsessed with him, with the same intensity as the old maid of an earlier generation.

The narrator, like other middle-aged women populating Munro's stories, is moderately successful in her career but is still rather fumbling in managing her relationships. The men in the story are no more adept at love, but their options are more varied. As Dennis, a friend of X, points out, men can choose young women and start a new life with a new family. Older women, faced with wrinkles and menopause, cannot deny their mortality as easily as a man with a young wife can. The narrator, reacting to the inevitability of the aging process, chooses new clothes and gets a haircut but realizes that "you have to watch out for the point at which the splendor collapses into absurdity. . . . Even the buttercup woman I saw a few days ago on the streetcar, the little, stout, sixtyish woman in a frilly yellow dress well above the knees, a straw hat with yellow ribbons, yellow pumps dyed-to-match on her little fat feet— even she doesn't aim for comedy." The narrator is a survivor and wills herself free of her obsession and depression: "At the same time I'm thinking that I have to let go. . . . There is a limit to the amount of misery and disarray you will put up with, for love, just as there is a limit to the amount of mess you can stand around a house. You can't know the limit beforehand, but you will know it when you've reached it." The narrator is ready, and able, to move on.

Summary

Alice Munro, writing about ordinary people in ordinary situations, creates a portrait of life in all its complexities. Munro, in her richly textured stories, explores the nuances of relationships, the depths of emotions, and the influence that one's past has on the present. With a few details, she is able to evoke someone's personality or an entire geographical region. She is a master at creating a short story that is as fully developed as a novel.

Bibliography

Blodgett, E. D. *Alice Munro.* Boston: Twayne, 1988.

Carrington, Ildiko de Papp. *Controlling the Uncontrollable: The Fiction of Alice Munro.* DeKalb: Northern Illinois University Press, 1989.

MacKendrick, Louis K., ed. *Probable Fictions: Alice Munro's Narrative Acts.* Downsview, Ontario: ECW Press, 1983.

Martin, Walter R. *Alice Munro: Paradox and Parallel.* Edmonton: University of Alberta Press, 1987.

Miller, Judith, ed. *The Art of Alice Munro: Saying the Unsayable.* Waterloo, Ontario: University of Waterloo Press, 1984.

Rasporich, Beverly Jean. *Dance of the Sexes: Art and Gender in the Fiction of Alice Munro.* Edmonton: University of Alberta Press, 1990.

Barbara Wiedemann

MURASAKI SHIKIBU

Born: Kyoto, Japan
c. 978
Died: Kyoto, Japan
c. 1030

Principal Literary Achievement

Murasaki is renowned as the author of *The Tale of Genji*, the world's first novel and generally acknowledged to be Japan's most important literary work.

Biography

Murasaki Shikibu was born in Kyoto, Japan, in or about 978. Little is known for certain about her life. The name by which she is known today was probably not her name while she lived. "Shikibu" means "Bureau of Ceremonies," a court position that her father, Fujiwara no Tametoki, once held, and "Murasaki" is a nickname derived from one of the main female characters in her novel, *Genji monogatari* (c. 1004; *The Tale of Genji*, 1925-1933). Her family belonged to a minor branch of the powerful Fujiwara clan that dominated Japanese politics during the Heian period (794-1160). Her father was a respected Confucian scholar who wrote poetry in both Japanese and Chinese. Her mother, Fujiwara no Tamenobu, was a member of another minor branch of this large clan. She died when Murasaki was an infant, and her death may account for some of the most poignant passages in *The Tale of Genji*. Genji, the central character, and the Murasaki of the novel, as well as other characters, suffer this early loss. Many people on both sides of her family were known for their literary talents, and her brother, Nobunori, became a well-known poet.

Of her early life, evidence indicates that in 996 Murasaki accompanied her father to a province north of Kyoto (Japan's capital at that time and the setting for *The Tale of Genji*), to which he had been appointed governor. Records show that by 998 she had returned to the capital to marry Fujiwara no Nobutaka, a man considerably older than her and who had a number of other wives. At that time, Japanese aristocrats and officials practiced polygamy, and romantic liaisons outside marriage were also common and to a certain extent condoned, which a reading of *The Tale of Genji* makes clear. Tradition has it that Murasaki's marriage was a happy one, although it did not last long. Her husband died in an epidemic only three years after their marriage and a year after the birth of their only child, a daughter.

After her husband's death, Murasaki was called to serve as a lady-in-waiting to

LA POÉTESSE MURA SAKI SIKI BOU.

Fac-simile d'un dessin de H. SOMM, d'après un livre japonais.

Akiko, a daughter of Fujiwara no Michinaga (the most powerful of the Fujiwaras) and a consort of the Emperor Ichigo. Then, as now, the Japanese emperor was the spiritual and social head of Japan but wielded little real political power. At court, the fine education that Murasaki had received from her learned father was useful. She could read Chinese and was familiar with the Chinese classics, and of course she practiced the traditional arts of Japan—painting, calligraphy, poetry, and probably music. With the exception of her knowledge of Chinese (which many courtiers considered inappropriate for women), these accomplishments were expected and appreciated in court circles.

Most accounts of Murasaki's life date the beginning of her work on *The Tale of Genji* from the five- or six-year-period following the death of her husband and before she entered service at court. Certainly by 1008, portions of it had been widely circulated, and her fame as a writer seemed fairly well established by the time that she was made lady-in-waiting to the emperor's consort. A short diary that Murasaki kept for about a year and a half describes both the pleasure she took from the respect that her writing received, as well as the jealousies that this respect provoked. Many of Murasaki's fictional characters suffer the jealous hatreds that trail in the wake of their accomplishments, especially if their court ranks are not high.

Murasaki continued in Akiko's entourage even after the death of Emperor Ichigo in 1011. The last definite mention of her at court is in 1013. She died in c. 1030 in Kyoto. Yet *The Tale of Genji* has continued to live. When changes evolved in the Japanese language, eventually making the original text difficult for all but scholars to read, it was translated into current Japanese. Its episodes have been dramatized on the stage, and Japanese poetry has drawn allusions from it from Murasaki's time to the present. It has also served as a model for many other works of Japanese fiction. Through her novel, Murasaki has joined the immortals.

Analysis

The Tale of Genji seems to invite analysis, and more than a thousand books interpreting it have been written in Japan. Since it has been translated into a number of Western languages, interpretive books and essays have appeared, and continue to appear, around the world. Probably nothing in the twentieth century has contributed more to its status as a world masterpiece than its translation into English by Arthur Waley, completed in 1933. Some scholars have criticized the freedoms that Waley took with Murasaki's text, but they all acknowledge that his translation is itself a classic of English prose. In 1977, Edward Seidensticker produced a more accurate translation, and English readers are fortunate in having both versions in print. For readers intimidated by such a long novel—*The Tale of Genji* is nearly twice as long as *Voyna i mir* (1865-1869; *War and Peace*, 1886)—abridged versions of both translations have been published.

Analyses of *The Tale of Genji* usually deal with the cultural breadth of its three-generational narrative and the psychological depths of its characterizations. Western commentators have admired Murasaki's romantic idealism, especially as it is combined with keenly observed social detail. In Japan, it has been especially admired for its expression of classic aristocratic values, values that continue to be reflected as major themes in Japanese literature.

Its most prominent themes are an intensely melancholic sense of life's beauty that grows from an awareness of its impermanence (*mono no aware*), the pain of unrequited love and the resignation of those bereft of love through separation or death, the impact of the passage of time on character, and the harmonizing of human moods and feelings with the seasons and other manifestations of the natural world. Other notable themes deal with social disillusionment, the limits to personal realization set by social circumstances, and the ultimate triumph of fate over desires and aspiration. For Buddhist Murasaki, fate reflects the working out of Karma—the belief that behavior in successive phases of a person's existence has consequences in this life. Genji frequently blames his bad fortune on his misdeeds in former lives.

Because *The Tale of Genji* is so long, Murasaki is able to dramatize the themes of her novel under various circumstances and over long stretches of time. The novel's three-generation time span makes backward glances to better or more promising days almost irresistible and manifestations of cultural decline, as well as personal loss, inevitable. The first third of the novel deals with the young prince Genji's triumphs and misfortunes as he contends for position in court and fulfillment in love. Although his father is the emperor, his mother is a relatively low-ranking concubine, and that makes Genji's court position shaky. This fact, and some indiscretions in his many amorous adventures, force him into self-exile when the emperor dies and his son by his principal wife ascends the throne. Genji's triumphant return to Kyoto and the great love of his life, Murasaki, when he is nearing his thirtieth year, is perhaps the high point of his life. Murasaki's languishing death in the fortieth chapter (two thirds of the way through the novel) sends Genji into seclusion. Two chapters later, he is dead, and the final twelve chapters, which take place eight years after Genji's death, deal with his world in decline. The main setting for these last chapters has shifted from the capital, with its dazzling pageantry, to a gloomy rural district on the Uji river several miles from Kyoto.

The love themes of *The Tale of Genji* have probably attracted more attention through the ages than those of social and personal disillusionment, although they are closely related. The patterns of courtship and love in the Heian court were every bit as elaborate and intense as those depicted in the medieval romances of Europe. Love affairs in the Heian court, like those in King Arthur's court, involve impassioned correspondence, seduction, adultery, and other forms of betrayal.

Yet unlike European medieval courts, which idealized the fealty and sacrifices of the chivalric lover, the Heian court tolerated a good deal of what Westerners would consider promiscuous behavior. As the people in traditional East Asian cultures did not find it difficult to embrace more than a single religious view (a Heian aristocrat was at once a Buddhist, Shintoist and Confucian), they saw nothing unnatural about being in love with more than a single person. In the West, men who seek many romantic adventures are usually considered shallow "Don Juans," but in classical Japan, if the feelings are sincere and the emotional commitments real, such behavior is not considered superficial. Genji, who was created as an ideal courtly lover, does not "love them and leave them." He does not fall out of love, and to the best of his ability he fulfills his emotional commitments and maintains his relationships throughout all of his life.

THE TALE OF GENJI

First published: *Genji monogatari,* c. 1004 (English translation, 1925-1933)
Type of work: Novel

At the height of Japan's aristocratic Heian period, Prince Genji and his successors strive for personal and social fulfillment through love affairs, friendships, rivalries, and political intrigue.

Except for a short diary, *The Tale of Genji* is Murasaki's only literary work, but it is generally considered Japan's most important literary achievement. While it is difficult to summarize its eleven hundred tightly printed but loosely plotted pages or to consider the nearly one hundred characters that move through this vast novel in a brief discussion, one can say that it focuses mostly on the life of its introspective hero, Prince Genji. The novel traces rather obliquely his rise, as the son of a minor consort of the emperor, to a position in society second in importance only to the emperor. It deals much more directly, however, with Genji's life as an adventurous exploration, even a quest, for the ultimate possibilities that can be realized in the cultivation of personal relationships—wisdom, excitement, love, friendship, rivalry, and the private and shared experience of beauty and joy, triumph and tragedy. Somehow, to the extent that one person can be fulfilled as a human being living by the values of the Heian court, Genji succeeds.

Genji's career consumes more than two thirds of the novel, during which he struggles to establish and maintain his position in court. Probably more significant to him, as well as more interesting for the reader, however, are his intimacies with a number of women. While still an adolescent, he falls in love with Fujitsubo, his stepmother and the emperor's consort. Their very secret affair results in the birth of a boy who, because he is presumed to be the emperor's son, eventually becomes an emperor himself. At about the same time that Genji is attracted to Fujitsubo, a marriage is arranged for him to the sister of his best friend, To no Chujo. Genji's relationship with his wife, Princess Aoi, is probably the least satisfactory in his long experience with women. Aoi dies shortly after giving birth to their son, Yugiri, when Genji is about twenty-three years old. After Aoi's death, Genji's most important relationship, and the main focus of his affection for the rest of his life, is Murasaki, the young niece of Fujitsubo. Since the Heian aristocracy was not only exclusive but also small, each character in the novel is related in one way or another to every other character.

Despite his abiding affection for Murasaki, Genji is intimate with many other women throughout his life. His most important liaisons are with Yugao (the mistress of his friend To no Chujo), Lady Rokujo (an imperious aristocrat whose jealousy results in the death of both Yugao and Aoi), and the secluded Lady of Akashi. Genji's daughter by Lady Akashi later marries an emperor, and their son, Niou, becomes a central character in the last section of the novel.

Toward the end of Genji's life (he dies during his fifty-first year), he is betrothed to Nyosan, the daughter of an emperor who wishes to see her well married before he retires. It was customary at that time for emperors to retire soon after they had reared an adolescent son. Nyosan deceives Genji by taking a lover, Kashiwagi, the son of Genji's friend To no Chujo. The child of this illicit relationship is Kaoru, another of the central characters of the last section of the novel. The Kashiwagi-Nyosan affair echoes Genji's affair with his stepmother and is viewed by him as a kind of Karmic retribution for his own transgressions. Many such relational echoes occur over the three generations of characters who inhabit *The Tale of Genji.*

After Genji's death, eight years pass before the narrative resumes. The main setting has shifted from the capital, with its dazzling pageantry, to a gloomy rural district near the Uji river, about ten miles from Kyoto. This last section, which for most readers is also the most compelling part of the novel, is integrated with the main section by having the spirit that ennobled Prince Genji continue to live, albeit divided and denatured, in the characters of his amorous grandson, Niou, and his son (or, more accurately, his wife's son by her lover), Kaoru. The creative tension generated in these sections by the hero's amorous impulses, on the one hand, and his concern for the properties of Heian society, on the other, is transformed into an unbalanced rivalry between the impetuous Niou and the sensitive but indecisive Kaoru. Still, with Genji gone, much of the life-enhancing spirit of romance has dissipated from court life, and with it respect for social forms also degenerates. While courtship retains its elaborate pattern and society its traditional form, these social structures grow ever emptier. Niou is no ideal courtier and lover but a dashing Don Juan bent on conquest for its own sake. The combination of Niou's unerring successes in court and in bedchambers, together with Kaoru's inability to exert his sensitive nature in any way that advances his own or anyone else's life, bears dramatic witness to a civilization's decline.

The novel ends inconclusively with the woman whom Niou and Kaoru having been courting for more than a hundred pages, Ukifune, contemplating the taking of holy vows and entering a Buddhist nunnery. The social and emotional stress of their courtship has so harassed her that she desires only to escape the complications of courtship and society for the simplicity of temple routines. That, too, recalls Prince Genji, who frequently contemplated "leaving the world" for Buddhist retirement. Only his responsibilities for others prevented him from following this path, the one followed by many Heian emperors and high officials. By Ukifune's time, Murasaki's tale suggests, there is even more reason to consider this retreat.

Summary

For the Japanese, *The Tale of Genji* depicts an ideal aristocratic society whose inhabitants loved elegance and were themselves paragons of grace, culture, and artistic skill. In barely a hundred years after it was written, Murasaki Shikibu's novel had become for them almost an object of religious veneration—an ideal representation of better days to which, following the collapse of Heian civilization and the civil unrest that followed, the Japanese people looked back nostalgically.

Since the novel's translation into English, Western readers have experienced similar responses. It is universally admired not only for the insight that it offers on a fascinating civilization but also for its intrinsic psychological interest, the beauty and intensity of its great scenes, and the artistry and penetration of its characterizations. Most particularly, it is admired for its profound expression of perennial human themes, not least of which is its celebration of human affection and emotional tenderness, feelings that make the pain of existence not only bearable but also meaningful for people in times and places far removed from the story's exotic civilization.

Bibliography

Field, Norma. *The Splendor of Longing in "The Tale of Genji."* Princeton, N.J.: Princeton University Press, 1987.

Morris, Ivan. *The World of the Shining Prince.* New York: Alfred A. Knopf, 1964.

Pekarik, Andrew, ed. *Ukifune: Love in "The Tale of Genji."* New York: Columbia University Press, 1982.

Puette, William. *Guide to "The Tale of Genji."* Rutland, Vt.: Charles E. Tuttle, 1983.

Shirane, Haruo. *The Bridge of Dreams: A Poetics of "The Tale of Genji."* Stanford, Calif.: Stanford University Press, 1987.

Dan McLeod

IRIS MURDOCH

Born: Dublin, Ireland
July 15, 1919

Principal Literary Achievement

Widely recognized as the most prolific and influential British novelist of her generation, Murdoch has emerged as an important and original theorist of fiction, as well.

Biography

Jean Iris Murdoch was born in Dublin, Ireland, on July 15, 1919, the only child of Anglo-Irish parents. Her mother, from a Dublin family, had a beautiful soprano voice and had trained to be an opera singer. She gave up her ambitions when she married a man of County Down sheep-farming people; it proved to be a successful marriage. Iris Murdoch was reared in London from the age of nine but returned to Ireland on holidays during a childhood that she has often described as happy. Yet she has said, "I feel as I grow older that we were wanderers, and I've only recently realized that I'm a kind of exile, a displaced person. I identify with exiles."

Murdoch attended the Froebel Institute, the progressive Badminton School in Bristol, and later entered Somerville College, Oxford. She read widely in ancient history and philosophy at Oxford and earned a degree in classics. There, along with many young intellectuals of the 1930's, she joined the Communist Party but later left it in disillusion.

Upon leaving Oxford, Murdoch followed in her father's footsteps and joined the civil service, entering the British Treasury in 1942. During this period she began to write novels; one was submitted to the British publishing house Faber but was rejected. In 1944, Murdoch left the Treasury and joined the United Nations Relief and Rehabilitation Administration in order to take a more active part in World War II. She worked in a camp for refugees in Austria, where she saw a "total breakdown of human society." Murdoch found it instructive; the experience provided her with models for the refugees and the homeless who appear frequently in her novels.

She worked in Belgium at this time also, where she met Jean-Paul Sartre, the French philosopher, novelist, and dramatist. His theories became the subject of her first published book, *Sartre: Romantic Rationalist*, which appeared in 1953, almost a decade after she had met him. The book explores Sartre's investigations into existentialism and his view of the novel as an important mode of human inquiry. Sartre's existen-

tialist concern for freedom in human action is a theme in many of Murdoch's novels.

After she left the United Nations in 1946, Murdoch spent an unsettled period reading and thinking in London and other cities in Europe. From 1947 to 1948 she studied philosophy at Newnham College, Cambridge, becoming particularly interested in the work of the Viennese-born British philosopher Ludwig Wittgenstein. During this time, she collected material for her book on Sartre and continued to write fiction.

Murdoch returned to Oxford in 1948 as Fellow and tutor in philosophy at St. Anne's College and kept this position until she gave up full-time teaching in 1963. Her first published novel, *Under the Net*, appeared in 1954 and earned warm acclaim from critics and the public. Two years later she married John Bayley, a literary critic and scholar who also wrote novels and poetry. He was appointed Thomas Wharton Professor of English Literature at Oxford. For many years the couple lived in Steeple Aston, a village near Oxfordshire. Their union became one of the most fruitful literary partnerships of the twentieth century. In 1986, they moved into a house in North Oxford.

From the mid-1950's onward, Murdoch's steady flow of fiction attracted more consistent attention than the work of any other postwar novelist. By 1965, critics were beginning to recognize the importance of her work. In that year, the critic A. S. Byatt's *Degrees of Freedom: The Novels of Iris Murdoch* appeared, an important study of Murdoch's early novels. By the late 1960's, Murdoch's novels grew longer and changed in tone but continued to appear almost annually.

After 1963, although she was a successful and widely read novelist, Murdoch continued to teach philosophy part-time at the Royal College of Art in London. Although she subsequently found it impossible to continue with a regular teaching post, she remained in close contact with the academic world through philosophical publications and well-attended lecture tours.

The Irish Academy elected Murdoch a member in 1970, heralding a decade in which she received much public recognition. She became an honorary member of the American Academy of Arts and Letters in 1975 and was appointed honorary Fellow of her former college, Somerville, in 1977. She was named Commander, Order of the British Empire, in 1976 and Dame of the British Empire in 1987.

Murdoch's individual novels similarly won acclaim. In 1973, *The Black Prince* appeared and won the James Tait Black Memorial Prize; *The Sacred and Profane Love Machine*, published in 1974, earned the Whitbread Award. With her international readership already established, Murdoch was awarded Britain's most prestigious literary award, the Booker Prize, for *The Sea, the Sea* in 1978.

In addition to writing more than two dozen novels, two plays, a volume of poetry, and three dramatic adaptations of her novels in less than forty years, Murdoch continued to publish technical papers in her academic specialty, moral philosophy. She wrote much about the Greek philosopher Plato, whose ideas often inform her fiction. She also published less technical papers linking aesthetics to moral and political concerns. One of the best known of these first appeared in *Encounter* in January of 1961. Originally titled "Against Dryness: A Polemical Sketch," the essay has been reprinted many times under the title "Against Dryness." In it, Murdoch illustrates her belief in the connection between art and morality, a key concept in understanding her work.

Murdoch's reputation continues to grow. All of her novels have been reissued in Danish and Dutch translations. More than three-quarters of her fiction has appeared in French, Spanish, Swedish, and Japanese, and she is a particular favorite among Russian readers. In addition to her publishing success, Murdoch continues to be an important presence on the British intellectual scene to a degree unusual among writers. The direction of her work represents a significant tendency of the contemporary novel.

Analysis

In her essay "Against Dryness," Murdoch writes:

> The connection between art and the moral life has languished because we are losing our sense of form and structure in the moral world itself. . . . [W]hat we require is a renewed sense of the difficulty and complexity of the moral life and the opacity of persons.

In novel after novel, Murdoch addresses the problems of living a moral life as her characters strive painfully to seek the Good. In a series of Gifford lectures delivered in 1982, Murdoch speaks about Plato's allegory of the cave and the sun. The soul, traveling through four stages of enlightenment, continues to discover that what it considered realities are only shadows of something else. Thus moral change may be considered a progressive discarding of the false "good," of images and shadows that are eventually recognized as false.

Central to this concept of moral change is the idea of Eros, or love. Sexual love and transformed sexual energy act as a major motif in Murdoch's novels, particularly in *A Severed Head* (1961), *The Italian Girl* (1964), *The Black Prince* (pb. 1973, pr. 1989), and *The Sea, the Sea* (1978). In novel after novel, love both blinds the characters and allows them a clearer vision of reality in a typical Murdoch dichotomy. Maturity is often achieved by falling "out of love." No other writer does a better job of evoking the changed consciousness that love brings.

Yet for all of their philosophical underpinnings, her novels provide a brilliant and satisfying entertainment. Murdoch has emphasized that she aims to write in the realistic tradition of nineteenth century English and European fiction. Prominent features of her plots include such time-honored novelistic devices as unexpected meetings, lost or found letters, forgotten keys, coincidence, and accident. All of these testify to the role of chance in human affairs.

Although critics have carped that her novels are "over plotted" and uneven, she has a gift for intricate double plots. This dual patterning is one of the characteristics of her fiction; the characters are frequently paired with one another symmetrically, such as the pairing of Martin and Antonia with Anderson and his halfsister, Honor Klein, in *A Severed Head*. The action itself is often repeated with slight variations, as in *The Bell* (1958) and *A Word Child* (1975).

As to the characters themselves, Murdoch tends to create upper-middle-class worlds peopled with certain types who reappear from novel to novel. Young, cunning women who are fierce in their pursuit of older men are often present. The older men are usually self-centered charmers who are weak, self-indulgent, and skeptical. They are often found out as adulterers and practice petty deceptions as long as they can. Her male characters are not of the conventionally firm, masculine kind—but they usually change during the novel.

Some of the most interesting of Murdoch's creations are power figures, whom Murdoch once called "alien gods." These are frequently men (although Honor Klein, in *A Severed Head*, falls into this category), and they are mostly Middle European refugees—rootless, suffering types. Sometimes Jewish, these figures are often demonic in their effects on others; when they do not function this way, they are simply mute, passive sufferers. Murdoch always keeps such characters at a distance, and the reader is never afforded an inner view of their nature.

The women in her novels cannot be classified as easily, although the vague, artsy "mistress" type does appear often. Murdoch's women are difficult to discuss because of their great variety. Although critics have remarked that her characters sometimes become subordinated to the plot of the story, at her best she lavishes a kind of love on the persons she depicts.

Murdoch has an intense, visual imagination and can describe people, places, houses, clothes, and even dogs with a luminous accuracy. London is a real presence in her novels; this tendency is most apparent in her first novel, *Under the Net* (1954), in *Bruno's Dream* (1969), and in *A Fairly Honourable Defeat* (1970). Because of her precise depiction of the city, including almost daily reports of the weather, she is considered the most important heir to the tradition of Charles Dickens.

One of Murdoch's most distinctive traits as a novelist might be called "transcendent realism." Her novels open with all the accepted realistic conventions of character, setting, and plot. Then within a set scene something outrageous, quirky, or fantastic will happen that seems far removed from the premise of the novel. Much of the humor of her novels flows from her characters' very British reserve in the face of the wildly fantastic. This intrusion of the unexpected is, for Murdoch, a testament to the richness of reality.

Murdoch's intense descriptive powers are not limited to the visual. She also excels at evoking the inner world of fantasies, projections, demonic illusions, and altered consciousness. She resembles no other contemporary novelist, partly because she is a religious fabulist whose fables are submerged in the conventional techniques of the novel.

A SEVERED HEAD

First published: 1961
Type of work: Novel

A vain wine merchant's wife leaves him for his best friend, after which he learns some hard truths about his own capacity for self-delusion.

A Severed Head, Murdoch's fifth published novel, is considered the best of the comedies of manners that Murdoch was writing early in her career. The cast of characters is largely restricted to the wealthy bourgeoisie; the decadent atmosphere is evoked by careful descriptions of richly decorated rooms, heavy drinking, and romantic misconceptions. The characters suffer frequently from languor and fatigue. Yet the structure of *A Severed Head* is Murdoch's own: A bumbling male protagonist lives through a series of events that destroy his complacency and teach him to recognize the separate reality of other people.

The protagonist, Martin Lynch-Gibbon, tells his own story. He is happily married to Antonia, a society beauty five years his senior. Martin's easy complacency is shattered when Antonia declares she is going to leave him for her psychiatrist, Palmer Anderson, who is Martin's close friend. Although Martin is repelled by Antonia's suggestion that he remain rational about the affair, he allows Antonia to live with Palmer and remains friendly with them both.

Unknown to both Antonia and Palmer, Martin has long kept a mistress, a young teacher named Georgie Hands. Although Martin professes to love Georgie, he has denied her the trip to New York on which her heart was set and encouraged her to have an abortion. After Antonia's revelation, Martin finds that he is extremely ambivalent toward his own mistress.

Events suddenly become more complicated when Antonia asks Martin to pick up Palmer's halfsister at Liverpool Station. In a scene both comic and portentous, Martin meets the dour Honor Klein on a rainy night that smells like "sulphur and brimstone." As they drive toward Palmer's house in dense fog, Martin almost collides with a truck. When Honor hangs her head out the window to see, Martin first apprehends her as a headless body.

Honor Klein falls into a category of the power figures that act as agents of change in many of Murdoch's novels. Loved and feared like the gods they mimic, they engender complications that, when finally resolved, leave other characters in closer touch with reality. Yet Honor is no caricature; she is entirely individualized. She is Jewish and has dark, almost oriental eyes and a cap of shiny black hair. She has devoted her life to the study of anthropology. Other characters recognize that she has mystical knowledge, perhaps gained from breaking the taboo of incest. She is the "severed head" of the title, an object of awe and veneration.

Although Murdoch carefully forecasts Honor's strange relationship with her half-brother, Palmer, Martin is too preoccupied with his own entanglements to notice. Indeed, he notices so little about Honor that when he discovers he has fallen desperately in love with her, he imagines that she is free of other ties and may even be a virgin. When he arrives without warning at her house in Cambridge to declare his love, he finds her in bed with Palmer. At this crucial point in the book, Martin realizes that his perception of Honor has been based on his own fantasies and has nothing to do with the real person.

The balance of power now shifts to Martin, since he knows Palmer's guilty secret. Antonia, sensing a change in Palmer, returns to Martin, who is still hopelessly in love with Honor. A short time later he is confronted with another confession: Antonia has had a long-standing love affair with Martin's brother Alexander. This final revelation shakes Martin to the core. He now realizes that his whole adult life has been based on self-delusion and an inability to see the truth about anyone else. Although he suffers great emotional pain, he also feels more sure about himself. Martin has grown up.

The end of *A Severed Head* is a fine example of Murdoch's device of pairing. In the last scene, Honor leaves Palmer and returns to Martin to accept his love or at least to take a chance on it. Georgie Hands, once Martin's mistress, goes to America with Palmer Anderson; Antonia is traveling in Europe with Martin's brother.

The theme of the novel is love, power, and the relationship between them. The plot resembles restoration comedy not only for its series of appalling revelations but also in the way it reveals love as war and power play.

A Severed Head appeared as a play in London in 1964, the script a collaboration between Murdoch and the popular British novelist and playwright J. B. Priestley. The play proved so popular that it was later made into a movie in 1971.

THE NICE AND THE GOOD

First published: 1968
Type of work: Novel

An investigation into a suicide at London's Whitehall affects the life of a group of friends on the Dorset coast.

In an interview, Iris Murdoch referred to her twelfth novel, *The Nice and the Good*, as the most open one she had done yet. This "openness" appears to refer to a looser plot structure and to more separate and free characters. The plot is really two equal subplots; one line follows John Ducane's investigation of an apparent suicide in the government offices at Whitehall in London, while the other follows a group of friends on a Dorset estate named Trescombe as they struggle toward an ideal of love.

Connecting the London plot and the Dorset plot are Octavian Gray, John Ducane's superior at Whitehall, who owns Trescombe and spends much of his time there with his wife Kate, and Ducane himself, who lives in London but is a frequent guest at Trescombe. Ducane is in love with Kate Gray, who encourages him yet confesses every secret kiss to Octavian.

In addition to Kate and Octavian, some of the characters at Trescombe are Mary Clothier, a widow; Mary's fifteen-year-old son, Pierce; Paula Biranne, a divorcé and schoolteacher; Paula's nine-year-old twins, who have "great souls"; Barbara, spoiled teenage daughter of Kate and Octavian; and Willie Kost, a refugee who has survived Dachau.

In his London life, Ducane is involved with Jessica Bird, his occasional mistress, and manipulated by Gavin Fivey, his manservant. In the course of his investigation, Ducane also becomes entangled with Richard Biranne, Paula's ex-husband; Peter McGrath, office messenger and blackmailer; and McGrath's wife Judy, a beautiful woman of dubious character.

John Ducane, a legal adviser, is one of Murdoch's flawed, culpable male protagonists, smart and successful but smug, who needs to think of himself as a good man. In addition to his investigation of the suicide and his quest for "the good," Ducane acts as confessor and adviser to the large group of "free" characters who live at Trescombe as friends of the Grays.

Much of the book is seen through Ducane's eyes. He is elevated to godlike status by many of those with whom he comes in contact, largely because of his ability to elicit confidence. Yet his predicament is complicated by a lack of personal decisiveness. He is appalled by his own muddled involvement with Jessica Bird and Kate Gray and is strongly attracted to Judy McGrath. Eventually, the surrounding characters come to perceive him as an ordinary mortal after all.

There are many motifs in the book, among them roundness. On the beach Ducane muses that "Everything in Dorset is round. . . . The little hills are round, these bricks are round . . . the crowns of the acacia, the pebbles on the beach. . . . Everything in Dorset is just the right size. This thought gave him immense satisfaction and sent out through the other layers and compartments of his mind a stream of warm and soothing particles." Octavian is described as round, and the cat, which is a striped cube, has the singular talent of being able to make its hair stand on end and become a fluffy sphere. Roundness indicates contentment, fulfillment, and proper proportion.

The theme of the novel is the search for a perfect proportion of the nice and the good in order to attain a rounded life, "nice" representing the claims of the body and "good" representing the spirit. Each of the adult characters except Kate and Octavian have guilty pasts because of the harm they have done to others. In every case, the harm was done by a failure of love. Mary Clothier regrets the death of her husband, who rushed out of the house after a marital spat and was hit by a car. Paula Biranne wrestles with a broken marriage and a love affair that led to her husband's mutilating her lover. Willy let two people die in Dachau through inattention.

Kate and Octavian live entirely in the flesh and are the hedonists of the group. Not only are they happy, but they make the people around them happy, too. This depiction does not diminish the distance between pleasure and virtue; it only suggests that life is not as simple as an allegory.

The ending of *The Nice and the Good* involves a carnival of reconciliation that resembles Shakespearean romantic comedy. When Ducane unravels the tangled causes of suicide and discovers that Richard Biranne was involved, he decides to dispense "private justice" and uses his knowledge to reconcile Biranne with his ex-wife, Paula. Ducane and Mary fall in love, teenaged Barbara returns Pierce's affection, Jessica pursues Willy, and even the dog and cat finally share a basket. As John learns when he and Mary discover they are in love, "it is the nature of love to discern good, and the best love is, in some part at any rate, a love of what is good."

THE BLACK PRINCE

First published: 1973
Type of work: Novel

A fifty-eight-year-old author develops a ruinous obsession for the twenty-year-old daughter of his best friend and protégé.

In *The Black Prince*, Murdoch returns to her preoccupation with love, exposing the sometimes horrifying face of the love god, Eros. Although Bradley Pearson, a novelist and the narrator, describes this work as "a simple love story," it is really his competitive friendship with successful writer Arnold Baffin that creates the tension at the core of the work.

What distinguishes Bradley from others in the novel is his sense of guilt and his prudishness. He insists that morality is a simple affair and is shown trying to live by these simplicities. Bradley is wrapped in self-righteousness, although it does not prevent him from acting badly. His friend Arnold, on the other hand, accepts life as it is and does not try to be perfect. He enjoys the self-satisfaction that Murdoch often uses as a second-best virtue.

The tension between the two men arises from their respective erotic entanglements and their different attitudes toward art. Aesthetically, Bradley believes in concentration and patience to achieve high art; he has published only three books. He believes that art is connected to the quest for a good life. Arnold writes prolifically, sells very well, and considers his work fun. Their erotic life echoes their professional rivalry. Bradley has a very brief liaison with Rachel, Arnold Baffin's wife, then later becomes involved with Arnold's daughter Julian. At the same time, Arnold is engaged in an affair with Christian, Bradley's former wife. Yet both men are doomed. At the end of the novel, Arnold is murdered by his wife, and Bradley, who is wrongly convicted of the crime, dies of cancer in prison.

The erotic and aesthetic themes mesh in Bradley's belief that a great love will induce him to produce a great book. His obsessive love for young Julian results in his writing *The Black Prince*, which he claims is the fruit of his passion. Readers must judge for themselves whether Eros has fertilized Bradley's muse. This realistic love story, however, is not all the reader has to consider. There are two forewords and six afterwords added to the narration; four of the afterwords are by characters involved in the story who feel the need to vindicate themselves and correct Bradley's narration. The enclosure of Bradley's tale by forewords and afterwords forces the reader into a world of multiple, sometimes conflicting, points of view. The resulting irony is the primary literary device in the framed structure of *The Black Prince*, yet the multiple viewpoints reveal more than the Bradley's ironic delusion. Irony is used to expose the ultimate duality of the human condition—the highly developed comic sense alongside the inevitable pain of human existence.

The experience of a violent passion is described in great detail in *The Black Prince*—the various phases of the passion, the transformation of the lover in the eyes of his friends, the delusions caused by the passion, and the moral consequences of such obsession. Although these moral consequences are serious enough to cause a suicide and a violent murder, one of the richest ironies is that the passion does result in a work of literary art.

William Shakespeare's *Hamlet* (c. 1600-1601) provides a touchstone for Murdoch in *The Black Prince*, but it, too, is touched with irony. Bradley and Julian's first innocent meeting is a discussion of the meaning of *Hamlet*. Quotations and allusions to the play run throughout the novel. Bradley's erotic energies are suddenly focused on Julian when she mentions that she once played Hamlet, thus identifying herself with the play's ambiguities. After several failures, Bradley manages to make love to Julian when she is fancifully dressed as Hamlet. Julian's interest in the play forces Bradley to think it through again, and in doing so he understands the pain of tragedy for the first time. Later, on his deathbed, Bradley realizes that his affair with Julian was not tragic after all, but ironic.

The black prince of the novel's title clearly refers to Hamlet and to Julian when she is dressed as Hamlet. *BP* are Bradley Pearson's initials, as well. Yet there is evidence that the black Eros, a dark god who is constantly evoked in the book, is the real black prince. As Bradley sees it, the catalyst that the talented creator needs, the god whom he awaits, is the mythic Eros. Eros rules not only the erotic life of all human beings but also the creation of art. Bradley thinks that after he encounters this god he will create a great work. Yet as the plot progresses it becomes apparent that Bradley completely misunderstands this god.

Many of Murdoch's readers consider *The Black Prince* her finest work. In the way it challenges its own conclusions in the afterwords and speculates on what fiction is, it is Murdoch's greatest departure from the realistic nineteenth century novel.

A WORD CHILD

First published: 1975
Type of work: Novel

Hilary Burde, the narrator, attempts to atone for a horrible mistake in his past but only repeats it.

A Word Child is a stylish novel in the gothic tradition of the nineteenth century that develops a brooding atmosphere of gloom and deals with aberrant psychological states. Murdoch's use of Gothic conventions is an exploration of the tensions between the interior world of the mind and the outer world of reality. The narrator of *A Word Child*, Hilary Burde, haunts himself with fantasies of power, possession, and betrayal. The narrative is divided into the days of a diary, reflecting Hilary's rigid approach to life.

Hilary is a prostitute's child who starts life as an illiterate orphan. After a schoolmaster discovers his linguistic gifts, he achieves a certain success at the University of Oxford under the patronage of don Gunnar Jopling and his wife, Anne, who also show unusual kindness to Hilary's half sister, Crystal. Hilary is obsessed with Crystal and, although he loves her, wields absolute power over her life. She is indeed a Crystal Burde in a less than gilded cage.

The relationship between Hilary and Gunnar is central to the narrative. While teaching at Oxford, Hilary falls in love with Anne Jopling and tries to persuade her to leave Gunnar and her young son. Anne, panicked by her recent discovery that she is again pregnant, provokes Hilary to crash his car in an accident that proves fatal to her. The Oxford careers of both men are ruined, and after a year of debilitation Hilary goes on to a dull civil service job in London.

After twenty years of self-inflicted suffering (and inflicting a certain discomfort on all who know him), Hilary finds that Gunnar has just been installed as head of the government department in which Hilary works. An unexpected chance for expiation of guilt arrives when Gunnar Jopling's second wife, Lady Kitty, approaches Hilary and tells him of Gunnar's similar preoccupation with the past. She suggests the two men get together to resolve their obsessions. Hilary, again infatuated, continues to meet Lady Kitty secretly. Murdoch skillfully distinguishes here between Hilary's fantasies about Lady Kitty's goodness and the reader's ability to see the foolishness of her behavior, particularly her suggestion that Hilary should provide her with a child. Gunnar surprises Hilary and Lady Kitty in the midst of a secret meeting, and in the scuffle that follows Lady Kitty is knocked off a jetty into the Thames and dies of overexposure. Hilary's struggle to atone for the death of Gunnar's first wife, Anne, leads instead to a doubling of his guilt.

Yet Hilary, despite the fact that he has nothing to show for his ordeal, has a changed perception of his own role in the order of things. At the end of the novel he realizes that a large part of everyone's life is ruled by chance. He is finally able to recognize that his involvement with the Joplings is not a tragedy in the Shakespearean sense since tragedy imposes too great an importance on his own part in the universe. Chance, rather than will, rules our lives. With this realization comes a hint that Hilary will, perhaps sometime in the future, be able to forgive himself.

A Word Child is a fine example of Murdoch's gift for intricate double plots, as well as an exploration of her concern with moral freedom.

Summary

The novels of Irish Murdoch comprise a rich chronicle of the manners of the mid- and late twentieth century British upper middle classes. Although considered a realistic writer, she is not afraid to take risks. In the carefully ordered, stable worlds she creates, the unpredictability of her characters stands out in bold relief. Saints and sinners, martyrs and mystics, villains and holy fools stumble toward an ideal of love in a modern age of terrors. Murdoch employs extremes of arbitrary coincidence, melodramatic manipulation of plot, and temporal compression to depict characters struggling for a vision of goodness in a secular world.

Bibliography

Baldanza, Frank. *Iris Murdoch*. New York: Twayne, 1974.

Byatt, A. S. *Iris Murdoch*. London: Longman, 1976.

Dipple, Elizabeth. *Iris Murdoch: Work for the Spirit*. Chicago: University of Chicago Press, 1982.

Johnson, Deborah. *Iris Murdoch*. Bloomington: Indiana University Press, 1987.

Rabinovitz, Rubin. *Irish Murdoch*. New York: Columbia University Press, 1968.

Todd, Richard. *Iris Murdoch*. New York: Methuen, 1984.

——————. *Iris Murdoch: The Shakespearian Interest*. New York: Barnes & Noble, 1979.

Wolfe, Peter. *The Disciplined Heart: Iris Murdoch and Her Novels*. Columbia: University of Missouri Press, 1966.

Sheila Golburgh Johnson

VLADIMIR NABOKOV

Born: St. Petersburg, Russia
April 23, 1899
Died: Montreux, Switzerland
July 2, 1977

Principal Literary Achievement

Nabokov, a novelist, short-story writer, poet, playwright, scholar-critic, translator, lepidopterist, and chess problemist, was a preeminent figure in twentieth century English and Russian literature.

Biography

Vladimir Vladimirovich Nabokov was born on April 23, 1899, in St. Petersburg, Russia. He was the eldest son of Vladimir Dmitrievich Nabokov, a prominent liberal politician and Anglophile aristocrat, and Elena Rukavishnikov, a member of a prominent family of industrialists. Young Vladimir, the favorite child, grew up amid great wealth and cultural privilege. Trilingual from childhood, he had live-in tutors and attended a private school. From his idolized father he inherited a love of nature, especially butterflies, and for chess; from his mother he acquired a passion for the visual arts, particularly painting, and for the marvels of memory and commemoration. His early life was divided between the family's elegant town house in the imperial capital of St. Petersburg and summers on its nearby country estate.

The young Nabokov published his first volume of poetry in 1916, soon following this with a second volume. The family's gracious existence ended when it was forced into exile following the Bolshevik Revolution of 1917. Its wealth vanished, but the cultural bounty acquired during those early years richly sustained Nabokov for the remaining sixty years of his life.

Although the Nabokov family settled in Berlin, the young poet was sent to England's University of Cambridge, where he spent the years from 1919 to 1923 before returning to Berlin, where he was to live until 1938. Tragedy struck when the father, now a newspaper publisher, was assassinated by right-wing Russian monarchists in 1922. Adopting the pen name V. Sirin, Nabokov published two further volumes of poetry while contributing poems, chess problems, the first Russian crossword puzzles, and reviews to the émigré Russian press. In addition to his journalistic endeavors, he supported himself by giving language and tennis lessons, working as a film extra, writing cabaret skits and plays, and translating. A handful of short stories pre-

ceded the first novel, *Mashenka* (1926; *Mary*, 1970), written soon after his marriage to Vera Slonim. Between 1925 and 1940, Nabokov established himself as the leading new writer of the Russian emigration with a string of nine novels, many stories, and poems. Following *Mary* were *Korol', dama, valet* (1928; *King, Queen, Knave*, 1968), *Zashchita Luzhina* (serial, 1929; book, 1930; *The Defense*, 1964), *Soglyadatay* (1930; *The Eye*, 1965), *Podvig* (1932; *Glory*, 1971), *Kamera obskura* (1932; *Camera Obscura*, 1936, revised as *Laughter in the Dark*, 1938), and *Otchayanie* (serial, 1934; book, 1936; *Despair*, 1937, revised, 1966). The best of the Russian novels were the last two: *Priglashenie na kazn'* (serial, 1935-1936; book, 1938; *Invitation to a Beheading*, 1959) and *Dar* (serial, 1937-1938; book, 1952; *The Gift*, 1963).

With the rise of Adolf Hitler, life in Germany was becoming increasingly difficult, and in 1938 the Nabokovs and their four-year-old son, Dmitri, emigrated to France. Nabokov sensed that his old European life was ending and now undertook his first original English-language novel, *The Real Life of Sebastian Knight* (1941). The Nabokovs were to spend only two years in France before fleeing once again just as the German forces were invading.

The Nabokovs arrived in New York in May, 1940. Nabokov's hard-won reputation as a Russian writer was meaningless in America. At forty-one, Nabokov started anew, this time as an American writer. First, however, he had to provide for his wife and son. During the early years, he both taught at Wellesley College and worked as a lepidopterist at the Harvard Museum of Comparative Zoology. In 1945, Nabokov became an American citizen. His responsibilities left little time for writing, but by 1947 he had completed his first "American" novel, *Bend Sinister*, a dark modernist fantasy about a philosopher who vainly tries to stand aside from political tyranny. More important for his American reputation was the series of autobiographical vignettes that appeared in *The New Yorker* in the late forties and early fifties. Several times revised, these were collected into what eventually became *Speak, Memory: An Autobiography Revisited* (1966), a revision of *Conclusive Evidence: A Memoir* (1951) and *Drugie berega* (1954). *Speak, Memory* is an intensely artistic exploration of the writer's first forty years. In 1948, Nabokov accepted a position as a professor of European literature at Cornell University, where he would spend the next decade. He taught in the winters, went on butterfly-collecting expeditions throughout the American West each summer, and continued his writing. Much of his time was devoted to the translation of Russian classics into English. The short novel *Pnin* (1957) was also done during the Cornell years, as was Nabokov's most famous work, *Lolita* (1955), the story of a young American girl and her perverted stepfather, Humbert Humbert. Only gradually did it emerge from the ensuing scandal that Nabokov had written an American masterpiece. The best-seller was eventually made into a major film. Suddenly, the wealth that Nabokov had lost thirty years before in the Russian Revolution was restored to him. He resigned his teaching post and returned to Europe for what was intended to be a visit. As time passed, however, the Nabokovs realized that a grand hotel in Switzerland would be their permanent home. At sixty, Nabokov was an international literary superstar. From his hotel suite in Montreux, there emerged a stream of brilliant books that would assure Nabokov's place as one of the great masters of twentieth century world literature: *Pale Fire* (1962), a stunning display of literary pyrotechnics taking the form of a commentary on a long poem; *Ada: Or, Ardor, A Family Chronicle* (1969), a richly embroidered fantasy of brother-sister incest that gained for its author a cover story in *Time*; the ghost story *Transparent Things* (1972); and *Look at the Harlequins!* (1974). As Nabokov's stature as an English author grew, interest reawakened in his Russian work, which now began to appear in English (and many other) translations. He died on July 2, 1977, in Montreux, Switzerland.

During Nabokov's lifetime, his writings were forbidden in his Russian homeland. With the coming of *glasnost* in the mid-1980's, Nabokov's works were republished in the land of his birth, where he was finally recognized as one of the great figures of Russian literature.

Analysis

Nabokov was often praised as a master of language and style but criticized for the perceived absence of general ideas, social relevance, and even morality in his novels. Russian literature has always had a strong moral, social, and political orientation. At times, this didactic tendency has overshadowed and even displaced the artistic element. First in his novel *The Gift*, and later in a collection of interviews, *Strong Opinions* (1973), Nabokov argued for the independence of art. That is not to say that Nabokov did not incorporate serious ideas and moral considerations in his art, but rather that they are secondary to artistic considerations. Such themes are deeply woven into the texture of Nabokov's works so that only the careful reader will recognize their presence.

It was only after Nabokov's death that his widow pointed to the presence of a master theme throughout her husband's work—a theme that she called "the hereafter." Is death the end of everything, or is there a hereafter? If so, does personal consciousness survive? Nabokov's novels rarely address these questions directly. Close examination shows that Nabokov's novels contain not one but two (or more) worlds. One of these is, within the framework of the novel, regarded by the characters as the one and only world. A chosen few of Nabokov's heroes, however, notice inexplicable coincidences and patterns, which lead them to suspect the presence of a controlling mind that has created them and their universe. This creator lives on another world. When these favored characters face death, either their own or that of a loved one, they become obsessed with the possibility of the hereafter, another world, that of their creator, with its promise of immortality and reunion with their loved ones. Intimations of a higher world are strongest in dreams and madness, but the real answer can come only at the moment of death. In some of the novels such as *Bend Sinister*, the controlling presence in the creating world—the author—reaches into the created world and rescues his hero. The character dies and returns to the mind of his author-creator and in doing so acquires the wider consciousness of his author. All the secret coincidences of the previous "fictional" universe are now explained. Implicit in this scheme is the idea of the artist as god. It is an art-centered view of the meaning of life, an extension of the relationship between the creator and his character to the realm of a personal philosophy.

Readers of *Speak, Memory* cannot help being struck by Nabokov's incredibly detailed recall of the minutiae of the past and his ability to bring it to life by the verbal precision of his writing. The theme of memory gains its greatest importance in connection with Nabokov's master theme of another, parallel world. The ability of Nabokov's heroes to detect signs and symbols hinting the existence of another world depends upon the power and precision of their memories. Without memory, everything happens as if for the first time and is meaningless. Most of Nabokov's fictional characters fail to recognize these signs of a master hand. In a sense, readers of Nabokov's novels are in the same position as his characters. They must recall the scattered details that constitute the patterns and coincidences signaling the other world.

Nabokov has remarked that the real history of a writer is the story of his style. Nabokov is indisputably one the greatest masters of both Russian and English style. Style is also what makes Nabokov a difficult writer for many readers. His novels are filled with word games and hidden allusions that sometimes hint at the presence of the other world or that add new dimensions of meaning. In the ghost story "The Vane Sisters" (1959), the doubting narrator's skepticism about the hereafter is undermined in his last sentence by an acrostic that he himself fails to notice. The acrostic is a message from the dead sisters of the story. More often, hints of the other world are in the form of allusions. In *Bend Sinister*, the presence of the other world is signaled by the recurrence of a footprint-shaped puddle that is the point of transition between the worlds of the author and his character. In *Ada*, the secret brother-sister relationship of heroine and hero is hinted by allusions to the English poet Lord Byron and the French writer François René de Chateaubriand, both of whom were rumored to have had incestuous relationships with their sisters. To appreciate fully Nabokov's novels, the reader should have a good grasp of Russian, French, and English literary history and, ideally, a knowledge of these languages.

Nabokov was a difficult, modernist writer who basically wrote for an elite audience. Such writers, although admired by literary specialists, are rarely read outside the classroom. The most amazing aspect of Nabokov's literary career is that he became a best-selling author, his name a household word. This development occurred in large part because of the scandal surrounding *Lolita*. His continued popularity, however, arose from literary qualities rare in a writer's writer. Nabokov's novels have strong, interesting plots and are marked by an elegant if often Rabelaisian sense of humor. They are enjoyed by a wide audience as well as by literary specialists.

MARY

First published: *Mashenka*, 1926 (English translation, 1970)
Type of work: Novel

A young Russian émigré learns that he must break with the past and seek his happiness elsewhere.

Mary, Nabokov's first novel, is set in Berlin's large colony of Russian émigrés who had fled the Bolshevik Revolution. The novel's events take place during the first week of April, 1924, in a boardinghouse whose residents, once well-off but now poor, live in a state of suspension. They feel that their real lives were left behind in the Russia of their dreams and desperately hope to return to their former lives. Meanwhile, they wait in a cold, alien city and dream of the past.

Ganin, the hero, is an ex-White officer who fought against the victorious Reds before escaping abroad. Although of sterner fortitude than his fellow lodgers, he too has fallen into an irritable malaise. He wishes to move on, perhaps to France, but lacks the resolve to break off a dreary love affair and go. The novel opens in a setting symbolic of the plight of its characters. Ganin and a new lodger named Alfyorov find themselves temporarily trapped in the dark between floors on an elevator. Alfyorov, an effusively cheerful vulgarian, tells the taciturn Ganin that his (Alfyorov's) wife, Mary, from whom he was separated by the Revolution, will at last be rejoining him. Later in his room, he shows Ganin her picture. Ganin leaves without a word.

The girl in the picture is Mary, Ganin's first love. For the next several days, Ganin walks the streets of Berlin in a trance, reconstructing, scene by scene, the entire story of their affair, the happiest time of his life. Ganin's memories reinvigorate him. He abruptly stops seeing his mistress and prepares to leave Berlin. At a party the night before Mary's arrival, Alfyorov, with Ganin's help, becomes very drunk and is put to bed. Mary's train is to arrive at eight o'clock in the morning, but Ganin sets Alfyorov's alarm for eleven. Early in the morning, Ganin sets off with his bags to meet Mary at the train station. The world once again seems new, full of possibilities. As he walks, Ganin comes to a sudden realization, whereupon he catches a taxi to a different train station and sets off alone to begin a new life.

Mary's theme is simple. Mary, Ganin's first love, is identified with his Russian homeland. His reawakened love for her is intertwined with his debilitating nostalgia for his lost past. Only after reliving that love can he put the past behind him and start anew. Like many first novels, *Mary* has a strong autobiographical element. As Nabokov indicates both in his introduction to the novel and in his autobiography, *Speak, Memory*, *Mary* is based on his own first love affair and even incorporates passages from letters that he received from Mary's prototype.

THE DEFENSE

First published: *Zashchita Luzhina*, 1929 (serial), 1930 (English translation, 1964)
Type of work: Novel

Luzhin, a Russian émigré and International Grand Master, engages in a losing chess game with madness and death.

The Defense, Nabokov's third novel, established him as the leading new writer of the Russian emigration. As the novel opens, Luzhin, a gloomy, friendless lad, learns that he must start public school in St. Petersburg. The boy soon begins cutting school to visit the home of his vivacious aunt, where he learns to play chess. When his father learns of his secretive son's gift, he launches the boy's career as a chess prodigy. Under the strain, Luzhin eventually falls ill and is taken to a German health spa to recuperate. As it happens, a major international chess tournament is in progress there, and the boy becomes an international star. Sixteen years pass before the reader again meets an unkempt, thirty-year-old Luzhin, who finds himself once again at this same resort. A homeless, international wanderer who can barely cope with life's ordinary demands, Luzhin has returned to the resort to prepare for a major tournament in Berlin. At the resort, the boorish, inarticulate Luzhin meets a young woman who is not put off by his eccentricities. After a bizarre courtship, Luzhin leaves for Berlin. For the first time in many years, he plays brilliantly, moving toward a play-off with his nemesis Turati, who has previously defeated him. Luzhin has even prepared a special defense against his opponent. At length, the final game begins, but Turati does not make the expected opening attack. When the game is adjourned for the night, the exhausted Luzhin vaguely hears a voice saying, "Go home." As he makes his way back to his hotel, he collapses.

Luzhin awakens in a rustic mental hospital, where a psychiatrist, together with the patient's fiancée, tells him that he must give up chess if he is to save his sanity. Out of his asylum window, Luzhin sees a scene reminiscent of the Russian countryside of his youth and thinks, "Evidently, I got home." Soon released, Luzhin marries and settles down with his new bride. He seems to have put chess out of his mind. All is well until Luzhin encounters a former schoolmate, who remembers him as a former chess prodigy. Luzhin denies his past, but that night he is plagued by a feeling that a secret attack is unfolding against him. Suddenly, he realizes that each stage of his new, chess-free life is subtly replaying one of the stages in his childhood that led to his initial encounter with chess and, ultimately, to his breakdown. He tries to devise a defense, but his every move is anticipated and thwarted by his unseen opponent. Recognizing his inevitable defeat, Luzhin resigns the hopeless game by leaping through a window to his death.

Nabokov often pointed to the similarities of the composition of chess problems and literary works. *The Defense* illustrates these similarities in many ways, but most prominently in its intricate plotting. The technical problem is to insert each of the subtly disguised repetitions of the key events leading to Luzhin's final breakdown in such a way that their essential similarity to a previous event is not immediately evident. This covert patterning sometimes extends to the smallest details. The good reader must be superior to Luzhin in recognizing the presence and implications of these patterns. Luzhin mistakenly believes himself to be a player in a chess game against madness and death. In reality, he is merely a pawn in a chess problem designed by his author.

INVITATION TO A BEHEADING

First published: *Priglashenie na kazn'*, 1935-1936 (serial), 1938 (English translation, 1959)

Type of work: Novel

Condemned to death in a mythic totalitarian society, the young hero struggles to attain the free world flickering in his imagination.

Invitation to a Beheading was Nabokov's next-to-last Russian novel. Cincinnatus, the hero, is a quiet rebel against the stifling mediocrity of imagination and consciousness of his world. He has an intuition of another world, one in which imagination is king and there are other people like him. Cincinnatus has been condemned to death for the crime of "gnostical turpitude," which seems to refer to his unique sense of unknown, unnamed things in a world where all things are already named and known to everyone.

The events of *Invitation to a Beheading* take place in a mythic country, with no indication of temporal or geographic setting, although the characters speak Russian. The story covers the last three weeks in the life of Cincinnatus, a youthful teacher of defective children. On the novel's opening day, Cincinnatus hears his death sentence pronounced and is remanded to the hilltop prison fortress, where he is to await the fall of the ax. At first, Cincinnatus is the only prisoner in the fortress, where he is attended by his bluff jailer Rodion; the unctious, frock-coated director Rodrig; and his lawyer Roman, who beleaguers him with inane legal formalities. The careful reader soon realizes that the three characters, like actors, sometimes exchange costumes and roles.

Cincinnatus wishes only two things from his jailers: the date of his execution and a last visit from his callous, unfaithful wife, Marthe, and their two deformed children. Nothing can be learned on either score. Cincinnatus is soon joined by a new inmate, the plump, complaisant Pierre, who intimates that he has tried to help Cincinnatus escape. A cheerful vulgarian who seems to enjoy odd privileges for a prisoner, Pierre forces his friendship upon Cincinnatus, who wishes only to be left alone to explore his thoughts.

Cincinnatus devotes himself to keeping a prison diary in which he explores his sense of his differentness from all others in his society and his intimations of another, better world: "I am the one among you who is alive—Not only are my eyes different, and my hearing, and my sense of taste—not only is my sense of smell like a deer's, my sense of touch like a bat's—but most important, I have the capacity to conjoin all of this in one point." This point is that he knows "a paramount thing that no one here knows." He has come to believe that the world in which he is imprisoned is an illusion. While still fearing the executioner's ax, Cincinnatus suspects that death is a doorway between this wretched, delusional world and another, brighter, real one. Through some ghastly mistake, he has been born into the "wrong" world, and only death will rectify the error.

The day of Cincinnatus' public beheading arrives, and he is escorted from the prison by Pierre, who proves to be the executioner. Strangely, Cincinnatus' cell starts to disintegrate and as they move toward the fatal square, statues and buildings begin to crumble like decrepit stage sets. As Cincinnatus ascends the scaffold, the crowd starts to fade into transparency. The ax falls, and "amidst the dust, and the falling things, and the flapping scenery, Cincinnatus made his way in that direction where, to judge by the voices, stood beings akin to him."

The intuitions of Cincinnatus, the quiet loner and heretic, have been confirmed. He has been trapped in a false, nightmare universe in which he is the only "real" person. His imagination and awareness, which make him a criminal in the eyes of his fellow citizens, also give him his intuition of a better world, to which he, with the help of his author-creator, gains entrance at the moment of his beheading. His death in the evil world is his birth into the ideal world fashioned by his creator.

Invitation to a Beheading, composed in a matter of weeks during 1934, is Nabokov's most poetic, artifice-saturated, and technically sophisticated novel. There is no pretense of realism in Nabokov's most overt venture into high modernism. There is no attempt to create rounded, believable characters; nor would they be appropriate to what is patently a false, antihuman fictional universe. The plot revolves around the relative reality of Cincinnatus' two universes—his prison world and the free world suggested by his imagination. Nabokov has interposed these two worlds into his dystopian novel in a subtle and ingenious way that is more evident in the Russian original than in the English translation. The presence of the two worlds is almost subliminally woven into the text through the use of the words "here" and "there" signifying the false and the real worlds. Cincinnatus' creator, Nabokov, has structured his story around these contrasting terms, affirming what his character can only suspect. Stylistically, *Invitation to a Beheading* is Nabokov's most brilliant novel.

THE GIFT

First published: *Dar*, 1937-1938 (serial), 1952 (English translation, 1963)
Type of work: Novel

A young Russian émigré poet and writer gradually masters his art and finds love in the Berlin of the 1920's.

The Gift, Nabokov's last and greatest Russian novel, is set in Russian émigré Berlin in the late 1920's. The hero, Fyodor Godunov-Cherdyntsev, is a young poet and writer who is seeking to find his own voice and his place in Russian literary tradition. The former aristocrat, forever barred from his homeland, leads a pleasantly precarious existence giving lessons, doing translations, and selling an occasional poem. *The Gift* has a dual plot line: the evolution of Fyodor's art, and the course of his love affair with his fellow émigré Zina Mertz.

As the novel opens, Fyodor, who just published his first book of poems, is settling in at a new rooming house. That evening, he goes to visit Alexander and Alexandra Chernyshevski, who have befriended the young poet after the suicide of their son. Exercising his artistic imagination, Fyodor tries to enter the mind of each of the people present. Alexander Chernyshevski is on the verge of madness, and through Alexander's eyes Fyodor sees the shadowy figure of his dead son, Yasha, among the guests.

A few months pass, and Fyodor receives a visit from his mother, who lives in Paris. They reminisce about their idyllic family life in Russia before the revolution. Their greatest concern, however, is the fate of Fyodor's father, a famous explorer who disappeared while returning from Tibet. Although he is presumed dead, both mother and son still hope for his return. Although an austere scientist as well as a man-of-action, Fyodor's father possessed an aura of secret knowledge that set him apart from others. Fyodor, who idolizes his father, decides to write his biography. After many months, he abandons the project, feeling that he is unable to capture his father's mysterious essence. Fyodor has not yet mastered the themes and techniques that will mark him as a great artist.

The young writer must once again change his lodgings, and he takes a room in the apartment of a Russian family named Shchyogolev. Zina, Mrs. Shchyogolev's daughter from an earlier marriage, proves to be a longtime admirer of Fyodor's poetry, and the young people are drawn together. Meanwhile, Fyodor, an accomplished composer of chess problems, has come across an excerpt from the diary of Nikolai Chernyshevski in a Soviet chess magazine. Nikolai Chernyshevski (who is not to be confused with the novel's other Chernyshevskis) was a radical nineteenth century Russian literary and political journalist who was exiled by the czar. The inept Chernyshevski became a political martyr revered by the liberal Russian intelligentsia. So respected was Chernyshevski that his primitive, social utilitarian aesthetic views came to dominate much of Russia's cultural development for more than a century. Fyodor, the young aesthete, sees Nikolai Chernyshevski as the bad seed of Russian cultural and political history and decides to write a book about him. The slight volume, which constitutes chapter 4 of *The Gift*, outrages almost all segments of the reading public and gains for Fyodor a certain notoriety.

Zina has served as Fyodor's muse throughout the writing of the Chernyshevski biography. The lovers, although living under the same roof, are never alone together. Their problem is unexpectedly solved when Shchyogolev obtains a job abroad and sublets the family apartment. Until the new tenants arrive, Zina and Fyodor can stay. The young lovers, whose relationship has remained unknown to the Shchyogolevs, see them off at the train station. As they spend their last money on dinner in a sidewalk café, Fyodor outlines the plan of his major novel, which proves to be *The Gift*.

The Gift is especially rich in themes. The most prominent is that of the artist's creative process. Fyodor's artistic development is illustrated through four stages: the early poems, the aborted biography of his father, the witty and elegant biography of Chernyshevski, and *The Gift* itself. In each case, the actual development of Fyodor's creative process is followed from its tiny, inconsequential beginnings to the finished work, for Nabokov's novel is a biographical study of the creative gift from which the novel draws its title. The second major theme is Nabokov's radical reassessment of Russian cultural history and literature. The theme is associated with Fyodor's withering biography of Nikolai Chernyshevski and with his relationship with a character named Koncheyev, poet and literary critic. It is in Fyodor's conversations with Koncheyev (all of which are imaginary) that Nabokov advances his own aesthetically based reevaluation of Russian literature. The third major theme is the hereafter. This theme centers upon Alexander Chernyshevski and, to a lesser extent, upon Fyodor and his father. The demented Chernyshevski at times believes that he is in touch with the spirit world, but at other times he rejects the idea. As he lies dying, listening to water drumming outside his curtained window, he murmurs, "What nonsense. Of course there is nothing afterwards. . . . It is as clear as the fact that it is raining." In fact, the sun is shining, and a neighbor is watering her plants. The theme surfaces again near the end of the book when Fyodor receives a night summons to come meet his returned father. The sequence proves to be a dream, but other clues throughout the novel suggest the ghostly presence of Fyodor's father.

The Gift, the most complex of Nabokov's Russian novels, is also the most deeply rooted in Russian history and culture. Beyond that, what at first seems to be a traditional realistic Russian novel in fact proves to be another example of Nabokov's artistic ingeniousness, for his novel is plotted on the model of a chess problem composed by Fyodor in the course of the book. *The Gift* is both a loving tribute to and a parody of the traditional Russian realistic novel. It is a fitting climax to Nabokov's career as a Russian writer.

Summary

The critic George Steiner suggested that many of the writers who have left lasting marks in twentieth century literature share a characteristic that he termed "extraterritoriality." In the past, writers were closely bound to their own countries and cultures. Their settings and their points of view were restricted to their own background. Vladimir Nabokov, like James Joyce, Samuel Beckett, and the Argentinian Jorge Luis Borges, lived in a multilingual, multicultural world. By drawing on his multicultural heritage, Nabokov revitalized the novel, creating master works for a new international audience.

Bibliography

Alexandrov, Vladimir E. *Nabokov's Otherworld*. Princeton, N.J.: Princeton University Press, 1991.

Boyd, Brian. *Vladimir Nabokov: The Russian Years*. Princeton, N.J.: Princeton University Press, 1990.

_____. *Vladimir Nabokov: The American Years*. Princeton, N.J.: Princeton University Press, 1991.

Johnson, D. Barton. *Worlds in Regression: Some Novels of Vladimir Nabokov*. Ann Arbor, Mich.: Ardis, 1985.

Juliar, Michael. *Vladimir Nabokov: A Descriptive Bibliography*. New York: Garland, 1986.

Lee, L. L. *Vladimir Nabokov*. Boston: G. K. Hall, 1976.

Pifer, Ellen. *Nabokov and the Novel*. Cambridge, Mass.: Harvard University Press, 1980.

Proffer, Ellendea, ed. *Vladimir Nabokov: A Pictorial Biography*. Ann Arbor, Mich.: Ardis, 1991.

Rampton, David. *Vladimir Nabokov: A Critical Study of the Novels*. Cambridge, England: Cambridge University Press, 1984.

Toker, Leona. *Nabokov: The Mystery of Literary Structures*. Ithaca, N.Y.: Cornell University Press, 1989.

D. Barton Johnson

V. S. NAIPAUL

Born: Chaguanas, Trinidad
August 17, 1932

Principal Literary Achievement
Described by many as England's greatest living writer, Naipaul explores the postcolonial world in his novels and nonfiction.

Biography

Vidiadhar Surajprasad Naipaul was born in Chaguanas, Trinidad, on August 17, 1932, of Hindu parents whose forebears had immigrated from India. Vidiadhar's father, Seepersad Naipaul, was reared in poverty because of the early death of his own father. After completing his education, however, Seepersad married into a large, powerful Brahmin family. At the time of Vidiadhar's birth, Seepersad was staff correspondent for *The Trinidad Guardian*, reporting on events in the small town of Chaguanas. There, he and his wife lived, along with dozens of relatives, all crowded into the large family home and dominated by his wife's mother. Two years after Vidiadhar's birth, when the crusading managing editor of *The Trinidad Guardian* lost his job, Seepersad was reduced to a position as stringer, or occasional writer. Lacking privacy or respect at home and deprived of the vocation that had given his life order and meaning, Seepersad had a nervous breakdown. For some years, he moved from one odd job to another and from one place to another, while his wife and children remained in the big house in Chaguanas.

Although his father was to be a major influence on his career, V. S. Naipaul says that he did not come to know him until 1938, when Seepersad was hired by *The Trinidad Guardian* to cover Port of Spain and moved his wife and five children to the city, where, for two years, they were finally able to live by themselves. During that period, which he calls the happiest in his life, the boy started reading his father's old press clippings, which gave him an insight into life in Chaguanas, as well as an interest in writing.

Later, the Naipaul family was again absorbed by relatives, living first in the country and then, when the war broke out, back in Port of Spain in a house crowded with family members who had come to the city to work. Because conditions at home were so chaotic during most of his childhood, V. S. Naipaul was developing a need for order, which he found at school and, interestingly, in reading draft after draft of the stories that his father was writing for his own pleasure. In this process, he came to

share his father's conviction that writing was the noblest vocation of all because it enabled one to work toward a just order in a chaotic and unjust world. By the time he was eleven, even though he himself had done no writing, V. S. Naipaul knew that he was to be a writer.

By the time Seepersad could finally buy a house for his family, V. S. Naipaul was fourteen years old. At eighteen, he left home. Having completed his studies at Queen's Royal College, he won a scholarship from the government of Trinidad, and in 1950, he left for Oxford, planning to study English in preparation for his career as a writer. Unfortunately, his father did not live to see his son's success. In 1953, at the age of forty-seven, Seepersad Naipaul died.

When he left Oxford a year after his father's death, Naipaul stayed in London, living meagerly on the income from a part-time position with the British Broadcasting Corporation's Caribbean service. In his "Prologue to an Autobiography," published in *Finding the Center: Two Narratives* (1986), Naipaul dates his writing career as beginning late one afternoon in the office where he worked, when, for no particular reason, he typed a sentence about someone named Hat shouting to his neighbor Bogart, back in Port of Spain. Naipaul's imagination was fired. He kept writing, and in time, he had finished a book. Although it was to be four years later, in 1959, that *Miguel Street* would be published, from the moment that Naipaul pecked out that sentence, with which the novel begins, he had begun to fulfill his father's dream. When he decided to remain in England after leaving Oxford, Naipaul was in effect choosing his lifetime home. In 1955, he married a British woman, Patricia Ann Hale, with whom he would live in historic Salisbury, near Stonehenge. Despite his long residence there and the acclaim that he has received from English readers, however, Naipaul always describes himself as an exile in England, in the same way that he would have been an outsider in Trinidad.

For his first four novels, however, Naipaul drew on the experiences of his childhood. *The Mystic Masseur* (1957), *The Suffrage of Elvira* (1958), *Miguel Street* (1959), and *A House for Mr. Biswas* (1961) are all set in Trinidad, and all have obvious autobiographical elements. *A House for Mr. Biswas*, for example, is the story of a poor man, much like Naipaul's father, who is doomed to live with his wife's relatives but determined to get a house of his own.

In 1962, Naipaul published his first nonfiction work, *The Middle Passage: Impressions of Five Societies—British, French, and Dutch—in the West Indies and South America*, which concentrates on the status of societies that, like the West Indies, are still influenced by their colonial heritage. During that decade, Naipaul wrote a variety of works, for example, the novels *Mr. Stone and the Knights Companion* (1963), set in England, and *The Mimic Men* (1967), about a West Indian expatriate in London, as well as short stories and other nonfiction books.

In the 1970's, Naipaul further broadened his scope, turning to Africa for his subject matter, with the novels *In a Free State* (1971) and *A Bend in the River* (1979), as well as to India, which he discusses in *India: A Wounded Civilization* (1977), after an extended visit to the home of his ancestors. During the 1980's, Naipaul continued to produce either a novel or a nonfiction book every year or two. Such works as *Among the Believers* (1981), the study of four Islamic countries, and *A Turn in the South* (1989), a travel book about the American South, illustrate Naipaul's continuing curiosity and flexibility.

Analysis

Although his works vary widely in subject, in form, and in tone, Naipaul's primary interest throughout his literary career has been the relationship of the individual to society. He is unlike such contemporary writers as Eudora Welty of Mississippi or R. K. Narayan of India, who write about the traditional societies in which they were reared. Naipaul does not deal with a static society, whose rules an individual must accept or defy, but with multicultural societies in which the various cultures themselves are changing because of the breakdown of old traditions, old beliefs, or the old, often colonial, governments that gave them stability.

Even a relatively peaceful society such as that described in Naipaul's Trinidad novels can be extremely complex. There are the white, Christian residents, the old governing class of the colonial period. Then there is a black majority, with its own customs, even its own language. Finally, there is the Indian minority, most of whom are descended from immigrants who worked out their passage as indentured servants, but who are now far from homogeneous. Some are rich, others are poor. Some are Hindus, some are Muslims. Some are religiously orthodox, others are not. As Naipaul indicates in "Prologue to an Autobiography," however, they do have one common quality: Most of them, even if they have abandoned their religious practices, still retain ties to an India that many of them have never seen. This fact is reflected in Naipaul's account of his grandfather, who, after spending his life in Trinidad, returned to India to die. The persistence of social prejudices brought from the older society is revealed in the conversation of Naipaul's elderly aunt, who remembers her cruel and miserly father with pride, because by inheritance he was of high caste. Yet, as Naipaul points out in the same essay, those very Indians who endured their exile in Trinidad by thinking of India as their real home often discovered that they were cherishing an illusion. He describes vividly the terror of the Indians who, ecstatic to be docking in Calcutta, were almost trampled by people who had been repatriated on the last boat and were now desperate to return to Trinidad.

Naipaul's characters are likely to be caught between two worlds, just as these immigrants were. His protagonist in *The Mimic Men*, for example, feels ill at ease in London, but when he returns home, he is just as much out of place as he was in England. One reason for his alienation is, of course, the fact that, while he has been absent, both he and his childhood home have changed. Certainly, this kind of experience is a universal phenomenon. The Indians who returned to an India they remembered, however, encountered not only the differences that the passage of time brings to any society but also the dizzyingly accelerated change resulting from the death of colonialism and the painful birth of a new society.

Much to the distress of some of his readers, Naipaul is not optimistic about attempts at democracy in formerly colonial countries. *The Suffrage of Elvira* is a comic treatment of the coming of democracy, defined as corruption; a West Indian island is the setting in *Guerrillas* (1975), a grim novel about the horrors of revolution. In his works about newly liberated African countries or about Middle Eastern Islamic countries, or about India itself, Naipaul stresses his own perception that twentieth century change does not seem to be resulting in progress and peace, but in disruption, violence, and the willful destruction of all that earlier generations have built.

Deprived of the support of traditional societies and stable governments, Naipaul's characters, like Naipaul himself, yearn for order in the midst of chaos. In some cases, like Man-man of *Miguel Street*, who decides to be crucified in order to prove his holiness, they are eccentric or mad enough to be doomed to failure, even in the most traditional society. In other cases, like that of Naipaul's own father and the protagonist of *A House for Mr. Biswas*, their problems seem to be the result of a number of factors, including chance, their own weakness or gullibility, and an encounter with particularly clever and vicious predators. In some of his works, however, such as *In a Free State*, the fate of the characters is a direct result of a breakdown of society. Such characters are totally isolated, separated from their native countries, their cultural traditions, and from one another. Such a vision, of alienated characters in a society that has lost its structure, may well be Naipaul's prophecy of the future.

Given the bleakness of his viewpoint, it would seem that Naipaul's works would hardly be rewarding reading. Yet although most of the characters in the early novels set in Trinidad are destined to fail, Naipaul's comic treatment of their problems and his satire of the social relationships with which they are so obsessed prevent his readers from taking either the characters or their entanglements very seriously. Not until *A House for Mr. Biswas* is there any hint of the tragicomic, or even tragic, tone of Naipaul's later novels. Even works such as *In a Free State*, however, whose vision of the future is extremely depressing, are compelling because of Naipaul's skill in constructing exciting plots, as well as his genius in creating fascinating, vital characters.

Naipaul's nonfiction works have much in common with his fiction. In both, there is brief, precise, and evocative description and a heavy reliance on accurately rendered dialogue. Whether his people are the fictional residents of Miguel Street or the real residents of the Deep South, Naipaul lets them speak for themselves. In the novels, dramatic dialogue keeps the plot in motion; in the nonfiction works, it also as effectively propels the reader forward to the next chapter, where there is sure to be an opposing viewpoint, or at least a marked variation in interpretation.

All of his technical virtuosity would be of little value if Naipaul did not have such valuable insights. Obviously, he believes that no efforts to produce a just order in society can succeed if they are based on illusions either about the past or about the present. If some misread Naipaul as yearning sentimentally for nineteenth century colonial society, they are ignoring the fact that he satirizes that world, and those who are nostalgic for it, just as clearly as he satirizes the simple-minded idealists who have underestimated the difficulty of creating new orders and who, in their foolish optimism, have permitted the rapacious and the vicious to take control of societies in which there is now neither order nor justice. What Naipaul says may not be pleasant to hear, but, like every worthy reformer, he must begin with the truth.

THE SUFFRAGE OF ELVIRA

First published: 1958
Type of work: Novel

In a new West Indian democracy, a candidate for office struggles to win, and to buy, the votes necessary for his election.

The Suffrage of Elvira, Naipaul's second published novel, has been described as a comedy of manners. Certainly, as the first chapter demonstrates, it is comic in tone. On one hand, Naipaul is dramatizing the desperate anxiety of Mr. Surujpat Harbans, as he drives his old truck up Elvira Hill, on the way to arrange support for his election to the legislative council. On the other hand, the omens that so terrify Harbans seem hardly to justify his fears. Two American women stop their bicycles so unexpectedly that Harbans cannot help sliding into them, and then later he hits and slightly injures a black dog, which is wandering about in the middle of the road with about as much sense as the women.

The fact that both the women and the dog do indeed prove to be recurring obstacles in Harbans' attempt to win the election not only unifies the plot but also points out the failure of democracy, that is, universal suffrage for adults, just four years after it was so nobly declared. Indeed, at the beginning of the second chapter, Naipaul defines what democracy has meant to the islanders: put simply, new possibilities for profit.

As a candidate, Harbans must try to win the election without spending so much money that the post will be unprofitable. As his backers, the Muslim leader, a tailor, and the Hindu leader, a goldsmith, try to spend as little of their own money as possible, while using the election to consolidate their power and, if possible, to get some immediate cash benefits. By rights, Harbans thinks, it should be a simple matter of paying these leaders a reasonable sum to deliver the votes. That is the way democracy should work.

Unfortunately, Harbans' opponent very nearly outwits him by benefiting from human irrationality. For example, the women on bicycles, who are Jehovah's Witnesses, persuade the Spanish voters, who were committed to Harbans, that God does not wish them to vote, since the end of the world is imminent. The dog, too, causes trouble. One of her puppies, which keeps appearing and disappearing, is seen variously as a curse and a blessing; to offset the harm that that puppy has done to the campaign, the dead puppies in the litter must be publicly displayed so as to discredit the Jehovah's Witnesses and send the Spanish voters on their way to the polling place.

Although *The Suffrage of Elvira* does not deal with courtly aristocrats as traditional comedy of manners does, it resembles that form in being both dramatic and satirical. Many of the passages consist of colorful dialogue, which has the quality of a scene from a play. Furthermore, the targets of satire are not only individuals but also universal types, such as the Muslim leader's haphazard son, whose schemes and slogans alike very nearly cost Harbans his victory.

Like audiences at comedies of manners, Naipaul's readers begin by laughing at foolish, ignorant people in a fictitious place; however, they should end by realizing that these characters actually exaggerate their own flaws. If no democracy has managed to exclude citizens who see that form of government merely as a means of enriching themselves, it is equally true that even the most principled electorate finds itself influenced by slogans, rumors, sexual scandals, calculated character assassination, appeals to religious convictions, even free drinks and parades. There is typical Naipaulian irony in the comment made about Elvira voters and intended to be the highest praise: Once they are bought, they stay bought. One wonders if that is the most that can be expected of a democracy, whether in the Third World or in the former colonial powers.

A HOUSE FOR MR. BISWAS

First published: 1961
Type of work: Novel

A poor man spends his life in the quest for self-respect, financial security, and, above all, a house of his own.

A House for Mr. Biswas, the fourth and last of the early novels, is important to the study of Naipaul for several reasons. Although it resembles its predecessors in that it is set in Trinidad, in this work for the first time the comic tone becomes more nearly tragicomic. While Naipaul still treats many of the characters satirically, his protagonist, Mohun Biswas, is likable, even admirable, in his struggle to gain self-respect and the respect of others and to make enough money to buy his own house. *A House for Mr. Biswas* is also important because it is Naipaul's most autobiographical work, reflecting closely his father's life and his own childhood. For this reason, the author comments in his foreword to the 1984 Vintage Books edition of the work that, of all of his books, this is the one that means the most to him. Naipaul's critics also place a high value on the novel. Many of them consider it to be his masterpiece.

Naipaul's initial chapters generally indicate the theme and the major motifs of his novels. The prologue to *A House for Mr. Biswas* is really the end of the story, describing as it does the disastrous ending of Mr. Biswas' life, when, at forty-six, the father of four children, penniless, debt-ridden, and ill, he is fired from his job and lies waiting to die in the ill-constructed house that was his life's goal.

In the first chapter of *A House for Mr. Biswas*, as in the prologue to *The Suffrage of Elvira*, Naipaul uses what seem like trivial events to set the pattern of the novel. Mohun's being born backward and having a sixth finger should not be blamed for his later troubles. It is soon evident, however, that the boy cannot keep his mind on his business, and through an improbable chain of events, his forgetting to watch a calf indirectly causes his father's death, which in turn sentences the family to poverty. As a poor young man, then, Mohun Biswas later becomes fair game for the predatory Tulsi family, which is always on the outlook for malleable sons-in-law.

The rest of Mr. Biswas' short life is spent in search of employment, prosperity, and a home of his own, where his wife and his children will treat him like the head of the house. Yet he fails in one job after another, and he also fails to make a home for his family. When he leaves the Tulsis, his wife refuses to go with him; when he stays with them, he is no more than a shadowy presence, who can assert himself only by sarcasm. The only relief that Mr. Biswas has from his despair comes in the developing love and loyalty of his son Anand, and even that is not enough to prevent his ultimate nervous breakdown. Like Seepersad Naipaul, Mr. Biswas eventually becomes a journalist in Port of Spain. He has, however, no real security. During his brief residence in the house that he knows is rickety, he looks back on his life, attempting to explain to himself every disastrous choice that he has made.

The story is tragic, but as the final paragraphs of *A House for Mr. Biswas* illustrate, Naipaul is writing now with a new complexity of tone. First, he treats the death of Mr. Biswas with appropriate compassion. Then, when the Tulsis, his favorite comic characters, invade the house at the time of the funeral, threatening its immediate collapse, the mood becomes farcical. Yet there is irony in the comedy; one realizes that the survival of the house despite the Tulsis is a symbolic triumph for the deceased. Finally, when Naipaul describes the return of the family to the empty house, the note is tragic. Naipaul was never again to write a purely comic novel; instead, he incorporated the comedy as merely one of a number of viewpoints from which his situations and his characters are to be seen.

A BEND IN THE RIVER

First published: 1979
Type of work: Novel

> Old residents try to prosper, or even to survive, in a newly liberated African state.

In *A Bend in the River*, as in all of his later works, Naipaul's dominant theme is alienation. The characters in this novel are not simply outsiders, such as Mr. Biswas among the Tulsis, but bewildered individuals attempting to survive in a rapidly changing society, where the rules are changed daily. The setting is a state in central Africa that has recently gone through a revolution and a civil war. The new government is under the control of a president, actually a dictator, who rules his country with the use of informers, youth squads, disappearances, and executions.

Into this reign of terror comes the protagonist, Salim, an East African Indian who has left the coastal area where his family has lived and traded for generations and bought a shop in an isolated village located on a bend in the river, which he believes should make it an ideal trading place. On his drive across Africa, as he bribes his way through road blocks, at times Salim questions his own sanity. He reaches his destination and settles down in the partially deserted village, hoping for peace and profit, but secure in the fact that he does have a home to which he can return. Unfortunately, he soon learns that his coastal village has been destroyed in a revolution and that his family has dispersed. Now Salim is truly marooned.

One of the points that Naipaul makes in *A Bend in the River* is that one does not have to be alone to be isolated. Salim is not alone. There are a number of expatriates in the village, Belgians, Greeks, Asians, and Indians, many of whom have remained through the turmoil, who now are waiting for life to stabilize. Every family, however, is preoccupied with itself and its own survival; though there is civility, there is no sense of community. Even his best friends, an elderly Indian couple, Shoba and Mahesh, are so preoccupied with themselves that they ignore the people and the country around them, seemingly convincing themselves that they are really living in India. When Salim visits them, there is no conversation; it is as if by ignoring the world outside their door, they can be safe from it. It is this kind of isolation that prevents the villagers from expressing outrage when the highly respected scholar and priest, Father Huismans, is murdered and mutilated, evidently because he had collected ritual masks and therefore seemed to be mocking the native religion. Many of the expatriates seem to see his death as an object lesson: this is what happens when one ventures forward, when one attempts to develop a community among peoples so different from one another.

For a time, the optimism of Father Huismans seems to be justified. Mahesh emerges from his isolation to acquire the Bigburger franchise. The president begins to construct a model town, the Domain, on the site of the old colonial suburb. Salesmen and consultants arrive from Europe, and Salim's childhood friend, the university-educated Indar, appears, a guest of the government, to work at the university-turned-polytechnic, whose chief function now is to train young men to be members of the president's staff. Salim's life becomes even more interesting when he has an affair with the wife of the president's white adviser. When he recognizes that he is beginning to believe the president's pronouncements, however, Salim feels the need to get some perspective and takes a trip to London.

When he returns to Africa, Salim finds that the promise of progress was an illusion. Caught between the oppressive president and his trigger-happy troops and a newly formed Liberation Army, everyone is terrified. Salim's business is nationalized, he loses most of his savings in the difficult process of getting money out of the country, and, finally, he is jailed, warned, and forced to flee the country.

The situation in *A Bend in the River* is what Naipaul finds characteristic of the Third World: For all the talk about a master plan, the leaders of these new countries have no real direction in mind. They cannot decide whether to destroy the vestiges of Europe or to mimic it, as the president did with his Domain, and they cannot seem to develop an orderly, progressive society. The only perceivable pattern is the survival of the vicious. As Salim says, to someone who does not live in these countries, their governments appear comic, and certainly there are many comic scenes in *A Bend in the River*. Yet, as Salim realizes, one who does choose to stay in the postcolonial chaos can lose everything, including one's life.

THE ENIGMA OF ARRIVAL

First published: 1987
Type of work: Novel

In rural England, an expatriate discovers that traditional societies are as susceptible to change as the Third World country from which he came.

In *The Enigma of Arrival*, Naipaul turns to the situation of the expatriate who lives as an alien in a traditional society. The narrator, a writer from Trinidad, has come to settle in the English countryside. From his cottage near Salisbury, he ventures forth to look at remnants of the past, prehistoric Stonehenge, deserted farm cottages, and rusting reminders of World War II, and to discover that even this seemingly unchanging landscape and the people who inhabit it are not exempt from change.

The structure of *The Enigma of Arrival* is more like that of an extremely digressive travel book than a work of fiction. One idea leads to another in the mind of the narrator, who is so close to Naipaul himself as to make it difficult to remember the distinction, and one anecdote suggests another. The connection is thematic and psychological, not chronological. Thus, in the second part of the book, the narrator moves from a journey to England that he has recently completed to his first journey out of Trinidad eighteen years before, while revealing his first impressions of airplane travel, of New York, and of London.

Although there is a great deal of lyrical description of nature in *The Enigma of Arrival*, Naipaul also tells the stories of people whom he has met along the way, such as Angela, an older, more worldly Italian girl at his London boardinghouse who became one of his closest friends. Late in his Salisbury stay, the narrator receives a letter from Angela, whom he has not seen for thirty years. Outside his window, the aspens sway, and he thinks of watching them grow, seeing two of them fall; inside, he sees the variations in Angela's handwriting, as she relates the events of her life, and he is acutely conscious of the fact that though one circles in life, sometimes returning, everything is in constant flux.

In the third segment of *The Enigma of Arrival*, symbolically entitled "Ivy," the narrator focuses on the people who have clung for decades to the area where he is living, and especially on those associated with the manor, such as the gardener Pitton, his elderly father, and the car-hire man, all of whom can describe what it was like on the estate when there were sixteen gardeners instead of only one. Then the reclusive landlord emerges from his seclusion and takes an interest in the world around him. The narrator gets to know the landlord's cousin, a personable man who calls himself a writer. There is a brief season when everyone seems to be happy.

Naipaul, however, always points out that the only thing on which one can rely is the certainty of change. The gardener is fired; the landlord returns to his isolation; the would-be writer becomes an alcoholic and commits suicide; the caretaker dies; his wife remarries; the little children's house on the estate is closed off with barbed wire; and the narrator knows that it is time for him to leave. In his epilogue, "The Ceremony of Farewell," he explains the new insights that came during his stay in Salisbury, involving primarily a new acceptance of the mystery of life itself.

Summary

Although he must be admired for his skill in plotting and characterization and for the beauty of his language, V. S. Naipaul is perhaps most important because he addresses the most difficult problem of modern humanity, the sense of alienation. Even in the early comic novels, Naipaul suggests how deeply his characters fear being expelled from the cultural groups that give them a sense of identity. Most of his later works take a realistic look at the Third World, where political and social change has deprived people of their identities, leaving them isolated in a chaotic and corrupt world. Only a writer of Naipaul's intellectual stature could have told the whole truth about this world; perhaps the knowledge of that truth will someday make possible some remedy.

Bibliography

Boyers, Robert. "V. S. Naipaul." *The American Scholar* 50 (Summer, 1981): 359-367.

Hamner, Robert D., ed. *Critical Perspectives on V. S. Naipaul.* Washington, D.C.: Three Continents Press, 1977.

McSweeney, Kerry. *Four Contemporary Novelists: Angus Wilson, Brian Moore, John Fowles, V. S. Naipaul.* Kingston, Canada: McGill-Queen's University Press, 1983.

Naipaul, V. S. "Prologue to an Autobiography." In *Finding the Center: Two Narratives.* New York: Vintage Books, 1986.

Sheppard, R. Z. "Wanderer of Endless Curiosity." *Time* 134 (July 10, 1989): 58-60.

Theroux, Paul. *V. S. Naipaul: An Introduction to His Work.* London: Heinemann, 1972.

Walsh, William. *V. S. Naipaul.* New York: Barnes & Noble Books, 1973.

White, Landeg. *V. S. Naipaul: A Critical Introduction.* New York: Macmillan, 1975.

Rosemary M. Canfield Reisman

EDNA O'BRIEN

Born: Tuamgraney, County Clare, Ireland
December 15, 1930

Principal Literary Achievement
O'Brien is most widely known for her lively fictions detailing the maturation of Irish girls and for her portrayal of Irish women encountering loneliness and loss in their search for love.

Biography
The youngest child in a shabby, genteel farm family, which included a brother and two sisters, Josephine Edna O'Brien was born in Tuamgraney, County Clare, Ireland, on December 15, 1930, and grew up in the rural West of Ireland. If her fictions are to be believed, and in broad outline the facts are substantiated by her on-the-record comments, her father, Michael O'Brien, drank too much, and her mother, Lena, fully assumed the classic martyr's role. O'Brien was educated at the local primary school in Scarriff and at the Convent of Mercy, Loughrea, County Galway. From this repressive, priest-ridden home and rural environment, with its many social and sexual taboos, she "escaped" in the late 1940's to Dublin to study pharmacy there in the work-study system then in vogue.

O'Brien's necessary physical departure from the West, and eventually from Ireland too, freed her, like many Irish writers in exile (James Joyce and Sean O'Casey, for example), to write about her homeland for a lifetime. Her best work, most readers agree, is set among the Irish and involves social and family relationships, searches and conflicts, not unlike O'Brien's own firsthand experiences, in a vanishing Ireland that she knows and re-creates extremely well.

Always a reader, in the city of Dublin she encountered for the first time, and with great delight, the stimulation of venturesome writers such as fellow Irish national James Joyce, and the realistic stories and plays of the Russian Anton Chekhov. She contributed pieces to the *Irish Press* newspaper. In 1954 O'Brien married the older, established writer Ernest Gebler. They had two sons, Carlo (a novelist in his own right) and Sasha (an architect).

The family moved to London, where she established permanent residence and wrote during their first month in England the very successful *The Country Girls* (1960). She followed this novel quickly with the other parts of the trilogy, *The Lonely Girl* (1962; reprinted in 1964 as *Girl with Green Eyes*) and *Girls in Their Married Bliss*

(1964). O'Brien and Gebler have argued in print over just how much help he gave her with the trilogy (the marriage was dissolved in 1964); whatever the truth behind their dispute, O'Brien was launched on a successful, jet-set, high-profile career, involving psychiatric counseling with the celebrated Dr. R. D. Laing and including frequent television appearances whenever a feisty, auburn-haired spokesperson for Ireland or for Irish women was called for. *The Lonely Girl* was made into a film, *Girl with Green Eyes* (1964), starring Rita Tushingham.

Based in London, successfully rearing her sons on her own, O'Brien had two most prolific decades of work, in a variety of genres. Her sexually explicit scenes, and criticism of Church personnel, caused for her some problems with the Irish censors. The novels accumulated: *August Is a Wicked Month* (1965); *Casualties of Peace* (1966); *A Pagan Place* (1970), her favorite work, and chosen by the *Yorkshire Post* as novel of the year; *Zee & Co.* (1971), which as a 1972 film starred Elizabeth Taylor, Michael Caine, and Susannah York; *I Hardly Knew You* (1977); and, after what was for O'Brien a long gap between major publications, *The Country Girls Trilogy and Epilogue* (1986) and *The High Road* (1988).

Between novels, beginning in 1962, and on the same general theme of love/loss and connection, she published dozens of short stories in a variety of magazines, including, principally, *The New Yorker*. Some of O'Brien's best short fictions appear in the following collections: *The Love Object* (1968); *A Scandalous Woman and Other Stories* (1974); *Mrs. Reinhardt* (1978; better known as *A Rose in the Heart*), from which the title story was made into a television drama (1981); *Returning* (1982); and *Lantern Slides* (1990).

Along with the prose fiction, O'Brien involved herself in journalism, writing travel books from her very personal experiences, including the provocative, eccentric *Mother Ireland* (1976), which is the best place to get an introduction to her work, editing the anthology *Some Irish Loving* (1979), and writing criticism of James Joyce. O'Brien also continued her interest in the theater: *A Cheap Bunch of Nice Flowers* (1962), *Time Lost and Time Remembered* (1966), *X, Y, and Zee* (1971), and *Virginia* (1981), about Virginia Woolf.

O'Brien's biography is, more than for many prolific writers, the avowed raw material for her fictions. In 1984 and 1986, she published in New York an elegant pair of matched volumes: *A Fanatic Heart*, largely from the best of her previously collected stories, and then what many consider her best work, a new edition of *The Country Girls Trilogy* with an entirely new *Epilogue*. This postscript's narrator is Baba, the more extroverted of O'Brien's dual heroines; the more introverted, Kate, readers are told, is dead. It seemed as if, as O'Brien approached sixty, the well of her previous inspiration was drying up, and she was putting her literary estate in order, or she was about to take a new direction, as represented by the confident "Baba" voice.

In 1988, however, after ten years of publishing no novels, she published, to very mixed reviews, *The High Road*, set again in the Kate-world of the expatriates' Mediterranean and its multinational cliques, and the new direction was denied. In 1990, O'Brien, most secure in her literary reputation in the United States, was back in New York, where she had been writer-in-residence at City College. At the Young Men's Christian Association (YMCA), she gave a dramatic public reading of "Brother," from her short-story collection *Lantern Slides*; it is the vengeful monologue of an Irish woman contemplating the arrival of her brother's new bride in the farmhouse that the two of them had shared alone together for many years. O'Brien, amid a crowd of fans, also signed copies of her very brief, autobiographical poem, "On the Bone."

Analysis

O'Brien's perennial concerns in her fictions are most readily accessible in her very eccentric, impressionistic travel/autobiography, complete with photographs by Fergus Bourke, *Mother Ireland*. This personal response to her dear, native land is not at all likely to be promoted by the Irish Tourist Board. Her Irishness is, however, something of which O'Brien is proud: "It's a state of mind," she claims. She is not, however, blind to Ireland's faults, appreciating that there must be something "secretly catastrophic" about a country that so many of its people leave. After an iconoclastic opening chapter on Irish history, with its uncanonized patron saint, Saint Patrick, and its paunchy Firbolgs, O'Brien continues with six chapters in which are sketched her dominant themes: loneliness and the search for love, the longing for adventure (often sexual), the repressive Irish Roman Catholic Church and rural society, the constraints of family ties (particularly as they involve a martyred mother and her daughter), and the courageous hopelessness with which life at best must be lived.

It would be a melancholy prospect indeed for her almost-always female protagonists ("Clara" from her short-story collection *A Rose in the Heart* has one of O'Brien's very rare male narrators) if it were not for O'Brien's saving graces of irony, sometimes at her own expense, and of humor. At her best, she skillfully roots her observations in the sensual details of an actual Irish world, now quickly vanishing. The late twentieth century proliferation of television antennae on cottage roofs, the problems of widespread unemployment, and other political issues make no inroads on the consciousnesses of her heroines. Problems of a practical nature (the need for grocery money) or of a provincial or national political nature (the Northern Ireland question) impinge not at all on O'Brien's fictional characters' search for fulfillment. Instead, her people, and her readers through them, inhabit an Ireland now almost gone. All five of their senses are engaged by a world of wet-batteries for radios, ink-powder to be reconstituted in school by highly favored students, private estate walls with fragments of bottles embedded in their tops to deter trespassers, Fox's Glacier Mints, orange-crate furniture, and lice fine-combed from a child's head onto a newspaper: in other words, the world of the 1940's and 1950's.

O'Brien's recurring themes, her experimenting with received forms and narrative stances in the pronouns used, and the feeling that she succeeds in communicating that this Irish microcosm has a universal significance are all clearly present in *Mother Ireland*, the most accessible and instructive work with which to make O'Brien's literary acquaintance.

Right from the beginning of her literary career, it appeared as if O'Brien had fallen upon, or decided upon, in whatever mysterious way inspiration works, the mechanism of splitting her heroines into two separate, complementary personalities. In *The Country Girls*, the shy and sensitive Caithleen tells her story, and she shares the action with her alter ego, the volatile and sometimes malicious Baba. They inhabit a world divided largely into warring camps: male and female, young and old, Church and laity, country and town—where Caithleen's aspirations toward romantic love are doomed to failure. Expelled from their repressive convent school for writing a ribald joke, the girls, in their late teens, come to Dublin. Caithleen's Mr. Gentleman, the first of a long line of largely unsympathetic men in O'Brien's work, disappoints her. With the ebullience and resilence of youth, she is "almost" certain that she will not sleep again. Yet she does, and in *The Lonely Girl* her education continues. Her tutor there is the cultivated snob whom she marries, Eugene Gaillard, whose initials, Grace Eckley noted in her *Edna O'Brien* (1974), are the same as Ernest Gebler's, O'Brien's husband at the time. At the novel's conclusion, the girls are still seeking their connection and sail on the *Hibernia* for Liverpool and London.

For the first time, in the third part of their saga, *Girls in Their Married Bliss*, Baba assumes the first-person narration, alternating with an omniscient voice distancing O'Brien and the reader from Kate's (as she now wishes to be known) role. The women are now in their mid-twenties, and there is a splendid, blustery, Celtic quality to the scapegrace Baba's style. The subject is still the female search for love in a healthy relationship with a man. In general it may be said, though, that, with few exceptions, the men whom O'Brien provides for her heroines are very poor risks, being either married already or in some other way unable to give themselves fully in any relationship. It is a doomed search on the evidence in *Girls in Their Married Bliss*, as readers observe Kate's marriage failing. Occasionally, as in the story "The Mouth of the Cave," *The Love Object,* or *The High Road*, O'Brien frankly offers a lesbian connection for her female narrator (not to be confused with the sisterly rapport between Kate and Baba). Still, it remains predominantly in a heterosexual connection that O'Brien's characters' hopes for happiness seem to lie.

In subsequent novels, O'Brien, like her characters, learns and develops her skills. Her protagonists shift back and forth between the two poles of experience, the two responses to life represented by the romantic Kate and the realistic Baba of her earliest works. In *August Is a Wicked Month*, the narrator, Ellen, is a Kate-like figure whose attempts at self-liberation, largely through her sexual activity, bring her great guilt and pain. The judgment is perhaps too clear in this novel to make it an artistic success. The balancing continues in *Casualties of Peace*, where Willa and Patsy are both victims of male violence. This novel is O'Brien's most Joycean up to this date; Patsy's love letters are reminiscent of the earliest of those exchanged between James Joyce and his eventual wife, Nora Barnacle, in their correspondence with each other.

After *A Pagan Place*, which is a rewriting of *The Country Girls* ten years later, in her *Zee & Co.*, where Zee is no patsy, and particularly in *Night* (1972), O'Brien's optimistic Baba-type character is back and on the offensive. This new attitude is best shown in *Night*'s Mary Hooligan, whose aggressive, courageous, night-long monologue forms the whole substance of the work. Family, community, and marriage settings are again explored. Mary, like Joyce's Mollie Bloom, or indeed Chaucer's Wife of Bath, is indomitable. Such an optimistic focus, however, does not last for O'Brien. With *I Hardly Knew You*, the narrator, Nora, takes readers back again to the violent world first encountered in the earliest works. "I am proud," says Nora, "to have killed one of that breed [men] to whom I owe nothing, but cruelty, deceit and the asp's emission," contradicting absolutely O'Brien's often-stated support for "human decency" and kindness among people of whatever sex.

This ambivalence, or offering of choices, continues between the *Epilogue* (1986), which seems to promise a return of Baba, and *The High Road*, which revives the old Kate figure in O'Brien's generic, less successful Mediterranean setting. In short, the graph of her fictional split personalities is by no means a straight line. What remains is that O'Brien is a writer from Ireland whose first thirty years there profoundly influence her view of the world. These effects are most clearly seen in her depiction of women's relationships. At her best, O'Brien's ability to re-create settings, particularly in Ireland, and her Joycean zest for language and humor reveal through her characters' poor choices her own support for those who dream of love achieved through kindness and decency.

THE COUNTRY GIRLS TRILOGY AND EPILOGUE

First published: 1986; includes *The Country Girls*, 1960; *The Lonely Girl*, 1962 (reprinted as *Girl with Green Eyes*, 1964); *Girls in Their Married Bliss*, 1964

Type of work: Novels

Two young girls make their escape from the repressions of the West of Ireland to Dublin, and eventually to love and marriage in London.

With *The Country Girls Trilogy and Epilogue*, Edna O'Brien served notice that there was a new voice on the literary scene. From the detailed, evocative first page, with its shock to the senses of the cold linoleum on bare feet (her bedroom slippers are, on her mother's orders, to be saved for visits to uncles and aunts), the twelve-year-old(?) Caithleen Brady arises to the smell of frying bacon. She is anxious; her father has not come home after his night out. Shy and sensitive, she tells her first-person story, and she shares the action with her friend and alter ego, the volatile and sometimes malicious Bridget Brennan (Baba). O'Brien quickly establishes what will be recurrent themes in her fictions: the dysfunctional family, with the drunken, brutal father and the martyred, overprotective mother; the search of her protagonist for a personal identity with which she can be happy, against the splendidly realized world of Ireland in the 1940's and 1950's.

It is a world divided into warring camps, male and female, Church and laity, country and town, where Caithleen's aspirations toward romantic love are doomed to failure. Her mother having drowned, Caithleen spends her mid-teen years boarding in a strict convent school, with its lingering smell of boiled cabbage, from which she and Baba contrive eventually to be expelled for writing a "dirty" note. In their late teens, joyously, they come to Dublin, Baba to take a business course, Caithleen to work as a grocer's assistant until she can take the civil service examinations. Loneliness, however, follows them: Baba contracts tuberculosis; Caithleen's man-friend, "Mr. Gentleman" (Jacques de Maurier), disappoints her. He is the first in a long line of rotters whom O'Brien's heroines encounter: the ugly father, Eugene Gaillard, and Herod and Dr. Flaggler. In O'Brien's fictions, such unsavory types far outnumber the few good men with decent inclinations: Hickey the servant-man and, in *Casualties of Peace*, the black man, Auro.

The Lonely Girl continues the girls's saga; Baba is healthy again. It is, however, largely Caithleen's story; again she is the narrator. The repressive effects of her family, her village community, and her convent education are again graphically shown. O'Brien has her heroine romantically involved with Eugene Gaillard, whose face reminds her of a saint and who is about the same height as her father; he is a cultivated snob and is often cold in bed and in the salon. He begins the further education of his still naïve, prudish "student." At the novel's conclusion, Caithleen, wild and feeling debased "because of some dammed man," is learning and changing. She is, as she says, finding her feet, "and when I'm able to talk I imagine that I won't be alone." Still seeking their connection, she and Baba sail for England and London. They effect their escape (physically, at least) from the constraints of their home environment. This development occurs despite the blandishments of a local suitor of Caithleen in the West, who declares to her, by way of enticement, "I've a pump in the yard, a bull and a brother a priest. What more could a woman want?" O'Brien's humor, and her ear for the best of conversational exchanges overheard, is a saving grace in an otherwise grim situation.

Girls in Their Married Bliss continues the story of the two women in London, where, for the first time, Baba assumes the first-person narration. She alternates with an omniscient voice, distancing both O'Brien and the reader from the role of Kate. (This is a technique that O'Brien will carry even further in *A Pagan Place*, 1970, where her heroine is removed and distanced to the second-person pronoun, "you.") The women, now about twenty-five years old, have not left all of their Irishness behind with their arrival in England. There is a splendid, Celtic rush to Baba's style. Kate, too, has her share of one-liners, word associations, epigrams, and zany metaphors. "Self interest," she observes, "was a common crime."

In these early novels, as she shows her heroines learning and developing, O'Brien is polishing and improving her writing skills. In *Girls in Their Married Bliss*, the topic is still the search for a loving connection, though the plot involves a very precisely observed, and psychologically sharp, account of Kate's marriage to Gaillard disintegrating. People, in the context of women's roles in society, are shown to rub exquisitely on one another's nerves; in the smaller context of bedroom politics, it is noted, "Men are pure fools." Marriage, at least for the reasons that women enter it in this story, is evidently not a solution to the quest for happiness; Baba makes a calculated move for comfort; Kate sees that her interest in people is generated solely by her own needs. They have both matured to the point where they no longer believe much in romantic plans. In the 1967 Penguin revision, this pessimistic tone is deepened when Kate has herself sterilized. She will not make the same mistake again; no further child of hers will in its turn become a parent.

In a reissue of the complete Country Girls Trilogy twenty-two years later in one volume (1986), in a brief *Epilogue* monologue delivered by Baba, O'Brien takes care of what might have been regarded previously as a split personality. The ebullient Baba brings readers up to date on past events. The despairing Kate is dead; she drowned, perhaps committed suicide, readers are led to think. This resolution of the split-heroine narrators in her fictions is, however, not final. In the weak *High Road* (1988), readers are thrown back once again into the narration of a "Kate" figure, a London-Irish woman who has gone abroad to try to forget a failed love affair, in the company of the jet-setters on the Mediterranean, an environment and group with which O'Brien is, as a whole, much less successful than she is with Ireland and the Irish, whose particularity and universality she feels and captures much more deftly and convincingly.

NIGHT

First published: 1972
Type of work: Novel

> In a solo harangue from her bed in England, Irish Mary Hooligan delivers a spirited, courageous account of her life and loves.

Night is O'Brien's most Joycean of novels, very clearly reminiscent of Mollie Bloom's concluding monologue in *Ulysses* (1922) in its mature female narrator, who is defiantly, and more optimistically than in Joyce's novel, taking stock of her situation and of her life and loves. It is indeed an exuberant tour de force in the zany realization of its narrator and in its stream-of-consciousness form.

Mary Hooligan, over the course of one winter night, which gives the novel its title, reviews her life and loves. Approaching middle age, divorced, with a grown son, Mary takes stock of her situation. O'Brien succeeds, for the moment, in fusing the spontaneous, activist Baba and the doomed dreamer Kate. For most of the work, however, it is the former voice that predominates. Mary is aggressively courageous in her determination to endure, and to enjoy without whining, whatever life sends her way. Her joy is everywhere manifest in her exuberant use of the English language: "I've had better times of course—the halcyon days, rings, ringlets, ashes of roses . . .

chantilly, high teas, drop scones, serge suits, binding attachments, all that."

She weaves time back and forth from the present as she remembers people and places significant in her life. The novel has no plot development in any traditional sense. Foremost in importance to Mary are her mother, Lil, whose specialty is the spittled-on mother's knot; her alcoholic father, Boss; her son, Tutsie, whom she realizes she loves too much; her former husband, the cold, authoritarian Dr. Flaggler, "one of the original princes of darkness"; and her childhood home in the Roman Catholic Barony of Coose, in the West of Ireland, rendered in all of its sensory detail of "occidental damp and murk." The arrival of dawn and a telegram announcing the imminent return of the owners of the house brings Mary's reverie to an end. "Moriarity, here I come," she says, projecting a reunion with her stonemason friend, with whom she feels she has a connection rivaling that of any family knot.

All O'Brien's perennial themes are evident, bound up in Mary Hooligan. At her best, which is often, Mary is a joy. Iconoclastic and frank, her sense of humor rarely fails to elicit sympathy for her blundering search for an enduring love relationship with a decent man. Reflecting on Nick Finney, the crooner back in the West of Ireland, with whom she first had sexual intercourse, she says, "It was St. Peter and St. Paul's day, and hence a holy day of obligation." Her words and syntax both rush along. At her worst, and that side of her personality is but hinted in her exchanges with her pessimistic friend Madge, she, or any woman, or any person, can become depressed and depressing. "Everyone has a grubby fantasy when you get past the bullshit," Madge says; such a person more often than not is a loser, is willing to settle for the possible. For Mary, "the puny possible has always belonged to others." Hers is the philosophy of excess. In her eclectic religion, free from the constraint of the Irish Catholic guilt of so many of O'Brien's heroines, Mary is relatively at peace with herself, her self-image relatively intact.

O'Brien did not easily achieve this positive realization of personality, nor would it last. Yet for this moment, and this enduring work, readers can rejoice that her verdict goes to Mary, and her progenitor Baba, discussed above. Employing her astonishing, imaginative, dramatic recall of places—particularly Irish places—O'Brien affirms people, their words, and the central importance of genuine self-knowledge and honesty. Such qualities foster hope, which Mary Hooligan only once, very briefly, considered abandoning. Quickly she retracted a death wish: "Do I mean it? Apparently not. I am still snooping around, on the lookout for pals . . . cronies of any kind, provided they . . . leave me . . . my winding dirging effluvias." Connection and involvement with others, in Mary's view and in O'Brien's, must be maintained, so that she, and her readers, may carry on.

A FANATIC HEART

First published: 1984
Type of work: Short stories

Drawn largely from her four previously published collections, these stories, below, reveal O'Brien's perennial themes of love and loss, most often narrated by Irish women.

The title of *A Fanatic Heart* is drawn from William Butler Yeats's "Remorse for Intemperate Speech," cited as an epigraph to introduce the volume. Indeed, in these lines are summarized O'Brien's ongoing, dominant themes of Ireland and the women of Ireland in their "maimed" search for loving relationships.

O'Brien continued to write short stories all of her life, and she published in this genre since the early 1960's. "Come into the Drawing Room, Doris" (ironically re-titled "Irish Revel" in *The Love Object*, 1968, and retained as such in *A Fanatic Heart*) first appeared in *The New Yorker* on April 25, 1962. Set in Ireland, this story, very clearly after the manner of James Joyce in "The Dead," in his *Dubliners* (1914), is an indictment of a whole society. Sprinkled with holy water by her overly protective mother, Mary, the heroine, who is observed by the omniscient narrator, sets off from her farm-home on her bicycle to the shabby Commercial Hotel in the village and to her first party.

It turns out to be a miserable work-party for her; the married artist with whom she had danced two years before, and about whom she had fantasized, is not there. Only eight locals are present for the roast goose and the liquor. Eithne and Doris are there—brash village girls who complement Mary's innate, refined naïveté; they amuse themselves "wandering from one mirror to the next." Doris is the name that the drunken, truculent O'Toole three times calls Mary, having spiked her orange drink, wanting her to come out of the room with him. Doris is an unlikely identity for the discreet Mary, but her image, O'Brien indicates, is in trouble anyhow: Her mother had already converted into a dustpan the sketch of her drawn by the artist whom she had romanticized. The party is a failure.

As the final paragraph indicates, "Mary could see her own little house, like a little white box at the end of the world, waiting to receive her." In this story, the family battle lines are not developed. The omniscient narrator leaves it at that, in a well-crafted tale, rich in the evocative minutiae of daily living and balky bicycles in the West of Ireland, in the 1940's. It is a picture rich in its natural descriptions of, for example, the blood-red fuchsia, and rich too in its cast of characters; they all have their stories. Some of them, such as Hickey, readers have already met (*The Country Girls*), and some will appear later. The themes suggested here—overprotective mothers, the unfortunate search for a companion, and an ignorant, brutal society set among natural beauties—will also recur as O'Brien increasingly and carefully works and reworks her fictions.

O'Brien's pessimism about much of the female condition shows little alleviation in her collection *A Rose in the Heart* (1978), or in *Returning* (1982), where the external topography in all nine stories is the familiar West of Ireland and the craggy community there. A young girl is present in all of them, either as the ostensible narrator or as the subject for more mature reflection on the part of a now-experienced woman. The American novelist Philip Roth isolates this then-and-now tension between the innocence of childhood and the experience of fifty years of living as the spring for these stories' "wounded vigor."

Summary

At her best, Edna O'Brien demonstrates, over a long writing career in many genres, the gift that she has worked hard to perfect: the capacity to transport her readers into the felt situation of her women—whether they are of the Kate type, sensitive, romantic losers, or of the Baba type, pragmatic, realistic winners. Her theme is love and loss. O'Brien, with the frequent saving grace of humor, and with a flair for the vivid use of the English language for what people, at their best, might say, particularly if they are Irish, opens for her readers a felt perspective on a gloomy situation to which her heroines and their society both contribute. The net effect of her best work is to encourage continued hope in those who still dream of love.

Bibliography

Dunn, Nell. "Edna." In *Talking to Women*. London: Macgibbon and Kee, 1965.

Eckley, Grace. *Edna O'Brien*. Lewisburg, Pa.: Bucknell University Press, 1974.

Guppy, Shusha. "The Art of Fiction, LXXXII: Edna O'Brien." *The Paris Review* 26 (Summer, 1984): 22-50.

Roth, Philip. "A Conversation with Edna O'Brien." *The New York Times Book Review*, November 18, 1984, 38-40.

Woodward, Richard B. "Edna O'Brien: Reveling in Heartbreak." *The New York Times Magazine*, March 12, 1989, 42, 50-51.

Archibald E. Irwin

SEAN O'CASEY

Born: Dublin, Ireland
March 30, 1880
Died: Torquay, England
September 18, 1964

Principal Literary Achievement

An internationally acclaimed dramatist, O'Casey was also a member of the pantheon of writers who established an Irish national literature in the early twentieth century.

Biography

Sean O'Casey was born John Casey in Dublin, Ireland, on March 30, 1880, to Michael and Susan Casey. He was the youngest of thirteen children, eight of whom died in infancy. Dublin at that time was among the most slum-infested cities in Europe, and the visual problems from which O'Casey suffered throughout his life began in this poverty-ridden environment. The family belonged to the least-known social class in the Ireland of the day, the Protestant proletariat. This fact led to the young O'Casey's sense of being an outsider. In addition, the early death of his father increased the family's difficulties, while making Susan Casey the dominant influence in the playwright's life. The interaction between economic difficulty and personal strength was to become a fundamental feature of the mature O'Casey's plays.

Despite the limitations of his background and personal circumstances, O'Casey was already a personage of some note in Dublin political circles before his first success as a playwright at the comparatively late age of forty-three. Although obliged to earn his living as a laborer, he involved himself in the various cultural and political activities of the time. The period in question, from 1891 to the establishment of an independent Irish state in 1921, is one that is distinguished not only by the triumph of Irish nationalism but also by the decisive and original influence of literature on the course of national life. This influence had its most important expression in the foundation of the Abbey Theatre Company, in effect Ireland's national theater, in 1904. An organization that appealed more than the Abbey to the young O'Casey was the Gaelic League. Founded in 1893, this organization was dedicated to the restoration of the Irish language. O'Casey's identification with this aim is preserved by his change of name, first to the Irish Sean O'Cathasaigh, and from that to a hybrid version. Settling finally on the hybrid name may be considered an expression of O'Casey's

Sean O'Casey

franconi 36

critical relationship with his times.

For somebody who was almost entirely self-educated, involvement with cultural organizations was instructive and influential. More important than this type of involvement, however, were O'Casey's political commitments. As a member of the working class, he became involved in Dublin labor politics. The rise of labor unions in Ireland was consistent with the general rehabilitation of national identity to which contemporary cultural organizations were dedicated. O'Casey became a prominent member of the most important union, the Irish Transport and General Workers Union. His commitment to the cause of labor found its most significant expression when he became secretary of the Irish Citizen Army, a militia formed to defend workers in the aftermath of the bitter strike and lockout of 1913. During the years immediately before the nationalist rebellion of Easter, 1916, O'Casey was a regular contributor to the organ of the labor movement, *The Irish Worker.*

Although he was no longer with the Citizen Army by the time of its participation in the Easter Rebellion, O'Casey wrote a brief history of the organization, *The Story of the Irish Citizen Army*, published in 1919. This work is his first publication of note, but by the time it appeared O'Casey was moving away from journalism and toward writing for the theater. After a number of rejections from the Abbey, his first play, *The Shadow of a Gunman*, was successfully produced there in 1923. There then followed the two other plays upon which O'Casey's reputation is largely based; these, along with *The Shadow of a Gunman*, constitute the most substantial act of witnessing and the most comprehensive artistic representation that the momentous political and social events in Ireland have received. These plays are *Juno and the Paycock*, produced in 1924, and *The Plough and the Stars*, produced in 1926, both Abbey productions.

The latter play irritated nationalist sensitivities in the audience to such an extent that riots plagued its weeklong first run. This reaction tainted O'Casey's reputation as a playwright, a development from which his career was never subsequently entirely free. Although the Abbey management supported O'Casey during *The Plough and the Stars* hostilities, it rejected his next play, *The Silver Tassie* (pb. 1878), a work that was a challenging dramatic and thematic departure from his initial successes and one that is his most important play apart from them. This rejection, which O'Casey brought to the attention of the press, was instrumental in the playwright's decision to settle permanently in England, which he did in 1928. He continued to write plays, but, though some of these—*Red Roses for Me* (pb. 1942), *Cock-a-Doodle Dandy* (1949), and *The Drums of Father Ned* (1959)—are striking for their artistic ambition, O'Casey never regained the strength of his early work. His nearest approach to doing so is to be found in his six-volume autobiography, the first volume of which, *I Knock at the Door*, appeared in 1939. Having cut himself off from Dublin, the only source of raw material that was of passionate interest to him, O'Casey identified with a naïve and sentimental communism. This ideology did not provide him with an adequate substitute for what he had left behind.

In 1927, O'Casey married Eileen Carey, an actress who had appeared in English productions of his work. They had three children. O'Casey spent his later years in Torquay, England, where he died on September 18, 1964.

Analysis

O'Casey's first three great plays set the tone for the rest of his work. In them, he portrays characters from society's lower levels entangled in conflicts that they cannot control, understand, or accept. Such fundamental conflicts form the basis of his plays.

Two important features make the conflicts in O'Casey's plays urgent and persuasive. One is his selection of character types. O'Casey's characters are generally poorly educated, powerless, and vulnerable. Typically, they are the people whom society considers ignoble and lacking in value. Basing his imaginative concerns on such characters was, at the time O'Casey did it, both artistically daring and culturally provocative. Doing so is an aspect of his contribution both to world drama and to the literature of his own country, whose originality can easily be overlooked. Moreover, while O'Casey was not the first playwright to put such characters on the stage, and not the first Irish playwright to do so, his insightful and vivid delineation of their lives and times gives them a stature that they otherwise have difficulty in attaining.

The second factor that makes the basic, age-old conflicts in O'Casey's work seem more immediate is its clear appeal to twentieth century audiences. The playwright's first three plays were each greeted with varying though undeniable expressions of keen interest. Yet as O'Casey's subsequent career in the theater reveals, their appeal is by no means confined to their own time, or even to Irish audiences. The continuing international success of *Juno and the Paycock* and *The Plough and the Stars*, in particular, confirms not only the wide appeal of their plots. These plays also remind their audiences of their own historical experiences. The basic drama of these two works concerns what happens when history comes knocking at the door. Modern audiences are especially well qualified to identify with that concern.

The conflicts that O'Casey dramatizes are those between the individual and history, between private need and public duty, and between principles and compromises. These conflicts are always enacted in a specific social context. As his absence from Ireland grew longer, O'Casey was unable to provide the action of his works with much particularity. Yet, even his late plays always carry a socially relevant message. O'Casey's consistent social awareness derives partly from his political orientation. It also reveals a debt to his most important theatrical mentor, George Bernard Shaw.

O'Casey's plays do not resolve the conflicts that they present. Rather than being resolved, problems are seen as forces that are impossible to tame. In these works, death often takes the place of peace. In general, the world of O'Casey's plays is not a particularly rational place. Events are brought about by complicated offstage actions. Typically, the plays open at a moment of difficulty. As the play develops, this moment becomes a state of crisis. The plays end when the full severity of this state has been experienced. The endings of O'Casey's plays usually represent conditions as being worse than they were when the action commenced.

Open and unresolved endings are a dramatically effective means of involving the audience in the fate of the characters. Solving the characters' problems would perhaps give the audience an experience of detachment and coziness. O'Casey's intention is to eliminate the artificial, formal barrier between observed and observer. By so doing, he reduces the gap between the audience's privileged social and cultural position and the downtrodden, neglected, and helpless condition of his characters. O'Casey's theater is democratic in spirit. One of the most powerful impacts that his plays make is through the spectacle of that spirit being frustrated or denied.

The social vision of O'Casey's plays is for the most part grim. The conclusion that Captain Boyle reaches at the end of *Juno and the Paycock* is that "the whole world is in a state o' chassis." The futility of his own career fully supports this point of view. The chaos, or "chassis," to which he refers pervades both the world of the play and the supposedly real, historical world outside the play.

As in many of O'Casey's works, violence and the threat of violence are never far away, and in his most important works, the action revolves around a violent incident and its inescapable repercussions. In O'Casey's view of the world, nobody gets away with anything, or gets away for long. While the depiction of shocking acts of violence is as old as the theater itself, O'Casey's presentation of them is modern in a number of important ways. He reveals violence as an instrument of official policy. Its application is unexpected, irrational, and unreasonable. It is also reckless in its disregard for civilians. By asking his audience to accept the reality of what he represents, O'Casey is also challenging public awareness to examine the implications or consequences of that reality. The note of shock, struck by the violence of O'Casey's work, is followed immediately by a note of interrogation and criticism, aimed, in effect, to stimulate the audience to reject much of what it has been shown.

Yet for every Captain Boyle, O'Casey also presents a Juno. He reveals a dual perspective, each element of which is equally significant. Strength of individual character offsets the world's difficulties and violence. This basic arrangement of forces may be seen in all the playwright's work. The arrangement draws attention not only to the comprehensive nature of O'Casey's vision. It also alerts the audience to the fact that, like many Irish playwrights of his generation, O'Casey's theater is one of character.

All of his plays are well populated, which, in the case of *Juno and the Paycock*, *The Plough and the Stars*, and *The Shadow of a Gunman*, incidentally helps to give a vivid sense of the crowded conditions and absence of privacy typical of tenement life. Despite the fact that virtually all O'Casey's characters come from the same social class, each of them is vividly distinguished from the others, an indication that social status in itself is not enough to stifle vitality. Even when the characters are not particularly admirable, their foibles and failings are treated unsentimentally and with the overall intention of depicting the variety of human nature. O'Casey does his characters the honor of taking them seriously, even when they appear to be caricatures. By doing so, he integrates his characters more plausibly with the serious concerns of his plots. As a result, the playwright also underlines his refusal to dismiss as unworthy of attention characters such as the ones whom he presents.

O'Casey paints his characters in broad strokes. In certain respects, they seem one-dimensional, distinguished by one obvious trait, such as laziness, cowardice, and deviousness. There again, however, he uses a dual approach. He escapes the risk of creating one-dimensional characters by the vivid language that he gives them. O'Casey's characters are dramatically intriguing and appealing as much for what they say as for what they do. O'Casey drew on the speech of the ordinary people among whom he lived. Yet his sense of language is not a matter merely of vocabulary. The violent events that destroy the lives of O'Casey's characters are often the product of something that has been said and cannot be unsaid. The essential artistic ingredient of O'Casey's theater, its language, is the means by which his characters are ensnared in the drama of their existences, and in the elemental conflicts that those dramas represent.

THE SHADOW OF A GUNMAN

First produced: 1923 (first published, 1925)
Type of work: Play

Illusion and reality clash violently and tragically in the Irish War of Independence.

Although it was not the first play that O'Casey wrote, *The Shadow of a Gunman* was the first play of his produced. It was premiered at the Abbey Theatre, Dublin, on April 12, 1923, and was an immediate success. The reason for its success is its setting, the Irish War of Independence. This war was fought, largely in guerrilla style, between volunteers of the Irish Republican Army and British forces. The nature of the war is very well reflected in the play's use of abrupt and vicious turns of fortune. These are reflected in the play's three central characters.

Donal Davoren, the poet, Seumas Shields, the opportunist, and Minnie Powell, the heroine, represent not only the twists of fate brought about by the action of the play. They may also be considered as an introduction to O'Casey's people. Most of the men in *The Shadow of a Gunman* are all talk. This quality is evident in O'Casey's decision to make Davoren a naïve, youthful, romantic versifier. Davoren's self-pity and self-involvement make him blind to the realities around him. Poetry, which is often thought of as a diagnosis of life's challenges, is Davoren's means of escape from those challenges. It is not surprising that his poetry is weak and inadequate.

Yet in this portrait of the artistic temperament, O'Casey is not only presenting a character for whom the image and self-deception define his relationship to the world. He is speaking to an audience of contemporaries who knew that many of the leaders of the Easter, 1916, rebellion were poets and dreamers. The violent circumstances of the play draw on the historical reality that was a direct result of that rebellion. In that sense, also, the gunman's shadow lies behind the activity of some of Irish nationalism's purest idealists.

Shields, on the other hand, is a down-to-earth exploiter of the main chance. He is Davoren's opposite, and the somewhat implausible fact of their sharing a room brings their differences into sharp focus. While Davoren does not fully appreciate the danger that his illusions can cause, Shields is fully alive to the perils that pass for normal life in a community at war. Seen in the larger context of the events that inspired the play, Shields may be seen as the unprincipled hanger-on, willing to do anything to survive. Shields never says that he knows there might be something amiss about the bag that Maguire leaves in his care. Although Shields is apparently Davoren's opposite, the result of both men's behavior is the same. Like Davoren, Shields talks about everything except what needs at all costs to be addressed. The magnitude of these costs is revealed when Minnie Powell pays with her life. She is the victim of Davoren's speech and Shields's silence. She is the one character in the play who attempts to take life as she finds it. As the play indicates, the challenge is to find something for which life is worth living, to emerge from the gunman's shadow. O'Casey's awareness of the severity of this challenge is one of the main reasons he subtitled *The Shadow of a Gunman* a tragedy.

In some respects, *The Shadow of a Gunman* reveals O'Casey as still something of an apprentice playwright. The plot is thin, and the minor characters sometimes seem to be too great a distraction from the main action. At the same time, however, these characters are necessary to enrich a sense of the play's theme. O'Casey compensates for such deficiencies by the richness of his characterizations and by his use of language. He not only equips his characters with colorful vocabularies but also bases much of the play's costly conflict on what people say and what they do not say, and on the moral consequences of the appropriate use of language. O'Casey's relentless exposure of self-deception, hypocrisy, and cowardice, however, enables the play to transcend its immediate context to become a potent reflection on the distorting and destructive effect of historical events on ordinary people.

JUNO AND THE PAYCOCK

First produced: 1924 (first published, 1925)
Type of work: Play

The tragedy of the Boyle family unfolds against the background of the Irish Civil War.

The Abbey Theatre production of *Juno and the Paycock* had its premiere less than a year after the successful staging of *The Shadow of a Gunman*, on March 3, 1924. The production consolidated O'Casey's reputation as the leading dramatist to emerge in the immediate aftermath of Irish independence. *Juno and the Paycock*, however, is far superior to the earlier work, in terms of its scope, its ambition, and its tragic impact. Yet, the play's opening sequence may strike the reader as a continuation of

The Shadow of a Gunman.

The time is two years later, and the historical context is the Irish Civil War, which followed the attainment of Irish independence in 1921. Johnny Boyle initially opposed Irish independence on the terms agreed to with England. He was unable to maintain this position, however, and this led to his betrayal of Robbie Tancred, his former comrade. The fact that Tancred was also a close neighbor brings home graphically the murderous intimacy of the Civil War. Yet it also sets the stage for the bitter domestic strife that consumes the Boyle family. Public and private experience are reflected in each other, as they are in *The Shadow of a Gunman*, though in a much more elaborate and assured manner.

Not only is Johnny's situation a public version of his family's inner conflicts; it is also reflected in what happens to his sister, Mary. At the beginning of the play, she too is presented as a person of principle. Yet she is unable to uphold her beliefs. The consequences of this failure are not as severe as they are in Johnny's case. At the same time, it is her affair with Bentham that brings about the final rift in the family, a rift that the end of the play does not suggest can be healed. When, at the end, Captain Boyle drunkenly intones that the blinds are down, he is referring to the custom in Ireland of lowering the window shades when there is a death in a household. The death in question is that of the Boyle family.

In *The Shadow of a Gunman*, O'Casey's emphasis is on the destructive force of political circumstances. In contrast, *Juno and the Paycock* concentrates on the economic facts of life. Johnny's contribution to the family's crisis is by no means insignificant, but it does not occupy the center of the work. Instead, the force that destroys the Boyles is money—or rather, money is the means by which the Boyles's vanity and vulnerability are exposed and exploited. The exchanges early in the play between the Captain, Joxer Daly, and Juno are often played as comedy. Yet what is being presented is a picture of a grim and hopeless state of economic affairs. Moreover, though Juno regards this economic reality in a light that is directly in contrast with the view of Joxer and the Captain, she also suffers economic oppression. That makes her, as a working woman, socially, as well as biologically, related to Mary. Thus, it is fitting that they should be the ones to continue working on their lives at the end of the play.

Such a perspective is necessary in order to understand why the family falls for Bentham. Everything about this character is fraudulent, from his appearance to his so-called education. That a spirited character such as Mary should fall for such a specimen suggests how desperate she is to improve her lot. She does not believe that this improvement can be made by the man from her own class and background, Jerry Devine. It is also because of its persistent experience of poverty that the family spends the money in a hasty and irresponsible way. The tragedy of *Juno and the Paycock* is based largely on the social and cultural poverty that prevents the Boyles from knowing how to handle the revolution in their private lives.

The only character unaffected by the actions of the play is Joxer. Like Seumas Shields in *The Shadow of a Gunman*, Joxer is interested merely in his own survival.

Such an outlook cannot be maintained by the Boyles. To that extent, they show how human they are. To the extent that they are human, however, they are vulnerable to vanity, gullibility, idealism, and a desire for improvement. The bleakness that results from their vulnerability is what the Captain acknowledges as "chassis," a world without order or coherence, a world in which hope for tomorrow turns out to be a cruel joke.

THE PLOUGH AND THE STARS

First produced: 1926 (first published, 1926)
Type of work: Play

The human consequences of historical events are depicted in the context of the Irish rebellion of Easter, 1916.

Set in the turbulence of the rebellion of Easter, 1916, *The Plough and the Stars* is a landmark in O'Casey's career for a number of reasons. First, it is the powerful conclusion of his Troubles Trilogy (the struggle for Irish independence is familiarly known as "the troubles"). It is also a more complex and far-reaching play, both formally and intellectually, than its predecessors. Unlike O'Casey's earlier plays, *The Plough and the Stars* draws on O'Casey's own personal experience as a member and subsequent critic of the Irish Citizen Army. *The Plough and the Stars* also gave the playwright his first taste of theatrical controversy in the hostile reaction of the audience to the first production, which was staged at the Abbey Theatre on February 8, 1926.

The play's title refers to the flag of the Irish Citizen Army. In this way, O'Casey identifies his principal characters in terms of their class and their organization. As a result, the social and economic vulnerability that has typically affected the characters of O'Casey's earlier works is less evident here. Nora Clitheroe not only aspires to respectability, which is what Mary Boyle expected Charles Bentham to provide in *Juno and the Paycock*; she can also afford some of respectability's trappings. This line of thought makes Uncle Peter, who is Nora's uncle, not entirely a figure of fun. Through him, O'Casey introduces the audience to working-class ritual and grandeur, though, in contrast to Jack Clitheroe's uniform, what Uncle Peter's regalia represents is laughably out of date.

These details establish a basis for introducing more important distinctions within the play's community of characters. O'Casey's view of the proletariat is striking in its range. Thus, Bessie Burgess is militantly opposed to the cause of Irish freedom. While Nora can entertain romantic dreams of nest-building, Mollser is dying of consumption virtually alongside her. For all of his ideological speech making about the working man, The Covey lacks the courage of drunken Fluther. The Irish nationalist known as The Figure in the Window has to share his scene with Rosie Redmond, a prostitute. It was this last contrast that caused audiences to riot in protest during the play's first production.

The strong sense of contrast that is provided simply by noting the range of characters in the play leads, in turn, to an appreciation of the play's central conflict. It takes place between the two characters who are least well-equipped to handle it, Nora and Jack Clitheroe. When the challenge to their marriage comes, each responds in the way that the other is least able to accept. With this human conflict as a focus, *The Plough and the Stars* both retains the immediacy of its historical context and rises above that context to appeal to audiences regardless of their background. The significance of the rift between Jack and Nora is emphasized, as in other O'Casey plays, by suffering. Nora and Jack are the play's only couple. Their being together offers a model of possibility, romance, and, above all, love, which is the opposite of war. The promise that they represent, however, is not realized. On the contrary, those with the most to live for lose the most as the play proceeds.

O'Casey dramatizes this emphasis on loss through the fate of Bessie Burgess. The character who seems least likely to behave in a neighborly way turns out to be the play's clearest example of Christian charity in action. Like Jack and Nora, she also suffers disproportionately for her attempt to make good what has been destroyed. Bessie's fate leaves only the remnants of the community at the mercy of the occupying forces. The contrast between the optimism and vitality of the play's opening and the scene of death and destruction with which it closes could hardly be more graphic. This contrast is brought out with devastating irony in the soldier's closing chorus, particularly as the stage directions indicate that, offstage, the city is burning. In *The Plough and the Stars*, O'Casey meshes the private chaos that befell Captain Boyle and the destructive forces that struck down Minnie Powell to produce his most powerful play.

MIRROR IN MY HOUSE

First published: 1956
Type of work: Autobiography

This six-volume experiment in autobiography is as noteworthy for its style as for its content.

O'Casey's experiment in autobiography, *Mirror in My House*, consists of six separately published volumes. The project began in 1939 with the appearance of *I Knock at the Door* and continues through *Pictures in the Hallway* (1942), *Drums Under the Windows* (1945), *Inishfallen, Fare Thee Well* (1949), and *Rose and Crown* (1952), before concluding with *Sunset and Evening Star* (1954). As though to confirm the significance of the author's Irish experiences, volumes 1 through 4 cover the first forty-six years of his life, from his birth to his departure from Ireland. His life in England up to 1953, roughly, is the subject of the two concluding volumes.

Some readers may be critical of *Mirror in My House* because it unequally divides attention between the two basic phases of O'Casey's life. It might be thought more appropriate to reverse the work's emphasis by concentrating less on the formative Dublin years and more on the period when O'Casey achieved international renown as a playwright and political notoriety because of his communist associations. Yet while critical opinion on the value and significance of *Mirror in My House* was divided as the individual volumes appeared, it is generally agreed that the overall project constitutes one of the more important literary autobiographies of the twentieth century.

One of the main difficulties of *Mirror in My House* is its experimental character. O'Casey's original approach to autobiography has two surprising aspects. The first and most important of these is that O'Casey refers to himself in the third person throughout. The effect is challenging and significant. It is one of the means by which O'Casey, who was generally skeptical of artistic innovation, associated himself with the works of some of his most illustrious literary contemporaries, such as William Butler Yeats and James Joyce. The works of those two writers reveal the fluctuations and variety of human personality. O'Casey acknowledges their relevance by the self-consciousness of his autobiographical presence. Over the course of six volumes, however, the justification for this approach is not sufficient to outweigh its tiresomeness.

The second important feature of *Mirror in My House* is its language. O'Casey adapts the verbal style of his characters to his narrative style. The effect is to give an extremely vivid picture of O'Casey's life and times. The accounts of hardship, suffering, and neighborliness in the work's opening volumes are particularly noteworthy. They also reveal the sources of the sympathy and revulsion that animate his plays. In addition, the exaggerations and poetic effects of the language in *Mirror in My House* are an interesting reproduction of how life seems in memory, rather than how life actually was. As is appropriate for a work of autobiography, the overall effect of O'Casey's verbal vitality is to create the history of a personal consciousness rather than a reliable chronicle of the author's life and times. He draws a sharp and culturally important distinction between biography and autobiography. Judged on its own terms, however, *Mirror in My House* remains one of the twentieth century's most elaborate, sustained, and artistically ambitious works of literary autobiography.

Yet, despite the depiction of the life of a sickly child in Dublin's Victorian slums, and other powerful scenes of poverty and pain, there remains a sense of striving too hard for effect. To some extent, this makes the work resemble those written by O'Casey in exile. Their thematic material is too heightened and lacking in a sense of authentic detail to be persuasive. It is not true to say that *Mirror in My House* lacks substance. Particularly in the later volumes, however, it lacks the texture and the sense of intimacy between author and material that is to be found in the Troubles Trilogy. Those three plays are the works upon which O'Casey's lasting reputation is deservedly based.

Summary

Sean O'Casey's long and prolific career is noteworthy for a number of reasons. In the first place, like all important writers, he drew the public's attention to ways of life and modes of perception that had previously not been considered subjects for art. In addition, his dynamic and colorful language subtly establishes and exposes the limits of his characters' worlds. The way people suffer when they have reached those limits is the overall theme of O'Casey's dramatic works. His greatest plays are suffused with an awareness of life's practical considerations, often presented from an economic point of view.

Yet these plays also remain sympathetically alive to his characters' human need to dream. The range of sentiment, action, and reflection evident in his plays, but especially in his first three major productions, is most vividly expressed in his use of language. This verbal skill disguises O'Casey's somewhat mechanical sense of plot and underlines his overwhelming responsiveness to the vagaries of human nature.

Bibliography

Kenneally, Michael. *Portraying the Self: Sean O'Casey and the Art of Autobiography*. Totowa, N.J.: Barnes & Noble Books, 1987.

Kilroy, Thomas, comp. *Sean O'Casey: A Collection of Critical Essays*. Englewood Cliffs, N.J.: Prentice-Hall, 1975.

Kosok, Heinz. *O'Casey the Dramatist*. Translated by Heinz Kosok and Joseph T. Swann. Totowa, N.J.: Barnes & Noble Books, 1985.

Krause, David. *Sean O'Casey: The Man and His Work*. London: Macmillan, 1960.

Lowery, Robert G., ed. *Essays on Sean O'Casey's Autobiographies*. Totowa, N.J.: Barnes & Noble Books, 1981.

Maxwell, D. E. S. *A Critical History of Modern Irish Drama, 1891-1980*. Cambridge, England: Cambridge University Press, 1984.

O'Casey, Eileen. *Sean*. London: Macmillan, 1971.

O'Connor, Garry. *Sean O'Casey*. New York: Atheneum, 1988.

O'Riordan, John. *A Guide to O'Casey's Plays*. New York: St. Martin's Press, 1984.

George O'Brien

GEORGE ORWELL

Born: Motihari, Bengal, India
June 25, 1903
Died: London, England
January 21, 1950

Principal Literary Achievement
Widely recognized for both his novels and his essays, Orwell, especially during the last decade of his life, worked "to make political writing into an art."

Biography
George Orwell was born Eric Arthur Blair in Motihari, Bengal, India, on June 25, 1903, the son of Richard Walmesley Blair, a minor official in the British government, and Ida Limouzin Blair. In 1904, Orwell's mother took him to England, where the family lived at Henley-on-Thames, Oxfordshire. Orwell had two sisters, one five years older and the other five years younger. According to his own account in his essay "Why I Write," Orwell, until he was eight years old, barely saw his father. Consequently, Orwell developed a habit of solitude that resulted from his developing "disagreeable mannerisms" that made him "unpopular" throughout his schooldays.

Orwell's schooldays were spent at Sunnylands, an Anglican convent school in Henley. He also spent time as a boarder at St. Cyprian's preparatory school in Eastbourne, Sussex, and as a King's Scholar at Eton. He attended one term at Wellington College in 1917.

Upon completing his formal education, Orwell prepared for the India Office examinations, after which he became assistant superintendent of police in the Indian Imperial Police in Burma, a position that he held from 1922 to 1927. Because of his disdain for British imperialism, reflected in such later essays as "A Hanging" and "Shooting an Elephant," Orwell resigned his post, moved to Paris, and gradually began his career as a writer.

His first works, written while he was working as a dishwasher in Paris and later as a hop picker near London, were published under his birth name, Eric Blair. These works include "A Scullion's Diary" (1931), which is an early version of *Down and Out in Paris and London* (1933), and "A Hanging." Perhaps the best overview of Orwell's early writing comes from Orwell himself. In "Why I Write," he recounts his first experiences as a writer. He says that he wrote his first poem, dictated to his mother, at the age of four or five. As Orwell reflects on this poem, he thinks it was

probably "a plagiarism of Blake's 'Tiger, Tiger.'" His first published poem, "Awake Young Men of England," is a patriotic poem written during World War I. It was printed in the local newspaper, the *Henley and South Oxfordshire Standard*, when Orwell was eleven years old. In his early years, Orwell also attempted a few short stories, but he considered the attempts "ghastly failures" and abandoned the genre.

Mostly, Orwell regarded his earliest writing as insignificant except insofar as he was aware that he wanted to be a writer. He begins "Why I Write" with an acknowledgment of that awareness:

> From a very early age, perhaps the age of five or six, I knew that when I grew up I should be a writer. Between the ages of about seventeen and twenty-four I tried to abandon this idea, but I did so with the consciousness that I was outraging my true nature and that sooner or later I should have to settle down and write books.

From 1932 to 1933, Orwell taught at a small private school in Hayes, Middlesex. It was then that he began to write books. In 1933, he published his first book, *Down and Out in Paris and London*, under his pseudonym George Orwell, a name that he used for the rest of his books. In the next seven years, eight of Orwell's books were published: *Burmese Days* (1934), *A Clergyman's Daughter* (1935), *Keep the Aspidistra Flying* (1936), *The Road to Wigan Pier* (1937), *Homage to Catalonia* (1938), *Coming Up for Air* (1939), *Inside the Whale and Other Essays* (1940), and *The Lion and the Unicorn* (1941). His two most highly acclaimed novels, *Animal Farm* (1945) and *Nineteen Eighty-Four* (1949), were yet to be written. During these years, prior to 1945, Orwell was gaining the personal and political experience that went into his final works.

In 1936, Orwell had married Eileen O'Shaughnessy; in 1944, they adopted a one-month-old baby. In March of 1945, Eileen died during an operation. Also in 1936, Orwell began a series of economic, social, and political experiences that gave him a deeper understanding of his earlier experiences in Burma and in Paris. For three months in 1936, he investigated working-class life and unemployment, a process that undoubtedly gave him insight into the despair that he felt at entering a hospital in Paris in 1929 during a time of personal poverty. He recalled the experience in his essay "How the Poor Die." During the summer of 1936, Orwell attended the Independent Labour Party Summer School. In early 1937, he was part of a detachment on the Aragon front in Spain. Orwell was wounded in the throat and honorably discharged.

Orwell says his experiences in 1936 and 1937 were a turning point:

> The Spanish war and other events in 1936-37 turned the scale and thereafter I knew where I stood. Every line of serious work that I have written since 1936 has been written, directly or indirectly, *against* totalitarianism and *for* democratic Socialism, as I understand it.

Politics and writing, for Orwell, had become interwoven. Orwell continued both his writing and his political involvement despite his ill health. In 1938, Orwell entered a tuberculosis sanatorium and later went to Morocco for his health. In 1940, back in London, Orwell joined the Local Defence Volunteers (Home Guard). From 1941 to 1943, Orwell was in charge of BBC (British Broadcasting Corporation) broadcasts to India and Southeast Asia. In 1945, he was a war correspondent for *The Observer* in Paris and Cologne. In June and July, he covered the first postwar election campaign. In August, 1945, *Animal Farm* was published.

Animal Farm is a culmination of Orwell's wide-ranging socioeconomic and political observations. In this novel, Orwell succeeds in making "political writing into an art." *Animal Farm* is followed by *Critical Essays* (1946; published in the United States as *Dickens, Dali, and Others*) and, finally, by *Nineteen Eighty-Four.* More than four hundred thousand copies of *Nineteen Eighty-Four* sold within the first year of its publication.

During the final years of Orwell's life, he was in and out of tuberculosis sanatoriums and other hospitals. In September of 1949, he was transferred from Cotswold Sanatorium, Cranham, Gloucestershire, to University Hospital in London. There, on October 13, only a few months before his death, he married Sonia Brownell, an editorial assistant with *Horizon.* Orwell died suddenly, on January 21, 1950, of a hemorrhaged lung. He was buried in the churchyard of All Saints, Sutton Courtenay, Berkshire.

Analysis

Orwell's writing of both novels and essays divides fairly distinctly into two parts, the periods prior to, and after, 1936. Orwell himself, in "Why I Write," makes the division, citing as the turning point his participation in the Spanish Civil War and alluding to other events occurring in the same year.

Orwell's writing up to 1936 includes essays recounting his experiences in Burma, India, Paris, and London. These works sharply criticize British imperialism, economic inequity, and class barriers. The works are highly analytical narratives, characterized by flashes of insight into humanity. In "A Hanging," for example, Orwell narrates his participation in the hanging of a man in Burma. As Orwell and the other executioners escort the condemned man to the gallows, the man sidesteps a puddle. At this moment, Orwell says, he realizes the "unspeakable wrongness" of cutting a man's life short when it is in "full tide." Again, in "How the Poor Die," Orwell recounts his experience of admitting himself, while impoverished, to a hospital in Paris. He concludes that the fear of hospitals that one finds among the poor is warranted. Yet again, in "Shooting an Elephant," Orwell narrates an experience in Lower Burma during which he unnecessarily destroys an elephant because he fears losing face with the natives. He suddenly realizes that he has no choice in his actions, that one of the effects of imperialism is that it changes him, as well as others like him, into a sort of "hollow, posing dummy." He acknowledges, during this flash of insight, "the hollowness, the futility of the white man's dominion in the East." Similarly, in his books during these early years, Orwell explores his experiences in Burma, India, Paris, and London. His first novel, *Down and Out in Paris and London*, explores in narrative his experiences as a dishwasher in Paris and as a hop picker in England; his second novel, *Burmese Days*, explores his experience as an officer in the Indian Imperial Police from 1922 to 1927.

Orwell's writing after 1936 is consciously focused political commentary, sometimes in works such as *Animal Farm* and *Nineteen Eighty-Four*, and other times in essays such as "Politics and the English Language." In "Why I Write," Orwell says that all of his serious work after 1936 is written "directly or indirectly, *against* totalitarianism and *for* democratic Socialism." His purpose, he says, is "to make political writing into an art."

Evident also in Orwell's later writings are other philosophical changes stemming from his sharply focused worldview. These later works often reflect a lack of faith in the human capacity to survive, and they point to the inevitability of oppression. To Orwell, oppression seems inevitable insofar as people are deceived by, and deceive others with, political language—that is, with discourse aimed at deception rather than expression. In *Animal Farm*, for example, the animals reject the totalitarian rule of the cruel humans and try to erect a democratic Socialism, only to become victims of new tyrants, the pigs and dogs. The oppressed animals are repeatedly deceived by clever political language and, thereby, allow themselves to be victimized. In the end, it matters little to the oppressed animals whether their oppressors are humans, hogs, or dogs.

Nineteen Eighty-Four explores these themes even more fully. Critics have called *Nineteen Eighty-Four* a satire, a dystopian novel, and a negative utopian novel. These labels all fit. They all capture the grim, cheerless worldview evident in this, Orwell's last novel. The protagonist, Winston Smith, tries to free his mind and body from the rigidly totalitarian controls of Big Brother, the figurative leader of Oceania. Smith struggles for freedom of thought, freedom to have an accurate picture of history, and freedom to love, only to discover that Big Brother has monitored his every move. Not only is Smith physically destroyed; he is, more horribly, also mentally remade into a creature without a will. His final submission is to acknowledge his love of Big Brother, who, mercifully, shoots Smith in the back of the head. The novel, often compared to Aldous Huxley's *Brave New World* (1932) and the Russian Yevgeny Zamyatin's *My* (wr. 1920-1921; pb. 1927, 1952; *We*, 1924), ends with the total defeat of humanity. Orwell depicts not only a society in which power is a means to an end but also one in which power itself is the end. The final image of total oppression, as in *Animal Farm*, is tied to the pernicious effects of political language. Smith himself has, ironically, spent his career rewriting history and erasing from the language those words that permit people to talk about or even think about freedom and humanity. He is left with only enough autonomy to admit to his beloved Julia that he has betrayed her. Orwell carefully interweaves the horror of oppression, the decay of language, and the loss of humanity.

These are themes that he explores in his nonfiction, as well. For example, in "Politics and the English Language," Orwell characterizes modern English prose as a "mixture of vagueness and sheer incompetence." His thesis is that "political speech and writing are largely the defence of the indefensible," that such language is used by people who want "to name things without calling up mental pictures of them." Orwell's conclusion in "Politics and the English Language," however, is not so grim as his conclusions in the final two novels are. The essay is, rather, a call to action to stop the decline of language, to reclaim its clarity.

In both his novels and his essays, Orwell succeeds in interweaving politics and language. More than that, however, Orwell the stylist holds a place in Western literature. He has, in fact, made political writing into an art. Often anthologized are such essays as "A Hanging," "Shooting an Elephant," "Why I Write," and "Politics and the English Language." Orwell is recognized as a careful stylist, conscious of his writing down to the word level, carefully using anthropomorphism in "Shooting an Elephant," painting scenes in Burma vividly with sensory images and fresh similes, and artfully sustaining dramatic moments. Readers are drawn to his strong narratives, his flashes of insight, and his clear analysis. Finally, his greatest appeal may be his honesty, his absolute candor with himself and others, what he calls his "power of facing unpleasant facts."

ANIMAL FARM

First published: 1945
Type of work: Novel

In what Orwell calls a "fairy story," animals overthrow the cruel humans only to fall into their own oppressive social structure.

George Orwell says of *Animal Farm*, a novel subtitled *A Fairy Story*, that it was the first book in which he tried, with "full consciousness" of what he was doing, "to fuse political purpose and artistic purpose into one whole." Set at Manor Farm, run by Mr. and Mrs. Jones, *Animal Farm* begins with a sketch of farm life from the perspective of the animals. Jones, who drinks excessively, and his nondescript wife do little to care for the animals while living off the animals' labor. It is old Major, the prize Middle White boar, who speaks in his old age of better times when the animals will set their own laws and enjoy the products of their labor. He tells the farm animals, "All the habits of Man are evil," and he warns them to avoid human vices, such as living in houses, sleeping in beds, wearing clothes, drinking alcohol, smoking tobacco, touching money, and engaging in trade. It is old Major who leads the farm animals in their first song of solidarity, which they sing so loudly that they wake the Joneses. Jones, hearing the ruckus and assuming that a fox is responsible for it, fires shots into the darkness and disperses the animals. Three nights later, old Major dies peacefully in his sleep. With him dies the selfless belief system needed to enact his vision.

As old Major has predicted, the overthrow of the Joneses and Manor Farm occurs.

Jones, increasingly incapacitated by alcohol, neglects the animals and the fields and finally leaves the animals to starve. In their desperation, the starving animals attack Jones and drive him off Manor Farm. Mrs. Jones flees by another way. Though the humans have been overthrown, it is not harmony but a lengthy power struggle that follows.

In this power struggle, essentially between the two young boars Snowball and Napoleon, one sees at first a sort of idealism, especially in Snowball, who speaks of a system that sounds much like Orwell's particular vision of "democratic Socialism." The animals begin by renaming Manor Farm as Animal Farm and by putting into print their seven commandments, designed primarily to identify their tenets and to discourage human vices among themselves. At first, the new order almost appears to work: "Nobody stole, nobody grumbled. . . . Nobody shirked—or almost nobody." In fact, Orwell's animals have human weaknesses that lead to their destruction. Mollie, one of the horses, is vain and does not want to forfeit ribbons and lumps of sugar. The sheep, hens, and ducks are too dull to learn the seven commandments. Boxer, a horse, believes blindly in the work ethic and the wisdom of Napoleon. Benjamin, a donkey, is cynical, refusing to act or become involved because he believes his actions are irrelevant. He believes "hunger, hardship, and disappointment" are "the unalterable law of life." In fact, the one action that Benjamin takes, a desperate attempt to prevent Napoleon from sending his friend Boxer to the glue factory, is futile. When he acts, his actions make no difference. Nothing changes.

Gradually, the pigs begin claiming the privileges of an elite ruling class. They eat better than the other animals, they work less, and they claim more political privileges in making major decisions. The outcome of the power struggle between Snowball and Napoleon is that Napoleon and his trained dogs drive Snowball into hiding. Snowball becomes in exile a sort of political scapegoat, a precursor to Emmanuel Goldstein in *Nineteen Eighty-Four* (1949). Napoleon, now the totalitarian ruler of Animal Farm, rewrites history, convincing the other animals that Snowball was really the cause of all their problems and that he, Napoleon, is the solution to them.

Under Napoleon's rule, Animal Farm declines steadily. As the pigs break the commandments, they rewrite them to conform to the new order. The sheep bleat foolish slogans in Napoleon's behalf. Napoleon's emissary, Squealer, a persuasive political speaker, convinces the increasingly oppressed animals that nothing has changed, that the commandments are as they always were, that history remains as it always was, that they are not doing more work and reaping fewer benefits. Squealer, in his distortion of history and his abuse of language for political purposes, is a precursor of Winston Smith and the other employees in the Ministry of Truth in *Nineteen Eighty-Four* who spend their days rewriting history and stripping the English language of its meaning. Ironically, all the animals pour their energy into creating a system that leads to their oppression.

The final decay of Animal Farm results from the pigs' engaging in all the human evils about which old Major had forewarned them. The pigs become psychologically and even physically indistinguishable from the humans. The pigs wear clothing, sleep in beds, drink alcohol, walk on two legs, wage wars, engage in trade, and destroy their own kind. Ultimately, despite old Major's vision, nothing has changed. The pigs and their dogs have become bureaucrats and tyrants: "neither pigs nor dogs produced any food by their own labour."

Though *Animal Farm* is antitotalitarian, it cannot really be called pro-democratic Socialism, except in the sense of a warning, because the animals have no choice; the course of their fate appears inevitable. Even if they had been given a choice, little in the novel indicates that it would have mattered. The final image in the novel is of the oppressed "creatures" outside the house looking through the window at the pigs and men fighting over a card game. They "looked from pig to man, and from man to pig, and from pig to man again; but already it was impossible to say which was which."

NINETEEN EIGHTY-FOUR

First published: 1949
Type of work: Novel

In the year 1984 in the oppressive society of Oceania, the protagonist Winston Smith futilely tries to preserve his humanity.

Nineteen Eighty-Four, a grim satire directed against totalitarian government, is the story of Winston Smith's futile battle to survive in a system that he has helped to create. The novel is set in 1984 (well into the future when the novel was written) in London, the chief city of Airstrip One, the third most populous of the provinces of Oceania, one of three world powers that are philosophically indistinguishable from, and perpetually at war with, one another.

Smith, thirty-nine, is in marginal health, drinks too much, and lives alone in his comfortless apartment at Victory Mansions, where he is constantly under the eye of a television surveillance system referred to as Big Brother. Smith's wife, Katharine, who lived with him briefly in a loveless marriage—the only kind of marriage permitted by the government—has long since faded from Smith's life, and his day-to-day existence has become meaningless, except insofar as he has memories of a time in his childhood before his mother disappeared. In the midst of this meaningless existence, Smith is approached clandestinely by Julia, a woman who works with him in the Ministry of Truth. She passes him a note that says, "I love you."

The next several months are passed with "secret" meetings between Winston and Julia. From Mr. Charrington, a shopkeeper from whom Winston has bought a diary and an ornamental paperweight, they secure what they believe is a room with privacy from Big Brother's surveillance. During these months together, Winston and Julia begin to hope for a better life. Part of this hope leads them to seek out members of the Brotherhood, an underground resistance movement purportedly led by Emmanuel Goldstein, the official "Enemy of the People." In their search for the Brotherhood, Winston and Julia approach O'Brien, a member of the Inner Party, a man who they believe is part of Goldstein's Brotherhood. Smith trusts only Julia, O'Brien, and Mr. Charrington. He feels that he can trust no one else in a society in which friend betrays friend and child betrays parent. Both he and Julia know and articulate their knowledge that, in resisting the government and Big Brother, they have doomed themselves. Still, they seem to hope, much as the oppressed animals in Orwell's *Animal Farm* embrace hope in a hopeless situation.

Winston and Julia's small hopes are destroyed when they are arrested by the Thought Police, who surround them in their "private" apartment. They are further disillusioned when they learn that Mr. Charrington is a member of the Thought Police and that their every movement during the past months has been monitored. Winston realizes further, when he is later being tortured at the Ministry of Love, that O'Brien is supervising the torture.

Evident in both the Ministry of Truth, where history is falsified and language is reduced and muddied, and in the Ministry of Love, where political dissidents and others are tortured, is Orwell's preoccupation with the effects of paradoxical political language. Even the slogans of the Party are paradoxical: "War Is Peace," "Freedom Is Slavery," and "Ignorance Is Strength." The Ministry of Truth, particularly, is concerned with reducing language, moving toward an ideal language called Newspeak. To clarify the purpose of the language purges, Orwell includes an appendix, "The Principles of Newspeak," in which he explains that Newspeak, the official language of Oceania, has been devised "to meet the ideological needs of Ingsoc, or English Socialism." Once Newspeak is fully adopted, "a heretical thought—that is, a thought diverging from the principles of Ingsoc—should be literally unthinkable." It is because Winston Smith still knows Oldspeak that he has been able to commit Thought Crime.

In the Ministry of Love, Smith comes to understand how totalitarian control works, but he continually wonders about the reasons for it. Why, for example, should Big Brother care about him? It is O'Brien who provides Smith with the answer: power. Power, as O'Brien explains, is an end in itself. Power will destroy everything in its path. O'Brien concludes that, when all else is gone, power will remain:

> But always—do not forget this, Winston—always there will be the intoxication of power, constantly increasing and constantly growing subtler. Always, at every moment, there will be the thrill of victory, the sensation of trampling on an enemy who is helpless. If you want a picture of the future, imagine a boot stamping on a human face—forever.

The purpose, then, of totalitarian government becomes only that of sustaining its feeling of power.

Still, even late in the novel, when O'Brien forces Smith to look into a mirror at his naked, tortured body and his "ruined" face, Smith clings to the idea of his humanity. He says to O'Brien, "I have not betrayed Julia." Yet Smith is stripped of this last tie to his humanity before Orwell's bleak vision is complete.

After a brief time of physical recovery, Smith wakes from a dream, talking in his sleep of his love for Julia. He has retained some part of his will and concludes of Big Brother and the Party: "To die hating them, that was freedom." Whatever he says in his sleep is, of course, being monitored by Big Brother. As a result, Smith faces his ultimate horror, the horror that makes him betray Julia. Physically and mentally ruined, Winston Smith is released from the Ministry of Love to await the death that O'Brien has promised him. Smith retains only enough self-awareness to tell Julia, during their final brief meeting, that he has betrayed her. She, too has betrayed him.

Winston's final defeat is encapsulated in the last words of the novel, seconds after the "long-hoped-for bullet" is "entering his brain." He has become convinced of the insanity of his earlier views; his struggle is finished: "He loved Big Brother."

SHOOTING AN ELEPHANT

First published: 1936
Type of work: Essay

In a narrative account of shooting an elephant unnecessarily, Orwell argues that the experience showed him the "real nature of imperialism."

Based on Orwell's experience with the Indian Imperial Police (1922-1927), "Shooting an Elephant" is set in Moulmein, in Lower Burma. Orwell, the narrator, has already begun to question the presence of the British in the Far East. He says that, theoretically and secretly, he was "all for the Burmese and all against their oppressors, the British." Orwell describes himself as "young and ill-educated," bitterly hating his job.

Orwell's job, in this instance, is to respond to a report of the death of a local man who was killed by an elephant in musth. Orwell finds the man "lying on his belly with arms crucified and head sharply twisted to the side." The corpse grins with "an expression of unendurable agony." At this point, Orwell feels the collective will of the crowd urging him to shoot the elephant, but Orwell, knowing that the elephant is probably no longer dangerous, has no intention of shooting the elephant. He begins to anthropomorphize the elephant, changing the pronouns from "it" to "he," referring to the elephant's "preoccupied grandmotherly air," and concluding that "it would be murder to shoot the elephant."

Despite Orwell's aversion to shooting the elephant, he becomes suddenly aware that he will lose face and be humiliated if he does not shoot it. He therefore shoots the elephant. The death itself is sustained in excruciating detail. After three shots, the elephant still does not die. Orwell fires his two remaining shots into the elephant's heart. He sends someone to get his small rifle, then pours "shot after shot into his heart and down his throat." Still, the elephant does not die. Orwell, unable to stand the elephant's suffering and unable to watch and listen to it, goes away. The elephant, like the Burmese people, has become the unwitting victim of the British imperialist's need to save face. No one is stronger for the experience.

Orwell candidly depicts his unsympathetic actions both in shooting the elephant and in the aftermath, when he is among his fellow British police officers. He is relieved, he admits, that the coolie died, because it gave him a pretext for shooting the elephant. As far as his fellow officers are concerned, he did the right thing. As far as the natives are concerned, he saved face. Yet Orwell concludes, "I often wondered whether any of the others grasped that I had done it solely to avoid looking a fool."

Throughout the essay, Orwell weaves his thesis about the effects of imperialism not only on the oppressed but on the oppressors, as well. He says that "every white man's life in the East was one long struggle not to be laughed at," that "when the white man turns tyrant it is his own freedom that he destroys," and that the imperialist "becomes a sort of hollow, posing dummy, the conventionalized figure of a sahib." Orwell's essay, however, is more than one person's riveting narrative about the beginning of an awareness. "Shooting an Elephant" captures a universal experience of going against one's own humanity at the cost of a part of that humanity.

POLITICS AND THE ENGLISH LANGUAGE

First published: 1946
Type of work: Essay

Orwell analyzes the corrupting influence of political language on clear thinking and concludes that "political speech and writing are largely the defence of the indefensible."

"Politics and the English Language," though written in 1946, remains timely for modern students of language. In this essay, Orwell argues that the English language becomes "ugly and inaccurate because our thoughts are foolish, but the slovenliness of our language makes it easier for us to have foolish thoughts." To illustrate his point, Orwell cites writing from two professors, a Communist pamphlet, an essay on psychology in *Politics*, and a letter in the *Tribune*. All of these examples, Orwell argues, share two common faults: staleness of imagery and lack of precision. In his follow-up analysis, he discusses general characteristics of bad writing, including pretentious diction and meaningless words. His purpose in the analysis is to show "the special connection between politics and the debasement of language."

Orwell maintains that, in his time, political speech and writing are "largely the defence of the indefensible." That is, the actions of ruthless politicians can be defended, but only by brutal arguments that "do not square with the professed aims of political parties." He gives examples of the British rule in India, the Russian purges and deportations, and the dropping of the atom bombs on Japan. In order to talk about such atrocities, Orwell contends, one has to use political language that consists "largely of euphemism, question-begging and sheer cloudy vagueness." Orwell translates for his readers the real meanings of such terms as "pacification," "transfer of population," "rectification of frontiers," and "elimination of unreliable elements." He concludes: "Political language—and with variations this is true of all political parties, from Conservatives to Anarchists—is designed to make lies sound truthful and murder respectable, and to give an appearance of solidity to pure wind."

This premise is one that Orwell explores more fully in his novels *Animal Farm*, particularly in the pigs Napoleon and Squealer, and *Nineteen Eighty-Four*, in Big Brother, Newspeak, and the Ministry of Truth. Orwell's conclusion in "Politics and the English Language" is less bleak than are his conclusions in the two novels. In the novels, the damage to language is irreversible. In the essay, Orwell calls his readers to action. He asserts that bad habits spread by imitation "can be avoided if one is willing to take the necessary trouble." He concludes that "one can even, if one jeers loudly enough, send some worn-out and useless phrase . . . into the dustbin where it belongs."

Orwell's 1946 essay is still calling readers to action. In 1974, for example, the National Council of Teachers of English began handing out its annual Doublespeak Awards for misuses of language with potential to cause harm or obscure truth. The awards, named in honor of Orwell, are meant to identify deceptive uses of language and to jeer them out of existence. Not surprisingly, perhaps, there is no shortage of nominees.

Summary

George Orwell's novels and essays have contributed to current literary and political writing an awareness of the connections among language and thinking and political actions. Particularly in his later works, Orwell focused his purpose on writing, merging art with politics, attacking the effects of the power motives of totalitarian governments in one's humanity, warning his readers of the dangers inherent in "groupthink" and "doublespeak," and grimly satirizing the human traits that have let oppressed peoples become the victims of those intoxicated by power. Though Orwell's writing career, by twentieth century standards, was fairly short, several of his essays and novels hold for him a place in Western literature and in political thought.

Bibliography

Connelly, Mark. *The Diminished Self: Orwell and the Loss of Freedom.* Pittsburgh: Duquesne University Press, 1987.

Gardner, Averil. *George Orwell.* Boston: Twayne, 1987.

Hunter, Lynette. *George Orwell: The Search for a Voice.* Milton Keynes, England: Open University Press, 1984.

Jensen, Ejner J., ed. *The Future of Nineteen Eighty-Four.* Ann Arbor: University of Michigan Press, 1987.

Muller, Gilbert H. *Major Modern Essayists*. Englewood Cliffs, N.J.: Prentice-Hall, 1991.

Richardson, J. M., ed. *Orwell × 8: A Symposium*. Winnipeg, Canada: Ronald P. Frye, 1986.

Carol Franks

JOHN OSBORNE

Born: London, England
December 12, 1929

Principal Literary Achievement
Osborne's powerful domestic drama, *Look Back in Anger*, established the character of the "angry young man" in modern British theater.

Biography
John James Osborne was born in Fulham, a grimy district of south London, England, on December 12, 1929, the only son of Thomas Godfrey Osborne, who worked as a copywriter for an advertising agency, and Nellie Beatrice Osborne, who worked as a barmaid. Osborne's father died when Osborne was twelve, and at least partially sentimental portraits of fathers and grandfathers figure prominently in Osborne's plays, as do unflattering portraits of mother figures (Osborne's relationship with his mother was not very satisfactory). His unhappy middle-class childhood and adolescence are vividly portrayed in the first volume of his autobiography, *A Better Class of Person, 1929-1956* (1981).

At fifteen, Osborne was expelled from St. Michael's, an undistinguished boarding school in Devon. Two years later, he was working as a journalist for trade magazines when he drifted into his theater career, which began when he took a job tutoring a company of juvenile actors. After working eight years in English provincial theaters, Osborne became an overnight sensation at the age of twenty-six when his third play, *Look Back in Anger* (1956), was accepted by the English Stage Company and performed at the Royal Court Theatre, London, under the artistic direction of George Devine.

Look Back in Anger opened on May 8, 1956, and in a review in *The Observer* on Sunday, May 13, the legendary critic Kenneth Tynan hailed Osborne's work as "the best young play of its decade," adding, "I doubt if I could love anyone who did not wish to see *Look Back in Anger.*" A Royal Court Theatre publicist described Osborne as an "angry young man," and that phrase came to designate a whole generation of British male writers, both playwrights and novelists, who came to be known as "the angry young men." Their work was typified by their working-class backgrounds, their irreverence for the traditional British establishment, and an intolerance for anything "highbrow" or "phoney." In the theater, Osborne's ruthless honesty with language and subject matter inspired a generation of vigorous British playwrights, including

Arnold Wesker, John Arden, Harold Pinter, and Tom Stoppard. *Look Back in Anger* ran for a year and a half, was transferred to New York, and for years enjoyed enormous success in various touring productions around the world.

Osborne's next two plays, *The Entertainer* (1957) and *Epitaph for George Dillon* (1958), were also big hits. In 1959, however, *The World of Paul Slickey* was a disaster. Many more plays, television scripts, and film scripts followed in the 1960's and 1970's, but the general impression created by Osborne's work was that he was not fulfilling the promise he had exhibited in *Look Back in Anger*. Highlights in this relatively disappointing period included *Luther* (1961), a dramatization of the life of Martin Luther; *Inadmissible Evidence* (1964), in which a middle-aged lawyer tries to justify his disappointing life; *The Hotel in Amsterdam* (1968), in which three couples meet in a first-class hotel and define their lives by their hatred of a tyrannical film producer; and his autobiography, *A Better Class of Person*.

In 1958, Osborne joined with Tony Richardson, the original director of *Look Back in Anger*, to form Woodfall Films. His greatest popular success in screenwriting was winning an Oscar for *Tom Jones* (1963), based on the 1749 novel by Henry Fielding. Among his many other projects, he successfully adapted three of his own plays for film: *Look Back in Anger* (1959), *The Entertainer* (1960), and *Inadmissible Evidence* (1968). He also received the New York Drama Critics Circle Award (1958, 1965) and the Tony Award (1963).

In 1958, Osborne bought a twenty-three-acre estate in Kent that served as a refuge for his reclusive way of life. In 1978, he married his fifth wife, Helen Dawson, a drama critic.

Analysis

It is traditional to say that Osborne's *Look Back in Anger* represents a turning point in the history of British theater, ending the era of the 1930's and 1940's and ushering in the new, more contemporary style of the 1950's and 1960's. In British theater, the 1930's, 1940's, and early 1950's had been dominated by the esoteric verse dramas of T. S. Eliot and Christopher Fry, the aristocratic drawing room comedies of Noël Coward, the commercial successes of Terence Rattigan, and the revivals of time-tested classics. In *Look Back in Anger* and subsequent plays, Osborne offered different fare.

His subject was not genteel, upper-class life but the life of contemporary, rough, and often unsophisticated working-class people. He was critical of British culture both past and present. Detesting the British elitism that emphasized class distinctions, Osborne questioned the conventional pride in England's Edwardian past and was equally critical of England's post-World War II welfare state, scoffing at anything "highbrow" or "phoney." His style was robust, even coarse, rather than elevated or dainty. These qualities of political attitude and style were the features that brought Osborne so much attention when he became a London phenomenon in the late 1950's. Since then, the more enduring feature of Osborne's drama has become the Osborne hero, modeled after the original "angry young man," Jimmy Porter. Ar-

chie Rice in *The Entertainer*, George Dillon in *Epitaph for George Dillon*, Bill Maitland in *Inadmissible Evidence*, Pamela in *Time Present* (1968), and perhaps even Luther in *Luther* are all, more or less, heroes in the Jimmy Porter mold.

Like Jimmy, these heroes are often outspoken and irreverent in their criticism of
contemporary British society, frequently angry, alienated, bitter, caustic, insensitive,
and critical of people and things around them. Sometimes these characters brutalize
those closest to them as they strike out from their personal pain. They are often
failures, but not simply because they suffer from class distinctions. Mainly, they suffer and fail because they experience the past as a terrible burden. They often look
back at their lives and find them very unsatisfactory. These are not genteel characters
one can analyze from a distance with a detached attitude. These characters demand
an emotional, complex, and often sympathetic response. In an oft-quoted statement,
Osborne has said, "I want to make people feel, to give them lessons in feeling. They
can think afterwards." The richness and complexity of Osborne's art in these characterizations is that in spite of their many unpleasant characteristics, these Osborne
heroes are often still compelling. They are what American critic Harold Ferrar has
called "the bastard we can't help caring about."

Yet the quality and prevalence in Osborne's drama of this kind of character also
constitute a literary deficiency. At his best, Osborne creates an unforgettable portrait
that may live forever in theatrical history; such a portrait was achieved in Jimmy
Porter. This sort of angry hero, however, often becomes so dominant in Osborne's
plays that other characters seem one-dimensional and cardboard-like in comparison.
This charge is sometimes even made against *Look Back in Anger*: Jimmy's friend,
Cliff, is seen as a cartoon sidekick; Alison's friend, Helena, is seen as an unconvinc-
ing contrivance of plot when she suddenly accepts the abusive Jimmy as a lover at
the end of act 2 and then gives him up just as suddenly in the last scene, when
Jimmy's wife, Alison, returns. Furthermore, the heroes that succeeded Jimmy Porter
generally pale in comparison with their startling original counterpart, and Osborne
seemed to be repeating himself without adding depth or dimension.

Some of Osborne's most interesting developments as a dramatist came later in his
career, when he seemed to be attempting to break from this focus on a single hero to
create more of an ensemble approach to drama, as in the 1968 play *The Hotel in
Amsterdam*. Immediately after *Look Back in Anger*, Osborne moved on to more technically innovative work, but the experiments were not always successful. *The World
of Paul Slickey*, for example, was a clumsy attempt at the musical form. A number of
works, such as *Luther* and *A Subject of Scandal and Concern* (1960), attempted to
employ historical materials for dramatic purposes but never achieved that blend of
past and present that makes such materials come alive onstage. In Osborne's bold-
est and most successful technical experiment, *Inadmissible Evidence*, Bill Maitland's
mental breakdown is portrayed in a dream sequence that locates the play's action in
the courtroom of Maitland's mind.

Osborne's historical importance is assured because *Look Back in Anger* altered the
style and subject matter of a whole generation of British writers. The great nine-

teenth century poet and critic Matthew Arnold insisted that historical importance should not be confused with artistic importance. *Look Back in Anger* is both a historical watershed and an artistic success.

LOOK BACK IN ANGER

First produced: 1956 (first published, 1957)
Type of work: Play

A pathologically unhappy and bitter young man vents his anger on all around him and is estranged from, but then eventually reconciled with, his wife.

Look Back in Anger opens on a lazy, mid-1950's Sunday afternoon in a one-room attic apartment in a town in the English Midlands. As usual, Jimmy Porter and his friend and business partner, Cliff Lewis, are reading the Sunday papers while Jimmy's wife, Alison, irons. As usual, Jimmy is verbally bashing everyone and everything around him, including Cliff and Alison—who seem to take his anger in stride.

What makes Jimmy so angry? To support a political reading of *Look Back in Anger*, critics cite Jimmy's famous speech near the end of the play, "there aren't any good, brave causes left," suggesting that Jimmy's anger comes from his disappointment that the faded Edwardian glory of England can no longer be real and felt with conviction and enthusiasm. This interpretation is supported by an earlier passage in the play in which Jimmy is quite nostalgic about the Edwardian world of Alison's father, Colonel Redfern: "all home-made cakes and croquet, bright ideas, bright uniforms . . . what a romantic picture." Jimmy admits that "if you've no world of your own, it's rather pleasant to regret the passing of someone else's."

In his contemporary England, Jimmy sees only political decay and the pretense of continued health. As an intelligent, articulate, and educated twenty-five-year-old, Jimmy has not been able to find work that matches his skills, so he earns a meager living running a streetcorner candy stand with Cliff as his partner. Part of him reaches for more success, symbolized most eloquently in his frequent, offstage riffs on his jazz trumpet, but part of him mistrusts success because he does not trust aspiration in a country where aspiration is associated with all that is false and hollow. From his demeaning social position, Jimmy lashes out at all the self-important people around him. His anger strikes at everything associated with British bureaucracy, but unhappily it also overflows into mistreatment of his wife and his friend Cliff.

A more psychological and domestic interpretation of the play often points to Jimmy's pain over his father's death. When Jimmy was ten years old, he spent a year watching his father die. To him, the rest of the family did not seem to care, and Jimmy sees a similar lack of sensitivity in Alison. He calls her "Lady Pusillanimous [cowardly]," a "monument to non-attachment," and in one of his verbal tirades even wishes that some catastrophe would shock her out of her lethargy, even something horrible such as having a child die. This is indeed what happens, and that tragedy serves, ironically, as the reconciling force in their marriage.

There are other interpretations of Jimmy's anger, but his complexity derives from the fact that the precise cause of his disease remains elusive. In fact, audiences and critics find Jimmy compelling because the richness of his pain defies final analysis.

Jimmy's anger cools a little at the end of the play but only because his conflict with Alison is resolved at a very great price. When Alison discovers that she is pregnant, an old friend, Helena Charles, comes to stay with the Porters, and Jimmy's badgering intensifies; his harassment is eventually directed toward Helena. In reaction, Helena convinces Alison that she should leave Jimmy and live again with her father, and Alison leaves. At the end of act 2, however, Helena is drawn by some strange attraction to Jimmy and offers herself to him, becoming his mistress. When act 3 begins, it is Sunday afternoon again and Jimmy and Cliff are once more reading their Sunday papers. Now, however in a mirror image of the opening of the play, Helena has replaced Alison at the ironing board.

Both the resolution of the conflict and the end of the play come as Alison returns, having lost both the baby and her fertility. In a scene that some critics find insufficiently motivated, Helena leaves and gives Jimmy back to Alison. The play ends with Jimmy and Alison reconciling, in part because Jimmy is satisfied that Alison's pain has brought her more in tune with his own suffering. The reconciliation is richly ambiguous. Have Jimmy and Alison repaired a marriage worth saving, or have they simply hid from problems they cannot face and handle? The enduring quality of *Look Back in Anger* is that either of these readings, and more, can be defended.

THE ENTERTAINER

First produced: 1957
Type of work: Play

A third-rate music-hall comic fails as the father of a thoroughly unhappy family.

In *The Entertainer*, Osborne's hero is Archie Rice, a pathetic music-hall performer whose domestic life is as much a failure as his comedy act. Himself an admirer of the English music hall and its vaudevillian traditions, Osborne alternates domestic scenes of the Rice family with scenes of Archie's coarse patter in the music hall to symbolize the decline of imperial England. In its late nineteenth and early twentieth century heyday, the music hall was an important expression of urban working-class pride, an entertainment that avoided anything "highbrow," serious, or intellectual. By the 1950's, the music hall had been replaced by cinema and television, degenerating into an even more decadent popular art, and in this mid-1950's music hall Archie is merely a comic setup man for a tacky striptease.

The family unit headed by Archie is equally disappointing. As a father, Archie is self-centered and insensitive, viciously ridiculing his own doddering father, Billy, who lives with them in their dilapidated and noisy slum apartment. Archie's wife, Phoebe, is a pathetic alcoholic who endures Archie's sexual infidelity by retreating mindlessly to the movies. The play's action takes place in 1956, during the Suez conflict, when Egypt seized control of the Suez Canal. Archie and Phoebe's elder son, Frank, is an unheroic conscientious objector, fresh from six months in prison, who works two menial jobs. Mick, Archie and Phoebe's younger son, has accepted the call for army service in Cyprus but has been captured and made a prisoner of war. Jean, Archie's daughter by his first marriage, is a more sensitive person, having thrown off the old-fashioned and sexist attention of her conservative boyfriend, Graham, but under the influence of a little too much gin she seems equally incapable of strengthening the family unit. As the family members squabble throughout the play, it is clear that they all exist in their own little worlds, seldom listening to, or really communicating with, one another. In many ways, *The Entertainer* can be seen as an English version of Eugene O'Neill's *Long Day's Journey into Night* (1957); both are portraits of profound domestic failure.

The climax of the action comes with the news that Mick, thought to be released and on his way home, has been killed. Compounded with that grief is the soon-to-follow funeral for Billy; Archie had attempted to get Billy back onto the music-hall stage in order to revive his (Archie's) own career. In the last scene, Archie is on stage, and the symbolic tax man, whom Archie has been cheating for the last twenty years, is waiting in the wings like death to take Archie to jail. Archie is supported in his last minutes by Phoebe, but there is no hopeful vision of an improved marriage as the lights snap out for the last time. Osborne's vision of the domestic future of the Rice family is as bleak as his vision of England's future as a world power.

One of the most interesting theatrical aspects of *The Entertainer* is that the famous British classical actor, Sir Laurence Olivier, took the role of Archie Rice in its initial London production. In *Look Back in Anger*, Osborne had made himself into a literary phenomenon by belittling the British establishment. Olivier was a significant member of that establishment's theater wing, but when he expressed an interest in Osborne's work, Olivier was cast as Archie Rice; Olivier's star status, along with a chillingly real performance, made *The Entertainer* a smash hit. It was soon transferred to London's West End and then was made into a successful film. After his first two plays, Osborne was himself a bonafide "star," part of a new establishment.

Summary

John Osborne's historical importance in modern British drama is seldom questioned. His *Look Back in Anger* gave a name, "the angry young men," to a whole generation of British writers. There is also no doubting the solid theatrical quality of his first big hit, since the compelling portrait of Jimmy Porter continues to command the stage wherever Osborne's play is revived. His prolific output includes more than forty other stage, screen, and television plays.

Bibliography

Anderson, Michael. *Anger and Detachment: A Study of Arden, Osborne, and Pinter.* London: Pitman, 1976.

Brown, John Russell. *Theatre Language: A Study of Arden, Osborne, Pinter, and Wesker.* New York: Taplinger, 1972.

Carter, Alan. *John Osborne.* Edinburgh, Scotland: Oliver & Boyd, 1969.

Ferrar, Harold. *John Osborne.* New York: Columbia University Press, 1973.

Goldstone, Herbert. *Coping with Vulnerability: The Achievement of John Osborne.* Washington, D.C.: University Press of America, 1982.

Hayman, Ronald. *John Osborne.* New York: Ungar, 1972.

Hinchliffe, Arnold P. *John Osborne.* Boston: Twayne, 1984.

Osborne, John. *A Better Class of Person: An Autobiography, 1929-1956.* New York: E. P. Dutton, 1981.

Taylor, John Russell. *The Angry Theatre.* New York: Hill & Wang, 1969.

Trussler, Simon. *The Plays of John Osborne: An Assessment.* New York: Humanities Press, 1969.

Terry Nienhuis

MAGILL'S
SURVEY
OF
WORLD
LITERATURE

GLOSSARY

Aesthetics: The branch of philosophy that studies the beautiful in nature and art, including how beauty is recognized in a work of art and how people respond to it. In literature, the aesthetic approach can be distinguished from the moral or utilitarian approach; it was most fully embodied in the movement known as aestheticism in the late nineteenth century.

Alienation: The German dramatist Bertolt Brecht developed the theory of alienation in his epic theater. Brecht sought to create an audience that was intellectually alert rather than emotionally involved in a play by using alienating techniques such as minimizing the illusion of reality onstage and interrupting the action with songs and visual aids.

Allegory: A literary mode in which characters in a narrative personify abstract ideas or qualities and so give a second level of meaning to the work, in addition to the surface narrative. Two famous examples of allegory are Edmund Spenser's *The Faerie Queene* (1590, 1596) and John Bunyan's *The Pilgrim's Progress* (1678). For modern examples, see the stories and novels of Franz Kafka.

Alliteration: A poetic technique in which consonant repetition is focused at the beginning of syllables, as in "Large mannered motions of his mythy mind." Alliteration is used when the poet wishes to focus on the details of a sequence of words and to show the relationships between words in a line.

Angry young men: The term used to describe a group of English novelists and playwrights in the 1950's and 1960's, whose work stridently attacked what it saw as the outmoded political and social structures (particularly the class structure) of post-World War II Britain. John Osborne's play *Look Back in Anger* (1956) and Kingsley Amis' *Lucky Jim* (1954) are typical examples.

Angst: A pervasive feeling of anxiety and depression often associated with the moral and spiritual uncertainties of the twentieth century, as expressed in the existentialism of writers such as Jean-Paul Sartre and Albert Camus.

Antagonist: A character in fiction who stands in opposition or rivalry to the protagonist. In William Shakespeare's *Hamlet* (c. 1600-1601), for example, King Claudius is the antagonist of Hamlet.

Anthropomorphism: The ascription of human characteristics and feelings to animals, inanimate objects, or gods. The gods of Homer's epics are anthropomorphic, for example. Anthropomorphism occurs in beast fables, such as George Orwell's *Animal Farm* (1945). The term "pathetic fallacy" carries the same meaning: Natural objects are invested with human feelings. *See also* Pathetic fallacy.

Antihero: A modern fictional figure who tries to define himself and establish his own codes, or a protagonist who simply lacks traditional heroic qualities, such as Jim Dixon in Kingsley Amis' *Lucky Jim* (1954).

Aphorism: A short, concise statement that states an opinion, precept, or general truth, such as Alexander Pope's "Hope springs eternal in the human breast."

Apostrophe: A direct address to a person (usually absent), inanimate entity, or abstract quality.

Archetype: The term was used by psychologist Carl Jung to describe what he called "primordial images" that exist in the "collective unconscious" of humankind and are manifested in myths, religion, literature, and dreams. Now used broadly in literary criticism to refer to character types, motifs, images, symbols, and plot patterns recurring in many different literary forms and works. The embodiment of archetypes in a work of literature can make a powerful impression on the reader.

Aristotelian unities: A set of rules for proper dramatic construction formulated by Italian and French critics during the Renaissance, purported to be derived from the *De poetica* (c. 334-323 B.C.; *Poetics*) of Aristotle. According to the "three unities," a play should have no scenes irrelevant to the main action, should not cover a period of more than twenty-four hours, and should not occur in more than one place or locale. In fact, Aristotle insists only on unity of action in a tragedy.

Assonance: A term for the association of words with identical vowel sounds but different consonants: "stars," "arms," and "park," for example, all contain identical *a* (and *ar*) sounds.

***Auto sacramental*:** A Renaissance development of the medieval open-air Corpus Christi pageant in Spain. A dramatic, allegorical depiction of a sinful soul wavering and transgressing until the intervention of Divine Grace restores order. During a period of prohibition of all secular drama in Spain, from 1598 to 1600, even Lope de Vega Carpio adopted this form.

Autobiography: A form of nonfiction writing in which the author narrates events of his or her own life. Autobiography differs from memoir in that the latter focuses on prominent people the author has known and great events that he has witnessed, rather than on his own life.

Ballad: Popular ballads are songs or verse that tell dramatic, usually impersonal, tales. Supernatural events, courage, and love are frequent themes, but any experience that appeals to ordinary people is acceptable material. Literary ballads—narrative poems based on the popular ballads—have frequently been in vogue in English literature, particularly during the Romantic period. One of the most famous is Samuel Taylor Coleridge's *The Rime of the Ancient Mariner* (1798).

Baroque: The term was first used in the eighteenth century to describe an elaborate and grandiose type of architecture. It is now also used to refer to certain stylistic features of Metaphysical poetry, particularly the poetry of Richard Crashaw. The term can also refer to post-Renaissance literature, 1580-1680.

***Bildungsroman*:** Sometimes called the "novel of education," or "apprenticeship novel," the *Bildungsroman* focuses on the growth of a young protagonist who is learning about the world and finding his place in life; a typical example is James Joyce's *A Portrait of the Artist as a Young Man* (1916).

Blank verse: A term for unrhymed iambic pentameter, blank verse first appeared in drama in Thomas Norton and Thomas Sackville's *Gorboduc*, performed in 1561, and later became the standard form of Elizabethan drama. It has also commonly been used in long narrative or philosophical poems, such as John Milton's *Paradise Lost* (1667, 1674).

Bourgeois novel: A novel in which the values, the preoccupations, and the accoutrements of middle-class or bourgeois life are given particular prominence. The heyday of the genre was the nineteenth century, when novelists as varied as Jane Austen, Honoré de Balzac, and Anthony Trollope both criticized and unreflectingly transmitted the assumptions of the rising middle class.

Burlesque: A work that by imitating attitudes, styles, institutions, and people aims to amuse. Burlesque differs from satire in that it aims to ridicule simply for the sake of amusement rather than for political or social change.

Capa y espada: Spanish for "cloak and sword." A term referring to the Spanish theater of the sixteenth and seventeenth centuries dealing with love and intrigue among the aristocracy. The greatest practitioners were Lope de Vega Carpio and Pedro Calderón de la Barca. The term *comedia de ingenio* is also used.

Catharsis: A term from Aristotle's *De poetica* (c. 334-323 B.C.; *Poetics*) referring to the purgation of the emotions of pity and fear in the spectator aroused by the actions of the tragic hero. The meaning and the operation of the concept have been a source of great, and unresolved, critical debate.

Celtic romance: Gaelic Celts invaded Ireland in about 350 B.C.; their epic stories and romances date from this period until about A.D. 450. The romances are marked by a strong sense of the Otherworld and of supernatural happenings. The Celtic romance tradition influenced the poetry of William Butler Yeats.

Celtic Twilight: Sometimes used synonymously with the term Irish Renaissance, which was a movement beginning in the late nineteenth century which attempted to build a national literature by drawing on Ireland's literary and cultural history. The term, however, which is taken from a book by William Butler Yeats titled *The Celtic Twilight* (1893), sometimes has a negative connotation. It is used to refer to some early volumes by Yeats, which have been called self-indulgent. The poet Algernon Charles Swinburne said that the Celtic Twilight manner "puts fever and fancy in the place of reason and imagination."

Chamber plays: Refers to four plays written in 1907 by the Swedish dramatist August Strindberg. The plays are modeled on the form of chamber music, consisting of motif and variations, to evoke a mood or atmosphere (in these cases, a very sombre one). There is no protagonist but a small group of equally important characters.

Character: A personage appearing in any literary or dramatic work. Characters can be presented with the depth and complexity of real people (sometimes called "round" characters) or as stylized functions of the plot ("flat" characters).

Chorus: Originally a group of singers and dancers in religious festivals, the chorus evolved into the dramatic element that reflected the opinions of the masses or commented on the action in Greek drama. In its most developed form, the chorus consisted of fifteen members: seven reciting the strophe, seven reciting the antistrophe, and the leader interacting with the actors. The chorus has been used in all periods of drama, including the modern period.

Classicism: A literary stance or value system consciously based on the example of classical Greek and Roman literature. While the term is applied to an enormous diversity of artists in many different periods and in many different national literatures, it generally denotes a cluster of values including formal discipline, restrained expression, reverence of tradition, and an objective, rather than subjective, orientation. Often contrasted with Romanticism. *See also* Romanticism.

Comédie-Française: The first state theater of France, composed of the company of actors established by Molière in 1658. The company took the name *Comédie-Française* in 1680. Today, it is officially known as the *Theatre Français (Salle Richelieu)*.

Comedy: Generally, a lighter form of drama (as contrasted with tragedy) that aims chiefly to amuse and ends happily. The comic effect typically arises from the recognition of some incongruity of speech, action, or character development. The comic range extends from coarse, physical humor (called low comedy) to a more subtle, intellectual humor (called high comedy).

Comedy of manners: A form of comedy that arose during the seventeenth century, dealing with the intrigues (particularly the amorous intrigues) of sophisticated, witty members of the upper classes. The appeal of these plays is primarily intellectual, depending as they do on quick-witted dialogue and clever language. For examples, see the plays of Restoration dramatists William Congreve, Sir George Etherege, and William Wycherley. *See also* Restoration comedy/drama.

Commedia dell'arte: Dramatic comedy performed by troupes of professional actors, which became popular in the mid-sixteenth century in Italy. The troupes were rather small, consisting of perhaps a dozen actors who performed stock roles in mask and improvised on skeletal scenarios. The tradition of the *commedia*, or masked comedy, was influential into the seventeenth century and still exerts some influence.

Conceit: A type of metaphor, the conceit is used for comparisons that are highly intellectualized. When T. S. Eliot, for example, says that winding streets are like a tedious argument of insidious intent, there is no clear connection between the two, so the reader must apply abstract logic to fill in the missing links.

Conversation poem: Conversation poems are chiefly associated with the poetry of Samuel Taylor Coleridge. These poems all display a relaxed, informal style, quiet settings, and a circular structure—the poem returns to where it began, after an intervening meditation has yielded some insight into the speaker's situation.

Cubism: A term borrowed from Cubist painters. In literature, cubism is a style of poetry, such as that of E. E. Cummings, Kenneth Rexroth, and Archibald Mac-Leish, which first fragments an experience, then rearranges its elements into some new artistic entity.

Dactyl: The dactylic foot, or dactyl, is formed of a stress followed by two unstressed syllables, as in the words "Washington" and "manikin." "After the pangs of a desperate lover" is an example of a dactylic line.

Dadaism: Dadaism arose in France during World War I as a radical protest in art and literature against traditional institutions and values. Part of its strategy was the use of infantile, nonsensical language. After World War I, when Dadaism was combined with the ideas of Sigmund Freud, it gave rise to the Surrealist movement.

Decadence: The period of decline that heralds the ending of a great age. The period in English dramatic history immediately following William Shakespeare is said to be decadent, and the term "Decadents" is applied to a group of late-nineteenth and early twentieth century writers who searched for new literary and artistic forms as the Victorian Age came to a close.

Detective story: The "classic" detective story (or "mystery") is a highly formalized and logically structured mode of fiction in which the focus is on a crime solved by a detective through interpretation of evidence and clever reasoning. Many modern practitioners of the genre, however, such as Raymond Chandler, Patricia Highsmith, and Ross Macdonald, have placed less emphasis on the puzzlelike qualities of the detective story and have focused instead on characterization, theme, and other elements of mainstream fiction. The form was first developed in short fiction by Edgar Allan Poe; Jorge Luis Borges has also used the convention in short stories.

Dialectic: A philosophical term meaning the art of examining opinions or ideas logically. The dialectic method of Georg Wilhelm Friedrich Hegel and Karl Marx was based on a contradiction of opposites (thesis and antithesis) and their resolution (synthesis). In literary criticism, the term has sometimes been used by Marxist critics to refer to the structure and dynamics of a literary work in its sociological context.

Dialogue: Speech exchanged between characters, or even, in a looser sense, the thoughts of a single character. Dialogue serves to characterize, to further the plot, to establish conflict, and to express thematic ideas.

Doppelgänger: A double or counterpart of a person, sometimes endowed with ghostly qualities. A fictional *Doppelgänger* often reflects a suppressed side of his personality, as in Fyodor Dostoevski's novella *Dvoynik* (1846; *The Double*, 1917) and the short stories of E. T. A. Hoffmann. Isaac Bashevis Singer and Jorge Luis Borges, among other modern writers, have also employed the *Doppelgänger* with striking effect.

Drama: Generally speaking, any work designed to be represented on a stage by actors (Aristotle defined drama as "the imitation of an action"). More specifically, the term has come to signify a play of a serious nature and intent that may end either happily (comedy) or unhappily (tragedy).

Dramatic irony: A situation in a play or a narrative in which the audience knows something that the character does not. The irony lies in the different meaning that the character's words or actions have for himself and for the audience. A common device in classical Greek drama. Sophocles' *Oidipous Tyrannos* (429 B.C.; *Oedipus Tyrannus*) is an example of extended dramatic irony.

Dramatic monologue: In dramatic monologue, the narrator addresses a persona who never speaks but whose presence greatly influences what the narrator tells the reader. The principal reason for writing in dramatic monologue is to control the speech of the major persona by the implied reaction of the silent one. The effect is one of continuing change and often surprise. The technique is especially useful for revealing characters slowly and for involving the reader as another silent participant.

Dramatic verse: Poetry that employs dramatic form or technique, such as dialogue or conflict, to achieve its effects. The term is used to refer to dramatic monologue, drama written in verse, and closet dramas.

Dramatis personae: The characters in a play. Often, a printed listing defining the characters and specifying their relationships.

Dream vision: An allegorical form common in the Middle Ages, in which the narrator or a character falls asleep and dreams a dream that becomes the actual framed story.

Dystopian/Utopian novel: A dystopian novel takes some existing trend or theory in present-day society and extends it into a fictional world of the future, where the trend has become more fully manifested, with unpleasant results. Aldous Huxley's *Brave New World* (1932) is an example. The utopian novel is the opposite: It presents an ideal society. The first utopian novel was Sir Thomas More's *Utopia* (1516).

Elegy: A long, rhymed, formal poem whose subject is meditation upon death or a lamentable theme. The pastoral elegy uses a pastoral scene to express grief at the loss of a friend or important person. *See also* Pastoral.

Elizabethan Age: Of or referring to the reign of Queen Elizabeth I of England, lasting from 1558 to 1603, a period of important developments and achievements in the arts in England, particularly in poetry and drama. The era included such literary figures as Edmund Spenser, Christopher Marlowe, William Shakespeare, and Ben Jonson. Sometimes referred to as the English Renaissance.

English novel: The first fully realized English was Samuel Richardson's *Pamela* (1740-1741). The genre took firm hold in the second half of the eighteenth century, with the work of Daniel Defoe, Henry Fielding, and Tobias Smollett, and reached its full flowering in the nineteenth century, in which great novelists such as Jane Austen, Charles Dickens, William Makepeace Thackeray, Anthony

Trollope, Thomas Hardy, and George Eliot produced sweeping portraits of the whole range of English life in the period.

Enlightenment: A period in Western European cultural history that began in the seventeenth century and culminated in the eighteenth. The chief characteristic of Enlightenment thinkers was their belief in the virtue of human reason, which they believed was banishing former superstitious and ignorant ways and leading to an ideal condition of human life. The Enlightenment coincides with the rise of the scientific method.

Epic: Although this term usually refers to a long narrative poem that presents the exploits of a central figure of high position, the term is also used to designate a long novel that has the style or structure usually associated with an epic. In this sense, for example, Herman Melville's *Moby Dick* (1851) and James Joyce's *Ulysses* (1922) may be called epics.

Epigram: Originally meaning an inscription, an epigram is a short, pointed poem, often expressing humor and satire. In English literature, the form flourished from the Renaissance through the eighteenth century, in the work of poets such as John Donne, Ben Jonson, and Alexander Pope. The term also refers to a concise and witty expression in prose, as in the plays of Oscar Wilde.

Epiphany: Literally, an epiphany is an appearance of a god or supernatural being. The term is used in literary criticism to signify any moment of heightened awareness, or flash of transcendental insight, when an ordinary object or scene is suddenly transformed into something that possesses eternal significance. Especially noteworthy examples are found in the works of James Joyce.

Epistle: The word means "letter," but epistle is used to refer to a literary form rather than a private composition, usually written in dignified style and addressed to a group. The most famous examples are the epistles in the New Testament.

Epistolary novel: A work of fiction in which the narrative is carried forward by means of letters written by the characters. Epistolary novels were especially popular in the eighteenth century. Examples include Samuel Richardson's *Pamela* (1740-1741) and *Clarissa* (1747-1748).

Epithet: An adjective or adjectival phrase that expresses a special characteristic of a person or thing. "Hideous night," "devouring time," and "sweet silent thought" are epithets that appear in William Shakespeare's sonnets.

Essay: A brief prose work, usually on a single topic, that expresses the personal point of view of the author. The essay is usually addressed to a general audience and attempts to persuade the reader to accept the author's ideas.

Everyman: The central character in the work by the same name, the most famous of the English medieval morality plays. It tells of how Everyman is summoned by Death and of the parts played in his journey by characters named Fellowship, Cousin, Kindred, Goods, Knowledge, Confession, Beauty, Strength, Discretion, Five Wits, and Good Deeds. Everyman has proved lastingly popular; there have been many productions even in the twentieth century. More generally, the term means the typical, ordinary person.

Existentialism: A philosophy or attitude of mind that has gained wide currency in religious and artistic thought since the end of World War II. Typical concerns of existential writers are humankind's estrangement from society, its awareness that the world is meaningless, and its recognition that one must turn from external props to the self. The works of Jean-Paul Sartre and Franz Kafka provide examples of existentialist beliefs.

Experimental novel: The term is associated with novelists such as Dorothy Richardson, Virginia Woolf, and James Joyce in England, who experimented with the form of the novel, using in particular the stream-of-consciousness technique.

Expressionism: Beginning in German theater at the start of the twentieth century, expressionism became the dominant movement in the decade following World War I. It abandoned realism and relied on a conscious distortion of external reality in order to portray the world as it is "viewed emotionally." The movement spread to fiction and poetry. Expressionism influenced the novels of Franz Kafka and James Joyce.

Fable: One of the oldest narrative forms, usually taking the form of an analogy in which animals or inanimate objects speak to illustrate a moral lesson. The most famous examples are the fables of Aesop, who used the form orally in 600 B.C.

Fabliau: A short narrative poem, popular in medieval French literature and during the English Middle Ages. Fabliaux were usually realistic in subject matter and bawdy; they made a point of satirizing the weaknesses and foibles of human beings. Perhaps the most famous are Geoffrey Chaucer's "The Miller's Tale" and "The Reeve's Tale."

Fairy tale: A form of folktale in which supernatural events or characters are prominent. Fairy tales usually depict a realm of reality beyond that of the natural world in which the laws of the natural world are suspended.

Fantasy: A literary form that makes a deliberate break with reality. Fantasy literature may use supernatural or fairy-tale events in which the ordinary commonsense laws of the everyday world do not operate. The setting may be unreal. J. R. R. Tolkien's fantasy trilogy, *The Lord of the Rings* (1955), is one of the best-known examples of the genre.

Farce: From the Latin *farcire*, meaning "to stuff." Originally an insertion into established Church liturgy in the Middle Ages, farce later became the term for specifically comic scenes inserted into early liturgical drama. The term has come to refer to any play that evokes laughter by such low-comedy devices as physical humor, rough wit, and ridiculous and improbable situations and characters.

Femme fatale: The "fatal woman" is an archetype that appears in myth, folklore, religion, and literature. Often she is presented as a temptress or a witch who ensnares, and attempts to destroy, her male victim. A very common figure in Romanticism, the fatal woman often appears in twentieth century American literature.

Figurative language: Any use of language that departs from the usual or ordinary meaning to gain a poetic or otherwise special effect. Figurative language embodies various figures of speech, such as irony, metaphor, simile.

First person: A point of view in which the narrator of a story or poem addresses the reader directly, often using the pronoun "I," thereby allowing the reader direct access to the narrator's thoughts.

Folklore: The traditions, customs, and beliefs of a people expressed in nonliterary form. Folklore includes myths, legends, fairy tales, riddles, proverbs, charms, spells, and ballads and is usually transmitted through word of mouth. Many literary works contain motifs that can be traced to folklore.

Foreshadowing: A device used to create suspense or dramatic irony by indicating through suggestion what will take place in the future. The aim is to prepare the reader for the action that follows.

Frame story: A story that provides a framework for another story (or stories) told within it. The form is ancient and is used by Geoffrey Chaucer in *The Canterbury Tales* (1387-1400). In modern literature, the technique has been used by Henry James in *The Turn of the Screw* (1898), Joseph Conrad in *Heart of Darkness* (serial, 1899; book, 1902), and John Barth in *Lost in the Funhouse* (1968).

Free verse: Verse that does not conform to any traditional convention, such as meter, rhyme, or form. All poetry must have some pattern of some kind, however, and there is rhythm in free verse, but it does not follow the strict rules of meter. Often the pattern relies on repetition and parallel construction.

Genre: A type or category of literature, such as tragedy, novel, memoir, poem, or essay; a genre has a particular set of conventions and expectations.

German Romanticism: Germany was the first European country in which the Romantic movement took firm grip. Poets Novalis and Ludwig Tieck, philosopher Friedrich Wilhelm Joseph Schelling, and literary theorists Friedrich and August Wilhelm Schlegel were well established in Jena from about 1797, and they were followed, in the second decade of the nineteenth century, by the Heidelberg group, including novelist and short-story writer E. T. A. Hoffmann and poet Heinrich Heine.

Gnomic: Aphoristic poetry, such as the wisdom literature of the Bible, which deals with ethical questions. The term "gnomic poets" is applied to a group of Greek poets of the sixth and seventh century B.C.

Gothic novel: A form of fiction developed in the late eighteenth century that focuses on horror and the supernatural. An example is Mary Shelley's *Frankenstein* (1818). In modern literature, the gothic genre can be found in the fiction of Truman Capote.

Grand Tour: Fashionable during the eighteenth century in England, the Grand Tour was a two- to three-year journey through Europe during which the young aristocracy and prosperous, educated middle classes of England deepened their knowledge of the origins and centers of Western civilization. The tour took a standard route; Rome and Naples were usually considered the highlights.

Grotesque: Characterized by a breakup of the everyday world by mysterious forces, the form differs from fantasy in that the reader is not sure whether to react with humor or with horror. Examples include the stories of E. T. A. Hoffmann and Franz Kafka.

Hagiography: Strictly defined, hagiography refers to the lives of the saints (the Greek word *hagios* means "sacred"), but the term is also used in a more popular sense, to describe any biography that grossly overpraises its subject and ignores his or her faults.

Heroic couplet: A pair of rhyming iambic pentameter lines traditionally used in epic poetry; a heroic couplet often serves as a self-contained witticism or pithy observation.

Historical fiction: A novel that depicts past historical events, usually public in nature, and that features real, as well as fictional, people. Sir Walter Scott's Waverley novels established the basic type, but the relationship between fiction and history in the form varies greatly depending on the practitioner.

Hubris: Greek term for "insolence" or "pride," the characteristic or emotion in the tragic hero of ancient Greek drama that causes the reversal of his fortune, leading him to transgress moral codes or ignore warnings.

Humanism: A human-centered, rather than God-centered, view of the universe. In the Renaissance, Humanism devoted itself to the revival of classical culture. A reaction against medieval Scholasticism, Humanism oriented itself toward secular concerns and applied classical ideas to theology, government, literature, and education. In literature, the main virtues were seen to be restraint, form, and imitation of the classics. *See also* Renaissance.

Iambic pentameter: A metrical line consisting of five feet, each foot consisting of one unstressed syllable followed by one stressed syllable: "So long as men can breathe or eyes can see." Iambic pentameter is one of the commonest forms of English poetry.

Imagery: Often defined as the verbal stimulation of sensory perception. Although the word betrays a visual bias, imagery, in fact, calls on all five senses. In its simplest form, imagery re-creates a physical sensation in a clear, literal manner; it becomes more complex when a poet employs metaphor and other figures of speech to re-create experience.

Impressionism: A late nineteenth century movement composed of a group of painters including Paul Cézanne, Édouard Manet, Claude Monet, and Pierre-Auguste Renoir, who aimed in their work to suggest the impression made on the artist by a scene rather than to reproduce it objectively. The term has also been applied to French Symbolist poets such as Paul Verlaine and Stéphane Mallarmé, and to writers who use the stream-of-consciousness technique, such as James Joyce and Virginia Woolf.

Irony: Recognition of the difference between real and apparent meaning. Verbal irony is a rhetorical trope wherein x is uttered and "not x" is meant. In the New Criticism, irony, the poet's recognition of incongruities, was thought to be the master trope in that it was essential to the production of paradox, complexity, and ambiguity.

Jacobean: Of or pertaining to the reign of James I of England, who ruled from 1603 to 1623, the period immediately following the death of Elizabeth I, which saw tremendous literary activity in poetry and drama. Many writers who achieved fame during the Elizabethan Age, such as William Shakespeare, Ben Jonson, and John Donne, were still active. Other dramatists, such as John Webster and Cyril Tourneur, achieved success almost entirely during the Jacobean era.

Jungian psychoanalysis: Refers to the analytical psychology of the Swiss psychiatrist Carl Jung. Jung's significance for literature is that, through his concept of the collective unconscious, he identified many archetypes and archetypal patterns that recur in myth, fairy tale, and literature and are also experienced in dreams.

Kafkaesque: Refers to any grotesque or nightmare world in which an isolated individual, surrounded by an unfeeling and alien world, feels himself to be caught up in an endless maze that is dragging him down to destruction. The term is a reference to the works of Austrian novelist and short-story writer Franz Kafka.

Leitmotif: From the German, meaning "leading motif." Any repetition—of a word, phrase, situation, or idea—that occurs within a single work or group of related works.

Limerick: A comic five-line poem employing an anapestic base and rhyming *aabba*, in which the third and fourth lines are shorter (usually five syllables each) than the first, second, and last lines, which are usually eight syllables each.

Linear plot: A plot that has unity of action and proceeds from beginning to middle to end without flashbacks or subplots, thus satisfying Aristotle's criterion that a plot should be a continuous sequence.

Literary criticism: The study and evaluation of works of literature. Theoretical criticism sets forth general principles for interpretation. Practical criticism offers interpretations of particular works or authors.

Lyric poetry: Lyric poetry developed when music was accompanied by words, and although the "lyrics" were later separated from the music, the characteristics of lyric poetry have been shaped by the constraints of music. Lyric poems are short, more adaptable to metrical variation, and usually personal compared with the cultural functions of narrative poetry. Lyric poetry sings of the self; it explores deeply personal feelings about life.

Magical Realism: Imaginary or fantastic scenes and occurrences presented in a meticulously realistic style. The term has been applied to the fiction of Gabriel

García Márquez, Jorge Luis Borges, Günter Grass, John Fowles, and Salman Rushdie.

Masque: A courtly entertainment popular during the first half of the seventeenth century in England. It was a sumptuous spectacle including music, dance, and lavish costumes and scenery. Masques often dealt with mythological or pastoral subjects, and the dramatic action often took second place to pure spectacle.

Melodrama: Originally a drama with music (*melos* is Greek for "song"). By the early nineteenth century, it had come to mean a play in which characters are clearly either virtuous or evil and are pitted against one another in suspenseful, often sensational situations. The term took on a pejorative meaning, which it retains: any dramatic work characterized by stereotyped characters and sensational, improbable situations.

Metafiction: Refers to fiction that manifests a reflexive tendency, such as Vladimir Nabokov's *Pale Fire* (1962), and John Fowles's *The French Lieutenant's Woman* (1969). The emphasis is on the loosening of the work's illusion of reality to expose the reality of its illusion. Such terms as "irrealism," "postmodernist fiction," and "antifiction" are also used to refer to this type of fiction. *See also* Postmodernism.

Metaphor: A figure of speech in which two dissimilar objects are imaginatively identified (rather than merely compared) on the assumption that they share one or more qualities. The term is often used in modern criticism in a wider sense, to identify analogies of all kinds in literature, painting, and film.

Metaphysical poetry: A type of poetry that stresses the intellectual over the emotional; it is marked by irony, paradox, and striking comparisons of dissimilar things, the latter frequently being farfetched to the point of eccentricity. Usually used to designate a group of seventeenth century English poets, including John Donne, George Herbert, Andrew Marvell, and Thomas Traherne.

Meter: Meter is the pattern of language when it is forced into a line of poetry. All language has rhythm, but when that rhythm is organized and regulated in the line so as to affect the meaning and emotional response to the words, then the rhythm has been refined into meter. The meter is determined by the number of syllables in a line and by the relationship between them.

Mock epic: A literary form that burlesques the epic by taking a trivial subject and treating it in a grand style, using all the conventions of epic, such as invocation to the deity, long and boastful speeches of the heroes, and supernatural machinery. Alexander Pope's *The Rape of the Lock* (1712, 1714) is probably the finest example in English literature. The term is synonymous with mock heroic. *See also* Mock hero.

Mock hero: The hero of a mock epic. *See also* Mock epic.

Modernism: A term used to describe the characteristic aspects of literature and art between World War I and World War II. Influenced by Friedrich Nietzsche, Karl Marx, and Sigmund Freud, modernism embodied a lack of faith in Western civilization and culture. In poetry, fragmentation, discontinuity, and irony were common; in fiction, chronological disruption, linguistic innovation, and the stream-of-consciousness technique; in theater, expressionism and Surrealism.

Morality play: A dramatic form in the late Middle Ages and the Renaissance containing allegorical figures (most often virtues and vices) that are typically involved in the struggle over a person's soul. The anonymously written *Everyman* (1508) is one of the most famous medieval examples of this form.

Motif: An incident, situation, or device that occurs frequently in literature. Motif can also refer to particular words, images, and phrases that are repeated frequently in a single work. In this sense, motif is the same as leitmotif. Motif is similar to theme, although the latter is usually more abstract.

Myth: An anonymous traditional story, often involving supernatural beings, or the interaction between gods and humans, and dealing with the basic questions of how the world and human society came to be. Myth is an important term in contemporary literary criticism. The critic Northrop Frye, for example, has said that "the typical forms of myth become the conventions and genres of literature." He means that the genres of comedy, romance, tragedy, and irony (satire) correspond to seasonal myths of spring, summer, autumn, and winter.

Narrative: An account in prose or verse of an event or series of events, whether real or imagined.

Narrator: The character who recounts the narrative. There are many different types of narrator. The first-person narrator is a character in the story and can be recognized by his use of "I"; third-person narrators may be limited or omniscient. In the former, the narrator confines himself to knowledge of the minds and emotions of one or at most a few characters. In the latter, the narrator knows everything, seeing into the minds of all the characters. Rarely, second-person narration may be used (an example can be found in Edna O'Brien's *A Pagan Place*, published in 1970).

Naturalism: The application of the principles of scientific determinism to fiction. Although it usually refers more to the choice of subject matter than to technical conventions, conventions associated with the movement center on the author's attempt to be precise and objective in description and detail, regardless of whether the events described are sordid or shocking. Naturalism flourished in England, France, and America in the late nineteenth and early twentieth centuries.

Neoclassicism: A term used to describe the classicism that dominated English literature from the Restoration to the late eighteenth century. Modeling itself on the literature of ancient Greece and Rome, neoclassicism exalted the virtues of proportion, unity, harmony, grace, decorum, taste, manners, and restraint. It valued realism and reason over imagination and emotion. *See also* Rationalism, Realism.

Neorealism: A movement in modern Italian literature, extending from about 1930 to 1955. Neorealism was shaped by opposition to Fascism, and by World War II and the Resistance. Neorealist literature therefore exhibited a strong concern with social issues and was marked by pessimism regarding the human condition. Its practitioners sought to overcome the gap between literature and the masses, and its subject matter was frequently drawn from lower-class life. Neorealism is associated preeminently with the work of Italo Calvino.

Nonsense literature/verse: Nonsense verse, such as that written by Edward Lear and Lewis Carroll, makes use of invented words that have no meaning, portmanteau words, and so-called macaroni verse, in which words from different languages are mingled. The verse holds the attention because of its strong rhythms, appealing sounds, and, occasionally, the mysterious atmosphere that it creates.

Novel of education: See *Bildungsroman.*

Novel of ideas: A novel in which the characters, plot, and dialogue serve to develop some controlling idea or to present the clash of ideas. Aldous Huxley's *Eyeless in Gaza* (1936) is a good example.

Novel of manners: The classic example of the form might be the novels of Jane Austen, wherein the customs and conventions of a social group of a particular time and place are realistically, and often satirically, portrayed.

Novella: An Italian term meaning "a little new thing" that now refers to that form of fiction longer than a short story and shorter than a novel.

Objective correlative: A key concept in modern formalist criticism, coined by T. S. Eliot in *The Sacred Wood* (1920). An objective correlative is a situation, an event, or an object that, when presented or described in a literary work, expresses a particular emotion and serves as a precise formula by which the same emotion can be evoked in the reader.

Ode: The ode is a lyric poem that treats a unified subject with elevated emotion, usually ending with a satisfactory resolution. There is no set form for the ode, but it must be long enough to build intense emotional response. Often the ode will address itself to some omnipotent source and will assume a spiritual hue.

Oxford Movement: A reform movement in the Church of England that began in 1833, led by John Henry (later Cardinal) Newman. The Oxford Movement aimed to combat liberalism and the decline of the role of faith in the Church and to restore it to its former ideals. It was attacked for advocating what some saw as Catholic doctrines; as a result, Newman left the Church of England and became a Roman Catholic in 1845.

Panegyric: A formal speech or writing in praise of a particular person or achievement; a eulogy. The form dates back to classical times; the term is now often used in a derogatory sense.

Parable: A short, simple, and usually allegorical story that teaches a moral lesson. In the West, the most famous parables are those told in the Gospels by Christ.

Parody: A literary work that imitates or burlesques another work or author, for

C

the purpose of ridicule. Twentieth century parodists include E. B. White and James Thurber.

Pastoral: The term derives from the Latin "pastor," meaning "shepherd." Pastoral is a literary mode that depicts the country life in an idealized way; it originated in classical literature and was a popular form in English literature from 1550 to 1750. Notable pastoral poems include John Milton's "Lycidas" and Percy Bysshe Shelley's *Adonais*.

Pathetic fallacy: The ascribing of human characteristics or feelings to inanimate objects. The term was coined by John Ruskin in 1856, who disapproved of it, but it is now used without any pejorative sense.

Persona: *Persona* means literally "mask": It is the self created by the author and through whom the narrative is told. The persona is not to be identified with the author, even when the two may seem to resemble each other. The narrative persona in Lord Byron's *Don Juan* (1819-1824, 1826), for example, may express many sentiments of which Byron would have approved, but he is nonetheless a fictional creation who is distinct from the author.

Personification: A figure of speech that ascribes human qualities to abstractions or inanimate objects.

Petrarchan sonnet: Named after Petrarch, a fourteenth century Italian poet, who perfected the form, which is also known as the Italian sonnet. It is divided into an octave, in which the subject matter, which may be a problem, a doubt, a reflection, or some other issue, is raised and elaborated, and a sestet, in which the problem is resolved. The rhyme scheme is usually *abba abba ced cde*, *cdc cdc*, or *cde dce*.

Philosophical dualism: A theory that the universe is explicable in terms of two basic, conflicting entities, such as good and evil, mind and matter, or the physical and the spiritual.

Picaresque: A form of fiction that revolves around a central rogue figure, or picaro, who usually tells his own story. The plot structure of a picaresque novel is usually episodic, and the episodes usually focus on how the picaro lives by his wits. The classic example is Henry Fielding's *The History of Tom Jones, a Foundling* (1749).

Pindaric ode: Odes that imitate the form of those composed by the ancient Greek poet Pindar. A Pindaric ode consists of a strophe, followed by an antistrophe of the same structure, followed by an epode. This pattern may be repeated several times in the ode. In English poetry, Thomas Gray's "The Bard" is an example of a Pindaric ode.

Play: A literary work that is written to be performed by actors who speak the dialogue, impersonate the characters, and perform the appropriate actions. Usually, a play is performed on a stage, and an audience witnesses it.

Play-within-the-play: A play or dramatic fragment performed as a scene or scenes within a larger drama, typically performed or viewed by the characters of the larger drama.

Plot: Plot refers to how the author arranges the material not only to create the sequence of events in a play or story but also to suggest how those events are connected in a cause-and-effect relationship. There are a great variety of plot patterns, each of which is designed to create a particular effect.

Poem: A unified composition that uses the rhythms and sounds of language, as well as devices such as metaphor, to communicate emotions and experiences to the reader.

Poet laureate: The official poet of England, appointed for life by the English sovereign and expected to compose poems for various public occasions. The first official laureate was John Dryden in the seventeenth century. In the eighteenth century, the laureateship was given to a succession of mediocrities, but since the appointment of William Wordsworth in 1843, the office has generally been regarded as a substantial honor.

Polemic: A work that forcefully argues an opinion, usually on a controversial religious, political, or economic issue, in opposition to other opinions. John Milton's *Areopagitica* (1644) is one of the best known examples in English literature.

Postmodernism: The term is loosely applied to various artistic movements that have succeeded modernism, particularly since 1965. Postmodernist literature is experimental in form and reflects a fragmented world in which order and meaning are absent.

Pre-Raphaelitism: Refers to a group of nineteenth century English painters and writers, including Dante Gabriel Rossetti, Christina Rossetti, and William Morris. The Pre-Raphaelites were so called because they rebelled against conventional methods of painting and wanted to revert to what they regarded as the simple spirit of painting that existed before Raphael, particularly in its adherence to nature; they rejected all artificial embellishments. Pre-Raphaelite poetry made much use of symbolism and sensuousness, and showed an interest in the medieval and the supernatural.

Prose poem: A type of poem ranging in length from a few lines to three or four pages; most occupy a page or less. The distinguishing feature of the prose poem is its typography: it appears on the page like prose, with no line breaks. Many prose poems employ rhythmic repetition and other poetic devices not found in prose, but others do not; there is enormous variety in the genre.

Protagonist: Originally, in the Greek drama, the "first actor," who played the leading role. The term has come to signify the most important character in a drama or story. It is not unusual for there to be more than one protagonist in a work.

Proverb: A wise and pithy saying, authorship unknown, that reflects some observation about life. Proverbs are usually passed on through word of mouth, although they may also be written, as for example, the Book of Proverbs in the Bible.

Psychological novel: Once described as an interpretation of "the invisible life," the psychological novel is a form of fiction in which character, especially the inner life of characters, is the primary focus, rather than action. The form has characterized much of the work of Henry James, James Joyce, Virginia Woolf, and William Faulkner. *See also* Psychological realism.

Psychological realism: A type of realism that tries to reproduce the complex psychological motivations behind human behavior; writers in the late nineteenth century and early twentieth century were particularly influenced by Sigmund Freud's theories. *See also* Psychological novel.

Pun: A pun occurs when words with similar pronunciations have entirely different meanings. The result may be a surprise recognition of an unusual or striking connection, or, more often, a humorously accidental connection.

Quest: An archetypal theme identified by mythologist Joseph Campbell and found in many literary works. Campbell describes the heroic quest in three fundamental stages: departure (leaving the familiar world), initiation (encountering adventures and obstacles), and return (bringing home a boon to transform society).

Rabelaisian: The term is a reference to the sixteenth century French satirist and humorist François Rabelais. "Rabelaisian" is now used to refer to any humorous or satirical writing that is bawdy, coarse, or very down to earth.

Rationalism: A system of thought that seeks truth through the exercise of reason rather than by means of emotional response or revelation, or traditional authority. In literature, rationalism is associated with eighteenth century neoclassicism. *See also* Neoclassicism.

Realism: A literary technique in which the primary convention is to render an illusion of fidelity to external reality. Realism is often identified as the primary method of the novel form; the realist movement in the late nineteenth century coincided with the full development of the novel form.

Renaissance: The term means "rebirth" and refers to a period in European cultural history from the fourteenth to the early seventeenth century, although dates differ widely from country to country. The Renaissance produced an unprecedented flowering of the arts of painting, sculpture, architecture, and literature. The period is often said to mark the transition from the Middle Ages to the modern world. The questing, individualistic spirit that characterized the age was stimulated by an increase in classical learning by scholars known as Humanists, by the Protestant Reformation, by the development of printing, which created a wide market for books, by new theories of astronomy, and by the development of other sciences that saw natural laws at work where the Middle Ages had seen occult forces. *See also* Humanism.

Restoration comedy/drama: The restoration of the Stuart dynasty brought Charles II to the English throne in 1660. In literature, the Restoration period extends from 1660 to 1700. Restoration comedy is a comedy of manners, which centers around complicated plots full of the amorous intrigues of the fashionable upper classes. The humor is witty, but the view of human nature is cynical. Restoration dramatists include William Congreve, Sir George Etherege, and William Wycherley. In serious, or heroic, drama, the leading playwright was John Dryden. *See also* Comedy of manners.

Roman à clef: A fiction wherein actual persons, often celebrities of some sort, are thinly disguised. Lady Caroline Lamb's *Glenarvon* (1816), for example, contains a thinly veiled portrait of Lord Byron, and the character Mark Rampion in Aldous Huxley's *Point Counter Point* (1928) strongly resembles D. H. Lawrence.

Romance: Originally, any work written in Old French. In the Middle Ages, romances were about knights and their adventures. In modern times, the term has also been used to describe a type of prose fiction in which, unlike the novel, realism plays little part. Prose romances often give expression to the quest for transcendent truths.

Romanticism: A movement of the late eighteenth century and the nineteenth century that exalted individualism over collectivism, revolution over conservatism, innovation over tradition, imagination over reason, and spontaneity over restraint. Romanticism regarded art as self-expression; it strove to heal the cleavage between object and subject and expressed a longing for the infinite in all things. It stressed the innate goodness of human beings and the evils of the institutions that would stultify human creativity. The major English Romantic poets are William Blake, Lord Byron, Samuel Taylor Coleridge, John Keats, Percy Bysshe Shelley, and William Wordsworth.

Satire: A form of literature that employs the comedic devices of wit, irony, and exaggeration to expose, ridicule, and condemn human folly, vice, and stupidity. Justifying satire, Alexander Pope wrote that "nothing moves strongly but satire, and those who are ashamed of nothing else are so of being ridiculous."

Scene: A division of action within an act (some plays are divided only into scenes instead of acts). Sometimes, scene division indicates a change of setting or locale; sometimes, it simply indicates the entrances and exits of characters.

Science fiction: Fiction in which real or imagined scientific developments or certain givens (such as physical laws, psychological principles, or social conditions) form the basis of an imaginative projection, frequently into the future. Classic examples are the works of H. G. Wells and Jules Verne.

Sentimental novel: A form of fiction popular in the eighteenth century in which emotionalism and optimism are the primary characteristics. The best-known examples are Samuel Richardson's *Pamela* (1740-1741) and Oliver Goldsmith's *The Vicar of Wakefield* (1766).

Shakespearean sonnet: So named because William Shakespeare was the greatest English sonneteer, whose ranks also included the earl of Surrey and Thomas Wyatt. The Shakespearean sonnet consists of three quatrains and a concluding couplet, rhyming *abab cdcd efef gg.* The beginning of the third quatrain marks a turn in the argument.

GLOSSARY

Short story: A concise work of fiction, shorter than a novella, that is usually more concerned with mood, effect, or a single event than with plot or extensive characterization.

Simile: A type of metaphor in which two things are compared. It can usually be recognized by the use of the words "like," "as," "appears," or "seems."

***Skaz*:** A term used in Russian criticism to describe a narrative technique that presents an oral narrative of a lowbrow speaker.

Soliloquy: An extended speech delivered by a character alone on stage, unheard by other characters. Soliloquy is a form of monologue, and it typically reveals the intimate thoughts and emotions of the speaker.

Song: A lyric poem, usually short, simple, and with rhymed stanzas, set to music.

Sonnet: A traditional poetic form that is almost always composed of fourteen lines of rhymed iambic pentameter; a turning point usually divides the poem into two parts, with the first part (octave) presenting a situation and the second part (sestet) reflecting on it. The main sonnet forms are the Petrarchan sonnet and the English (sometimes called Shakespearean) sonnet.

Stanza: When lines of poetry are meant to be taken as a unit, and the unit recurs throughout the poem, that unit is called a stanza; a four-line unit, a quatrain, is one common stanza. Others include couplet, *ottava rima*, and the Spenserian stanza.

Story line: The story line of a work of fiction differs from the plot. Story is merely the events that happen; plot is how those events are arranged by the author to suggest a cause-and-effect relationship. *See also* Plot.

Stream of consciousness: A narrative technique used in modern fiction by which an author tries to embody the total range of consciousness of a character, without any authorial comment or explanation. Sensations, thoughts, memories, and associations pour forth in an uninterrupted, prerational, and prelogical flow. For examples, see James Joyce's *Ulysses* (1922), Virginia Woolf's *To the Lighthouse* (1927), and William Faulkner's *The Sound and the Fury* (1929).

***Sturm und Drang*:** A dramatic and literary movement in Germany during the late eighteenth century. Translated as "Storm and Stress," the movement was a reaction against classicism and a forerunner of Romanticism, characterized by extravagantly emotional language and sensational subject matter.

Surrealism: A revolutionary approach to artistic and literary creation, Surrealism argued for complete artistic freedom: The artist should relinquish all conscious control, responding to the irrational urges of the unconscious mind. Hence the bizarre, dreamlike, and nightmarish quality of Surrealistic writing. In the 1920's and 1930's, Surrealism flourished in France, Spain, and Latin America. (After World War II, it influenced such American writers as Frank O'Hara, John Ashberry, and Nathanael West.)

Symbol: A literary symbol is an image that stands for something else; it may evoke a cluster of meanings rather than a single specific meaning.

Symbolism: A literary movement encompassing the work of a group of French writers in the latter half of the nineteenth century, a group that included Charles Baudelaire, Stéphane Mallarmé, and Paul Verlaine. According to Symbolism, there is a mystical correspondence between the natural and spiritual worlds.

Theater of Cruelty: A term, coined by French playwright Antonin Artaud, which signifies a vision in which theater becomes an arena for shock therapy. The characters undergo such intense physical and psychic extremities that the audience cannot ignore the cathartic effect in which its preconceptions, fears, and hostilities are brought to the surface and, ideally, purged.

Theater of the Absurd: Refers to a group of plays that share a basic belief that life is illogical, irrational, formless, and contradictory, and that humanity is without meaning or purpose. Practitioners, who include Eugène Ionesco, Samuel Beckett, Jean Genet, Harold Pinter, Edward Albee, and Arthur Kopit, abandoned traditional theatrical forms and coherent dialogue.

***Théâtre d'avant-garde*:** A movement in late nineteenth century drama in France, which challenged the conventions of realistic drama by using Symbolist poetry and nonobjective scenery.

Third person: Third-person narration occurs when the narrator has not been part of the event or affected it and is not probing his own relationship to it but is only describing what happened. He does not allow the intrusion of the word *I*. Third-person narration establishes a distance between reader and subject, gives credibility to a large expanse of narration that would be impossible for one person to experience, and allows the narrative to include a number of characters who can comment on one another as well as be the subjects of commentary by the participating narrator.

Tragedy: A form of drama that is serious in action and intent and that involves disastrous events and death; classical Greek drama observed specific guidelines for tragedy, but the term is now sometimes applied to a range of dramatic or fictional situations.

Travel literature: Writing that emphasizes the author's subjective response to places visited, especially faraway, exotic, and culturally different locales.

Trilogy: A novel or play written in three parts, each of which is a self-contained work, such as William Shakespeare's *Henry VI* (*Part I*, 1592; *Part II*, c. 1590-1591; *Part III*, c. 1590-1591). Modern examples include C. S. Lewis' Space Trilogy (1938-1945) and William Golding's Sea Trilogy (1980-1989).

Trope: Trope means literally "turn" or "conversion"; it is a figure of speech in which a word or phrase is used in a way that deviates from the normal or literal sense.

***Verismo*:** Refers to a type of Italian literature that deals with the lower classes and presents them realistically using language that they would use. Called *verismo* because it is true to life, and, from the writer's point of view, impersonal.

Verse: Verse is a generic name for poetry. Verse also refers in a narrower sense to poetry that is humorous or merely superficial, as in "greeting-card verse." Finally, English critics sometimes use "verse" to mean "stanza," or, more often, to mean "line."

Verse drama: Verse drama was the prevailing form for Western drama throughout most of its history, comprising all the drama of classical Greece and continuing to dominate the stage through the Renaissance, when it was best exemplified by the blank verse of Elizabethan drama. In the seventeenth century, however, prose comedies became popular, and in the nineteenth and twentieth centuries verse drama became the exception rather than the rule.

Victorian novel: Although the Victorian period extended from 1837 to 1901, the term "Victorian novel" does not include works from the later decades of Queen Victoria's reign. The term loosely refers to the sprawling works of novelists such as Charles Dickens and William Makepeace Thackeray, which are characterized by a broad social canvas.

Villanelle: A French verse form assimilated by English prosody. It is usually composed of nineteen lines divided into five tercets and a quatrain, rhyming *aba, bba, aba, aba, abaa*. The third line is repeated in the ninth and fifteenth lines. Dylan Thomas' "Do Not Go Gentle into That Good Night" is a modern example of a successful villanelle.

Well-made play: From the French term *pièce bien faite*, a type of play constructed according to a "formula" that originated in nineteenth century France. The plot often revolves around a secret known only to some of the characters, which is revealed at the climax and leads to catastrophe for the villain and vindication or triumph for the hero. The well-made play influenced later dramatists such as Henrik Ibsen and George Bernard Shaw.

*Weltanschauung***:** A German term translated as "worldview," by which is meant a comprehensive set of beliefs or assumptions by means of which one interprets what goes on in the world.

Zeitgeist: A German term meaning the spirit of the times, the moral or intellectual atmosphere of any age or period. The *Zeitgeist* of the Romantic Age, for example, might be described as revolutionary, restless, individualistic, and innovative.

LIST OF AUTHORS

LIST OF AUTHORS